ABOUT BRITAIN

ABOUT BRITAIN

A Journey of Seventy Years and 1,345 Miles

Tim Cole

BLOOMSBURY CONTINUUM
LONDON • OXFORD • NEW YORK • NEW DELHI • SYDNEY

BLOOMSBURY CONTINUUM
Bloomsbury Publishing Plc
50 Bedford Square, London, WC1B 3DP, UK
29 Earlsfort Terrace, Dublin 2, Ireland

BLOOMSBURY, BLOOMSBURY CONTINUUM and the Diana logo are trademarks of Bloomsbury Publishing Plc

First published in Great Britain 2021
Paperback 2022

A catalogue record for this book is available from the British Library

Library of Congress Cataloguing-in-Publication data has been applied for

ISBN: PB: 978-1-4729-3728-5; eBook: 978-1-4729-3729-2; ePDF: 978-1-4729-3727-8

2 4 6 8 10 9 7 5 3 1

Typeset by Deanta Global Publishing Services, Chennai, India
Printed and bound in Great Britain by CPI Group (UK) Ltd, Croydon CR0 4YY

In fond memory of my father Edwin Roger Lloyd Cole (1942–2020) and my paternal grandparents Herbert Aubrey Cole (1911–84) and Elizabeth (née Lloyd) Cole (1910–2004) who first took me About Britain.

Contents

About Britain

This is the story of an unexpected journey. Like many things I end up doing, it began with a serendipitous discovery. There's an Oxfam bookshop that lies between my office and another building where I often have meetings. If I've got a few minutes spare, I'll drop in for a quick look. One afternoon I was scanning the travel shelves when I came upon a slim volume shedding its dust jacket. The torn cover combined the muted green and brown shading of a topographic map with the sharp red lines of a road map. The box in the top left-hand corner announced that this was *About Britain No. 1. West Country. A New Guide Book with a portrait by Geoffrey Grigson*, while the black-and-white Festival of Britain logo in the bottom right-hand corner revealed it was published in 1951. It was only 50 pence so I bought it, largely on account of the painting of the distinctive red cliffs of south Devon that I'd visited as a child, reproduced in vivid colour on the title page.

Of course, as always happens, having bought this volume I started spotting others from the same series. Charity bookshops seemed to stock nothing else. The guide to the West Country was quickly joined by others. Priced at 'a reasonable' three-and-six for those lacking 'ten shillings or fifteen shillings to spend on a fat topographical volume', these were short, mass-market guidebooks with an average initial print run of 50,000 copies.[1] Plenty were produced and plenty are still around. Before long I had a complete set of all thirteen volumes and my thoughts turned to what I might do with these guides. After the watercoloured title page, photograph-topped contents page and a few words on 'using this book' came an opening essay about the region as a whole. These lengthy 'verbal portraits', although penned by different authors, covered more-or-less the same range of subjects and were interspersed with photographs that both accompanied the text and were found in a central section of full-page images carefully arranged in pairs. Next came six – or in some cases a few more – mapped-out driving tours around the region, before a gazetteer and short reading list completed things in just under a hundred pages.

I'm not a book collector, but something was starting to draw me in. I decided to begin where any historian would: in the archives. Sitting at a numbered desk in the National Archives in Kew, I read the minutes of the meetings of the various Festival of Britain committees that developed the books that I'd been amassing. From these, I was able to piece together the backstory of the way these guides were created to encourage domestic and foreign visitors to see more than simply the main Festival of Britain exhibition in 1951. Championed by the post-war Labour government, the festival was intended as a rerun of the 1851 Great Exhibition and a chance to showcase Britain as a country that was successfully rebuilding after the trauma of the Second World War. Those putting the festival together mainly focused on developing content for the exhibitions on the South Bank that would show that 'British initiative in exploration and discovery is as strong today as it ever was' but they were also keen to get visitors out of London, onto the road, and about Britain.[2]

As is so often the case, things did not turn out quite as intended. The original plan was to develop a series of special coach tours during the festival year. Sample itineraries were drawn up covering 'Upper Thames and East Midlands', 'Upper Thames and West Midlands' and 'Lower Severn, Gloucester, Somerset, Welsh Marches, Cotswolds', each in five and a half days. These were planned with an eye to selecting 'sites, areas and activities which would give the visitor a memorable, enjoyable and balanced picture of life as it is lived in the British Isles' and to 'preserve a balance between urban and rural life'. Visits to historical sites such as Blenheim Palace or the 'Colleges and College Gardens with tea break' in Oxford were mixed with experiences of contemporary industry such as 'opencast iron mining at Corby'. Although these coach 'Tours of Britain 1951' would be led by expert guides drawn from geography departments in British universities, the Festival Office wished to produce accompanying 'Tour Guide Books' to 'supplement' the guides' narrative. With an eye to the future, they also realized that guidebooks would not simply 'replace the guide-managers and local guides in cases where visitors prefer to tour unescorted in their own vehicles' but also guarantee 'a permanent record, and guide in the future, of the Festival theme' once the events of 1951 were over.[3] It was a good job they made this provision. Plans for coach tours quickly fell by the wayside and the guidebooks and motor car became the sole means of conveying visitors across the country.

Digging into the files, I discovered that there was another twist to this tale. Those putting these volumes together soon became aware that others also had plans to produce 'a series of General Guide Books' to coincide with the Festival of Britain. Rather than creating two competing series, it made better sense to combine forces. Therefore, in November 1949, the Brewers' Society came on board as sponsors. By the time the Festival of Britain Council was belatedly informed of this collaboration it was a fait accompli. The offer that the guidebooks 'be produced under the full editorial control of the Festival Office but free of all cost to the Festival' was one that was simply too good to be turned down by the budget-conscious Festival Council. However, that didn't stop at least one of their members from expressing his concern that allowing 'a commercial enterprise to produce Festival guide books' might result in 'a deterioration of Festival standards'.[4]

The Brewers' Society certainly brought their own editorial vision with them to the project. The main liaison between the Festival Office and those putting the guidebooks together – the wonderfully named Colonel Penrose Angwin – insisted that 'responsibility for factual accuracy would rest with the Festival Office' under guidance of the newly created 'Tours Advisory Panel' that was largely filled with academics. However, while the precise content was to be determined by this group of experts, the Brewers' Society and their editorial team at Holdens determined the look and feel of these mass-market guidebooks and took an increasingly leading role. Reading through the minutes of the meetings of both the 'Tours Advisory Panel' and the 'Guide Books Editorial Committee' during the rest of 1949 and into 1950 offered a glimpse of the lengthy and often vigorous debates over what these guidebooks should contain, as well as what they should be called. Initially known in-house as the 'Happy Travellers Guides for the Festival of Britain', a number of potential names were considered and dismissed – 'The British Way', 'British Ways', 'Portrait of Britain', 'British Portrait', 'Britain at Home' and 'Britain on View' – before settling on *About Britain*.[5]

All archives are places of presences and absences, and the paperwork relating to these guidebooks was no exception. The minutes of the various committees that met during 1949 and 1950 survived, but there was much less information available when it came to the later stage of test-running aspects of the guides in the summer of 1950. Publication deadlines were pressing and so men and women with 'a wide knowledge and affection for the area' were hired to check the proposed motor tours.[6] However, the surviving paperwork that I worked through tended to be limited to initial contracts, letters of acceptance and details of payment or correspondence quibbling over what were seen as excessive claims for contingencies. It seemed that the budget was clearly in the minds of those in the Festival Office in London in 1950 and so all they kept was the paperwork of financial transactions. Archives can be frustrating places. Time and time again you are left wondering why someone kept this paperwork but not that. I've long been interested in the creative potential of working with the constraints that archives always present, but I realized that reading the paperwork about these guidebooks would only get me so far.[7]

Sitting silently in Kew – pencil in hand – my mind drifted to the roads that those with 'a wide knowledge and affection for the area' had driven in the summer of 1950, and visitors had carefully retraced the following year. Although the paperwork I looked at was mainly concerned with how much meals had cost en route, it contained enticing details of these first journeys. I was drawn to a letter sent from the Festival Office, on my birthday as it happened, to a geography lecturer in Manchester, Norman Pye. In July and August, he checked the six tours included in the guidebook to Yorkshire and Lancashire, pausing in Scarborough, Harrogate, Rotherham, Lancaster, Warrington, Glusburn and York for his one shilling and six pence lunch.[8] Reading through this litany of lunch spots not only made me hungry, but desperate to leave my desk in Kew and head out on the road to follow in his tyre tracks. Pye was no longer alive, but the places he drove through were still there.[9]

And so I decided to follow one route randomly drawn from each of the twelve volumes. I began with the guidebook I'd first chanced upon. It had twelve, rather than the customary six, tours in the back. Most were marked out on strip maps self-consciously styled on the first road maps produced by John Ogilby in the seventeenth century, but I settled on the map-less seventh tour.[10] Simply entitled 'Barnstaple–Exeter–Torquay, 76 miles', it offered up a route that 'crossed the country of Devonshire from north to south, from the Bristol Channel to the English Channel'. I decided that a May Bank Holiday Monday would be a fitting day for this first journey, with the kids in the back of the car. Once completed, I then began working my way first eastwards, and then northwards.

I set out to try to immerse myself in a specific moment that came just a few years after the end of the Second World War. Along each route, I was intrigued by what those putting the tours together thought was worth seeing and what this suggested about the ways they saw post-war Britain during its rebuilding and reimagining. This meant doing the kinds of things that come naturally to a historian: reading all the different elements making up these multi-media guidebooks, which combined textual and visual clues, as well as exploring the material related to their production in the National Archives. Along some journeys I discovered contradictions and ambivalences in how modern Britain was thought about in 1951.

But as well as trying to immerse myself in the past, I was conscious that I was attempting to retrace these routes in the present. Driving along the same roads just under 70 years after these books were first published I discovered what had changed and what had stayed the same. Rather than trying to write about all aspects of continuity and change, I embraced the limits the guidebooks imposed upon me. It is not only archives that creatively constrain. Itineraries also do. Each region was restricted to a small number of tours. Each tour directed me along this road, not that, and I chose to follow it in this direction, not that, flagging some places (to the exclusion of others) as worth seeing along the way. Rather than working against the constraints of a linear tour drawn up by someone else, I decided to work with them and stick as far as I could to the original route writing only about the landscape that lay directly along either side of the road. It felt like an experiment in following a series of tunnels, or wormholes perhaps, chosen by someone else.

Working primarily with the landscape, I wanted to see what it suggested of the stories of post-war Britain. Those stories cover a range of what might be dubbed social, cultural, environmental, economic and political histories. But rather than privileging one of these lenses, I decided to start with the roadscape that I passed along and work from that. This does mean there are plenty of gaps. I intentionally only drove those roads chosen for me by those in the Festival Office in 1950, rather than all roads – and specifically the yet-to-be-built motorways – criss-crossing Britain. I focused on what I passed along the sides of these roads, only stopping to explore on foot occasionally. In short, I did not – metaphorically or literally – stop, knock on the door of a house, enter and adopt the methods of a social historian who might conduct oral history interviews with the inhabitants. Instead, when I did go on foot, I sought to work more with the methods of the environmental historian or historical geographer and to adopt what one historian memorably described as the 'archive of the feet'.[11]

But, in reality, I did very little walking and rather a lot of driving. Adding the totals from all twelve journeys together came to a little over 1,300 miles, but sometimes I ended up lost or came upon a red 'Road Closed' sign and was forced to follow another route. Rather than adopting the 'archive of the feet' I chose mainly to follow the archive of the steering wheel and tyre tracks. This was intentional. These guidebooks were primarily aimed at motorists, with Britain offered up as a landscape to be driven through. And so I drove along the roads, sometimes alone and sometimes with others. I wanted the car not only to be the vehicle that I used to access past and present, but also an object of study in its own right. As well as thinking about the ways that people imagined the world in 1951, and exploring histories of continuity and change over seven decades, this book is also a reflection on our changing relationship with cars and roads and travel in general.

Retracing twelve itineraries put together in the summer of 1950 took me to places both familiar and unfamiliar, making me think afresh about what Britain meant then and means now. Of course when I followed these routes it was not in the immediate aftermath of the Second World War but in years dominated first by debates and preparations for Brexit, and later the spread of a global pandemic. Starting close to my Bristol home, before heading first east, and then north, it became clear that the answer to the question of what Britain is, was as, if not more, complex than when the Festival Office first set out to answer it in 1951. It also quickly became apparent how much has changed in Britain in the course of the three score years and ten of a human lifespan.

Barnstaple–Bishop's Tawton–Eggesford–Witheridge–Tiverton–Bickleigh–Silverton–Killerton House–Poltimore House–Exeter–Telegraph Hill–Teignmouth–Babbacombe–Torquay

I

West Country

Barnstaple–Exeter–Torquay (76 miles)

I left Barnstaple via the inner ring road that seemed to be the only way not simply around, but also out of, town. I had tried to see everything the gazetteer at the end of the *About Britain* guide had picked out as particularly significant in this 'busy market town and shopping centre with a well-known pottery'. The '14th-century bridge', church with a 'twisted' spire and the 'little colonnaded building with a statue of Queen Anne' were still there, although a new bridge meant that the medieval one was now bypassed by most traffic.[1] But the pottery had closed. Brannam Pottery, established in the middle of the nineteenth century, had been sold in the late 1970s and moved from the centre of Barnstaple to an industrial estate on the edge of town. The business had since ceased trading entirely and the old Brannam Pottery works on Litchdon Street – resplendent with its decorative facade, which was guaranteed preservation after gaining listed status in the late 1980s – was up for sale with a new residential future mapped out given its 'potential' for conversion into four flats.[2]

By the time I reached the road that motorists were directed to follow in 1951, I was almost at the first place on the itinerary: Bishop's Tawton. The route had been checked on the ground in the summer of 1950. In mid-May, Penrose Angwin – who oversaw all aspects of the process from the Festival Office in London – contacted a fellow colonel, James Stuart, to invite him to test-run some of the provisional tours near his Exeter home. 'I was looking forward to doing it myself,' Angwin explained, 'but time presses hard and I simply cannot make it.' Desperate to get the job done quickly, he used a mixture of enticement – 'you will enjoy doing it enormously' – and flattery. It was his latter strategy that interested me in particular, given that it revealed something of his understanding of what these tours were meant to achieve. Angwin explained that the job 'can only be done by one who not only has a wide knowledge of and affection for the area, but who also has an appreciation of the relationship between the people and the land – what grows on it and comes from it, and has done in the past' before adding to ensure Stuart's compliance, 'you have all these things so I hope you really will do it'.[3]

The idea that there was a 'relationship between the people and the land' was mentioned time and again in the opening essays of the guides. That is not surprising as it was also there in the 'steering script' drawn up by the committee to ensure that the various authors of these opening 'verbal portraits' were on message. Starting with the deep history of geological time, they were to reveal the underlying bedrock in each region before moving on to more recent human-led 'historical transformations'.[4] It was also there in the Festival's South Bank exhibition that showed 'the Land and the People'. Scholars have disagreed over whether this represented the continuation of neo-romantic ideas of a 'Deep England' or was a more 'democratic . . . space within which to explore the way the nation had shaped its environment and been shaped by it'.[5] But whether reactionary or progressive, both the guides and the Festival assumed that the underlying geology was the literal bedrock on which Britain was built. And so, following roads that Stuart had driven in the early summer of 1950 armed with a 'letter to the Regional Petroleum Officer which should secure you enough petrol for the job', I was primed to look out for 'what grows on' and 'comes from' the red soils of Devon.[6]

The road I took was not simply signed the three-quarters of a mile to Bishop's Tawton and the 31 miles to Crediton, but brown signs emblazoned with a red rose transformed it into a 'Tourist Route' all the way to Exeter. Brown road signs first made an appearance in the 1980s after being introduced in France a decade earlier to signal sites of tourist interest during the explosion of post-war leisure time and car ownership. Some, like this one, identify a longer stretch of road as a 'tourist' or 'scenic' route that traverses natural or historic landscapes. Others, like the second brown sign jostling for attention at this turn-off, direct traffic to specific 'tourist destinations': in this case the seven miles to the wonderfully alliterative Cobbaton Combat Collection.

This route has a history of being seen as well worth driving. In the late 1920s it was highlighted by John Prioleau, the motoring correspondent for the *Spectator*, in a book of weekend drives for new car owners. Rather than following the road north to south as I did, Prioleau had his readers take this stretch in reverse. Driving from Eggesford to Barnstaple, he informed them that they would not be disappointed by driving along the Taw Valley that 'follows the rivers' twistings faithfully' and offered the chance to see 'one of the most beautiful valleys in the south'. 'It is all peaceful country with that warm look which gladdens the heart of the Devonshire lover,' Prioleau gushed, before alerting his readers that 'any temptation to drive fast must be most sternly repressed'. Although he thought it 'not likely that the occasion will arise' he warned the new breed of middle-class motorists to 'be on your guard against it for you will miss countless treasures unless you keep to a positive crawl'.[7]

Prioleau's advice came on the cusp of a major change in speed limits on Britain's roads. In 1903, the Motor Cars Act had introduced what was seen at the time as a liberal maximum speed limit of 20 mph. This seemed incredibly fast compared to the earlier speed limit of only 4 mph in rural areas. The interim loosening of this restriction in 1896 when the speed limit was raised to 14 mph was a cause for celebration for motorists who took to the roads on the inaugural London to Brighton run. Although widely flouted, the speed limit of 20 mph persisted through the 1910s and 1920s until it was finally abolished in the 1930 Road Traffic Act. A period of relative deregulation followed for a few years, before the 1934 Road Traffic Act introduced a maximum speed limit of 30 mph in 'built-up areas'. Once out of towns and cities, speed was only limited by the power of the engine and the self-control of the driver. It was not until the second half of the 1960s that maximum speed limits were introduced to the new motorways and to A-roads like this one.

Despite Prioleau's admonition to keep the foot off the gas, I kept the pace well above that of the recommended 'crawl' but below the 60 mph speed limit spelled out in black and white. I was driving this 'tourist route' on a Bank Holiday Monday in an era of mass car ownership, a world away from the age of an emerging middle-class motoring elite. When Prioleau sent his weekend drivers along this road, he was in the middle of two decades that saw a remarkable twenty-fold increase in car ownership. In 1919 there were just over 100,000 cars on Britain's roads. Two decades later there were over 2 million. This rapid increase in car owners created the market for the many motoring books – like those penned by Prioleau – published between the wars. However, while the 1920s and 1930s saw increasing numbers of motorists taking to Britain's roads, motoring tended to be for an elite. That began to change after the Second World War as the cars first bought by the middle classes in the 1920s and 1930s became affordable for working-class motorists in the second-hand car market of the 1950s and 1960s. This period also saw the mass production of new cars and prices fell in an increasingly competitive market. Between 1949 and 1965 the number of cars tripled. By 1970 there were over 12 million cars on Britain's roads.[8]

Half a century later – my wife and I in the front and the kids in the back – I was driving one of the just under 40 million cars registered in Britain. An estimated 10 per cent of those cars were on the road on this sunny Bank Holiday Monday in the late 2010s, but few of them were on this stretch of road that ran through tunnels of deciduous trees in their late spring light green, new leaf growth, with occasional glimpses of the river that ran alongside.[9] Further along I passed dark green plantings of conifers on either side of the road, as well as a sawmill. In 1951, motorists were alerted to 'much State afforestation on both sides of the valley'. That phrase 'State afforestation' was repeated many times in the captions that ran alongside the route maps in the *About Britain* guides. It reflected the interest in what grew from the soil, but it was also a chance to celebrate the transformation of what was seen as unproductive land.

Reaching Eggesford, I left the main road, crossed the railway and drove up the hill into Flashdown Wood. I was in search of the earliest 'State afforestation' in Britain. Established by the 1919 Forestry Act, the Forestry Commission sought to promote the planting of trees across Britain. Eight commissioners were appointed to oversee this mission. Among them were two aristocratic landlords – Lord Lovat, who was the commission's first chairman, and Lord Clinton – who were keen to ensure they were the first to plant Forestry Commission trees on their estates. There is a story, possibly apocryphal, which tells of a race to plant by these two as soon as the inaugural meeting of the commissioners ended. Lord Lovat immediately took the night train north with plans to plant on his Monaughty estate the following day. Lord Clinton headed west and was met at Eggesford station by a hastily convened tree-planting party. Once Clinton and his team had planted beech and larch saplings on his estate, they sent the news to Lord Lovat in a telegram that greeted him as he alighted at Elgin station.[10]

Finding those first trees wasn't easy. I was helped by a dog walker who had lived in the area her whole life, and whose brother worked for the current Lord Clinton as a stockman on his Hewish estate. She was on her way to visit the garden centre with her elderly mother and father and had decided to stop off at 'Lord Clinton's trees' as she called them, knowing that it would be nice and cool in their shade. However, these turned out not to be the original trees, but an avenue of copper beeches planted to celebrate the Forestry Commission's golden jubilee in 1969. I walked through them with my wife and daughters, the leaves' colours moving from light to dark in layers up each tree. It was one of my daughters who finally found the small grove of beeches and larches planted here in 1919, spotting the bronze plaque that spelled out their significance as 'the first planted by the Forestry Commission in the United Kingdom'.

Although these historic trees were here in 1951, the plaque wasn't. It was put up in 1953 during what one newspaper article described as a 'Forest Birthday'. Reading on, it was clear that just over three decades of 'State afforestation' was primarily being celebrated in economic terms. From this handful of beech and larch trees 'Britain's new forests' had delivered nearly £2 million to the nation's coffers in 1951.[11] Most of these were not beech or larch, but fast-growing Sitka spruce that promised a rapid return on investment. Describing Eggesford in the early 1950s, the Forestry Commission's in-house *Journal* boasted that this recently planted forest that 'extends to 1,000 acres' already formed 'an impressive sight on each side of the main road from

Exeter to Barnstaple' given that 'some of the Sitka spruce planted in those early days, though still only thirty-five years old, have already topped 100 feet'.[12]

While speed was not of the essence when it came to driving through this forest, it was when it came to afforestation, which was very much a commercial venture. The emergence of the Forestry Commission immediately after the end of the First World War was no coincidence. It grew from the discussions of the 'Home Grown Timber Committee' – chaired by the Devon landowner Sir Francis Dyke Acland whose former estate was on the guidebook itinerary in 1951 and therefore mine today – that had mobilized as much timber as possible for the war effort. Close to 500,000 acres of forests were felled during the war to produce everything from pit props for the coal mines, which fuelled industry and the navy, to timber for the miles of trenches constructed on the Western Front. War had highlighted the dangers of relying so heavily on imported wood. The recommendation of Acland's forestry subcommittee that existing British woodland be better managed and further woodland planted to ensure self-sufficiency during any future war was accepted and the Forestry Commission created to oversee both.

Acland's subcommittee set their sights on planting over a million acres of new forest by the end of the 1950s and almost double that by the end of the century.[13] They reached the first milestone in 1956. As the press pointed out, a million acres was a lot of land and a lot of trees. It was equivalent to a decent-sized English county, with Essex and Kent suggested as comparisons. In terms of trees, the estimates were that anything from 1,500 million to 2,000 million trees had been planted by hand.[14] To celebrate, the Forestry Commission decided to return to where it all began and headed once more to Eggesford Forest.

It was another helpful dog walker who pointed me in the right direction, and I made my way through another Forestry

Commission car park to the roadside verge where I found the Queen's Stone set back, but still visible, from the main road running between Barnstaple and Exeter. The dog walker tooted her car horn and waved cheerfully as she passed me a few minutes later as I stood on the verge looking at the stone unveiled by the Queen in 1956. The original plaque had recently been stolen, but it had been replaced with a new and shiny version contrasting with the dulled plaques at the base of each of the five trees ceremonially planted by the gathered 1950s VIPs.[15]

Between the time when the Forestry Commission was established and the day in May 1956 when the Queen had marked the planting of the millionth acre of new forest, Britain had once again been at war. Thoughts had again turned to the importance of self-sufficiency in timber and plans were drawn up for another post-war campaign of afforestation. This time the goals were even more ambitious. The plan was that by the end of the century Britain would be covered by 5 million acres of commercial woodland made up from 2 million acres of better-managed existing woodland and 3 million acres of newly planted forests. By 1976, the Forestry Commission reached their next major milestone and celebrated the planting of 2 million acres of woodland with a plaque unveiled in the Forest of Dean.[16] But their ambitious plans for 5 million acres of commercial woodland by the end of the century were never quite realized. In the opening decades of the twenty-first century, I drove through a country with close to 3 million acres of woodland. Although not quite on the scale imagined, Britain did look different as a result of commercial afforestation. When the Forestry Commission was set up, around 5 per cent of land was woodland. Just under a century later, it was around 13 per cent.

While the *About Britain* guides were enthusiastic about 'State afforestation' not everyone was so sure. During the 1950s there was already widespread feeling that foresters were 'much too fond of conifers' and that the 'alien' Sitka spruce, which originated from the west coast of North America, was changing the British landscape for the worse. One author of a number of books on forestry in the 1950s leapt to their defence on the grounds that demand for softwood outstripped the need for hardwood and the land being devoted to forestry was what he called 'only "conifer land"'. He drew an imaginary line across Britain that divided it into deciduous and 'conifer land'. Reassuring his readers in southern England that 'in recent years more broadleaved trees have been used', he explained that 'the proportion of hardwoods to softwoods planted by the Forestry Commission south of a line from Ipswich to Gloucester' was roughly fifty–fifty.[17] What was happening north and west of this line that I crossed over on future journeys was another matter entirely. 'State afforestation' continued to mean the mass planting of Sitka spruce through the 1950s, 1960s and into the 1970s: of the 77 million trees planted in 1971, 44 million were Sitka spruce.[18]

But there wasn't a single Sitka spruce in sight around the plaque unveiled to mark the first million acres of the reforestation of Britain. Instead, the stone was encircled by five oaks, one of them planted by the then Minister of Agriculture, Derick Heathcoat-Amory, who was MP for Tiverton. His constituency was just a few miles from Eggesford and the next stop on my itinerary. I left the oak tree he planted in 1956, turned off the 'tourist route' to Exeter and drove through Witheridge towards Tiverton on a beautiful stretch of road that took me from one valley to the next. Then, as now, it 'climbs and passes through farm land' and at one point I was stuck behind a tractor pulling a large trailer piled high with freshly cut grass that spilled down whenever we entered a tree-lined tunnel. Out of the wooded tunnels, there were views to either side over farmland and forest with the occasional wind turbine in the far distance. Dropping down into Tiverton, I was on the lookout for the 'old buildings of Blundells School' and 'the early nineteenth century textile factory' that motorists were instructed to 'observe' in 1951.

The textile factory was easy to spot, although the original building had been destroyed by fire and completely rebuilt in the 1930s. I pulled in to the yard to visit the factory shop, but the guard on the gate told me that the lights were only on because they were stocktaking. Despite not being open to the public on this Bank Holiday Monday, it was clear that Heathcoat Mill was still very much in business. It had recently celebrated its 200th birthday by re-enacting the walk of hundreds of lacemakers from John Heathcoat's original mill in Loughborough to the old woollen mill that he had bought in Tiverton. The relocation from Leicestershire to Devon took place after Luddites attacked Heathcoat's mill where he had pioneered machine-made lace. Heathcoat left Loughborough, taking a number of his workers with him. The mill in Tiverton had been producing military uniforms but failed to adjust to the changes brought by peacetime. This mill became the largest employer in town, producing machine-made lace, and then diversifying into a range of other high-end fabrics – crêpe de Chine, georgette, marocain – in the twentieth century. When the then royal princess, Elizabeth, married in 1947, she wore a veil manufactured in Tiverton. There was a longer-standing royal connection with the Heathcoat-Amorys before the Queen and Derick Heathcoat-Amory each planted an oak on the verge of the main road running through Eggesford forest.

But this factory did not survive the twentieth century simply by diversifying into new fabrics for high-end fashion and the world of ballet. In wartime the mill had expanded its output, producing munitions during the First World War and parachute silk and parts for Spitfires in the second. It has continued these connections with the military, producing high-tech uniforms alongside parachute fabrics for a global military market, bringing this factory in Tiverton squarely within the global military-industrial complex. Heathcoat Mill has been reimagined in the early twenty-first century as a leader in 'engineered textile solutions' that extends to weaving transmission belts for the automotive industry.[19]

A little further on I came across another mill that had also reinvented itself in the late twentieth century, not as a site of production but consumption. Bickleigh Mill was – like Heathcoat Mill – built in the eighteenth century, but as a corn mill, set within the surrounding agricultural land of the Bickleigh Castle estate. After devastating floods in the autumn and winter of 1960, the mill ceased grinding corn. It now offers 'three floors of retail therapy'. From one look at the crowded car park it seemed that few could resist the delights of 'one of Devon's largest and most exciting rural shopping, eating and recreation destinations', which 'blends the traditions of a bygone age with contemporary living and offers out of town shopping and dining in the most idyllic of settings'.[20] Perhaps I should have stopped to savour this intoxicating mix, but the *About Britain* guide predated such delights and advised me instead to 'visit the church for Carew monuments and the castle (privately owned) if open'.

When motorists passed by in 1951, Bickleigh Castle could be visited for one week in the summer, or at other times 'by appointment' with one shilling gaining access to the 'Saxon chapel; guard room and armoury'. By the 1970s, the attractions on offer six afternoons a week were expanded to include not only the 'Tower, Great Hall, Chapel, Guard Room and Armoury' but also a Tudor 'Maritime Museum' and a collection of 'spy and escape gadgets' all washed down with 'Cream teas in thatched barn'. Writing approvingly of the owners' desire to 'give . . . children not only instruction but also a really enjoyable time', one journalist extolled that 'this can be accomplished . . . without turning the garden into a mini-funfare but by using the facilities of the castle itself, and its environs, to the best advantage' allowing youngsters to 'indulge in the simple and yet mind-broadening jollifications so often denied the modern child'. These additions brought day trippers in by the carload. In the late 1970s and early 1980s just under 10,000 visited this heritage attraction each year. By the end of the 1980s this had doubled.[21] This growth came during a period, as I would see on later journeys, of the blossoming of the heritage industry fuelled in part by rising car ownership.

Bickleigh Castle continued to be open to the public through the 1990s, but this was a period when the heritage industry was beginning to wane and so many of the places that had already been reinvented once were due a second reinvention. When it went back on the market in the early 2000s, the castle was bought by an events organizer who re-badged Bickleigh as a luxury wedding venue. This new lease of life came after the deregulation of the wedding market following the passage through Parliament in 1994 of an amendment to the 1949 Marriage Act. The original Marriage Act had limited where marriages could take place; either under the watchful eye of the church or the state with its network of Registry Offices. In Bickleigh, it was the church with its monuments to the former owners of the castle that continued to have a wedding monopoly through the 1950s. But in the mid-1990s all that changed. Anywhere approved by the local authorities could now host weddings. Thousands of venues took up the opportunity offered by the privatisation of marriage ceremonies, and it seemed that I passed at least one alongside all the routes that I followed. This provided a new, and very lucrative, market for Bickleigh Castle, which hosted 'up to thirty' weddings a year in its latest reimagining as a site of 'dream' nuptials.[22]

No one was getting married at Bickleigh Castle on that Bank Holiday Monday, so I continued on through the village that was crowded with people sitting outside the 'cluster of fishing inns' on either side of the bridge that I crossed just before noon. Dropping down to the river, I caught a glimpse of rows of vines planted on the south-facing slope of the valley. I had passed the turning to the vineyard – marked by a grape-laden, brown tourist destination sign – just before reaching Bickleigh. A temporary banner on the side of the main road advertised that this was the start of 'English Wine Week'. But it turned out that Yearlstone Vineyard was closed on this Monday, like all other Mondays, regardless. It meant that I could only see the vines from afar, rather than taste the wines of the first commercial vineyard established in Devon.

The arrival of vines into this corner of Devon was unimaginable in 1951 when it was resolutely still a 'cider-orchard district' as the notes accompanying this tour described. When Gillian Pearkes planted the first vines here in the mid-1970s, she continued making two 'cyders' and a perry from the orchard here, but also added one red and three white wines. After Pearkes's death, Yearlstone was bought as an ongoing business and it continues to combine a cider orchard with a seven-acre vineyard. Pearkes had been bullish about the potential for transforming Devon from 'cider-orchard district' into 'the vineyard of England', boasting that 'the wines produced here have a character imparted from the vines, which are grown on old soils and rocks, in contrast to the cold clay farther east'. However, Yearlstone remains something of an outlier. By the mid-1980s there were around 50 commercial vineyards in the south-west – including a cluster in south Devon – but it was the chalky soils of the south-east – land mirroring the Champagne region – that attracted the most significant investment during the rebirth of the British wine industry in the post-war decades.[23]

As motorists were following these routes, commercial vinegrowing was tentatively being re-established after three decades of absence following the abandonment of the last British vineyards at Castell Coch in South Wales in 1920. In the second half of the 1940s, two pioneers – Ray Barrington-Brock, who established a Viticultural Research Station at Oxted in Surrey in 1946, and Edward Hyams who planted an experimental vineyard in Kent and published *The Grape Vine in England* in 1949 – experimented with finding grape varietals to suit British soils and climate. Writing in the late 1980s, Gillian Pearkes, who planted the vineyard at Bickleigh with vines from Oxted, reflected back nostalgically on those early days when 'Ray Barrington-Brock's open days in September were the greatest possible draw. Magical days – to see grapes actually ripening on vines in the open and to be given a glass of wine from these many separate varieties while talking to the handful of people then actually growing vines in England was a great experience.'[24]

Vines from Oxted were planted in the first commercial vineyard created on three and a half acres in Hambledon, Hampshire by Sir Guy Salisbury-Jones in 1952. The novelty of his venture made it newsworthy, with photographs of the former Marshal of the Diplomatic Corps in his vineyard cropping up in the press in the 1960s. A larger, five-acre, commercial vineyard was planted in 1960 at Beaulieu, again in Hampshire, by Colonel Robert and Mrs Margaret Gore-Browne. As Prue Leith wrote in the mid-1970s, the dozen or so 'veterans' of the industry who had planted the first vineyards tended to be 'upper middle class people who were worldly enough to know about wine, and rich enough to risk money at growing it'.[25]

Salisbury-Jones saw the economic potential of British vineyards. Having secured an off-licence, he started selling his wine to restaurants and shops as well as directly to members of the public at 18 shillings a bottle during 'open days' held at the vineyard in August and September. Moreover, as president of the English Vineyards Association – founded in 1967 – he lobbied for government aid to be allocated to the wine industry, which he estimated contributed more than £1 million in excise duty in 'a good year'. In particular he was critical of the practice of putting the same excise duty, more than a quarter of the total sale price, on English wine as the much inferior 'fortified brew of imported concentrate, water and sugar' made in industrial quantities.[26]

From Salisbury-Jones's original parcel of three and a half acres of vines, there are now close to 3,500 acres of vineyards across England and Wales. This story of growth has been patchy. When Pearkes planted two acres of vines at Yearlstone, she joined pioneering growers producing wine from a few hundred acres. The number of vineyards increased during the 1980s and early 1990s, reaching just under 500 covering over 2,600 acres. However, following several decades of continuous growth, there was a period of decline in the second half of the 1990s when many small vineyards went out of business. A decade later, things picked up again with the planting of new smaller vineyards. Although an English and Welsh wine industry has emerged in the last 70 years, it accounts for less than half a per cent of all the bottles bought in a country that is one of the world's biggest importers and consumers.[27]

I left Bickleigh and its orchard turned vineyard behind, and drove on through Silverton, entering into what the *About Britain* guide flagged up as the 'cider-orchard district'. When motorists drove across Devon in 1951, they made their way from north to south through a county with over 20,000 acres of orchards. However, not all was well that autumn. The difficulty of sourcing sugar as rationing continued meant that cider makers left thousands of tons of apples to rot in the orchards. But over the course of the following decades the situation worsened. Orchards were abandoned, replanted with other crops, or dug up to make way for new housing on the edge of villages. Since the 1960s, over 60 per cent of orchards have disappeared across Britain as a whole, with even higher rates of decline in some regions. In Devon, 90 per cent of orchards disappeared in half a century.[28] There were occasional glimpses of apple trees overhanging hedgerows or through gates as I drove through mid-Devon, but these were few and far between.

Things had got so bad by the early 1990s that orchards became an environmental battleground. A group named Common Ground drew attention to the fate of this vanishing landscape. Founded in 1983 by three leading members of Friends of the Earth, Sue Clifford, Angela King and Roger Deakin, Common Ground aimed to refocus the environmental movement on what it saw to be a range of threatened landscapes. On 21 October 1990, Common Ground celebrated the first National Apple Day at the old Apple Market in London's Covent Garden, long since stripped of its fruit-selling function to become a shopping destination like Bickleigh Mill. As well as bringing a cider bar and 100 traditional varieties of apples to central London, Common Ground also displayed images of West Country orchards by the photographer James Ravilious who had been recording the threatened sites since the 1970s.[29]

There has been a resurgence of cider makers in Devon and further afield. I found locally made cider on sale in the National Trust shop at Killerton House, along with an orchard containing a collection of traditional varietals. But it was not this orchard that the *About Britain* guide directed visitors to admire. In 1951, there were cider orchards aplenty, and visitors were directed to Killerton to see the 'remarkable' gardens with their 'fine collection of specimen trees and . . . rhododendrons and azaleas, which are in flower during May and June'. The gardens there looked particularly fine that year. To 'ensure' that 'English gardens' made 'an appropriate contribution to the Festival of Britain' the National Trust had worked with the Festival to guarantee that five of their gardens – one of which was Killerton – were 'in first-class condition'. Those heading there in May 1951 were not disappointed, but were greeted by 'the spring blossom at its best'.[30]

Given that it was late May, I decided to follow the guidebook's advice and stop to see the gardens. I was obviously not the only one keen to see the rhododendrons and azaleas. The main car park near the house was full, so I had to park in the overflow parking in a field just beyond. I dropped in to the house with my wife and kids after eating the last pasties in the cafe. It was not open to visitors in 1951 because it had been 'let to the Workers' Travel Association'. In the 1930s, 1940s and 1950s, the Workers' Travel Association had, as its official history expressed it, put 'great and famous houses to a new and inspiring purpose'.[31] By 1960, they had a portfolio of 18 holiday centres across the country, including the house at Killerton among a number of former stately homes. These were gradually shed as the association moved through a series of name changes from the 1960s onwards before being wound up in the late 1980s. Killerton moved from housing the Acland family, to workers on holiday, then student teachers from St Luke's College, before being opened to visitors during the heritage industry boom in the late 1970s that Bickleigh Castle had capitalized on.[32]

I passed many former country estates that are now National Trust properties. When Sir Richard Acland handed over the Killerton and Holnicote estates, it was the largest-ever gift the National Trust had received. These two estates brought the National Trust's total landowning to almost 100,000 acres as it celebrated its jubilee in 1945, and was signalled as 'a notable indication of the increasing importance' of the organization. Seventy years later, it owns well over six times as much land across England and Wales. When Acland gifted Killerton to the National Trust, he did so at a time when, as their Annual Report phrased it, 'owners of large houses are becoming more and more convinced that many of them may have no future whatever as private residences'. Faced with the costs of upkeep and death duties, the trickle of houses ending up in the hands of the National Trust became a flood in the decades following the 1940s.[33]

But Acland was motivated by more than simply a concern with keeping the estate intact. Even the right-of-centre press recognized that his gift was 'dictated partly by a desire to give some practical expression to his political theories'.[34] Like his father, Acland had entered Parliament as a Liberal. First standing unsuccessfully for the seat of Torquay (my final destination today), he was elected MP for Barnstaple (where I began my journey) at the second attempt in 1935. But in 1942 he left the Liberal Party to form the Common Wealth Party with J. B. Priestley before later joining the Labour Party – which in 1945 was committed to a policy of land nationalization – and became MP for Gravesend in 1947, a seat he fought and lost as an independent in 1955, before going on to be a co-founder of the Campaign for Nuclear Disarmament in 1957.[35]

Acland explained to his soon to be former tenants what had made him and his wife decide to give Killerton to the National Trust: 'Rightly or wrongly, it has been my growing conviction in these last years that we have now reached such a point in history that the private ownership of large properties of all kinds, including large landed estates, is impeding the Christian and economic development of our country.' He confessed that his landownings had become 'an increasingly heavy burden on my conscience'. But he clearly also had at least half an eye on the thing worrying many other landowners, expressing his relief that with his bequest the Killerton estate would remain 'safe for ever' on his death, rather than being broken up to pay death duties.[36] However, in the 1970s the safety of the estate would be called into question.

Lying stretched out on the grass in sight of the rhododendrons heavy with flowers, I became aware of a distant hum. The wind was coming from the east and brought with it the sound of traffic passing less than a mile away on the motorway. I glimpsed the flashes of light reflected off successive windscreens so decided to walk over to the M5 which cuts the Killerton estate in two. I followed the path through parkland, along the edge of the cider orchard, before reaching the thatched Budlake Post Office, now decked out as if in the 1950s, complete with a vegetable garden reflecting the moment when rationing drew to an end. Just beyond the post office, I stood on the bridge looking down on the Bank Holiday traffic crawling past.

The route of the M5 was surveyed in the mid-1960s, and work began on the final stretch to Exeter later that decade. In July 1971, a public inquiry opened into the proposed route running from the Cullompton bypass to Poltimore straight through the Killerton estate. Opposing what he saw as inflicting 'a fearful scar' on Killerton, the director general of the National Trust expressed his fears that riding roughshod through the estate would 'undermine the public's confidence in the Trust's ability to protect and hold its properties inalienably', which might 'have the most adverse effects on the faith of past benefactors and on the intentions of prospective donors'. He spoke these words not simply in the abstract, but with one of those past benefactors, Sir Richard Acland, who had spoken of Killerton now being 'safe for ever', sitting listening to him. Ultimately, his words were in vain. However, having lost the battle to keep the motorway from the Killerton Estate, the National Trust was quick to cash in on the opportunities presented by a large construction project on its doorstep. It requested planning permission to quarry gravel on the estate.[37] The motorway I looked down upon from the bridge was not simply built through the Killerton estate but also using material dug up from its grounds.

I avoided the motorway, taking the recommended 'by-roads' from Killerton towards Poltimore House, but I managed to miss a critical turning, so ended up on the outskirts of Exeter, bypassing the house entirely. Although the *About Britain* guide made clear that Exeter 'compels a pause in the journey', I was running late after my earlier stops so followed the ring road around the city, crossed over the river and headed south. The changes to the urban roadscape were glaring. Here, as in every town and city I drove around, was the combination of edge-of-town strip mall and supermarket alongside chain restaurants and a Starbucks Drive Thru. I probably should have Driven Thru for an experience unthinkable in 1951, but kept going on the widened road that emerged from the end of the motorway.[38] Heading up Telegraph Hill I passed, as the *About Britain* guide informed me, acres of dark conifers to left and right, with occasional flashes of purple rhododendrons in flower.

I left the main road, passing a solar farm and wind turbine before going down into Teignmouth. It was late afternoon and I found the last parking space along the promenade, walking back towards the Grand Pier while glancing down on reddening bodies stretched out on the red sand beach below. The pier looked less than grand. The ballroom closed long ago, and the red and yellow ladybirds of a children's ride lay beyond the barrier that stopped me walking the remaining two-thirds, which was closed off to the public after storm damage. All that remained of the stump of a pier was a packed amusement arcade with its ageing fortune-telling machine. Teignmouth – 'with its charming Georgian houses and terraces' in 1951 – was not the only seaside resort I drove through that seemed a little tired; forgotten as the range of holiday destinations have expanded. But there was something lovely about taking my shoes off and walking back to the car along the shore, trousers rolled up, ankle-deep in the bracing water.

Back in the car, I crossed the River Teign on the bridge that was 'only freed from toll charges in 1949'. I was sure these were words penned by James Stuart, drawing on what Angwin had called his 'wide knowledge of and affection for the area'. Like Stuart before me, I ended this coast-to-coast route in Torquay. I parked on the palm-tree-dotted promenade to the west of the main harbour, where boats were returning to the marina after a Bank Holiday Monday at sea and teenage boys jumped off the harbour walls into the chilly water. It was getting late, so I found a place serving upmarket fish and chips overlooking the harbour. The market-special whiting had sold out, so my wife, kids and I ordered hake, gurnard and monkfish alongside haddock and cod, served with tartare sauce tarted up with four Cornish seaweeds. I was very much hoping to sample a glass of Yearlstone white but sadly they didn't have any English wines on the menu, so I had to settle for a West Country cider instead.

Driving across Devon, I'd been primed by Angwin's letter to Stuart to pay attention to what grew out of the soil. Stuart's description of the route picked out Forestry Commission trees, National Trust rhododendrons and azaleas and the apple trees in the central 'cider-orchard district'. The Forestry Commission trees are not only still there, but there are more of them and they are a lot taller. At Killerton, it was clear from the crowded gardens that these exotics are still an attraction in late spring, although I was to discover on a later journey that not everyone is quite as fond of rhododendrons. But cider orchards were decidedly thin on the ground, and it seemed that in some cases vineyards had been planted not simply alongside them, but also in their place. New things have come out of Devon's red soils.

Landscapes change. But there are times, as with Common Ground's campaign to halt the decline in traditional orchards, that those changes are resisted. What struck me reading the words of Sue Clifford – one of Common Ground's founders

– was how she saw the loss of orchards as the disappearance of a 'cultural landscape'. 'When you lose an orchard you sacrifice not simply a few trees,' Clifford argued, 'but you might lose fruit varieties particular to that locality, the wildlife, the songs, the recipes . . . the look of the landscape, the wisdom gathered over generations about pruning and grafting. In short the cultural landscape is diminished by many dimensions with one blow.'[39] Her words echoed Angwin's belief in the connections between people and the land. There was a shared thread of romanticism running through the Festival of Britain, the *About Britain* guides I was trying to retrace and Clifford's elegy for the Devonian cider orchard.

But as well as this continuity in thinking about the land I'd also encountered the emergence of a new way of valuing orchards. Drawing on ecology rather than historical geography, saving and replanting orchards could be seen as anything from a way to overturn the environmental damage caused by the agro-miles of 'importing just over 400,000 tons of dessert apples into Britain' consuming 'fourteen million litres of fuel' in the process, to preventing 'priority habitat' loss that threatened biodiversity.[40] It was not simply the case that the land and what grew from it had changed since 1951. As I was to discover on subsequent journeys, there had also been a profound change in how that land and its products were imagined and valued.

Southampton–South Stoneham–Chandler's Ford–Otterbourne–Compton–Winchester–New Alresford–Bishop's Sutton–Chawton–Alton–Basing–Basingstoke–Worting–Overton–Laverstoke–Whitchurch–Longparish–Wherwell–Stockbridge–King's Somborne–Romsey–Cadnam–Brook–Fordingbridge–Breamore–Salisbury

2

Wessex

Southampton–Whitchurch–Salisbury (104 miles)

The beginning of each *About Britain* tour was marked on the map with the symbol of a hand and the words START HERE. Yet it was hard to work out exactly where to begin this journey. The hand hovered to the west of Southampton. A sketch of the medieval Bar Gate beside the bottom of the map hinted that this might be the place to set out from, but traffic no longer runs through this gate and, given where I was headed, I decided to try to start where the River Test enters Southampton Water.[1] However, it was impossible to catch a glimpse of the water, let alone get to it. I approached the 1930s 'Dock Gate No. 8', but it was closely guarded by a man and woman in high-vis jackets so I could go no further. Beyond the guarded gate lay the New Docks, or Western Docks, opened in 1934. Since then, there has been further expansion westwards. In the late 1960s, a container terminal was opened; it has grown as the quantity of goods being transported globally by container ships has risen. It now handles around 1.5 million containers a year. Only its rival port over on the east coast, Felixstowe, handles more.

Rather than trying to reach this dock-lined stretch of the River Test, I drove parallel to it. The port lay hidden behind fencing and guarded gates off to the left, but there were occasional glimpses of what lay just beyond this boundary. There was a wonderfully ironic moment when I saw rows of new cars waiting on the dockside and immediately behind them a pile of brightly coloured metal from cars that had been scrapped and crushed. On the other side of the road, I passed the glass pyramidal front of the Harbour Hotel, the headquarters of the cruise line Carnival UK, and the distinctive blue and yellow of an IKEA store in the edge-of-town mix of shopping, dining and leisure. Carnival UK's headquarters is well located. It lies a short drive from the largest cruise-ship terminal in the country where Carnival operates a fleet under the names of two long-established companies they have acquired: Cunard and P&O.

One of Cunard's liners – the *Queen Mary* – took pride of place in a full-page photograph in the middle of the *About Britain* guide to Wessex. The caption underneath explained that Southampton was the 'home port of the largest oceanic liners' and the site of 'exits and entrances' to the Continent and the Americas.[2] But this iconic ship can no longer be found here. In October 1967 the *Queen Mary* left Southampton for the last time, bound for California where she began a new life as a permanently moored hotel in Long Beach. Her place as the flagship of Cunard's fleet was taken over by the *Queen Elizabeth 2*, followed by the newly launched *Queen Mary 2* in 2004. But the vast *Queen Mary 2* was not at her berth in Southampton that morning. She must have been out at sea, perhaps in the middle of a luxury round-the-world cruise.

When motorists drove by the much smaller port here in 1951, they did so at a time when liners like the *Queen Mary* were the only means of transcontinental travel. All that changed in the 1950s with the start of the jet age. In a familiar story of technology developed for military purposes during the Second World War being repurposed for civilian life, the jet engine transformed travel. During the 1950s the British-built de Havilland Comet and the American-built Boeing 707 dramatically sped up long-haul travel. It became possible to get from London to New York in a matter of hours rather than days and by the end of the 1950s more passengers flew, rather than sailed, across the Atlantic for the first time. In 1957, close to a million crossed the Atlantic to and from Britain by sea. Fifteen years later this number had fallen to around 30,000, compared with the over 4 million who chose to fly.[3]

In order to survive, ocean liners had to change. While for the *Queen Mary* this meant being transformed into a hotel, for most others a new lease of life came with being used as cruise ships. Cunard's rival P&O, which formed a separate company – P&O Cruises in 1977 – converted two of their ships from liners going between Southampton and Sydney into cruise ships sailing via a series of ports, entertaining and feeding their passengers along the way. Rather than the ship being a way of getting from A to B, the on-board journey itself was rebranded as the experience.

These developments in Southampton were mirrored elsewhere, most notably on the other side of the Atlantic, which became the centre of the growing cruise industry. In the late 1960s and early 1970s, three big players emerged to dominate the global cruise market: Norwegian Cruise Line, Royal Caribbean International and Carnival UK's sister company Carnival Cruise Lines. These companies began ordering new, purpose-built cruise ships designed not for speed but with all the trappings of floating resorts. Over the last four decades the size and number of ships has grown considerably. Passenger numbers globally more than doubled between 2000 and 2010.[4] The cruise terminal at Southampton typically handles well over a million passengers a year.

Passing this vast port on the left, I found myself on a series of short motorways: first a stretch of the M271, then a slightly longer run of the M27, before it became the M3. Once on these motorways it appeared impossible to escape from them. I decided to stop at the services for a coffee. I'd been joined for this trip by two friends and colleagues, Barney and Lucy, who I'd worked with on a number of projects, including developing a series of sound journals called *Mayfly*, named after the insect that lives for only a few minutes to a couple of days after hatching.[5] It was early June and part of this road trip followed the River Test where I'd heard there was a good chance of finding mayflies so I'd invited them to join me. Coffee in hand, I stood with them flicking through the books on the table enticing customers into W. H. Smith. Having read the captions that ran alongside the strip map, I knew I was on the hunt for watercress as well as mayflies. I couldn't find a recipe for watercress soup in the *British Food* recipe book on display, but did find a photograph of the common mayfly – *Ephemera vulgata* – in the RSPB's *Nature Watch* and took this as an omen that I'd find mayflies although watercress might be in short supply.

According to the *About Britain* guide I should have taken the 'main road through Otterbourne and Compton' that 'follows the old Roman road into Winchester', but I chose to stay on the M3 a little longer. In part this was an opportunity to experience a few more miles of what the Thatcher government had boasted was the biggest road-building programme since the Romans.[6] But there was also pragmatism in my decision. I knew that the road the guidebook mentioned had since been dug up and replanted as a wildflower meadow. Reading back through my notes on these few minutes driven at 70 mph, I realized how my experience of the landscape had been reduced to a patchwork of contrasting colours I'd jotted down: dark green coniferous plantations speckled with pale purple rhododendrons, white chalk showing through young green planting.

I left the motorway at the next junction, headed west and claimed the last parking space in the Garnier Road car park just as it was vacated by returning dog walkers. Accompanied by my friends, I followed the path down to the Itchen Navigation Canal where wader-clad engineers from Southampton University were demonstrating the qualities of an inspection boat to a camera crew. I began chatting with a man who had paused to watch the scene. He turned out to be a keen fisherman who lived locally, so talk soon moved on to mayflies. He told me that his previous car had been black and how, in some years, swarms of mayflies had mistaken it for the dark surface of the water and started laying their eggs on it, something that had only stopped after he swapped his black car for a silver one. Our conversation soon shifted from mayflies to the stretch of motorway that I'd just driven along. It became clear where he stood on the question of extending the M3 from Southampton, a topic that had dominated local – and national – debate from the 1970s to the early 1990s. 'It's chalk not granite,' he told me and explained that they could 'have cut a tunnel with a teaspoon' rather than dig out the deep chasm in Twyford Down that I'd just driven through. As he left, he pointed the way towards the bridge crossing this controversial stretch of motorway, darkly warning me to cover my ears when I reached it.

The motorway lay on the other side of St Catherine's Hill, so I couldn't hear any traffic noise as I made my way along the towpath. Here I glimpsed my first mayflies: initially one and then another, then more floating downstream. Most looked spent, but one or two rose up briefly from the water to flutter a little before returning to rest on the surface. As I rounded the base of the hill and came to the valley that led towards the bridge, the sound of birdsong merged with the sound of traffic, which was now all too audible. Traffic noise soon dominated as I made my way up the valley and then climbed the chalk track onto the road that crossed over the motorway. I stood with Barney and Lucy in the middle of the bridge above the stream of cars and lorries travelling in both directions; we were greeted by one lorry driver honking his horn and giving us a friendly wave. Looking through the railings that kept me from the six lanes of traffic down below, I could just make out faint traces of erased graffiti. It was faded, but I could read one name: 'Mr Malone'.

I found his name again, just the other side of the bridge. It was etched on a chalk megalith that lay on the grass beside the fence that separated the eastern half of Twyford Down from the steep-sided cutting and the motorway down below. THIS LAND WAS RAVAGED the chalk megalith recorded in capitals for emphasis, before listing the perpetrators, starting with 'G. Malone' – Conservative MP for Winchester in the early 1990s – and then moving on to a mixture of familiar and less familiar names: 'J. MacGregor, R. Key, J. Major, D. Keep, C. Parkinson, C. Patten, M. Thatcher, C. Chope'. At the turn of the century English Heritage had recommended that this stone receive official protection through listing, but in a rare move their request was rejected by the government.[7] Unlisted and unprotected, it lay fallen on its back with an empty Red Bull can next to it. I saw the drink as a libation of sorts, but perhaps I was reading too much into this place where ribbons had been tied to the motorway fence and fluttered in the stiff breeze that blew over this interrupted downland.

Both the megalith and the cutting were the products of more than two decades of wrangling over how to speed up traffic running to and from the expanding docks at Southampton. Although a bypass had been built to the east of Winchester just before the war, and opened just after, it was quickly seen as insufficient for the growing number of vehicles. In particular, the 'bottleneck'-causing traffic lights at Hockley were demonized as the 'only signal-controlled crossing between Southampton and Edinburgh' leading to demands that they be removed. In 1991 Christopher Chope, then Conservative MP for Southampton

Itchen and Minister for Roads and Traffic – whose name appeared among the list of 'ravagers' featured on the megalith – claimed in the ultimate example of time costs money that the 'Hockley Jams' were costing the country a million pounds each month through the delays they caused.[8]

During the 1970s, a number of routes to extend the motorway all the way to Southampton were proposed, countered and newly proposed. Initially, a route to the west of Winchester was favoured, but this was rejected largely because of the opposition of local landowners. After a decade of failed attempts to identify a suitable route closer to the city, a new route was proposed in the early 1980s that went much further east, literally through the middle of St Catherine's Hill. At the first of two public inquiries held in the mid-1980s the option of building a tunnel underneath, rather than a cutting through, St Catherine's Hill was raised. As the fisherman I'd met made clear, there were still many who saw a tunnel as the preferred option. The idea of a toll tunnel through the middle of Twyford Down continued to be discussed during the late 1980s but was ultimately dismissed on the grounds of cost. In early 1990, the government announced that the motorway would go through a cutting deep into Twyford Down. This was seen by the president of the Twyford Down Association that mobilized to oppose these plans, as nothing less than 'the greatest single act of visible destruction ever worked on the scenery of southern England'.[9]

Building a motorway here was also seen as doing great archaeological and ecological damage. The proposed route for the motorway cut through land that had been granted protected status in the post-war era. It threatened to damage parts of two Scheduled Ancient Monuments, a Site of Special Scientific Interest, and cut through an Area of Outstanding Natural Beauty. These last two categories were by-products of the decision to create National Parks in the late 1940s, seeking to limit development on land seen as worth preserving because of its natural or cultural value. Twyford Down was therefore something of a triple whammy. But this was not the only place where it seemed that these state-sponsored designations were dispensable. In 1990, it was estimated that over 600 Sites of Special Scientific Interest had been lost or damaged in the previous decade, and that close to another 400 were threatened by road-building plans.[10]

Opponents of the Twyford Down scheme sought to call upon a higher authority than the seemingly schizophrenic British state. In 1990 they brought a legal case against the British government on the grounds that it had failed to implement the Environment Impact Assessment Directive. This led to a very public spat between the European Environment Commissioner and the Conservative government over questions of sovereignty that chimed with wider Eurosceptic sentiment and meant this appeal was ultimately unsuccessful. In 1992 preliminary works on the site began. It was at this point that opposition to road building moved beyond the rooms of public inquiries and offices in Brussels. A political battle took place on the ground during the general election that spring, with a partially successful tactical voting campaign that saw Chope defeated in Southampton Itchen, although Malone took the Winchester seat for the Conservatives.

The battle to save Twyford Down also moved to a new phase on St Catherine's Hill as initial peaceful protests by Friends of the Earth shifted to tactics employed by Earth First! activists. Earth First! had emerged in America in the early 1980s. In Britain their initial focus was not on anti-roads protest, but direct action to blockade nuclear power stations and halt imports of hardwoods from the rainforests. However their attention moved to a call to 'Reclaim the Streets' that culminated in the protest at Twyford Down.

In the summer of 1992, protesters occupied the site, claiming a connection with its past inhabitants by calling themselves the Dongas Tribe. This name came from the ancient hollow-ways crossing the landscape used by drovers, but also drew on a tradition of Celtic tribes – or what were claimed as 'indigenous Albions' – who opposed the Romans. In an attempt to stop construction, the Dongas set up camp on Twyford Down until they were forcibly evicted at the end of the year and the road I'd just driven along was completed.[11] However, the opening of this road did not spell the end of protests. What began at Twyford Down was repeated across Britain during the 1990s. Direct action against new road building – from the Newbury bypass to Fairmile near Exeter – became a familiar story in the British press, with Daniel Marc Hooper, better known as 'Swampy', emerging as its unlikely figurehead.

It did not spell an end to the Dongas either. After their camp was broken up, some took to the road as travellers. In the mid-1990s, the Dongas called for a revival of the Tan Hill Fair in Wiltshire, announcing a 'Tribal gathering – all folk welcome to join the growing tribe living in benders on the hill forts, backways and woodlands of Wessex . . . travelling by foot, horse, donkey, bicycle and handcart, celebrating our stolen countryside, the right to live together tribally and celebrate the seasons!'[12] Both the Dongas' choice of the ancient name of Wessex and series editor Geoffrey Grigson's choice of Wessex as the title of the *About Britain* guide to this region seemed to be attempts to turn back the clock to a distant and mythical past.

The Dongas ultimately achieved some success in their efforts to halt change. The battle for Twyford Down marked an important shift in thinking about both road protests and roads. During the 1980s, there had been broad acceptance of the need for new, larger roads to carry more and more vehicles with protesters simply questioning precisely where these were sited or seeking to mitigate the impact of new roads. Later, protesters began a more fundamental critique of the desire to build new roads. The occupation of Twyford Down took place in the same summer that the 'Earth Summit' was held in Rio de Janeiro. This saw a change in environmental concerns from opposing a road to the much bigger question of reducing global vehicle emissions.[13] After Twyford Down, road-building policy in Britain was never the same again. It spelled the end of a policy of 'predict and provide' that fuelled the government's 1989 white paper, which called for a 'step change' in road building in order 'to provide additional capacity in support of growth and prosperity'. In its place, a more critical policy emerged that recognized that road building was part of the problem as it led to increased demand. Royal Commission on Environmental Pollution reports in the 1990s called for a more fundamental turn away from car dependency, although these remain more aspirational than delivered on.[14]

I headed back – ironically perhaps – towards the car. To get there I had to cross over the road taken by motorists driving from Southampton to Winchester in 1951. The tarmac had long been broken up and the site filled in with chalky soil taken from the nearby cutting and the whole area grassed over. In an attempt to transfer habitat down the hill, turf was cut from Twyford Down with seeds, plants and butterfly eggs in situ, and replanted in the old transport corridor on the eastern side of St Catherine's Hill.[15] This was an attempt to restore the former Site of Special Scientific Interest land that had been displaced, and the species – especially of butterflies – found on it. I walked with my colleagues along this former road now replanted as wildflower meadow listening to Galliano's song 'Twyford Down' playing on Barney's phone. The sound of the motorway faded as I rounded the base of St Catherine's Hill. In the valley, I passed a grazing deer as I walked back down to, and then along, the Itchen Navigation Canal to the car.

Leaving the car park, I bypassed the southern edge of Winchester, 'the ancient capital of England', and made my way along a farm- and tree-lined road towards Ropley. Entering the village I passed a former pub – the Anchor – now remodelled as a Thai restaurant. Leaving the village I spotted another – the Chequers Inn – boarded up and awaiting demolition to make way for nine new homes. In the next village – Four Marks – another roadside pub from the 1930s had been converted into a Co-op. Closed and repurposed pubs were a familiar sight along the roads that I retraced; the Campaign for Real Ale's claim that eighteen pubs a week were closing was made materially visible.[16]

Things had been very different seven decades or so earlier. Ropley's former roadside pubs were typical of the new lease of life given to village inns as the car opened up new leisure and dining destinations for inter- and post-war urban motorists. Rather than being restricted to those places where train tracks ran, roads opened up the rural interior. In the early years of middle-class motoring, the car was imagined as 'the "magic carpet" of modern life' that could transport travellers through time and space on 'tours of exploration through old-world towns and villages where castles, churches and inns breathe their messages from the dim past'.[17] But as well as bringing new trade to old pubs, the increasing number of cars also led to the building of new pubs and the renovation of the old. This had been the case with the Chequers Inn in Ropley. Photographs from the early part of the twentieth century show a more modest coaching inn on this spot.[18] This was replaced during a period of interwar building that saw mock-Tudor coaching inns appearing like this one.

Given the link between roads, motorists and the rebirth of the village inn, it is perhaps no surprise that the *About Britain* guides were sponsored by the Brewers' Society who had a vested interest in encouraging motorists to head out for a whole day and stop off for something to eat and drink. Although it had been an offence to be 'unfit through drink' when driving since the 1930s, and the 'motorway code' warned drivers that 'even small quantities of alcohol or drugs may affect your judgment', it was not until 1967 that the law was tightened and a maximum alcohol limit introduced along with the breathalyser to enforce the new law.[19] But the closure of roadside pubs had less to do with the tightening of drink-driving laws, than with other changes taking place. In part the building of the motorway network during the 1960s and 1970s – and beyond – took long-distance motorists away from A-roads like this. They were more likely to stop, as I had done earlier that morning, at a motorway service station for something to eat or drink, than visit a roadside pub. There was also a change in where drinking took place, as it relocated from the roadside pub to the home.

I continued towards Alton, mistakenly bypassing Chawton and the Jane Austen's House Museum in the process. It seemed that those putting this route together had also omitted Austen. Her former home had been bought and opened as a museum in 1949, but Austen was absent from the caption midway along this section of the route map, although the gazetteer at the back of the guidebook picked out Chawton as 'a place of pilgrimage for lovers of Jane Austen'.[20] The guide was more interested in someone else, even though this lay just off the itinerary. Below an illustration of Selborne Church, the caption informed motorists that 'some 5 miles south-east of Alton is Selborne, where Gilbert White (1720–1793), the author of *The Natural History of Selborne*, was vicar.' Living in this part of Hampshire, White was familiar with mayflies. They made an appearance on his 'Naturalist's Summer-Evening Walk' and I hoped that they'd also appear on this June day centuries later.[21]

At Alton, I turned off towards the 'busy railway and agricultural centre' of Basingstoke. As if on cue, the road ducked under a bridge carrying the railway line that had run parallel to me for the last few miles. Known as the 'Watercress Line', this stretch of railway has closed, and then reopened, since motorists were directed underneath it in 1951. First built in the 1860s, this secondary line was one of the many miles of track identified for closure just under a century later as part of the so-called 'Beeching cuts' that ended roughly a third of all passenger services across the country. However, rather than accepting the end of this service, a group of rail users battled closure through a series of public inquiries in the late 1960s and early 1970s. Ultimately they were unsuccessful. In 1972, the decision was made to close the line and introduce a bus service.

This was not to be the end of this line. Just as one campaign to save the railway from closure was drawing to an unsuccessful close in 1972, a new campaign began. While those who battled to keep this line open in the late 1960s wanted to maintain a daily rail link for commuters and shoppers living in the villages along the track, those fighting to reinstate the line in the early 1970s saw a new future for the railway as a heritage attraction. With limited funds, three miles of track between Alresford and Ropley were reopened in the late 1970s. The nostalgic steam-train service each summer weekend proved hugely popular. Over 50,000 tickets were sold in the first season. This success meant that during the 1980s the remaining stretches of the line were restored. If I'd been here at the weekend, I could have joined the Saturday night 'Real Ale Train' from Alton through Four Marks and Ropley to Alresford – and then back again – sampling two local ales at 'pub busting prices' in the restored bar carriage.[22]

As I was to discover elsewhere on these journeys, the 1970s were, ironically, something of a new golden age of rail. The axing of miles of the rail network and phasing out of steam trains in the 1960s coincided with a rising interest in – and nostalgia for – Britain's disappearing industrial past. The more than 100 rail preservation societies that emerged not only set out to buy up miles of track like the 'Watercress Line' but also to purchase steam locomotives that had been dispatched to a scrapyard in South Wales. By the mid-1970s, enthusiasts had rescued around 1,000 steam trains from being broken up, and the National Railway Museum had opened in York as the home for the most prized examples. As well as allowing passengers to ride steam trains, the sound of steam was brought into British living rooms through the popular series of Transacord recordings, which at their peak reached sales figures of 40,000 records a year.[23]

But I stuck to the road rather than following the rails, and made my way towards Basingstoke. On the outskirts of town, I crossed under the motorway thundering above me and ended up on the ring road. I should have headed east to take the detour carefully marked out in the *About Britain* guide to include 'the ruins and earthworks of Basing House, the ancient seat of the Paulet family' that are now part heritage attraction, part wedding venue. But I headed west around the ring road to begin the return journey along the River Test.[24] Here I passed a massive out-of-town leisure complex where opportunities for fun were piled one on top of another: an Aquadome, Bowlplex, Odeon multiplex cinema, Planet Ice, Indoor sky diving and Milestones museum – complete with a recreated 1940s sweet shop – all washed down with Drive-Thru Costa coffee. It was half term and the car parks were packed, but I kept going, following the first of many brown tourist signs simply stating 'Bombay Sapphire'. The sides of the road were strewn with the white of cow parsley and hawthorns in full flower and at one point the flowery verge offered the final resting place of a dead deer, which had attracted birds of prey circling above it.

I stopped in Overton in search of both watercress and lunch. Given the Brewers' Society sponsorship of the *About Britain* guides, I felt duty-bound to eat at the local pub. The White Hart had a 'Watercress and Old Winchester salad' on the menu, but it only came as an accompaniment to the steaks. When asked about its provenance, the man behind the bar simply told us that it came from 'our suppliers' so I opted for 'locally-smoked' trout instead. After lunch I walked around the village with Barney and Lucy but could find no signs of the once-flourishing watercress industry. The closest I got was some wild watercress growing in the clear waters of the river and a bottle of Twisted Nose watercress gin, made just down the 'Watercress Line' in Old Alresford, on sale in the local wine merchants. According to the Winchester Distillery, started in the mid-2010s amid a revival of interest in gin, Twisted Nose offered 'an intensely herbaceous yet delicately floral spirit with soft sweet citrus notes and spicy undertones finishing with a peppery finish'.[25]

While those putting the captions together described Overton as 'a village of watercress-growing', elsewhere in the guide Grigson was more dismissive. It was not the only place where the authors of these opening 'verbal portraits' and those in the Festival Office putting the tours together differed in their opinions. Overton didn't even make it into the gazetteer Grigson created: there was literally nothing to see here. And in his opening essay, he made it quite clear that watercress growing did not meet with his aesthetic approval. While quick to claim that the hillsides of eastern Hampshire 'measured out with hop poles' were perhaps as, if not more, 'attractive formally than a vineyard in southern France or along the Rhine', 'the growing of watercress' was 'another matter' entirely. Describing what was 'one of the minor industries of our time . . . without much charm' Grigson declared watercress beds 'insipid and unlovely objects as one can see quickly enough in Eastern Hampshire at Alresford and Basing'. The only saving grace was that 'watercress is not grown on a scale great enough to interfere with the general delights of the eye'.[26]

You get the sense reading Grigson that he would not have been sorry to see watercress growing disappear from Overton. The highpoint in this industry came in the mid to late nineteenth century, when watercress was a 'cheap staple' in the diet of the urban working class. The 'Watercress Line' was named after the goods transported from the chalk-stream-fed watercress beds in Alresford to Basingstoke and then on to cities in the Midlands and northern England. But during the 1950s the industry fell into decline following the outbreak of Crook root disease. From over 1,000 acres of watercress beds in 1940s, there were less than 150 acres 60 years later. Most, like those in Overton, had simply been abandoned.[27] Watercress was relegated to a garnish rather than a staple.

In the last two decades watercress has made something of a comeback. In the early 2000s, growers launched a cheeky 'Not just a bit on the side' advertising campaign and Alresford began holding an annual Watercress Festival to kickstart National Watercress Week each May. The increased publicity worked. Watercress production and sales doubled in the 2000s.[28] This revival did not take place in Overton but further west along the Test and its tributaries. Ten miles away, St Mary Bourne is home to the largest watercress farm in Europe. However, the rise in popularity of this 'superfood' bred another set of challenges. To meet demand, supermarkets sourced watercress grown in Spanish polytunnels rather than English chalk-stream-fed pools. Local growers fought back in the 2010s and successfully argued their case that the European Union make a distinction between 'watercress' – a 'traditionally grown crop . . . cut from flowing water' – and what could now simply be called 'land grown cress'.[29] This was not the only case of claims to the importance of *terroir* that I'd come across. It reminded me of Angwin's words to Stuart that argued for the importance of the soil and what grew in and out of it. However, that connection has more recently been spectacularly severed, as I would discover on my next journey.

I left watercress-less Overton and continued along the 'London Road' following yet more brown signs towards Bombay Sapphire's new home in Laverstoke. When motorists drove through here in 1951, this was the place where 'paper for Bank of England notes' had 'been made . . . since 1724, in mills belonging to the Portal family'. Just a few miles from Overton where I'd stopped for lunch, is the technology centre for De La Rue, which is the world's largest producer of banknotes and passports. But they no longer make banknotes in Laverstoke, but rather 'every drop of Bombay Sapphire gin' instead. Traces of the building's past as a paper mill are visible. A small display in the lobby included a copy of a watermark produced here to celebrate the Festival of Britain. But the mill stopped making paper in the 1960s, fell vacant in the 2000s and was bought by Bacardi and turned into a distillery and visitor centre offering a range of 'experiences' in the 2010s. The bar was crowded with retirees sipping their end-of-tour gin and tonics and gin cocktails. Chatting with the guy on the front desk, it was clear that these numbers were typical for a mid-week afternoon at this distillery and had been visited by around 65,000 'experience seekers' the year before.

Rather than join them, I stood with my colleagues looking across the River Test that runs by and through the mill to the Thomas Heatherwick-designed glasshouse, which has been added on to the red-brick paper mill to encase the ten botanicals that flavour this gin. There was no sign of watercress, and the only mayflies I saw were the few that were either dead or dying and floating on the water, so I decided to move on and follow the

River Test to search for mayfly in Stockbridge. After parking up on the wide main street, I followed the advice of the wine merchants in Overton who'd told me to take the path that ran beside Lillies' tea rooms into the water meadows. That, they reckoned, would give me the best chance of finding mayflies while the temperatures were still a little on the cool side. My fellow mayfly hunters and I arrived in the water meadows just as the sun came out from behind the clouds and the day was at its warmest. I glimpsed a few mayfly along the Test but when heading back to the high street we came across a looping dance of mayflies and were enveloped in literally hundreds of large specimens with their distinctive triple tails, one shorter in the middle. They rose and then glided back down, resting now and then on a fence post or wire, or on reeds or grasses beside the stream.

Back on the High Street, I suggested that we drop into the Grosvenor Hotel for a cup of tea. From our table by the bar we watched, helplessly, as a single mayfly desperately attempted to climb up the inside of a locked, double-glazed window that looked out onto the street before falling down and then trying to repeat this action again and again. This dying mayfly was mirrored by the framed cases of tied fishing flies that covered the walls of the downstairs bar as well as the corridor leading to the gents. No doubt there were more upstairs in what the *About Britain* guide described as the 'HQ of the celebrated "Houghton Club" for fly-fishermen' that occupies the rooms above the bar, having been co-founded by the landlord of the then Grosvenor Arms in 1822. When Grigson wrote his introductory essay, he described the Grosvenor Hotel as home to 'Britain's most select and exclusive circle of anglers'.[30] It still is.

The Houghton Club not only owns this hotel, but close to 15 miles of both banks of the River Test either side of Stockbridge. With fishing rights along the Test changing hands for £600 per foot, the value of this riparian strip is eye-watering. It proved just as difficult to get down to the river here as along the fenced-off industrial zone by the Southampton docks. The wine merchants in Overton had suggested I take the path beside the tearooms in Stockbridge for a reason – this was one of the very few places where anyone can access the river. Grigson explained that the 'chalk streams of Wiltshire and Hampshire' offered 'some of the most delicate, rewarding, and incidentally most expensive by the yard of any fishing to be had' before adding 'I should hesitate to estimate the cost per trout per season for a rod on one of the best beats of the Test or the Itchen.' Little has changed. Gaining access to the Test during the season remains prohibitively expensive. And in the case of the long length of the riverbanks owned by the Houghton Club, it remains impossible, except to a very narrow group of less than 30 members, which includes the Duke of Northumberland among a select list of the landed and business elite.[31]

I left Stockbridge following the Test south. 'Below King's Somborne', the caption alongside this stretch of the route explained, 'the road and railway both follow the easiest natural route by clinging to the river valley.' The road still clings to the river valley, but the Sprat and Winkle Line went the way of the Watercress Line and was closed in the mid-1960s as part of the Beeching cuts. Rather than being restored as a steam railway, the former railway line makes up part of the Test Way long-distance footpath. Just past King's Somborne, the trail passes between a converted station and platform, complete with a 1920s carriage, which functions as a railway enthusiast's wedding venue.[32] Although the Test Way follows the course of this famous river from the South Downs to Southampton Water, it doesn't get close to these treasured and privately owned riverbanks very often.

I stuck to the road, rather than walking a stretch of the Test Way, and drove on to Romsey. Here several of the 'fine old inns' seemed to have been converted into a dental surgery, shop or restaurant. I had almost made it back to Southampton, but this route didn't return back to where it had started out. Instead, it headed north-east to finish in Salisbury, which had been chosen as the centre for the next series of tours. Heading towards Cadnam I spotted a brown tourist sign to the Rufus Stone that was illustrated on the route map in the guide. Following it meant that I ended up on the dual carriageway that emerged from the end of the M27 in the middle of rush hour. Pushed along by the flow of traffic, I quickly passed signs to the Rufus Stone services and then the Rufus Stone itself. This sign pointed off to the right. I had to make my way across two lanes of busy traffic.

Once I reached the other side and crossed over a cattle grid, I entered into what seemed like another world. I drove past ancient oaks, and stopped at the Rufus Stone, which stood erect unlike that other memorial stone on St Catherine's Hill I'd visited earlier that day. A Forestry Commission guidebook to the New Forest produced in 1951 promised those who turned off the main road a 'wilderness of wood and moor, where oaks and beeches that number their years by centuries stand beside heaths that the plough has never broken', and a return to 'primeval England'.[33] Standing by the Rufus Stone perhaps this wasn't quite the case, but there was something peaceful about this place.

In 2005, the New Forest became the ninth National Park in England, and the fourteenth in the country. It wasn't the only National Park I'd visited that day. Earlier that morning I'd strayed into the very edge of the fifteenth, and newest National Park, which includes a swathe of the South Downs running from St Catherine's Hill eastwards to the edge of Eastbourne. Both were latecomers to the attempt to open up access to large areas of 'relatively wild country'.[34] The first National Parks in 1951 were Dartmoor, the Lake District, the Peak District and Snowdonia. Some authors in the *About Britain* guides mentioned them in their opening essays. In the guidebook to the Home Counties the naturalist Richard Fitter expressed his disappointment that 'the only proposed national park within fifty miles of London' – on the South Downs – was 'not among the first . . . designated'.[35] Fitter was to remain disappointed for the rest of his life. The South Downs only became a National Park five years after his death.

When John Dower drew up his preferred list of National Parks in 1945, he deliberately excluded the South Downs and the New Forest. This was because he was 'reasonably satisfied that they would, in future, be adequately dealt with by other agencies; the South Downs by the county and local authorities, and the New Forest by the Forestry Commission.' But it was also more negatively framed. Dower explained that 'both have, unfortunately, suffered considerably in places from past misdevelopments' and he was also convinced that 'large-scale afforestation . . . cannot be successfully combined with National Park requirements'.[36] That the New Forest had a history as a commercial forest would have been clear to visitors driving through in 1951. They could read a new guidebook published by the Forestry Commission, which made explicit reference to the forest's wartime exploitation, when 'great quantities of timber had to be felled to meet urgent national requirements'. Attempting to paint a picture of just how much timber had been removed during the Second World War, the guidebook explained that it was enough wood to 'provide a decking . . . one inch thick and nine feet wide' for a bridge reaching from nearby Southampton all the way to New York.[37]

The loss of the timber was no doubt still visible in 1951, but visitors were reassured that the last few years had seen 'much natural seeding, and replanting, so that the scars should soon be covered up', in part at least by fast-growing conifers that promised a quick return.[38] But the route took me not through the forest, but rather across grazing land on my way to Fordingbridge where I stopped to let the ponies and cattle that have 'a prior right over any car' cross the road before me.[39] I left this forest shared by foresters, grazers and their cattle as well as tourists, and crossed over a new river: the River Avon. Approaching Salisbury on the road that ran parallel to the river, I saw the spire of the cathedral standing tall above the city in the light of the setting sun. I caught glimpses of the view from the south, west and north as I made my way around the inevitable ring road encircling this city that the *About Britain* guide described as 'perhaps the most beautiful county town in England' and so just the kind of place for motorists to spend a couple of nights, interspersed with a circular round-trip of 100 miles taking in Stonehenge and Avebury, before heading the next day the 78 miles to Dorchester. But I needed to head home so couldn't hang around.

Driving back, my thoughts turned to time and in particular how we measure it. These thoughts were triggered by the mayflies I'd seen. As the Latin species name *Ephemera* makes clear, the mayfly is best known for the brevity of its life. I was conscious that this journey had brought multiple timespans together. At one extreme lay the day or two of a mayfly's life. In between were the 70 years since the Festival of Britain that marked a human lifespan. At the other extreme lay geological time seen in the chalk that I had driven through, walked on, and that had shaped the rivers with their trout and mayflies. Time can be measured at all these different scales and ideas of continuity and change vary accordingly. From the perspective of the chalk – the cutting into St Catherine's Hill aside – not much had changed along this journey. The same was true at the other end of the scale. Not much changes as far as human history – if not entomological history – is concerned, in the few hours or days of a mayfly's life.

But as I retraced these routes, I had chosen to work with the perspective of a human lifespan. Working with 70 years changes become more visible. Things looked different along the sides of the roads that motorists had driven in 1951. But adopting the measure of the human lifespan did not only make me think about change, it also highlighted continuity. It was now impossible to get to the mouth of the River Test because of the changes wrought by containerization and the movement of millions of tons of goods by sea. But it was also impossible to get to the stretches of the River Test upstream because of the persistence of elite cultures that had successfully navigated post-war Britain and stayed afloat. Driving from Southampton to Salisbury, it seemed that Britain was both very different and yet in some ways still much the same.

*Canterbury–Lower Hardres–Stanford–Westenhanger–
Lympne–West Hythe–Dymchurch–Hythe–Sandgate–
Folkestone–Dover–Ringwould–Walmer–Deal–
Sandwich–Ramsgate–Broadstairs–Kingsgate–Margate–
St Nicholas at Wade–Herne Bay–Swalecliff–Whitstable–
Faversham–Sheldwich–Leaveland–Wye–
Chilham–Thanington–Canterbury*

3

Home Counties

Canterbury–Margate–Canterbury (104 miles)

'The route leaves Canterbury past St Lawrence cricket ground' explained the *About Britain* guide, so I dutifully made my way around yet another inner ring road – this one shaped by the line of the city's walls – and headed south.[1] A cricket ground not only began this journey, but also heralded the beginning of the Home Counties guidebook. The watercolour on the title page, intended to provide a visual clue to the region as a whole, showed a village cricket match rendered in whites and greens.[2] It was not the only cricketing image in the book. A photograph in the centre spread showed fans celebrating the 'popular victory when West Indian cricketers beat England at the Oval in 1950'. The West Indies hadn't simply beaten England. They had thrashed them by more than an innings in this last match of a series they had won convincingly. The symbolism of this first Test series win against England in what the caption underneath described as 'a world as well as an empire capital', was clear.[3]

Half of the journeys at the end of the guidebook began in what was still, just, the 'empire capital London'. They offered day trips that worked their way counter-clockwise around the city with an emphasis on the Home Counties that lay to the north. The other six focused attention on the land south of the capital, dipping a frequent toe into south-coast resorts as motorists made their way from and between Canterbury, Tunbridge Wells and Brighton.[4] I was due to visit Canterbury to speak at the university, so I decided to follow the first of the tours that began and ended there, hugging the Kent coastline en route. I'd driven from Bristol early that morning, so by the time I reached the cricket ground I wanted both a coffee and a chance to stretch my legs.

The St Lawrence cricket ground is no longer named simply after its location on the edge of the city. In 2013 it was renamed the Spitfire Ground, St Lawrence, not directly in honour of that most famous of wartime British aircraft, but rather more indirectly, driven by the marketing copy of its sponsors, Shepherd Neame brewery. Large advertising banners showing a bottle of 'Spitfire Gold – the Bottle of Britain' – were wrapped around the columns of each of the five large floodlights that looked down on the ground. A day–night game – another innovation alongside sponsorship – was scheduled for the following week. But with no match today, two men doing some work on the ground told me I could get pitch-side if I headed through the Lime Tree Cafe. After circling the boundary that used to include a lime tree before it succumbed to a fungal rot in the 1990s and was finished off by a storm in the 2000s, I headed back through the cafe that celebrates this odd arborial pitch invasion to the car.

I followed the road around the ground before driving – carefully as the sign instructed – through Lower Hardres. This sign, like others that I passed, adopted the widespread practice of incorporating 'a road safety message, of no more than 5 words' from the various options on offer: 'Please drive slowly, Please drive safely, Please drive carefully, Welcomes careful drivers, Welcomes slow drivers, Welcomes safe drivers' and 'Thank you for driving carefully'.[5] From Lower Hardres, I followed the line of the old Roman road of Stone Street that 'runs straight for nearly ten miles without even a village': something reinforced by the rod-straight inset route map that began with a straight line running directly south from Canterbury. The road was straight, very straight. When I finally reached the first major bend in the road just before Farthing Common it came as something of a surprise, forcing me to slow down after getting used to running straight without the usual slowing down for bends in the road or villages strung along the road with their 'Welcomes careful drivers' signage. The only thing that changed my pace were the few tractors that I came upon on this road dappled with sun and shade and lined with alternating stretches of hedged fields and tunnels of trees. Enticing brown tourist signs pointed off to either side but I kept going, enjoying the views off to the right, 'across the valley to the Wye Down', from this old road perched up on the edge of the ridge.

At Farthing Common, the road started to descend and I caught sight of what the *About Britain* guide promised was 'one of the best landscape views in east Kent . . . from the hill above Monks Horton'. It was the first view of the Kent coastline that today's route closely followed. One addition to that coastline since 1951 that the Festival of Britain would have approved of, given their celebration of nuclear fuel as the energy source of the future, was particularly visible: the large rectangles making up Dungeness nuclear power station. The first structures appeared in the 1960s and the last will be here for some time still; it is likely to take up to a century before the Dungeness plant is fully decommissioned and demolished.

Once down on the coastal plain, the main road veered off to the left just before Stanford but I followed Stone Street into the village. On the map in the guide the road was shown continuing, bisected by the railway that ran underneath it before running past 'Westenhanger Castle on the right, once a magnificent 14th century fortified mansion' and on to Lympne. But things have changed since 1951. Once through the small village, my progress was abruptly halted by a tall wire fence. On the other side lay the traffic-filled lanes of the M20 motorway. Getting out of the car I discovered that it wasn't only a section of the old road that was missing. A faded poster fixed to the fence informed me that Marmite the cat – from the photograph, black, as the name suggests – had also disappeared. Standing in the middle of Stone Street, peering through the chain-link fence and past the scrubby verge that has grown up across the route of the Roman road over the last three decades, the midday Monday traffic flashed past. Originally built as far as Maidstone in the late 1960s, the M20 was extended further east to connect with the newly built Channel Tunnel in the early 1990s.

The traffic doesn't always race past here on its way to, or from, France. Since the late 2000s, this stretch of motorway has been occasionally repurposed as a vast car park. Under so-called 'Operation Stack' the motorway was closed to regular traffic and thousands of trucks parked nose-to-tail whenever the Channel Tunnel or Dover ferry port were temporarily closed by anything from bad weather to industrial action. To prepare for similar future events as well as potential delays resulting from the creation of a hard border between Britain and the European Union, plans were drawn up following the 2016 Brexit referendum result to build a massive lorry park to hold up to 3,600 trucks.[6] Two potential sites either side of Stone Street were investigated. But the chosen site that lay just west of where I stood was opposed by the owners of the wedding and events business at Westenhanger Castle, and these plans were shelved. Instead, a former airfield was used as a temporary lorry park. Rather than closing the entire motorway, waiting lorries were now parked on the eastbound carriageway and cars directed to use two lanes in each direction on the westbound carriageway. But on that sunny morning the M20 was a blur of traffic – much of it lorries headed across or underneath the Channel – rather than a vast, Brexit-ready, parking lot.

Seventy years ago, there was no motorway to stop motorists' progress along Stone Street. Instead, they were more likely halted in their tracks by the sight of planes landing and taking off from the 'busy airport' that lay beside the road. All that now remained of this transport hub was the Airport Cafe with its green roof, blue sign and two space-age 1960s pods out front. I was hungry after an early start, so went inside to order a set breakfast and mug of tea that I ate outside under a burgundy umbrella shading me from the mid-morning sun. After finishing my all-day-breakfast I headed off to look for remnants of the former airport, but the most I could find were a couple of old hangars at the back of the car park of the offices of Holiday Extras whose major business, ironically given their location, is selling airport parking.

The former military airfield here was repurposed at the end of the war as one end of an 'Air Ferry' that transported thousands of motorists and their cars, two-by-two, to France for summer touring. In mid-July 1948, the first car – an Armstrong Siddeley Lancaster – was loaded onto a Silver City Airways Bristol Freighter plane and flown across the Channel to Le Touquet in France. Over the next few years demand rapidly increased. Those driving by in the summer of 1951 had a good chance of seeing a plane coming in to land or take off, as this happened on average every fifteen minutes. Looking back on their first four years of crossings, Silver City Airways was confident that having carried over 20,000 cars and 80,000 passengers, its Air Ferry was 'now firmly established as the modern way of taking a continental holiday by car, motor or pedal cycle'.

The attraction, as the brochure pointed out, was the ease and speed offered by the opportunity to 'fly to the continent with passenger, luggage and your car'. But it wasn't cheap. The cost of getting a car there and back was between £24 and £48 (equivalent to roughly £750 to £1,500 today) depending on the size of the vehicle. There were cheaper ways to get your car to the Continent in 1951. It could be loaded onto a boat at one of the Channel ports, and then unloaded in France. But this was a lengthy process in the days before roll-on, roll-off ferries. The petrol tank needed draining, and the electrics disconnecting before the car could be hoisted onto the cargo deck. It certainly could not compete with the speed offered by Silver City Airways, which boasted that, with only a 20-minute flight, half an hour beforehand to clear customs, and then brief formalities on arrival, motorists could be 'on the road in France within an hour of arriving at Lympne'.

In the early 1950s, it seemed there was a bright future for transporting motorists and their cars to the Continent by plane. Silver City Airways quickly expanded from their initial base in Lympne and started new services from Eastleigh, Southend and Gatwick. However, they were forced to abandon Lympne airfield in 1954 because the grass runway had become unusable after heavy rain. The last plane took off from the airfield in October with the final two of well over 50,000 cars that had made the short flight over the previous six years. But this was not their last flight from south Kent. Silver City Airways simply moved down the road to a new purpose-built airport – Ferryfield – in Lydd near Dungeness, complete with dual concrete runways, where they continued operating into the early 1960s.

With the departure of Silver City Airways, a new airline moved in and offered a coach–air service that connected London and Paris, via Lympne and Beauvais in the mid-1950s. Skyways' service proved popular and during the second half of the 1950s additional routes were added taking passengers from London to Lyons, Vichy, Montpelier, Dijon, Fréjus, Tours, Brussels and Antwerp by coach and plane. During the early 1960s the range of destinations increased, with the company awarded licences to operate charter flights to Barcelona, Basle, Luxemburg, Lyons, Palma, Perpignan, Pisa and Venice. Late in the 1960s a new concrete runway and terminal building were built and the airport was officially reopened as Ashford Airport. The Skyways Coach–Air brochure from 1969 proudly introduced the renamed airport offering eleven daily services between Ashford and Beauvais in the summer months, the first leaving at 8.15 in the morning, the last at 9.15 at night. The forty-five minute flight was the short leg of a journey of five hours from Victoria coach station to Paris. An off-peak return fare came in at £11 11 shillings – or roughly £160 today. However, despite initial optimism, this was the beginning of the end. Skyways ceased operations in the early 1970s, and the airport closed a few years later and was redeveloped as an industrial estate in the 1980s.[7]

Rather than driving into the industrial estate, I rejoined Stone Street and headed towards the sea at Hythe. I dropped down the steep hill with views back to the old sea cliff where Lympne Castle looks out towards the coast. I was a day too late for Sunday cream teas at Lympne Castle which, like Westenhanger Castle, does most of its business hosting weddings. Now, as then, the road 'follows the twisting dykes of Romney Marsh' in marked contrast to the long straight stretch of Roman road that delivered me here, give or take the detour around the motorway. In this watery landscape, I crossed over the Royal Military Canal as well as the Romney, Hythe and Dymchurch Railway line, before reaching the main road that runs parallel to the coast.

At first I couldn't see the sea. Coastal access was blocked by the Hythe Ranges, used for practising live firing out to sea since the mid nineteenth century. It was the first, but not the last, military landscape that I'd drive by on these journeys and it was clearly in use that morning. A red flag was flying and I could hear the sound of shells through my open side window on a day that was getting warmer. Once past the ranges and the anaemic rows of military housing, I reached Hythe where road, miniature railway and canal – filled with boats in the sunshine – ran side by side. Just beyond the town, the road finally dropped down to the shore and I got my first glimpse of the sea at close quarters. The water was choppy and it was clearly high tide. A few pensioners dipped their toes in the waves from the narrow strip of pebble beach at Sandgate where a man sat watching his three fishing lines straining out into the sea. After a short while the road turned away from the coast again and climbed the hill before dropping down into Folkestone where I ended up on the one-way system that deposited me opposite a large office building, which appeared to be the main office of the travel and financial services company Saga.

Founded in Folkestone in 1951, the company had its origins in the decision of Sidney and Margery De Haan to buy a twelve-bedroom hotel – the Rhodesia – in Folkestone with a view to cashing in on the expected rise in holidays in the post-war years. In order to fill vacant rooms over the long winters, the couple began offering cheap, off-season, full-board holidays to older people. Rising demand meant that they quickly bought another hotel before expanding and shifting from hoteliers to tour operators focusing solely on this age group. They made use of empty university halls of residence outside term times, offered up passport-free day trips to France and popularized travel to the Algarve in the 1960s. Over the following decades, Saga added long-haul holidays and cruises to their list of travel options. They advertised their first three-month round-the-world cruise, but more numerous were month-long, off-peak, all-inclusive holidays to Benidorm for anywhere between £70 and £90 (roughly £500 to £700 today). The company grew rapidly in the mid-1970s, tripling its turnover in two years. By the mid-1980s they were taking 250,000 pensioners on holidays near and, increasingly, far. In the decade before the end of communism, Saga boasted that it was the world's largest tour operator to Transylvania.[8] But it was not just their holidaymakers who were extending their horizons. The company was too, diversifying from travel to financial services and insurance, all aimed at retirees.

The De Haans and Saga rode the wave of one of the major demographic changes that took place in modern Britain. The post-war period saw the continued rise in life expectancy. Men and women born in 1911 could expect to live – on average – until their early and mid-fifties respectively. By 1951, this had risen a decade or more to their mid-sixties for men and early seventies for women. By 2011, this upward trend continued, with life expectancy rising to the high seventies for men and low eighties for women.[9] Britons were living longer. During the first half of the twentieth century this was largely the result of improved health for the young, but during the second half of the century medical advances tended to be focused more on the elderly – for example with developments in treating heart disease. As a result, the proportion of the population over the age of 65 rose by almost three-quarters between 1951 and 2000, reaching a total of over 9 million.

But it was not simply the case that Britons lived longer and were healthier in the second half of the twentieth century. They were also – and this was critical to Saga's success – in many cases getting wealthier. When the De Haans first started attracting older people with cheap off-season breaks in the late 1940s and early 1950s, old age was, for most people, a period of life when they had relatively little money. In the 1950s, it was the other end of the lifespan – the emerging teenager – that was the focus of consumer spending. But seven decades later, Britain not only has more people over 65 than it does under 18, but they also tend to be wealthier. During the post-war decades, growing affluence among many, if not all, older Britons led to the coining of the phrase the 'grey pound' that companies like Saga successfully capitalized on by offering luxury cruises rather than a week at the Rhodesia during a Folkestone winter. Saga is smart to target the over-50s. After all, they own around 80 per cent of the wealth, have 60 per cent of the savings and 40 per cent of the disposable income in contemporary Britain.[10]

But it is clear that this healthier, wealthier older population are busy doing more than simply sampling the travel offered by Saga during their retirement. Half of those in their mid-50s to mid-70s volunteer, and I met some of that army of an estimated 6 million volunteers when I pulled off into the car park of the Battle of Britain Memorial perched on the clifftops just above Folkestone.[11] I'd been tempted by the brown tourist sign as well as the fact that my morning had started with advertising posters of the 'Bottle of Britain' at the Spitfire ground in Canterbury. Nipping to the gents in the visitor centre, I found Shepherd Neame advertising posters adorning the walls: 'Downed all over Kent like the Luftwaffe' read the one over the sink where I washed my hands.

This memorial, sited on a former Second World War-era Royal Artillery battery, was created in layers as money came in for a privately funded venture spearheaded by a former Battle of Britain pilot eager that these events were not forgotten half a century later. 'The National Memorial to the Few' – a statue of a lone young airman looking out to sea – was unveiled in the early 1990s. He sat in the middle of white paving slabs which etched the distinctive shape of the Spitfire propeller, flanked by a replica Mark 1 Spitfire and Mark 2 Hurricane. Walking around I met another visitor who told me that I should take a look from the cliff edge, telling me 'with the cliffs you can just imagine them coming home'. Standing on the edge, I looked along the white chalk cliffs that stretched around to Dover on my left, down to Folkestone harbour on my right, before walking back to the visitor centre, opened in 2015.[12] Its gift shop was filled with model Spitfires – from large ones priced at several hundred pounds, down to an Airfix model to make and paint for £10 which was pegged at skill level 1 – and bottles of Spitfire Heritage 1930s Botanical Gin with its ingredient list of symbolic botanicals: 'Rosemary for Remembrance, Borage for Courage, Blood Orange for the Sacrifice, English Rose Petals for the ATA girls'. I got chatting to one of the volunteers who bemoaned the fact that the centre's largest donation had not come from the British government, but the King of Bahrain.

Back in the car, the road climbed the cliffs and crossed over the route taken by the Channel Tunnel deep below me. Although there had been talk of a tunnel under the Channel during the nineteenth century, the idea only started to gain currency in the late 1950s and early 1960s after the post-war rise in travel between Britain and the Continent. During the 1960s and early 1970s, a number of proposals were considered and came close to approval. However, the new Labour government shelved the project, before it was taken up again by the Thatcher government in the late 1970s and early 1980s. Thatcher's preference was for a subterranean motorway, given her favouring of the private car and, as I'd discovered on the previous journey, new roads. Cars were imbued with an ideology of independence. Trains carrying groups of passengers and their cars seemed a shade too close to public transport. Although the idea of individuals driving under the Channel was rejected due to the safety risks presented by ventilation in a tunnel that would stretch more than 30 miles, the Thatcher government did ensure that this was a private venture rather than a state-funded project. It meant that the rising costs of construction were borne by the company given a 55-year concession on the tunnel when the treaty giving the go-ahead was signed in my starting point, Canterbury, in the mid-1980s. Originally estimated to cost just under £5 billion, the final cost of construction was almost double that.

When it opened in 1994 the tunnel not only speeded up journey times across the Channel, it also transformed the relationship between Britain and France in a subtle but significant way. Rather than a frontier on either side of the international waters, there was now a land border between the two nations.[13] But this land link, soon to become a harder border between Britain and France in the wake of Brexit, lay hidden deep beneath the chalk as I went down into Dover – the 'nearest port to the Continent' – where the castle loomed up on the hill ahead. Down near the harbour, a large mural painted by Banksy after the Brexit referendum result covered the end wall of a terrace; it showed a man up a ladder, chipping away at one of the stars on the European Union flag.

I followed the road beside the port, being careful to keep in the right-hand lane to avoid ending up in the ferry terminal where two large ships were moored up awaiting their next sailing to Calais. The introduction of ferries that motorists could simply drive onto and then off again at the other end made the process of transporting cars across water faster just as the car-ferry flights from Lympne had first done in the late 1940s and early 1950s, and the Channel Tunnel did in the mid-1990s. Originally developed for the mode of transport of the nineteenth century, the train, the technology was reworked for the newly dominant mode of transport: the car.

The earliest large car ferry to operate out of Dover was built for the newly nationalized British Railways in 1951 and began regular service between Dover and Boulogne the following year. Unlike the planes crossing the Channel from Lympne with two cars at a time, the *Lord Warden* could take up to 120 cars and 1,000 passengers. From the mid-1950s to the mid-1960s, the number of cars taken across the Channel by ferries more than doubled, reaching well over 300,000. In the following years, things really took off. By the end of the 1960s, some 4 million passengers were making their way across the Channel each year. This growth continued through the 1970s making Dover, by the 1980s, the busiest passenger port in the world. It remains busy, despite the addition of the Channel Tunnel. Although the tunnel quickly gained just under 20 million passengers a year in the late 1990s, things slowed down a little in the 2000s after a price war with cross-Channel ferry companies and the competition posed by the new low-cost airlines. By the 2010s, more or less the same number crossed the Channel each year by train and ferry (a little over 20 million using the former and a little under 20 million using the latter), a combined figure ten times that of half a century earlier.[14]

The road from Dover climbed through a gap in the white cliffs, with signs reminding drivers coming off ferries to drive on the left. Once on the clifftop, I drove above the sea through farmland before dropping down to the promenade in Walmer. I passed the castle pictured in the guide and then the former home of 'The Royal Marines and the Royal Naval School of Music', which the *About Britain* guide informed motorists 'are at Deal'. They aren't any longer. The barracks closed in the mid-1990s and the band moved to Portsmouth.[15] The former barracks along the front are now town houses and apartments and I walked through this upmarket housing estate in search of traces of the former barracks and one building in particular. Finally I found the remains of the former chapel destroyed by an IRA bomb attack in 1989. I arrived in the small memorial garden that lies at the foot of the one wall left standing as three older men were leaving. There was a much more public memorial to these events in the gardens by the promenade. Here the bandstand bore the names of the eleven band members who died. In the summer it hosts weekly concerts, but I was a day too late for the Broadstairs and St Peter's Band which played on Sunday, sponsored by the Fish Bar, which I passed as I drove along the front where a few old guys in black swimming trunks braved the chilly water.

The road once more left the sea and ran through arable land where one field was dominated by a huge, many-tentacled water sprayer. I passed a PYO – pick your own – farm, but was too late for asparagus and too early for strawberries. PYO farms first grew up in the 1970s, before experiencing a second wave of popularity in the 1990s and 2000s. While they had been initially a way of getting hold of large quantities of cheap fruit that could be stored in the new chest freezers in a growing number of British homes, their later revival was driven more by – in the words of one Kent farmer – the desire for 'a recreational experience'.[16] The image of middle-class families heading to the fields for a few hours' fruit picking as a weekend leisure activity offered a strange continuity with one of the photographs in the *About Britain* guide I had on the passenger seat beside me. This showed a group of 'hop-pickers' above a caption explaining that 'London's connections with the Home Counties are manifold'. But this particular connection was restricted by class. 'Hop-picking in Kent' was, according to the guidebook, 'an outing with pay for whole families of poorer people'.[17] By contrast, PYO farms offered an opportunity for labour as leisure to the late twentieth-century urban middle classes, and if the sign was anything to go by, they still do.

Farmland briefly gave way to townscape. I caught a glimpse of the attractive market square in Sandwich, before making my way towards the next in the string of ports. The road to Ramsgate was dominated by industry rather than agriculture. First was the sprawling 'State of the Art Lab Space' at the Pfizer pharmaceutical factory that opened in the 1950s, best known as the place where Viagra – reportedly the most popular medicine on Saga cruises – was created.[18] Pfizer moved their research and development plant from here to Cambridge in 2011, and the company was now just one tenant of this home to high-tech industries: 'Discovery Park'.[19] A little further on, past a vast car auction site, came recycling works and metal fabrication plants, before the road dropped down to the coast once more at Pegwell Bay.

Driving through Pegwell Bay it was simply impossible to miss the large, replica Viking ship – bow and stern picked out in yellow paint – that stood within a black, iron-fenced enclosure in the middle of the strip of grass between road and clifftop. I slowed down when I saw it and pulled in to the small car park to take a closer look. The *Hugin* ended up here by a circuitous route. It started its journey in Denmark in 1949 when the Danish National Travel Association commissioned a replica of the Gokstad Viking ship in order to re-enact the first landing on British shores 1,500 years before as a 'publicity scheme' to boost post-war foreign tourism to their country. A crew of 53 were selected with an eye to choosing those matching popular perceptions of Vikings: sailors tended to be tall and bearded. Dressed in costumes borrowed from the Danish Royal Opera House, these modern-day Vikings started out in early July 1949 watched by a smattering of the Danish political elite, the international press and – as the photographs of the occasion show – a large and enthusiastic crowd. After working their way down the Danish coast, stopping off for banquets thrown by local town councils and a meeting with the Danish king and queen, they finally left on what one journalist dubbed their 'voyage to "invade" Britain'.[20]

On the morning of 28 July, the crew rowed ashore at Broadstairs beach. It was crowded with an estimated 30,000 holidaymakers who had gathered to witness what one paper dubbed 'D-Day plus 1,500 years'. The next day, the crew made a second landing at neighbouring Ramsgate. That the *Hugin* made two invasions highlighted the bitter rivalry between these two coastal resorts. Reporting the 'genial invasion' of Broadstairs, journalists were well aware that the choice of initial landing site was 'much . . . to Ramsgate's chagrin' with one writing how he 'could imagine Ramsgate dignitaries biting their nails at the thought that they were not to be invaded until tomorrow'. Although Broadstairs won the victory in the fight to be invaded first, they did not win the battle to buy the ship when the Danish Travel Association put it up for sale. The plan had always been that this was to be a one-way voyage with the replica ship then sold off at half price to whoever wanted it. While Broadstairs and Ramsgate both put in an offer for the ship, in the end a 'third party' – the *Daily Mail* – bought the *Hugin* and announced that it would make a tour of British seaside resorts as well as inland towns and cities, before being given to Broadstairs and Ramsgate 'to share' in a new permanent home 'to be agreed upon' by both.[21]

And so the ship set sail again, this time without its Viking crew, along the south coast of England, stopping off at crowded seaside resorts. After a summer at sea the *Hugin* took to the road on the back of a lorry. Children were let out of school to watch the ship as she made her way north through Staffordshire and Lancashire, navigating narrow roads that I would later take in reverse as I drove from Stafford to Oxford. In mid-September the *Hugin* arrived in Blackpool for the start of the famous illuminations. This was not simply another year of lighting up the promenade of this northern seaside resort, but its post-war revival after a decade of darkness as a result of the war in 1939, and its long shadow that ran through the second half of the 1940s. In 1949 the illuminations became highly symbolic: a light in the post-war darkness, with an estimated 800,000 turning up during the opening weekend to see the attractions, which included the *Hugin* lit up from bow to stern. After touring the north-west, the ship finally reached its new permanent home in the summer of 1950. The *Daily Mail* reporter who had accompanied it on its tour of Britain reported that the *Hugin* was now lying 'bright and perfect on the green cliff-top' near Ebbsfleet where I came across it seven decades later. During its first summer here, both Ramsgate and Broadstairs were quick to claim this clifftop addition, with Ramsgate assuming the title the 'Home of the *Hugin*', and Broadstairs highlighting 'the Famous Viking Ship *Hugin*' as an additional attraction in this 'ideal family resort'.[22]

It is clear that this replica Viking ship caused quite a stir in post-war Britain, although not enough to be covered by the *About Britain* guide. After its journey of 1,500 miles 'on sea and land' it was claimed that the *Hugin* had been 'seen by millions of people'.[23] Even if the reporting of the ship's new owners tended towards hyperbole, there was clearly something going on which prompted commentators to try to make sense of this. The *Daily Mail* read the 'enormous interest in the oar-driven Viking ship *Hugin*' alongside a 'return to pursuits like sailing, fishing and riding' as 'a subconscious reaction from a scientific and mechanical age' and a retreat from the very modernity that the Festival of Britain was so keen to celebrate.[24] But for Cyril Frank, writing in the *Observer*, it seemed this ship reached much further back and touched on something almost primordial. 'Perhaps something in our bloodstream responds to the Viking longship,' he suggested, 'as it responds to bare winter branches and a nip in the air. As an idea, lodged even in minds which successfully resisted the main body of historical instruction, it has a bleak Northern romance. Like the angular grey gannet, it belongs to Northern waters.'[25]

Some saw the arrival of the Viking ship as a chance to connect Britain with shores much further north than those lying across the Channel. The clearest example of this came in the speech given by the owner of the *Daily Mail*, Viscount Rothermere, when handing the ship over to Broadstairs and Ramsgate. He made reference to another memorial stone – 'a stone cross in a meadow, marking the reputed landing-place of St Augustine' – that the *About Britain* guide pointed out to the motorist driving through Ebbsfleet, rather than the Viking boat less than a mile away. Rothermere brought both together claiming, 'that the spiritual benefits from St Augustine's landing were in some respects equalled by the benefits of blood that resulted from the invasions of the Norsemen'.[26] Telling a story of Britons as a 'race', it was clear that Rothermere looked north not south, and saw the *Hugin* as a reminder of a kind of Nordic purity.

However, the author of the opening essay in the *About Britain* guide, Richard Fitter, was dismissive of such claims. Describing Kent as 'the gateway to England' he recounted the 'constant stream of invaders, Stone Age men, Bronze Age men, Celts, Belgae, Romans, Jutes, Saxons, Normans' that 'have landed on the open shores of Kent and Sussex'. Not only did Fitter omit the Vikings that Rothermere – and before him, Victorian Britain – was so fond of, he also dismissed any claims to racial purity. Rather, he claimed – in language typical in mid-century Britain – that the 'mongrel race of the English' had 'emerged' from this long stream of incomers and was all the better for it, being 'fertile in ideas and achievement as only a cross-bred race can be'.[27]

The faint traces of one of those 'fertile . . . ideas' lay just beyond and beneath the Viking ship. I only found it because the *Hugin* had forced me to slow down, stop and leave the car for a closer look on foot. Walking around the ship, I noticed a steep set of concrete steps that dropped down beneath a steel walkway to the edge of the sea. I thought I'd follow them to see where they led. On the shoreline, I discovered a large stretch of tarmac with clumps of shrubs and plants bursting through the flat surface. Although faded, I could just make out the regular white parallel lines marking out parking places. It was clear that this had once been a very large car park right on the edge of the Channel next to a wide, concrete slipway stretching down into the water.

For just over a decade Pegwell Bay was the home of Hoverlloyd's futuristic hoverport. Swedish-owned Hoverlloyd had begun their first international hovercraft service just down the coast, where two 36-seater hovercraft made a total of 1,000 flights between Ramsgate and Calais during the summers of 1966 and 1967. Grasping for analogies from the more familiar experience of driving, one journalist described the rough outward journey as like driving 'a road somewhere in the Balkans' while the smoother return leg was 'more like being on an English B-road'. By 1967, Hoverlloyd were ready to expand their service, and boasted that the introduction of much larger SRN4 hovercraft, which could carry 30 cars as well as 250 passengers, would – again drawing on an analogy from the world of motoring – create 'next summer's new motorway to France'. These large hovercraft would depart from the purpose-built 'splendid new terminal' in Pegwell Bay, the faint traces of which could still be seen in the marked-up concrete.

Ultimately this 'new motorway to France' did not materialize quite as quickly as expected. Plans to build the large terminal on a rare stretch of 'unspoiled coast', which included a Site of Special Scientific Interest and was close to a planned British Railways-owned hoverport in Dover, led to two public inquiries before planning was approved. It was, one newspaper editorial suggested, 'a notable bout in the continuous contest between the impetus of technology and conservation of the natural environment', which it saw as deservedly won by technology given the chance to establish not simply a hoverport but a 'shop window for an important British invention with a large export potential': albeit one ironically supplied by a Swedish company.[28]

First developed in the 1950s by British engineer Christopher Cockerell, the hovercraft was initially greeted as something of a wonder vehicle given that it could travel over both water and land. In the late 1950s there were high hopes for it. The press was rapt. During the first half of the 1960s, when plans for a Channel tunnel crossing were being seriously considered, the hovercraft was being touted as an alternative 'Channel Link'. When the large terminal was being built at Pegwell Bay, Cockerell saw the short Channel crossing as only the beginning, predicting that within two decades hovercraft would run between Britain and Belgium, Denmark and 'perhaps Norway and Sweden' and at the height of enthusiasm over nuclear power imagined the 'ocean hovercraft' of the future 'powered by an atomic engine'. When Hoverlloyd readied themselves for business in the summer of 1969, they offered not simply a speedy, 40-minute crossing, but a chance to experience 'one of the century's greatest adventures' and 'the century's greatest travelling sensation' in 'the world's newest, easiest, most revolutionary method of transport'. It seemed that the hovercraft had 'captured the imagination of the British public more than any other invention since the war', something explained by contemporaries as partly because it was 'an attractive and ingenious idea' and partly because it was a British one.[29]

Over 250,000 passengers and their more than 30,000 cars were carried to and from Pegwell Bay during that first summer. Numbers rose through the 1970s, reaching close to 1 million passengers and 150,000 cars by the middle of the decade when hovercraft carried around a third of all passengers across the Channel. However, despite these impressive figures all was not well. Even in the autumn of 1969, Hoverlloyd's boss reflected that, 'perhaps we were too enthusiastic in investing so heavily at the start'. One in four flights were cancelled, customers complained of the 'bumpy ride, noise and flying spray' and the company reported a loss of around £250,000. Things improved a little and by the early 1970s Hoverlloyd were reporting a small profit, which rose in the second half of the decade.

But the rising price of oil proved to be the undoing of the 'fuel intensive' hovercraft, which could not compete with more economical ferries, and in the late 1970s the company was put up for sale. In the early 1980s, Hoverlloyd merged with their British Railways-owned and fellow-loss-making competitor Seaspeed to form Hoverspeed and all operations moved along the coast to Dover. The hoverport in Pegwell Bay was kept on for a decade or so as a maintenance base before being demolished in the mid-1990s. It was not simply that the busy hoverport here came and went, so did the Hovercraft Age. By 2000, hovercraft crossings between Dover and Calais ended because they could not compete with cheaper, larger ferries or the speedy transit times of the recently opened Channel Tunnel.[30]

I walked back up the steps to the clifftop, leaving the shrub-strewn forecourt to the few dog walkers out on this sunny evening, and made my way back to the car. I could see the gleaming freshly painted Viking ship in my rear-view mirror as I went in search of the other memorial that the guide directed motorists to in 1951. I found it off a minor road at the northern edge of a golf course in a freshly mown meadow: a late nineteenth-century 'Saxon' cross that referred to a much earlier event offering another story of landings and origins along this stretch of coast.[31] Returning to the main road, I headed towards Margate. Dropping down, first to Broadstairs, and then a little further along down to Margate, I got a clear view of the ranks of wind turbines out to sea that make up the Thanet Offshore Wind Farm that, when it opened in 2010, was the largest in the world.[32]

Described in the caption alongside the map as 'the most famous of all Kentish seaside towns, with fine sands and safe bathing', H. G. Stokes was a little more reserved about Margate in his gazetteer at the end of the guidebook, stopping short of using the adjective 'fine' to describe the beach in this place of 'sands, bands, cliff walks and a very bracing air'.[33] The cool east wind was blowing hard when I got out of the car by the seafront and the long beach was almost empty: no one it seemed was braving the waters. I walked over to the Turner Contemporary art gallery that opened here in 2011, but it was closed on a Monday so I could only walk around it, looking out to sea for a glimpse of Antony Gormley's *Another Time*. It was high tide and Gormley's sculpture of a human figure on Fulsome Rock was submerged, so I returned to the car and left this seaside resort reimagined as a site of cultural tourism.

I quickly managed to get lost. I blame it on what looked like a cluster of massive, glowing greenhouses off to the left. Road signs pointed the way to 'Thanet Earth'. The sign was black, not brown, so it was clear that this was an industrial rather than a tourist site, but I kept going regardless. At first, I saw two large buildings, then more appeared. They were all enormous, and as I got closer I realized that these were indeed gigantic greenhouses. It was market gardening on a radically different scale compared with the polytunnels that I'd passed as I headed towards Sandwich. When they picked the first crop of cucumbers from just one of the greenhouses at Thanet Earth in 2009, they harvested around 250,000, and they can fit 500,000 tomato plants in just one of the largest greenhouses here. Given these numbers it is perhaps no surprise that more than 10 per cent of all the tomatoes, cucumbers and peppers eaten in Britain originate from this site.[34]

Driving along, the arable land seemed, superficially at least, relatively unchanged, aside from the machinery that I was stuck behind on the road earlier in the morning or saw in the fields. The 1950s and 1960s had seen increased mechanization as horse finally gave way to tractor, something the *About Britain* guides celebrated as I discovered on my next route. But this enormous plant was more than simply another stage in the mechanization of agriculture, it represented the industrialization of agriculture.

Thanet Earth was more factory than farm, having dispensed with the most basic element of arable farming: the soil.

When he introduced this region, Richard Fitter bemoaned the fact that some of the 'richest soil in England' was being 'dug away for the sake of the gravel underneath' as market gardens were turned into gravel pits and 'this fertile land' was made infertile in the rush for, among other things, road building. As I'd reflected after both of my earlier journeys, the underlying rock often loomed large in these opening essays that began with geological time and told the prehistoric story of the layers of 'chalk . . . sands and clays' that humans subsequently exploited. But when Thanet Earth was built, all the top soil was stripped away and salad vegetables were now grown in nutrient-watered, sterile rock wool in this hydroponic 'farm'.[35]

Thanet Earth is not only farming removed from the soil, but also largely removed from the weather. Sunlight is supplemented by carefully controlled artificial heat and light and nutrient-rich water is piped in, rather than relying on the vagaries of rainfall. Whatever the weather outside, the growing conditions inside are always at their peak and offer a year-round growing season for 'British-grown' tomatoes that are constantly available for customers clamouring for the same vegetables and fruit rather than accepting the limits of seasonality. While in the 1980s and 1990s these demands were satisfied by importing fruit and vegetables, in the late 2000s and 2010s they were increasingly met by the artificially lit, heated and fed greenhouses in this corner of Kent. In a sense, this factory farm could be anywhere. The plants grow removed from the soil beneath, and the wind, sun and rain on the other side of the greenhouse glass. There is no connection with local *terroir*. Rather than chalky soils drawing twenty-first-century farmers here, proximity to motorway networks are more important in ensuring the steady supply of year-round tomatoes to customers similarly detached from time and place.

After my detour past Thanet Earth, I finally made my way back to the right road and followed it towards Whitstable where I stopped to eat fish and chips sitting on the beach in the evening sun, surrounded by flint pebbles, bleached oyster, mussel and crab shells, and whitened fish bones. Business appeared to be still going strong in this place 'world-famous for oysters' in 1951 and they featured on the menu at the harbourside restaurant. Back in the car, I almost ended up on the motorway as I tried to get to Faversham, but finally made it through the centre of the town where I passed the Shepherd Neame brewery whose advertising slogans had punctuated the earlier part of my day. It seemed that most of the other 'modern industries' referenced in the *About Britain* guide had long gone, with one former factory now home to a supermarket that no doubt stocked punnets of tomatoes grown in the new factories of food production down the road. After passing Thanet Earth, the guide's description of the route 'south of Faversham' through land where 'brick earth and good loam cover the chalk, providing excellent fruit-growing country, where cherries and hop gardens flourish' seemed positively quaint. But I did pass hop poles, oast houses and signs off to the national fruit collection grown in the soil of Brogdale Farm, before following a beautiful road towards Wye on a perfect evening.

At Wye, I criss-crossed the river, waited for a train to pass, and then drove on to Chilham in search of the 'picturesque village square' that earned a place in the final image alongside the route map as well as the final lengthy caption. It was deserted and beautiful, with half-timbered houses and inns along three sides, and the castle that had been visited by *Hugin*'s 'Vikings' in the summer of 1949 along the fourth. The castle was available to hire as a wedding venue, and the gardens were open one day a week but I arrived a day too early for that. It was getting late, so I dragged myself away from Chilham and dropped down back to the main road, passing Chartham Vineyard and its rows of vines planted on the slopes off to the left. I crossed over the river, before making my way along the riverbank into Canterbury, past the familiar ring of out-of-town shopping, and towards the cathedral tower that dominated the cityscape.

On this journey following the Kent coastline, I had expected to come face to face with the long history of comings and goings between Britain and France. The stretch of sea between this island nation and the European mainland is narrow, yet it appeared to be widening in the run-up to Brexit and ever more frequent stories of the tragic deaths of migrants in flimsy and overcrowded dinghies. Standing on the cliff edge looking out to sea I couldn't quite glimpse the French shore, but the traces of past transport technologies were a reminder of France's proximity and its distance, as well as 70 years of inventions to get more and more people – and their cars – there quicker. It was clear that much had changed along this coastline. In the post-Channel Tunnel era, flying cars across the Channel appeared as odd as the far more recent, ill-fated experiment using hovercraft running out of Pegwell Bay.

But Pegwell Bay surprised me not only because of what had been and gone in the course of the last 70 years, but also because of what was still there. It seemed anachronistic to find a brightly painted replica Viking ship just above the former site of a futuristic hoverport. But it was clear that the *Hugin*'s recreation of an ancient invasion had touched a chord in the post-war years just enough to mean that the ship was still there. What struck me most exploring this story of a stunt to attract foreign visitors to Denmark was the way that some people used this as a way of emphasizing Nordic roots. Yet there was as little agreement in the 1950s about who the British were as there is now. Standing on the island shore, questions of connections past and present come to the fore. Questions that, as Banksy's stencil on the end wall of a house in Dover showed, remain just as potent as ever.

But there was something else about the *Hugin* that interested me. In direct contrast to the enthusiasm expressed for modernity by the Festival of Britain, the *Daily Mail* saw the *Hugin*'s popular appeal as a rejection of modernity and an opportunity to seek comfort in tradition. One thing these journeys revealed was an ambivalence towards modernity in post-war Britain that continues into the present. The embrace of the hovercraft as the vehicle of the future was typical of a moment in the 1960s and 1970s that briefly embraced technological modernity. Yet Britain appears to have been attracted to the past as much as to the future.

But technological modernity was not simply to be found hovering above water and earth, but closer to the ground in the vast greenhouses of Thanet Earth. My sense was that these would have presented more of an imaginative leap for those putting the guidebooks together. As I saw on earlier journeys, the *About Britain* guides were interested in the earth beneath our feet and what grew out of it. Their assumption was that geology determined what happened where. There was a certain comfort in this notion of fixity: that things would not change too much because the underlying bedrock of Britain was unchanging. I wondered what Angwin would make of farming that cleared away the very soil that he wanted visitors to pay attention to. But I also wondered what he and his contemporaries in 1951 would make of another change in thinking about the land that I found on my next journey.

Cambridge–Madingley–Caxton Gibbet–Eltisley–Godmanchester–Huntingdon–St Ives–Needingworth–Earith–Haddenham–Wilburton–Stretham–Wicken–Soham–Stuntney–Ely–Littleport–Mildenhall–Brandon–Mundford–Northwold–Stoke Ferry–Wereham–Downham Market–South Runcton–Setchey–Wiggenhall St German–Wiggenhall St Mary the Virgin–King's Lynn

4

East Anglia

Cambridge–Littleport–King's Lynn (124 miles)

Leaving Cambridge along the Madingley Road, the concrete facade of Churchill College set back from the rush-hour traffic among green lawns was the first sign of the post-war expansion of this university city. Founded in 1960, Churchill was one of seven new colleges built since 1951. When motorists left Cambridge during that year, they would have passed some of the 8,000 students there. Ninety per cent of them were men, with women only admitted to the university a few years before in 1948. Heading west seven decades later I passed a few of the more than 18,000 students – 7,000 of them international – cycling to their lectures on a crisp October morning. There is now almost parity of men and women, although Cambridge still lags behind other British universities where women students make up a small majority.[1]

Elsewhere, the growth of British universities has been more marked. On the other side of Cambridge, the former Anglia Polytechnic, which became Anglia Polytechnic University in 1992 and Anglia Ruskin University in 2005, teaches almost twice as many students as Cambridge University. And in other towns and cities I drove through the rise in student numbers has been even more dramatic. In Loughborough, where I went later, student numbers grew from 1,500 in 1950 to 17,000 by the mid-2000s: a more than ten-fold increase, rather than the doubling seen in Cambridge. But if the number of students had not risen as much as in other British 'univercities' it was clear that Cambridge University had physically grown, and was still expanding. As they left town in 1951, motorists were instructed to look out for 'the University Observatory, containing the Northumberland Telescope designed by Airy in 1835' 'one mile out of Cambridge'.[2] I passed the driveway down to the observatory just after Churchill College, but far more visible were the cranes towering over the west Cambridge site. Work was underway to build a second, larger Cavendish Laboratory to join the earlier one built here in the 1970s. Once complete, it would add more lab space to the epicentre of research into everything from nanoscience to advanced photonics.

Once on the other side of the M11, I followed the old Cambridge Road along the bottom of Madingley Hill where, as the *About Britain* guide pointed out, 'lies an American cemetery of World War II'. I pulled in to the car park and walked up the hill with my wife and younger daughter (both holders of American passports) who had joined me on this trip, the low sun accentuating the flashes of red on the trees planted among the thousands of stark white graves. Madingley is one of a number of American military cemeteries worldwide. In 1923, the US Congress established the American Battle Monuments Commission in recognition of the shift in geopolitics taking place in what was seen as America's century. The commission was charged with maintaining military cemeteries in those places where American troops had fought since 6 April 1917, the day America entered the First World War.

At the end of the conflict, eight American cemeteries were established, mostly in France, but including one at Flanders Field in Belgium and another at Brookwood just outside Guildford. Nearly 500 men were buried at Brookwood, but it was clear walking up the hill that many more were buried at Madingley. There were 3,812 graves and the names of another 5,127, listed as missing, were engraved on the memorial wall that runs alongside the chain of reflecting pools stretching from the flagpole to the chapel. These numbers bear witness to the far greater scale of American participation in the Second World War, and in particular the massive numbers of American troops based in Britain, prior to the D-Day landings. Over 2 million men made their way through Britain during the war, with over 1.5 million stationed here in June 1944.[3]

Madingley was one of hundreds of temporary burial grounds created during the Second World War. At the war's end most were closed down and the remains either repatriated or reinterred in one of the 14 sites chosen to be permanent American military cemeteries. Madingley was one of these. When motorists passed here in 1951, the new graves had been dug but the landscaping was still only sketched out on paper in the offices of Boston architecture practice Perry, Shaw and Hepburn and the celebrated landscape architectural firm Olmstead Brothers, famous for creating Central Park in New York. During the first half of the 1950s, the landscaping and building work was completed and the cemetery officially opened in 1956.[4] It was both aesthetically and, following the transfer of the land, literally a small piece of America in the Fens and not the last that I'd pass today. That this was American soil was clear as I walked past the Stars and Stripes fluttering on the white flagpole back down the hill with views over the motorway to Cambridge and beyond, as the chapel chimes rang out the hour before shifting to a jaunty rendition of 'America the Beautiful'. I drove into Madingley with the tune still ringing in my ears.

Just at the edge of the village I passed one of the many triangular, red-edged warning signs that flank British roads. But in the middle was something I'd not noticed on earlier journeys.

Nestled within the red frame was the black silhouette of a toad. According to the Department for Transport, this sign can be sited at any 'approved . . . migratory toad crossing' site, but 'only during the migratory period' in the early spring. This stretch of road has long been a crossing site for common toads on their way to spawn in the lakes in the gardens of Madingley Hall. But the sign should have come down or been covered over in the summer months once the toad's breeding season ends. There weren't any toads on this autumn morning, and there wouldn't be any for a few months yet, although warmer winters associated with climate change have meant that the original timespan identified for these temporary signs has been extended.[5]

A digital map created by the conservation group Froglife revealed that more was being done to help Madingley's migrating toads cross the road than simply erecting a sign directed at motorists. On the map the toad symbol on the southern edge of the village was shaded green, not purple, showing that this was the site of an 'active patrol'. It has been so for some time. In the late 1980s, William Seale first started carrying toads across the road here. Since then he has gathered an army of volunteers, which reached 150 at its peak. Madingley Toad Patrol has been busy catching and releasing common toads each spring for over four decades, helping tens of thousands to get to the other side between the traffic flows, with a record number of well over 1,000 on a single night. This local hands-on activism has sought to overturn decades of decline that led to the common toad being listed as a threatened species in 2007. Numbers had fallen dramatically in the 1950s and 1960s because of habitat loss before the decline slowed down during the 1970s. However, things worsened again in the 1980s, when it seemed that the cars of evening commuters were mainly to blame.[6]

From the warning signs that I passed on other journeys, it was clear that toads aren't the only animals straying on to British roads. Signs warned of ducks by the village green in Hutton in Lancashire, and deer in Cannock Chase in the Midlands. Elsewhere, they pointed out cattle, sheep and wild horses. They will soon be joined by another. In 2019, the Department for Transport introduced a new 'small wildlife sign' to fill what they saw as the 'gap between warning signs about smaller animals such as migratory toads and wild fowl, and large animals such as deer and livestock'. The choice of a hedgehog to represent all small and medium-sized animals no doubt owed much to the lobbying power of the British Hedgehog Preservation Society and its efforts to halt the steep decline in hedgehog numbers. But when the new sign was unveiled, it was clear that the department were more concerned about the safety of motorists, and particularly motorcyclists, than hedgehogs. It is estimated that around 100 motorists have been killed, and 14,000 injured in accidents involving animals on the road in just over a decade. Introducing the new sign the Transport Minister was hopeful that 'the new small mammal warning sign should help to reduce the number of people killed and injured' before adding, perhaps as something of an afterthought, 'as well as helping our precious small wild mammal population to flourish'.[7]

Although toads wouldn't be crossing here until January at the earliest, I drove carefully past the impressive gateway to Madingley Hall, home to the University's Institute of Continuing Education as well as the spawning ground for thousands of toads. I left the village through the cluster of 1930s council houses on its edge, crossed over the main road and followed the old St Neots Road that runs parallel to the dual carriageway through Hardwick. On the left were the nondescript buildings of DVSA Hardwick: the motorcycle driving test centre for Cambridge. Although driving licences were introduced after the 1903 Motor Car Act, it was three decades before British car or motorcycle drivers had to pass a test to get their licence. The 1930s saw increased state regulation following two decades of growth in car ownership. Yet test centres like the one in Hardwick were not established until later. In the second half of the 1930s would-be drivers simply arranged to meet their examiner for the half-hour test at a central location such as a railway station.

Past Hardwick, the old road came to an abrupt end at a roundabout, so I ducked underneath the dual carriageway, before continuing parallel to it once more. Here I slowed down for a rolling road closure. They were replacing the catseyes in the middle of the road. It is a relatively common scene given that these reflectors only last two or three years before they need replacing. They, like driving licences, were a product of the 1930s and the rising number of cars on British roads. Patented in 1934 by Percy Shaw, their name drew on his experience of driving through the West Yorkshire fog at night and spotting the reflection of his headlights in the eyes of a cat standing thankfully by the side, rather than in the middle, of the road. In 1935, he set up Reflecting Roadstuds to manufacture catseyes, which became mandatory markings in the middle of British roads in the late 1940s.[8]

Once past the construction crew, I saw the first signs of the population growth that has taken place around Cambridge in recent decades. The former wartime airfield at Bourn was slated for a massive new housing development, and a little further on more houses were being built in Cambourne. Here I passed a van parked in a layby with the driver busily rearranging the piles of parcels in the back ready for delivery to the increasing number of homes in west Cambridgeshire. Delivery vans seemed particularly numerous that morning. With the commuter traffic gone the roads were fairly quiet and the ratio of vans to cars had shifted.

Over the last two decades, the number of miles driven by delivery vans on Britain's roads has increased by 50 per cent compared with much more modest increases in car mileage. This rise is due to the growth of online shopping. There is something almost cyclical about this; from delivery by first horse and then van in the early part of the twentieth century, through the rise of the out-of-town supermarket with large car park for the motor age that I'd seen on the edge of every town, to a return to van delivery in the digital age, and the acceleration of online shopping, compounded by the global pandemic. Once more, rather than going to the shops, goods are increasingly coming directly to us in the backs of thousands of vans making what the logistics industry calls the 'last mile' from warehouse to doorstep.[9]

Once through Cambourne, I briefly left the old road for the new dual carriageway before turning onto a Roman road. It stretched off straight into the distance, but I didn't stay on it long because I wanted to stop at the Caxton Gibbet Park Service Area. Pulling into the car park it was clear why it had this name. A wooden gallows stood, somewhat incongruously, on the grass verge in front of the McDonald's Drive Thru. The gallows was here in 1951, although it was not the one used to hang the 'many highwaymen' at this spot where 'the road crosses the Roman Ermine Street' but a more recent addition. According to the archaeologists called in prior to the building of the new service area, it was 'probably a nineteenth-century replica' placed here 'to attract passing trade' to the Gibbet Inn built around a hundred years after the last public execution on this spot. Although its somewhat macabre advertising was still there, the Gibbet Inn had long gone, and so had the Yim Wah House Chinese restaurant that followed it, to be replaced instead by a choice of twenty-first-century British roadside eateries: McDonald's, Subway and Costa Coffee.[10]

I wasn't particularly hungry or thirsty, so I headed back to the roundabout. Here I made a mistake. Rather than taking the first turning to follow the route marked in the *About Britain* guide towards Eltisley, I went straight over and continued along

Ermine Street towards Papworth Everard. It was later that I realized the cause of my confusion. The captions running along either side of the strip map referred to both places: Eltisley with its 'charming village green with cricket pavilion and 17th century houses' and Papworth with 'the first village settlement for tubercular patients and their families' whose 'industries include leatherwork which is exported'.

Papworth became home to the Cambridgeshire Tuberculosis Colony in 1918, with discharged soldiers making up most of the first group of 17 patients suffering from the disease housed in Papworth Hall. During the interwar decades the number of patients grew to over 300, and the renamed Papworth Village Settlement transformed a small village into a centre of medical treatment and industrial enterprise. Given that tuberculosis was, as a 1946 film about Papworth expressed it, 'as yet untamed', patients were provided with treatment, housing and 'suitable' work in factories that produced everything from leather suitcases to the bodies of cars and trucks. But things were already changing when motorists directed by the *About Britain* guide skipped Papworth in favour of Eltisley.

The founding of the National Health Service in 1948 meant that the state took over the role of providing medical treatment from private doctors or charities like the Papworth Village Settlement. Initially Papworth Hospital continued to focus on chest disease, but by the mid-1950s they had begun pioneering heart surgery. The Papworth Village Settlement – renamed the Papworth Trust in 1963 – continued to provide housing and work. But when TB became treatable with antibiotics available freely under the NHS in the 1950s, they started housing a broader range of disabled and then older persons. As a result, Papworth became home to an increasingly older population and by the 1980s this was a village very much in decline, with its former industries sold off.[11]

While the village was declining in the 1970s and 1980s, the hospital on its southern edge was rapidly expanding. In 1979, the first successful heart transplant in Britain was performed at Papworth. A few years later, in 1986, the first successful triple heart, lung and liver transplant in the world was undertaken there. In its centenary year, what had started out as Cambridgeshire Tuberculosis Colony received the royal stamp of approval and was renamed the Royal Papworth Hospital. But the hospital was boarded up when I drove through Papworth, and the sign marking the exit from the roundabout where I'd taken the wrong turning had been partially scrubbed out to cover the large, white-on-blue capital 'H' for hospital. I stopped and chatted with the security guards who told me that a Chinese developer had been in talks to buy the site and redevelop it, but had pulled out because the asking price was too high. Although no longer here, the Royal Papworth Hospital hadn't moved far. It reopened 16 miles away on the massive Cambridge Biomedical Campus site close to Addenbrookes Hospital on the southern edge of Cambridge in 2019.

The old hospital wasn't the only place boarded up in Papworth. I passed an abandoned church as I drove, ironically, to Godmanchester and then on to Huntingdon past freshly ploughed fields and the sluice gates on the River Great Ouse. Crossing the river, I followed the signs towards Hinchingbrooke House that was marked on the *About Britain* map and was given the longest caption alongside it. The lengthy reference may have been because of the house's former residents. 'Probably both Charles I and Cromwell spent some of their boyhood in Hinchingbrooke House' the caption explained, before adding that it was 'now the home of the Earl of Sandwich'. As with so many other former aristocratic homes I passed, the aristocrat had long gone. Since the 1970s, it has been part of Hinchingbrooke School, passing through various iterations of grammar school, comprehensive, specialist sports college and academy according to changing government education policy. But the old house was also an events space that hosted the usual mix of conferences, dinner dances and weddings. When I was there in late October, it had temporarily been turned into 'Horror at Hinchingbrooke House' offering the chance to be 'hunted by axe wielding freaks, chainsaw maniacs, killer clowns, demonic creatures and more' each evening in the week before Halloween.[12]

It was just before midday and I didn't stop to wait until nightfall. I was beginning to realize that going to Hinchingbrooke House had been a mistake. It seemed that all the roads around it were being dug up, in a county where construction was taking place everywhere to smooth the way for the burgeoning population of Cambridge's hinterland. I decided that it was probably best to make my way back the way I'd come and then into and through Huntingdon. I skirted the town, passing a packed car park by a strip mall that was home to the staples of twenty-first-century British urban retail: Next, Sports Direct, TK Maxx, Sainsbury's and an M&S Foodhall. My daughter needed new leggings and socks so I pulled in, eventually found a parking space, and made my way with her into TK Maxx.

From its first store in the United States in the late 1970s, this American discounter has become a major player in what is rather quaintly known in the age of online shopping as the 'bricks and mortar' retailing sector. Since opening its first British store in Bristol in the mid-1990s, TK Maxx now has 270 shops across the country, including this one in the redeveloped Chequers Shopping Centre in Huntingdon. Plastered all over the window were orange signs assuring shoppers that the items they'd find inside would be priced at discounts of up to '60% off RRP'. The emergence of RRP – recommended retail price – and discounters selling goods well below it, signalled an important shift in the last 70 years as power shifted from manufacturers to retailers.

When motorists drove from Cambridge to Huntingdon in 1951, the shops they passed sold most items at prices fixed by the companies making them. Around half of the money spent by British consumers in the early 1950s was on products that were priced exactly the same regardless of where they were bought as a result of resale price maintenance agreements by manufacturers. This practice of effectively fixing prices came under increasing political scrutiny in the second half of the 1950s, before being abolished in all sectors outside books and medicines in the mid-1960s. After the 1964 Resale Prices Act, manufacturers could set a recommended retail price for a product, but it was now left to the retailer to decide if they sold it at this price, or far below it.[13]

This apparently minor change had a dramatic impact. With discounting possible, new stores opened to sell goods at reduced prices. One example was the ill-fated electrical goods discounting chain Comet, which opened its first superstore in Hull in the late 1960s. These shops tended to be larger and were often built with car parks on the edge of town as retailing became concentrated in fewer, larger shops. But as well as deciding what price to sell goods at, shops also began commissioning, making and marketing their 'own-brand' products. By the mid-1980s, well over half of all sales in Sainsbury's were of own-brand goods. The rise of own-brands saw retailers moving into manufacturing, or at least subcontracting it out. This represented a shift in the balance of power between retailers and manufacturers. Rather than manufacturers telling shops what to charge, shops were now telling manufacturers how much they were willing to pay for goods, and those shops were more than happy to take their business elsewhere to the lowest seller. Such was the change taking place on the high street and in shopping centres like the one I'd stopped at, that one scholar equates the passing of the Resale Prices Act with the abolition of Corn Laws over a century earlier, suggesting that '1964 was for the relationship between manufacturers and retailers what 1846 was for the political dominance of manufacturing over landed interests'.[14] Over two centuries, economic power in Britain has shifted from the land, to the factory, to the shopping centre and, latterly, the online retail site.

Chief among those online retail sites, as the delivery vans that I'd seen that morning revealed, is Amazon.com. Its sales figures of close to $300 billion when I drove through East Anglia dwarf the 'bricks and mortar' business of the TK Maxx I'd just left with my daughter, the proud owner of some discounted socks. Amazon's rise to power in Britain owed much to the technological changes that came with the development of the internet and the shift in regulation marked by the collapse of the Net Book Agreement. At the beginning of the twentieth century the Net Book Agreement was an attempt by the Publishers Association to control the price that certain 'net books' were sold at in the shops. From a small number of titles, this grew to include fiction after the First World War. Post-1964, publishing was the only industry – aside from medical goods – where the tradition of manufacturers setting the purchase price continued.

However, by the 1990s this consensus in the publishing industry had begun to break down. A number of large bookshops began discounting. A few publishers caved in and by the end of the decade discounting was the norm. Amazon capitalized on this with deep discounting of loss leaders as they began selling books online in the United States in the mid-1990s and in Britain towards the end of the decade.[15] It meant that on my way back to the car, I could have dropped in to Sainsbury's to pick up not only some own-brand groceries but also a heavily discounted book from the bestseller list. But I wanted to make it to Wicken Fen by lunchtime so instead I took the road towards St Ives.

I drove on through an increasingly flat and watery landscape. The route clung to a narrow strip of land perched between a lake on the left and the marina on the right with the River Great Ouse just beyond. I passed a National Trust sign pointing down to Houghton Mill, the last working mill on the Great Ouse, but was on the lookout for another National Trust sign. I found it in St Ives and followed the brown sign with the oak leaf to Wicken Fen past new housing on the edge of town. The *About Britain* guidebook was a little ambivalent about where precisely along this road the flat coastal plain of the Fens began. 'Between St Ives and Earith the soil darkens, turning to the dark peat of the fens' the caption just below St Ives informed motorists. But the one immediately above pushed the boundary a little further north and signalled that 'the iron bridge at Earith over the New Bedford River' marked 'the entry into the fens'.

Driving towards Earith it felt like I was on the cusp of flat, watery, peaty fenland. Once over the concrete bridge that replaced the original nineteenth-century 'iron bridge', I found myself on the first of many roads raised well above the surface of the neighbouring fields. The causeway undulated gently up and down, responding to the movement of the shrinking peat. I passed farms with wooden crates piled up in the yard ready for the next harvest of potatoes and sugar beets, the farm names stamped on each one. Hand-drawn signs at the side of the road warned of 'Mud on Road' and the car squelched through piles of ink-black peaty mud on the road surface. I briefly left the low-lying land behind and ascended the 'island' of Haddenham. But dropping down from this high point I was soon immersed once more in the flat and watery landscape of the Fens, crossing over the River Great Ouse and then the River Cam in quick succession, before turning off to take a narrow lane that reached a dead end at Wicken Fen.

It was no surprise that those drawing up the *About Britain* tours included Wicken Fen on one of the itineraries. During early discussions, Wicken Fen had been flagged up as just the kind of place to be included alongside 'the names of towns and villages' in the gazetteer at the back of each guidebook.[16] And so on the penultimate page it received its own short entry where it was described as 'one of the few remaining pieces of natural fen, this is now preserved by the National Trust as a sanctuary for birds, plants, insects, etc.'. This description was repeated more or less word for word in the caption alongside the route map. There, Wicken Fen was described as 'an area of original and undrained fen owned by the National Trust' and home to 'rare birds, plants, and butterflies, including the Swallowtail'. Another reference came in the introductory 'verbal portrait' penned by the novelist Ralph Mottram, who explained that 'the 680-acres of Wicken Fen' was one of 'several surviving scraps of fenland' that 'may be turned into National Nature Reserves'. Rather than the Swallowtail, Mottram was more interested in the 'Large Copper' butterfly, which 'wavers around' in Wicken and Woodwalton Fens where it had been 're-introduced' although he added rather darkly that 'its future is doubtful'.[17] All the writers of this guidebook were in agreement that Wicken Fen was important, so I decided to stop at what is the 'most species-rich site' in the country and home to around 9,000 different plants and animals.[18]

It was late October, so any chance of seeing butterflies at Wicken Fen was out of the question. The large copper only emerges in high summer, and the swallowtail a little earlier in May through to July, with a second wave in August to September during some seasons. But the lack of butterflies was not simply a result of being there at the wrong time of year. More fundamentally I had arrived here far too late. The native large copper went extinct in the 1840s as a result of the drainage of the Fens for arable farming. In 1927, the Dutch variant was introduced at Wicken Fen and Woodwalton Fen 30 miles to the north-west, but Mottram was right to be gloomy. In the post-war era, large coppers disappeared from Wicken Fen and struggled on at Woodwalton Fen for only a little longer. The same was true of the swallowtail. The population died out here in the 1950s. There were attempts to reintroduce them in the 1970s and then again in the 1990s, but both proved short-lived. From being widely found in East Anglia as well as further afield during the nineteenth century, the habitat of Britain's largest and rarest butterfly gradually retreated across the course of the twentieth century. To find swallowtail butterflies, you now need to travel 100 miles or so north-east to the Norfolk Broads. This story of reducing habitat and numbers has been mirrored in other native species of butterfly with more than a third placed on an endangered 'Red List' in the last decade.[19]

The disappearance of the swallowtail from Wicken Fen was a result of changes in this landscape not immediately visible on the ground. Driving through Britain, some changes were conspicuous. Something like the building of the motorway network was clear to see wherever I went. But other changes were far less obvious and this was particularly true when driving through rural farmland like this tour through East Anglia or walking around Wicken Fen. That something had changed here was clear from the loss of the swallowtail butterfly, but I only discovered what lay behind this local extinction after I returned home.

I'd found a reference to an article from the late 1980s on 'The Recent History of Wicken Fen' that I thought would be worth a look. As a historian, I assumed the phrase 'recent history' would refer to the post-war decades I was interested in. But ecologists work with a different sense of time and so recent history meant the last four centuries. That article led me to a book on Wicken Fen, which I found online and ordered from a second-hand bookshop that was, inevitably, one of Amazon's sellers.

Through a series of seven pie charts, the authors told a story of changing land use here since the early seventeenth century that was less immediately visible when walking around the Fen.

The first three charts – stretching from 1600 to 1870 – told the story of drainage for agricultural use. While in the seventeenth and eighteenth century Wicken Fen was roughly a third peat bog and two-thirds grassy sedge, by the late nineteenth century around a quarter of the land had been drained.[20] Beyond Wicken Fen, drainage took place earlier and more thoroughly. As the *About Britain* guide boasted in a series of photographs showing agricultural productivity, the Fens had been 'largely reclaimed from water-logged marshes in the 17th century' and turned into 'the richest farm-land in England'.[21]

In an attempt to halt further drainage of Wicken Fen after the market for sedge used in thatching declined, Victorian naturalists started buying up strips of land. At the end of the nineteenth century, a small part of Wicken Fen became the National Trust's first nature reserve. It received the state's stamp of approval following reports on National Parks and the creation of the Nature Conservancy in 1949. Wicken Fen, 'an outstanding relic of the ancient fenlands of eastern England, containing many plant and insect species which are not found, or are exceedingly rare, elsewhere' became National Nature Reserve 63.[22]

But all this protection did not put an end to landscape change as the final four pie charts showed through snapshots of land use in 1900, 1936, 1956 and 1981. The proportion of drained land is more or less the same now as it was in the 1950s and was almost a century before. During the Second World War, parts of the fen were drained and farmed as part of the war effort, but when motorists made their way to Wicken Fen in 1951 it was reverting back to wetland. However, these pie charts showed changing land use despite attempts at preservation. In 1900, sedge covered the majority of the Fen. By the 1950s, this had shrunk to roughly 12 per cent of the fen and by the 1980s sedge made up only a tiny sliver of the pie. In its place scrub woodland, or carr, had taken over. By the late 1990s, about 75 per cent of what was still named Sedge Fen was actually carr, and only around 10 per cent sedge. It is only in the last couple of decades that the National Trust tried to reverse this encroachment by clearing away areas of scrub to make room for more sedge.[23]

But the damage, as far as the swallowtail was concerned, had been done. It died out here in the 1950s because its food plant, the milk parsley, disappeared as a result of scrub invasion in the fen and falling water levels because of continuing drainage well beyond it. 'More was required', at Wicken Fen, 'than simply erecting a perimeter fence and advertising the designation of a nature reserve' to quote the words of the government's Biodiversity Action Plan from the mid-1990s.[24] That 'more' has included the rise of active management of the site to limit the 'natural' processes of scrub growth. But it has also resulted in increasing attention being paid to what is happening on the other side of the reserve fence. When they were first set up, the National Nature Reserves were seen as islands to be safeguarded from changes taking place elsewhere as a result of suburbanization, road building and intensive agriculture. But over the last few decades there has been recognition that something needs to be done about the land between these islands.

In 1899, the National Trust bought a couple of acres of Wicken Fen. Over the following decades, as a result of donations and bequests, the reserve grew to over 700 acres. But this pales in comparison with plans that aim to transform the reserve from a few hundred acres to part of a massive 20-square-mile corridor running south-west from the main road that I'd driven in on, along the course of the River Cam and all the way to the edge of Cambridge. Rather than protecting natural habitats piecemeal by creating discrete nature reserves, the National Trust's Wicken Fen Vision self-consciously aims to 'deliver on a landscape scale' in order 'to give nature the space it needs'.

This grand scheme is not simply driven by a desire to safeguard fauna like the swallowtail. While safeguarding specific species and increasing biodiversity continue to be matters of concern, the Wicken Fen Vision focuses on something dubbed in contemporary jargon 'ecosystem services'. This represents what is seen as 'a utilitarian turn in conservation' less concerned about the intrinsic value of milk parsley or the swallowtail butterfly, and more with the functional value of nature measured in pounds and pence. Peatland restoration here, as elsewhere, is seen as a chance to 'stimulate a sustainable tourism economy, creating opportunities for jobs and local businesses' and 'to promote and protect the precious benefits ecosystems provide such as storing flood waters and mitigating global warming as a means to support a healthy sustainable environment.'[25]

These plans represent a radical rethinking of the Fens compared with that found in the *About Britain* guide. In the full-page photographs in the East Anglia volume images of intensive agriculture dominated. On one page a photograph of a 'Fenland horizon' showed a large, flat, freshly ploughed field of dark peat, stretching into the far distance. On the opposite page there was a close-up of a tractor pulling a plough. As with many of these photographs the placement was intentional. The left page showed the results of previous centuries of reclamation that turned unproductive 'water-logged marshes' into the 'richest farm-land in England' that 'in parts . . . gives a yield of wheat from every acre four or five times the average in the USA'. On the right, the caption – 'Land reclamation, 20th century' – boasted that land was still 'being converted to production'.[26]

This story of highly productive, mechanized, intensive farming – a process that resulted in the ripping up of hedgerows to create larger, machine-friendly fields – was one that the Festival of Britain was keen to tell. When the editorial committee met in London in May 1950 to discuss the mock-up of the East

Anglia guidebook, the choice of photographs was 'the subject of considerable comment'. Reading the minutes in Kew, it was clear that there was concern 'that over much attention had been paid to picturesqueness at the expense of modernity' with 'the absence of illustrations of agricultural machinery and reafforestation and the excess of horse pictures . . . especially noted'.[27] Not all pictures of horses were cut from the final East Anglia guidebook. Racehorses at Newmarket made an appearance, as did 'Suffolk Punch stallions'. And while it did not include a horse, the opening image on the title-page of a horse-drawn 'East Anglian farm cart', by Barbara Jones, looked more to the past than the future of agriculture. But while not all horses were erased, the final guidebook was careful to include a photograph of 'Fordson Tractors in the factory at Dagenham', as well as the image I'd seen of 'Land reclamation, 20th century' being undertaken by tractor, not horse, power. As the book explained to visitors to this region, 'farming is probably nowhere more highly mechanized'.[28] This mechanization was not only made visible in the pages of *About Britain* but also still visible on the surrounding roads. Just after leaving Wicken Fen I passed a tractor pulling a trailer laden with peat-covered root vegetables.

But the Wicken Fen Vision offers an alternative future. The sums have quite literally been done and the losses from ending arable production are more than outweighed by the gains offered by what jargon terms 'nature-based recreation, grazing, flood-protection . . . reduced greenhouse gas emissions . . . pollination services, improved water quality, improved soil quality, and several cultural services' as peat is re-flooded for carbon storage and sequestration rather than drained for growing sugar beet.[29] Vastly enlarging Wicken Fen is not the only such project on the table. More than 200 peatland restoration – or rewilding – projects are underway across the country. Just to the north-west of Wicken Fen, there are plans to create a 15-square-mile wetland buffer zone linking Woodwalton Fen with the nature reserve at Holme Fen. And a little later on that day, I passed signs directing tourists to Lakenheath Fen nature reserve where the RSPB boasts that they have 'transformed former carrot fields into a magical wetland home for kingfishers, cranes, otters and watervoles'.[30]

Such a future for the Fens would have been unimaginable and hopelessly backward looking in 1951 when intensive agriculture was celebrated. The guides I was following were published two decades before the language of ecosystem services appeared, and another two decades before ideas of carbon offsetting emerged. Back then the Festival of Britain was busy celebrating fossil fuels, pairing an image of a watermill with one of a massive new coal-fired power station on the edge of Ipswich, above a caption that explained 'the rivers still help to furnish power, but by enabling coal to be brought cheaply to such vast items in the National Electric Grid system as the new Cliff Quay Power Station'. In 1951 the present was seen to be coal-fired and the immediate future was nuclear.[31] The two black-bodied, white-sailed windmills I passed as I made my way into and through Wicken represented the past of power in 1951, rather than its present, let alone its wind-turbined future.

I saw another windmill – signposted in brown as a site of heritage tourism – as I avoided yet another bypass and took the old road through Soham. The houses were brick-fronted, but flint-sided, revealing what lay deep beneath the peat. Rejoining the bypassed traffic at the edge of town, I got my first glimpse of Ely Cathedral. But on reaching the outskirts of Ely I was forced off to the left and around the city like so many others with their inner ring roads encircling one-way streets and pedestrianized zones. This mini ring road eventually deposited me on the other side of the cathedral, which remained visible in the rear-view mirror for a while longer as I drove through the flat landscape to the architectural hodge-podge town of Littleport that straddled the road. Bridging the Great Ouse once more, I headed towards Mildenhall past freshly ploughed fields of black peat off to the right and a thin stand of poplars off to the left. The road I was on was raised above the surrounding fields and I passed a rather ominous warning sign that showed a car falling off the road into water. I kept both hands firmly on the steering wheel as I navigated this narrow causeway through a watery landscape flecked with flint-edged houses and peppered with potatoes. Above the horizon, my eye was drawn to a plane in the big sky that banked hard to the right as it came in to land on the runway at RAF Mildenhall.

I passed the runway a few minutes later as I drove between perimeter fence and uniform rows of base housing. Although the red-edged sign informed me that this was RAF Mildenhall, the entrance gate signage made clear that this site was shared with the US Air Force. The American presence was visible on and along the road. American flags flew over a car sales lot and a roadside sign informed me that I could 'sell or trade . . . US car spec here'. A stream of large, left-hand-drive cars were entering and leaving the base, as they were at RAF Lakenheath a few miles away. I initially ended up on the wrong side of the vast airfield at Lakenheath, having turned off too soon. Rather than driving along its eastern edge, I arrived at the main entrance on the west but quickly stopped when I saw signs warning that ID was needed to go any further. I turned around in a street of military housing dressed for Halloween with a mixture of orange and black banners and fake cobwebs. It looked more like a street in the American suburbs than western Suffolk where the Fens meet Breckland.

Having retraced my steps I entered into the landscape of Breckland. Off to the right, gnarled Scots pines bordered a silver birch speckled, bracken-brown heath that was a radically different landscape from the black peat of the morning. Motorists were alerted to this changing landscape in 1951, just as they were earlier on in the tour when entering the Fens at Earith. A new boundary was crossed, 'between Mildenhall and Brandon' where 'the route enters the "Breckland" region of sand and heath now being afforested by the Forestry Commission'. As with the reclamation of the 'water-logged marshes' of the Fens for productive purposes in the seventeenth century, the *About Britain* guide approved of the twentieth-century reclamation of 'the sandy desert of the high Breckland'. Mottram drew attention to the planting of '60,000 acres . . . with Scots and Corsican pine' creating 'one of the nation's main reserves of soft wood' that was already being put to good use in the poles carrying 'many of the telephone wires of Great Britain'. A little further along this stretch of the route, the motorist was instructed to look out for 'timber yards in clearings close to the road'.[32]

But driving through Breckland it was clear that more was going on than simply pastoral farming and commercial forestry production. On the opposite side of the road from grazing sheep and Scots pines lay a double line of perimeter fencing keeping me out of RAF Lakenheath. I drove along the edge of the runway before turning left at the end of the fenced boundaries to follow the signs to the designated 'viewing area'. Getting out of the car, the fact that I was now in Breckland rather than the Fens was plain to see. Sand, not peat, blew along and out of the narrow gap between tarmac and grass where I parked. I was not the only one here. A long line of cars and vans were parked on both sides of the narrow road. One man was up on the roof of his van that doubled as a viewing platform, poised for action with his camera and long lens trained on the runway that lay beyond the fence. Just around the corner, a burger van was parked up and doing a brisk trade serving up snacks for those waiting for planes taking off or landing. I was nothing like patient enough. After a few minutes staring through the wire fence, I returned to the car and headed back to the main road and into the woods. Driving through the tunnel of trees, I heard the roar of a plane low overhead.

The two bases at Mildenhall and Lakenheath had both been active during the Second World War and were still functioning when motorists drove through here in 1951. But the guide was more interested in Mildenhall because of its proximity to West Row where 'the Mildenhall Treasure, now to be seen in the British Museum, was found during World War II'. While neither air base received a mention, motorists were alerted to the fact that they were driving through a military landscape. On this stretch of road between Mildenhall and Brandon, those following this tour were informed that 'War Office training operations are conducted in this region, known as the "Stanford Battle area".'

The 'Stanford Battle area' was part of the wider transformation of East Anglia for military use during the Second World War. More than 100,000 acres were taken over by the army in 1942 to train thousands of troops in the run-up to the D-Day landings. Most was returned after the war was over, but around a quarter remained in the hands of the military and the Stanford Training Area lying to the north-east of the road to Brandon continues to be used for live-fire military training. That the 'Stanford Battle area' did not disappear entirely at the end of war owed much to the fact that a new, Cold, war began soon after 1945. This left its mark. A mock German village – with the very un-German name of 'Eastmere' – was built in the 1960s in the middle of the Breck as Stanford Training Area was repurposed for preparing troops for urban combat in central Europe. That scenario never materialized, but in the aftermath of the Cold War the village shifted imaginatively eastwards as a site of preparation for urban warfare in the Middle East.[33]

This changing story of post-Second World War geopolitics was visible from the road that once ran through 'Stanford Battle area' and now follows the perimeter fence of RAF Lakenheath. Lakenheath was one of hundreds of airfields hurriedly built across East Anglia during the war. Construction started here in 1941 and building was still going on at the end of the war on this 'half-finished aerodrome'. Just what would happen with this wartime airfield was a matter of concern for local MPs troubled by the spread of the site across the former road between Lakenheath and 'their shopping town of Brandon'. Most airfields built in East Anglia during the war reverted to agricultural use at the war's end, but Lakenheath and Mildenhall assumed a new, and controversial, role. Neither base had been home to the US Air Force during the war.[34] But all that changed in the middle of 1948, when American B-29 bombers first arrived at Lakenheath.

By 1951, as motorists were driving along the road to Brandon, the US Air Force had taken over administrative control of this base, as well as joint operation of that at Mildenhall. This was a playing out of an agreement reached by first Atlee, and then the new prime minister, Churchill, with President Truman in late 1951 and early 1952 that 'the use in an emergency of bases in this country by United States forces was accepted'. The 'emergency' in question was the beginning of the Cold War, and Lakenheath became part of an archipelago of American military sites on British soil. What this meant in practice was a source of political conflict across the post-war decades. In particular, the key question frequently asked but never fully answered in Parliament was whether the British government had a right to veto what happened on American military bases like Lakenheath. This was especially the case when U2 reconnaissance aircraft left British soil to fly over the Soviet Union in the early 1960s, prompting one MP to ask whether 'the British government are in a position to forbid the use of these bases for activities of a provocative or risky character'. But it was not only spy planes that were based here. It was also bombers carrying nuclear weapons that came under increasing public and political scrutiny.[35]

The end of the Cold War did not spell the end of the American military presence. At the close of the twentieth century, there were 13,000 American visiting forces in 30 bases across Britain, with more than half of them stationed at these two bases in East Anglia.[36] Madingley cemetery is not the only bit of American soil in East Anglia. These bases are, and look set to continue to be, a little bit of America complete with everything from a US Post Office to an American high school. They stand as a concrete expression of the so-called 'special relationship' that has dominated British foreign policy in the post-war decades. That special relationship has not come under much scrutiny, aside from a brief period in the 1980s when the Labour Party unsuccessfully called for the closure of American nuclear bases.[37] This lack of scrutiny contrasts with another special – or perhaps less special – relationship. As a number of scholars astutely note, 'the absence of public debate on the structure of the UK–US relationship since the transformation of Britain's international environment after the end of the Cold War contrasts sharply with the detailed (and often suspicious) scrutiny of every aspect of Britain's engagement with institutionalized Europe' during the same period.[38]

Leaving this little piece of America, I entered Brandon past a Tesco store, followed by a fish and chip shop, a closed-down and boarded-up Bingo Hall, a couple of betting shops, and then Aldi. Gone was the bustling centre of 'dressing of rabbit skins for the felt and hat trades' that the *About Britain* guide portrayed. Both the felt hat industry and the trade in rabbits have long gone: the former to changing fashions, the latter to the outbreak of myxomatosis just a couple of years after 1951. The first signs of the disease came with the discovery of a few dead rabbits on a farm in Kent in 1953. By the end of the following year the disease had spread across the country, killing the majority of wild rabbits in the process. An estimated population of around 100 million wild rabbits before the outbreak was reduced to perhaps as few as 1 million by the end of the 1950s, much to the delight of farmers and foresters if not the country as a whole, which was still dependent on wild rabbit as non-rationed meat.[39] The rabbit population has since rebounded, although not to anything like their pre-myxomatosis numbers, nor their former place in the British diet.

Just after Brandon I left Suffolk and crossed into Norfolk. Since the bicentennial of Lord Nelson's death at the Battle of Trafalgar, Norfolk – as the sign at the county boundary declared – has been 'Nelson's county'. This association with Nelson, who was born in Norfolk, came after a request was made by the Norfolk Nelson Liaison 2005 Committee and the cost of the new signs was paid for by another son of the county, Bernard Matthews. Matthews pioneered intensive turkey farming in Norfolk in the 1950s, first in the bedrooms of an old stately home – Great Witchingham Hall – and then, as the business expanded, in sheds on former Second World War airfields across East Anglia. From being the preserve of the upper-middle-class Christmas dining table in the pre-war period, mass production allowed this American bird to become the British Christmas dinner staple. Intensive farming also made turkey a cheap meat that found its way into a wide range of products produced by Matthews's company, transforming turkey from a once-a-year product into a daily mainstay, including the much-vilified 'Turkey Twizzler'. But it isn't only the Turkey Twizzler and intensive poultry farming in Norfolk that have come under criticism. Given his defence of slavery, Nelson has since been dubbed 'a white supremacist'.[40] On the roads entering Norfolk, Nelson remained celebrated for the time being at least, although those road signs may yet go the way of the Turkey Twizzler.

I drove into Norfolk along a straight road lined by beech and silver birch trees. At regular intervals, tracks ran perpendicular to the road off into the Forestry Commission woods to either side. Bypassing Stoke Ferry, I left Breckland and returned into Fenland once more. I wanted to follow the original route that crossed the river and passed the then 'new pumping station at St Germans', which drained the Middle Level that runs down to the causeway at Earith that I'd driven along earlier that morning, but the road was closed. There were no other roads across the watery landscape and so I had no choice but to follow the main road towards King's Lynn where I parked up and walked into town to find something to eat and drink. Over hot chocolate and cakes I talked about the journey with my wife and younger daughter. Our conversation turned, perhaps unsurprisingly, to the very visible American presence found in this corner of Britain. The day began with a cemetery where close to 4,000 American servicemen were buried and ended alongside a US Air Force base where 5,000 work. The American entry into global affairs in the twentieth century is not only part of the past here but also the present.

But the more I thought back on this journey as I returned home and began reading up on what I'd seen along the way, the more I was struck by the past, present and future of Wicken Fen. The plans for expansion of National Nature Reserve 63 signalled a different way of imagining nature and what conservation means, as well as a different way of thinking about the value of the Fens as a productive landscape. For those putting the *About Britain* guides together, productivity was seen through the lens of intensive agriculture. The more recent turn to talk of 'ecosystems services' still has an eye on productivity, but recasts the Fens as a site of carbon capture and eco-tourism.

What struck me was how this appeared to be a case of turning back the clock to the years before seventeenth-century drainage that would have been unimaginable in 1951. The Festival of Britain proudly showcased the products of progress. These could be, and were, rooted in the past, but they were seen as an improvement on what had gone before. The present was celebrated as faster, cleaner, better, and the assumption was that this trajectory would continue. That sense of naive confidence has disappeared. The future imagined for the Fens is a rewilding that attempts to reverse the damage done by the very 'progress' that the guides celebrated.

Stafford–Colwich–Rugeley–Lichfield–Sutton Coldfield–Birmingham–Edgbaston–Bournville–Cotteridge–Solihull–Hampton in Arden–Meriden–Coventry–Marton–Long Itchington–Southam–Ladbroke–Mollington–Banbury–Adderbury–Deddington–Woodstock–Oxford

5

Chilterns to Black Country

Stafford–Coventry–Oxford (104 miles)

From a quick glance at the *About Britain* guide, it seemed that this journey through the middle of England would be heavy on ecclesiastical architecture. A sketch of the medieval interior of St Chad's in Stafford appeared beneath a fragment of the 'Bombed Coventry Cathedral'. On the next page a carved 'Dragon with knotted tail' at Adderbury Church was joined by a drawing of 'Carfax Tower' in Oxford, which is all that remains of the twelfth-century St Martin's Church. Interspersed between these images, captions drew attention to 'Lichfield Cathedral . . . the smallest cathedral in England', 'the new cathedral tower' in Coventry and the 'parish church (1797), designed by Robert Cockerell' in Banbury. Some of these ecclesiastical buildings were highlighted as sights to admire from the road with mention of a 'wonderful' or 'handsome' facade. But in other cases the sketches of interiors invited motorists to stop and venture inside.

However, the guides were never intended to merely direct visitors from one old church to another but to be a new kind of guidebook for a Britain 'ready for the future', which celebrated modern industrial factories alongside ancient cathedrals.[1] This carefully chosen route from Stafford to Oxford was no exception. Coventry was to be visited not only to see the site of a 'new cathedral tower . . . rising from the ruins of this magnificent old cathedral' but also to experience the 'vigorous way of life' of a city with 'great motor-car factories'. And in Banbury, motorists were told to look out for 'the huge works of the Northern Aluminium Company' on the way into town and 'extensive open-cast ironstone workings' on the way out of town, as well as the late eighteenth-century parish church in the centre.[2] The ecclesiastical and industrial were two sides of the same coin.

In order to navigate this landscape, I decided that I should take a vicar along. A good friend of mine is a theologian who spent his childhood in the Midlands. I picked him up outside the modern station on the western edge of Stafford before negotiating a series of roundabouts and heading out along the Lichfield Road through the typical landscape of urban edges. 'I hate this kind of place, bungalow land,' Matthew thought out loud, as I drove through rows of bungalows, past the sign to the mid-1960s municipal crematoria off to the left and more recently built DIY and grocery stores off to the right.

However, once through Weeping Cross and then on to Milford Common, we entered a rather different space. In 1951, motorists were invited at this point to look up from the road to 'the Royal Forest of Cannock Chase' that 'rises to nearly 800 ft. on the right'. Seven years later, this became Cannock Chase Area of Outstanding Natural Beauty and land for the people rather than monarchs. The first cluster of Areas of Outstanding Natural Beauty – the Gower Peninsular, Llyn Peninsular and Quantock Hills – were all designated in 1956. In 1958, Cannock Chase was the fourth place added to a list that has now grown to encompass more than forty parts of the country deemed officially beautiful and accessible.

I crossed in and out of National Parks and Areas of Outstanding Natural Beauty time and again. These were products of a post-war desire to conserve natural landscapes and open them up for urban populations. But in the eyes of their creators, there was clearly an A list and a B list and Cannock Chase was on the latter. When he drew up his wish list of future National Parks in 1945, John Dower saw Cannock Chase as an 'isolated patch' of 'wildness' that was simply too 'small' for National Park status and so he put it on his list of 'Other Amenity Areas NOT suggested as National Parks'. The National Parks Committee that reported two years later followed Dower's lead.[3] So rather than becoming a National Park, Cannock Chase became an Area of Outstanding Natural Beauty. Despite this different designation, the hope was to ensure that this 'isolated patch' of 'wildness' remained that way.

But driving through Cannock Chase it was clear that the wild was not entirely safe. I passed a triangular warning sign like those I'd seen on other rural roads. These now-familiar signs are relative newcomers to the British landscape. They started to appear after the 1963 Worboys Report recommended that the jumble of signs that had accrued over decades be replaced with a unified set of modern signs. New signs had already been designed for the building of motorways in the late 1950s. Graphic designers Jock Kinneir and Margaret Calvert tested new signage on the Preston bypass in 1958. Drawing on practice in Germany and the United States, they rejected the use of capital letters and instead adopted upper and lower case letters in their new font appropriately called Transport.

In the mid-1960s, new road signs were erected with new fonts, lower-case lettering and shorter lines of text. 'Slow – Major Road Ahead' was replaced with the much shorter instruction to 'Give Way' and the command to 'Halt' was replaced by 'Stop'. As the county surveyor of Oxfordshire enthusiastically proclaimed, 'the adoption of the word STOP to replace HALT finally brings this country out of the horse-and-buggy era, and acknowledges the appropriateness of a command used for many years in both Europe and America, to describe what is required of drivers of motorized vehicles.' That he pointed to borrowing from practice beyond Britain was significant. The decisions of the 1931 Geneva Convention Concerning the Unification of Road Signals – and a later 1949 Geneva protocol – clearly shaped the recommendations of the Worboys Report that nudged Britain increasingly into line with Europe as the country began the process of applying for entry to the European Community.[4]

The influence of European practice was visible in the warning signs I passed. As they developed them, the Worboys Committee had two different traditions it could look to. Across the Atlantic, America had adopted the yellow diamond. Across the Channel, Europe had chosen the red triangle. While a United Nations Commission stated its preference for the American model on the basis that the colour yellow was more arresting and the diamond shape offered more room to play with for deploying a variety of symbols, the British Road Research Laboratory decided that the red triangle was more suitable. In adopting red triangular warning signs containing a symbolic pictogram without the use of any additional legend, the Worboys Committee made clear where its allegiances lay.

While the red triangular road sign could be seen as the unification of the British roadscape into the wider European one, this convergence was not total. In some cases, pictograms were copied wholesale from European road signs, but in other cases new pictograms were designed by Kinneir and Calvert. This was the case with the British deer that I saw flashing up on the road sign I sped by. European signs showed a small, static deer facing to the left, with all four feet planted on the ground, centrally placed in the triangle. By contrast, the larger deer with more clearly defined antlers adopted in Britain leapt across the sign, from left to right, in mid-flight with two legs in the air and two on the ground. It seemed about to break out of the frame, with its legs intruding onto the red border.

It was a sign that captured not only a dynamic stag in motion, but also a nation that was becoming more closely aligned with Europe while maintaining a distinct and separate identity. However, it seems that even this dynamic image of a British stag leaping from the edges of an über-European sign has failed to keep cars and deer apart. This short stretch of road through Cannock Chase is one of the hotspots for accidents between deer and vehicles in the Midlands. Given that half a century of warning motorists has not been entirely successful, attention has more recently turned to warning deer rather than drivers. There was a hint to me, the naive motorist, that something was going on because of the jarring appearance of wordy signs – complete with now unfamiliar block capitals – that warned of 'ANIMAL DEATHS' for the next few miles and the implementation of a 'deer safety project'. But the precise nature of that 'deer safety project' remained hidden in the forest and invisible from the road. Among the trees, 'Deer Deter DD430' technology, developed in Austria and used elsewhere in Europe, had been deployed. When roadside sensors were triggered by approaching headlights, alarms and blue and yellow strobe lights were set off to startle any deer and keep them off the road.[5]

I was tempted to pull off the road and search for a leaping British stag. But this was a day for driving not walking, so I kept going along the route that a strip map enforces, neither deviating to the left nor the right, at least not at this point. I pressed on along the Trent Valley towards Rugeley, drawn by the distinctive sight of four cooling towers and a large chimney in the distance. Two huge power stations were built here after motorists drove by in 1951. But one had already gone, and it turned out that the other was soon to follow. Chatting with the security guard on the gate, he told me that the long process of decommissioning Rugeley B was well underway.

The twentieth century saw a shift in Britain from dispersed private electricity power production to one increasingly centralized from the mid-1920s and ultimately nationalized in the late 1940s, before being broken up and re-privatized in the 1990s. These changing conceptions of the role of the state in energy production have been shaped by both ideology and war. It is perhaps not surprising that the shift to create some kind of countrywide 'national gridiron' and then a 'national grid' came in the wake of the two wars. In the aftermath of the Second World War, and particularly the power shortages in the winter of 1946, the decision was made by the Labour government to nationalize the industry. In 1948, a new British Electricity Authority – renamed the Central Electricity Generating Board a decade later – was created to oversee not only transmission, but also generation, of power.

When the Central Electricity Generating Board opened the 600-megawatt-output Rugeley A in the early 1960s, and then the 1,000-megawatt-output Rugeley B in the early 1970s, they did so in a joint venture with another recently nationalized industry: coal. Technological advances meant that it became cheaper to move power around the grid than transport coal to power stations. As a result, large coal-fired power stations like Rugeley were no longer sited close to urban areas where power was used, but near the coalfields and rivers needed for its production. Rugeley was built next to the newly opened Lea Hall Colliery, with coal taken directly to the furnaces by conveyor belt. The nearby River Trent provided water for cooling for this power station, built along what became known as Megawatt Valley. The distinctive modernist architecture of concrete cooling towers transformed the landscape of the Trent Valley, which became, for a few decades, home to the greatest concentration of power stations anywhere in Europe.[6]

Things began to change in the 1990s. Lea Hall Colliery was closed, and coal had to be delivered by rail from much further afield. Rugeley power station also came under new ownership as a result of privatization. But the changes here were not just about who produces power but more about how power is produced. Rugeley A was demolished in the mid-1990s and I arrived at Rugeley B just a few years after electricity production had stopped and a few months before what the site's owners described as the 'first controlled collapse demolition event' was to take place.[7] It is not only Rugeley that is on its way out. In the next few years all these 'great temples to the carbon age' will have gone as a result of the 2001 European Large Combustion Plants Directive, which limited the lifespan of power stations unable to adapt to new limits on airborne emissions. The demolition of coal-fired power stations along the Trent Valley marks the end of the age of coal. On the riverine edge of Rugeley, I was reminded of walking along the decaying tarmac gradually being reclaimed by flora in Pegwell Bay. Both are places where a temporary technology has come and gone in the course of the human lifespan.

Once this power station is gone, there are plans to replace it with a 'sustainable village' powered by solar rather than fossil fuel. Judging by the other side of the bypass where Rugeley A once stood, few traces of the power station will remain. I got quickly back into the car after being told off by a different security guard for taking photographs. The only hint of what once stood on the other side of the road was a sign informing me that this was Towers Business Park, the centrepiece of which is a 700,000-square-foot Amazon 'fulfilment depot'. They offer regular customer tours here, but I hadn't booked ahead and so wasn't able to get inside this huge warehouse. Instead I counted the rows of loading doors along the roadside edge of this distribution depot, sited strategically in the middle of England where the majority of the nation's population can be reached within a half-day's drive.[8]

Making my way towards Lichfield, the landscape quickly changed from warehouses to green-hedged fields. Although agriculture was clearly the dominant industry there were hints of diversification but the 'wedding barns' I drove past were empty. Entering Lichfield, I saw the three spires of the cathedral as I dropped down into the city and tried my best to navigate towards them. But the inner ring road and one-way system meant that I had to settle for a glimpse of the spires rather than the 'wonderful west front' of Lichfield Cathedral. My decision to press on was partly due to an enticing brown tourist sign pointing the way towards the Staffordshire Regiment Museum. Normally I would have ignored this and pressed on, but Matthew persuaded me not to. His granddad had served in the Staffordshire Regiment during the First World War and he'd just returned from retracing his footsteps through Belgium. As it turned out, I probably shouldn't have listened to him. These brown signs took me away from the original route, along the Tamworth Road – rather than the Birmingham Road – to Whittington Barracks and into the museum's empty car park.

The last time I visited a regimental museum was on a primary school trip and my one abiding memory was seeing a bar of chocolate from the First World War. So at this museum I asked the welcoming staff if they had any First World War chocolate on display. They didn't, but they did show me a display case from the last Gulf War that included a couple of Yorkie bars, one marked 'It's not for civvies'. 'They all love their sweets,' one of the staff told me, but explained that in the desert heat Haribo trumped chocolate.

It was clear that regimental museums have changed a lot in the last forty years. This was not simply the result of evolving museum display practices, but also efforts to keep pace with the national curriculum introduced by the Thatcher government in 1988. While industries like power or coal were no longer dealt with by the state the opposite was happening in education. The state increasingly determined what would be taught, and in the case of history this meant deciding what 'a coherent knowledge and understanding of Britain's past and that of the wider world' was, and was not. The heritage industry adapted to this selective choice of which past was worth studying and this museum has been very successful in attracting thousands of school visits each year to their 'Great War Trench' and 'Blitz Experience'. These offer younger children 'an aspect of a theme in British history that extends pupils' chronological knowledge beyond 1066' and older children an understanding of the 'challenges for Britain, Europe and the wider world' between 1901 and the present day.[9]

There weren't any school parties booked in that morning, so one of the museum's enthusiastic guides offered to show Matthew and myself around. We happily followed our guide, Rob, through the Coltman Trench – double-width and fitted out with plastic barbed wire to meet accessibility and health and safety requirements – and then into the Anderson Shelter complete with the sounds of planes overhead and bombs exploding in the distance. I had missed the west front of Lichfield Cathedral, but chanced upon a little piece of the Western Front recently carved into the soil of Staffordshire instead. The trench's presence here was not as anachronistic as it might seem: model trenches had been dug down the road in Cannock Chase by troops before they headed to France. It was hard to pull Matthew away from Rob and his colleagues, but I needed to get going. We headed back to the Birmingham Road, pausing to buy petrol on the way. Inside the shop I spotted Yorkie bars among the ranks of brightly coloured wrappers so decided to buy a couple. Chomping chocolate, I drove beside the M6 Toll road for a few minutes, before eventually crossing over it.

The idea of building what was originally known as the Birmingham Northern Relief Road first surfaced in the 1980s during the Thatcher government. With traffic use on the M6 more than double earlier projections, what was in effect a motorway bypass was proposed. Originally the plan was that it would be publicly funded, but in the age of privatization the government announced that it would be financed by a private company, which would be given fifty years to recoup their investment. In the early 1990s, the government considered introducing toll-charging across the motorway network. However, by the time construction started on this 27-mile stretch of motorway, following a number of public inquiries and legal challenges, this idea had been dropped. In 2003, Britain's first, and only, motorway toll-road finally opened: the M6 Toll. Its owners were keen to recoup their hefty investment and make a profit. They assured drivers that the 'M6 toll isn't just a road. It's a stress-busting, time-saving, congestion-free escape route. A gateway to gigs, a protector of business meetings, even a shortcut to your own bed.'[10]

While the M6 Toll remains an exception, toll roads were the norm in previous centuries. A network of turnpikes was built across Britain in the seventeenth and eighteenth centuries, complete with toll-houses and gates, some of which are still visible. In the late nineteenth century the burden of maintaining roads was passed to the state in the guise of the newly created county councils. When motorways were first built in Britain in the late 1950s, the principle that building and maintaining roads was the responsibility of the state continued, although under the oversight of national, rather than local, government. In 2053, the 'shortcut to your own bed' will return to state ownership, spelling the end of this late twentieth-century experiment. However, charging for road use may not be confined to the past; it is possible that tolls will become the new way of paying for roads when the vast sums generated by fuel duty trickle away, as we change first to hybrid, and then to fully electric, vehicles.

Those 27 exceptional miles of the M6, and the miles that run both north and south of them, stretch further than I thought. In

1975, the European Agreement on Main International Traffic Arteries identified a network of major roads connecting Europe from north to south, and from east to west. One of these – the E05 – runs from Scotland to southern Spain and includes this stretch of the M6 that therefore does not simply connect north and south Birmingham, but ultimately Glasgow with Cadiz. However, there was nothing to suggest that this was the E05 as I made my way over the M6 Toll. According to European rules, there should be green rectangular signs spelling out that this is a major north to south European traffic artery. But these are absent from the British stretches. As with the wild animal warning sign that I'd passed, British adoption of European road signs has been far from complete.

Leaving the British motorway to make its way past Birmingham, I carefully followed the old road in order to try to drive straight through the middle of the city. I entered leafy suburbia and then the heart of the lovely old coaching town of Sutton Coldfield, before exiting through more leafy suburbia and making my way to Erdington. Here I saw Birmingham stretched out beneath me. I dropped down Gravelly Hill, and ended up beneath the Gravelly Hill Interchange, better known by its mid-1960s nickname 'Spaghetti Junction'. Jammed between the river and canal, the M6 raced over my head. Without meaning to, I found myself on a brief stretch of elevated urban motorway with views of Aston Villa's ground – Villa Park – off to the right before entering the 'Heartlands' of Aston dominated by the high-rises making up Aston University and science park. I soon entered office and apartment block-lined Birmingham proper, where I followed a series of tunnels through and underneath the city.

Driving out of each subterranean section offered a brief glimpse of a slice of the city on either side before being plunged back into gloom. Birmingham was reduced to a series of short vignettes. I saw a flash of the shining steel of the new shopping centre around the Bull Ring, a sign to the National Trust's Back to Backs (houses), a glimpse of the Chinese Quarter, followed by a sign pointing towards Gay Village, which points to a bigger story of change following the decriminalization of homosexuality in 1967. In what seemed no time at all I reached Edgbaston where the '325 foot high clock tower which distinguishes the buildings of Birmingham University' could still be seen, but it now peeped up behind the facade of the vast new Sport & Fitness club built in the post-fees era when students are seen first and foremost as consumers.

Thinking back on this experience of driving through Birmingham, it seemed strangely appropriate that I had only really seen the city from the top of Gravelly Hill. While the guidebook celebrated both modern factories and medieval churches, those commissioned to write the opening essays were sometimes voices of dissent. This was certainly true of the historical geographer W. G. Hoskins who introduced this volume that covered the Chilterns to the Black Country. He recommended that motorists view Birmingham and the Black Country from afar, preferably from the A4123 which offered a 'superb general view of this industrial concentration' from the west. From the safety of their car, Hoskins wrote, motorists could peer down on this landscape that,

> forms a plateau, and one sees it stretching away level beneath its canopy of smoke unbroken to the horizon: factory-chimneys and cooling-towers, gasometers and pylons, naked roads with trolley-bus wires everywhere, canals and railway-tracks, greyhound racecourses and gigantic cinemas; wide stretches of cindery waste-land, or a thin grass where the hawthorns bloom in May and June – the only touch of the natural world in the whole vast scene; plumes of steam rising all over the landscape,

> the pulsing sounds of industrial power coming across the dark waste; and the gaunt Victorian church-spires rising above the general level, or completely blackened towers receding into the smoky distance.

'This is the Black Country, well and truly named,' concluded Hoskins, whose sympathies clearly lay with a more green and pleasant land. It came as no surprise that he chose to end his essay by directing his readers' gaze away from 'the noise and ugliness of the blackened busy towns' to the timeless 'unravished Midland countryside' of 'some willow-hung, slow-moving Warwickshire stream'.[11]

His dislike of industrial urbanity went against the grain of the Festival of Britain project. But Hoskins's views were widely shared. The next stop on my route, the model factory village of Bournville, represented the nineteenth- and early twentieth-century ambivalence towards urban modernity articulated by Hoskins and others. The village and factory are still there. But from the road signs etched in both industrial black and tourist brown, it was clear that this was not simply a chocolate factory but also a chocolate destination. There were two entrances: one signed in black for lorries making deliveries to this factory that produces 20,000 bars of chocolate each hour, the other signed in brown for cars and coaches making their way to Cadbury World and the shop selling some of those bars. I chose brown, parked up and had a quick walk along paths lined with fences painted in Cadbury purple.

Leaving Bournville I got lost. The strip map was no help at all. After driving around for a while I chanced upon Solihull Lane, which offered the promise of taking me to my next destination. I passed the gates of the Land Rover factory as planes roared in above me on their descent into Birmingham International Airport. Just beyond the airport entrance I reached the road to

Hampton in Arden and after crossing over yet another motorway drove slowly through the village. It turned out that they were celebrating their eighth annual scarecrow competition, this time around the theme 'music', which explained why Elvis peeped out of one front garden and the Blues Brothers strutted in another. Leaving this collection of musical icons stuffed with straw behind, I continued on to Meriden, passing under the proposed route of the High Speed 2 rail line.

If, and when, it is built, the track will go to the planned Birmingham Interchange station near to the airport that I'd just driven by. Running at up to 250 mph, HS2 aims to reduce the travel time between London and Birmingham to around 50 minutes. Envisioned as the sister of the first high speed line that I'd crossed underneath in Kent, HS2 has been bogged down in spiralling costs, delays and environmental protest. It is unlikely to reach Birmingham before 2030 and Manchester and Leeds before 2040. When it does make it here, it will pass over a stretch of road with a longer history of being a place for speed. Just a little further on I came to a stretch of road known as the 'straight mile', which was the interwar site of Sunday morning unofficial motorcycle races, complete with stewards, starters, spectators and racers.[12]

But I kept the speed down as I came into Meriden. In the notes alongside the strip map, this was simply 'another of the old forest villages' passed through on the road from Birmingham to Coventry: in short, a place to be driven through and viewed, alongside Hampton in Arden, as an example of a settlement dating back to when this whole area 'was once the great Forest of Arden'. But the gazetteer at the back of the *About Britain* guide reported Meriden's claim to be 'the centre of England' so I stopped for a closer look. I parked in front of the sadly closed fish and chip shop, buying sandwiches from the Co-op instead, and sat down with Matthew to eat them on a triangular village green in the middle of England.

Whether Meriden is the centre of England or not has long been a moot point. The guidebook acknowledged that in the 1950s this accolade was fought over by a 'wayside' oak tree in Lillington and the 'cross at Meriden on the Coventry-Birmingham Road'. Most saw Meriden's claim to be the stronger of the two. When the journalist Paul Bewsher wanted to take the temperature of the nation's public opinion in 1938, he justified heading to Meriden on the grounds that 'if you mount a map of England on cardboard, you can balance it on a pin at the tiny dot marked Meriden'. However, it seems that middle England may lie a little further north-east. Using computer modelling, rather than trying to balance a map on a pinhead, the Ordnance Survey determined that the true centre lay in a field on Lindley Hall Farm, rather than the village green in Meriden where the copper plaque in front of the eroded sandstone cross proudly proclaimed that I had reached 'the CENTRE OF ENGLAND'.[13]

When motorists drove through Meriden in 1951, this cross was on the move. Given fears that the 'crumbling' cross was dangerously close to what was 'said to be the busiest highway in the country', it was decided to move it from the side of the road to a safer location in the heart of the village green. Reporting that 'The Centre of England is to be Moved', the job of 'strengthening' the cross, 'surrounding it with low railings, and a flower-bed; and for the first time, putting up a plaque to say what it is' was estimated to take a week at most. However, as with many things, it took a little longer. In large part this was because the cross travelled much further than first planned. In the early spring of 1952, it was taken to London, and erected at the heart of a new post-war 'English village' showcasing 'People's Houses' recently built by the council in Leicestershire, alongside 'an ideal village pub' reconstructed in Olympia for the *Daily Mail* Ideal Home Exhibition. Here, as one reporter wrote during this period dominated by post-war rebuilding, 'the ancient stone, whipped temporarily from its home in Warwickshire to London's Olympia by magic undreamed of centuries ago, once more stands squarely at the heart of the matter – a very different matter – housing.'[14] After the exhibition closed, the cross returned to its new location in the centre of the village green in Meriden. The plaque says that 'the cross was rebuilt on this site when the green was improved in celebration of the Festival of Britain. AD 1951'.

The cross was not the only monument on this green. Looming over it was a much larger, grey-granite column. Funded through public subscriptions, the Cyclists War Memorial was unveiled in 1922. Meriden, with its claims to be at the centre of Britain, was chosen because of its accessibility to amateur cyclists converging here from north, south, east and west. And they did, in vast numbers. Thousands came for the unveiling of the memorial with the press publishing photographs not only of the crowd on the green, but also their bicycles parked en masse in the fields around. And they continued to congregate here in thousands on the anniversary of the unveiling throughout the 1920s and into the 1930s. There were a few cyclists there when I drove through. They had also stopped to buy something to eat from the Co-op, propping their bikes up near the memorial. Matthew and I sat near them on a bench dedicated to '50 years service to cycling by John Hunt' eating our sandwiches while looking at the medieval stone cross encircled by neat municipal planting, the cyclists memorial beyond, and the Birmingham–Coventry road.

Once the 'busiest road in England', today it was relatively quiet. I saw none of the lorries that the parish council feared might collide with the sandstone cross. Like everywhere else, Meriden has its bypass. But when it opened in the late 1950s, it was not without teething troubles. A month after opening, one of Birmingham's MPs asked the Minister of Transport if he was aware of the congestion that the old Birmingham–Coventry road still faced at certain times of the day. It turned out that the minister did know that 'difficulties had arisen' at one junction 'mainly at the closing time of the Triumph Engineering Company's factory when large numbers of workers travel towards Coventry' before reporting that he was 'trying to find a more satisfactory permanent solution'.[15] There was certainly no congestion when I was there, but then again there was no longer a motorcycle factory.

Triumph had moved here during the Second World War after the original factory in Coventry was bombed. But in the early 1970s, the company decided to close the Meriden factory and move up the road in an attempt to cut costs in a market increasingly dominated by Japanese motorbikes. In protest, the workforce began a sit-in.[16] It was partially successful and in the mid 1970s a worker's cooperative bought and reopened the factory. But this was to prove only a temporary stay of execution. Meriden's post-war motorcycle history was reduced to a memorial plaque on the corner of the aptly named Bonneville Close, which led into the housing estate built on the site of the former factory. It was a place among many where manufacturing industry had been and gone since motorists first followed this route.

This was particularly true in Coventry, which 'welcomed' me a little further along the old Birmingham–Coventry road. I entered the city past a 1930s roadhouse – the Tollgate – whose name drew on the history of toll-charging on British roads. I faithfully followed the brown signs to 'Historic Coventry' and ended up parking beneath a large tower block that was now a 'Student Village'. A short walk away I found the Coventry Transport Museum, which spelled out the rise and fall of what was once Motor City UK. Among the rows of bicycles, motorcycles, lorries and cars made here, I tried to find a car made in Coventry in 1951. There wasn't one. Most cars built in

Britain in the early 1950s ended up being exported, with around 80 per cent bought overseas as Britain briefly became the largest exporter of cars in the world.[17]

Writing in 1951, Hoskins explained that 'something like 40 percent of the working population' of Coventry worked in the automobile industry. It was, he noted, the importance of the city's industry which 'by 1940 had turned over very largely to making aircraft and aircraft parts' that explained why Coventry had been bombed so heavily during the war. Although the war was over, Hoskins hinted at new dangers facing Motor City. Presciently, he saw the reliance on car manufacturing in Coventry – as well as in the other motor towns of Oxford and Luton – as leaving it 'dangerously dependent on this one great industry' and warned that 'a slump would have serious effects on their whole economy'.[18] Ultimately Coventry did not just experience a slump but a dramatic fall. Sitting in the back of a Coventry-built taxi at the end of the exhibition, a film transported me around the former sites that were once car factories and are now retail parks and housing estates.

The car industry's disappearance from Coventry seemed unimaginable in the 1950s when Britain was second only to America in terms of the numbers of cars made. By the 1970s, the rise of European and Japanese car industries meant that Britain lagged behind not only America, but also Japan, France and West Germany. Coventry took a big hit. As plants closed, and unemployment rose, Coventry was reduced, as the local band the Specials phrased it in their 1981 number one hit, to a 'Ghost Town'.[19] The 1980s was the low point here, as in other towns and cities dependent on manufacturing industry. In the 1990s, there was a short-lived revival as foreign companies opened up new factories. Next to the taxi I sat in stood one of the last Peugeot 206s to come off the production line at the Ryton factory, closed in the mid 2000s. Although the London Taxi Company continues to make taxis in Coventry like the one I sat in, and a futuristic display featuring a prototype Aurrigo self-driving car pod hinted at a high-tech car manufacturing future, the 'vigorous way of life' of the car industry that motorists were invited to experience in 1951 had been largely reduced to a museum display.

Alongside the rows of cars once manufactured here, this museum to the industrial past also offered a nostalgic take on Britain's 'finest hour'. Matthew and I were treated to an unexpected second Blitz experience of the day, with a soundtrack of air-raid warnings, planes overhead, bombs falling, and flashes of light as they landed, but the Anderson Shelter – unlike the one Rob had led us into – was roped off so there was nowhere to hide. Leaving the museum and walking to the newly built Coventry Cathedral, next to the bombed-out remains of its ancient predecessor, I realized that I was cutting it fine; it was later than I'd planned, and they were just about to close for the day. I was glad that Matthew was with me. He played the vicar card and we got in to see the early 1960s interior decorated by a Who's Who of mid-century British artists: Graham Sutherland, John Piper, Elizabeth Frink, Jacob Epstein. After a quick look round this temple of 'Peace and Reconciliation' we left the cathedrals old and new, and headed back to my – Japanese – car parked in the centre of a twice-destroyed city: once by war and once by shifts in the global economy.

Leaving Coventry, I passed the Prologis Park industrial estate built on the site of the factory where the Peugeot 206 had been made. They still make cars here, but rather than turning out mass-produced vehicles, Jaguar Land Rover has opened a bespoke manufacturing centre. In one corner, Special Vehicles Operations make 'high-end, luxury bespoke commissions' that include, among other things, the option of armour-plating. In another, the Classic Works Facility offers those with the money an opportunity to 'own a part of history' by purchasing a fully restored Land

Rover Series 1, first made between 1948 and 1957. Automobile heritage was not only on display at the motor museum but was also being remade 500 classic Land Rovers at a time. As I found elsewhere, they are still making things in post-industrial Britain, but the industries that have survived have – like the farmers with their wedding barns – diversified and specialized.

Leaving Coventry, I drove through a number of villages towards Banbury. In 1951 motorists entered from the north, past 'the huge works of the Northern Aluminium Company', which the caption explained 'flank the road on the descent into Banbury'. Having missed a turn, I came in from the east, so headed north to make sure I didn't miss out on the industrial as well as the ecclesiastical delights of Banbury. However, the aluminium factory closed in the mid-2000s. Only a few key elements – the 1931 gates, the 1936 office building with its aluminium windows, and the war memorial – were guaranteed a future through listing, as these art deco industrial premises are turned into a boutique hotel.[20]

Once in the centre of Banbury I went in search of the famous Banbury cakes mentioned in the gazetteer at the back of the *About Britain* guide. Asking around, I discovered that Chandler's Cafe on Church Lane was the best place to try what one shopkeeper described as a 'flatter' version of an Eccles cake. But when I found the cafe they had already closed for the day. The 'original Banbury cake' shop – Brown's – that claimed to have been baking Banbury cakes for 200 years and motorists had no doubt visited in 1951, closed their doors in the mid-1960s. Walking past it, it was clear that not only had the business gone but the medieval building housing the shop on Parson's Street had also been demolished, despite local protest. But this wasn't quite the end of the Brown family's connection to Banbury cakes. Philip Brown, an inheritor of his great aunt's tradition and recipe, now bakes Banbury cakes 20 miles away in Hook Norton. If I'd planned ahead, I could have ordered them from his online shop, had them delivered to my home in Bristol and packed a box of six to bring with me to eat outside the former site of Brown's on Parson's Street.[21] But that seemed overly complicated so I settled for chocolate wafer biscuits from a Polish shop. Matthew and I ate them admiring the ancient Banbury cross and more recent neighbouring statue of a fine lady riding a cock horse, complete with rings on her fingers and bells on the horse's feet of nursery rhyme fame.

It was only when I returned home that I discovered that Banbury was not only visited by motorists in 1951 but also British sociologists. They were inspired by the work of their American colleagues Robert and Helen Lynd who had immersed themselves in the lives of the inhabitants of Muncie, Indiana in the 1920s and 1930s. Dubbing this place 'Middletown', the Lynds saw Muncie as a lens through which to explore the wider changes affecting America.[22] In the late 1940s, British sociologist Margaret Stacey discovered her own Middletown in Banbury. She and her team were here when motorists armed with their copy of the *About Britain* guide drove past the aluminium works and into town in 1951. After publishing her first study in 1960, Stacey made a return visit and published a follow-up study in the mid-1970s, which laid the basis for sociologists interested in the processes of social change. Once back home, I ordered Stacey's books as well as any follow-on studies I could find. Reading these was a little like the experience of discovering the pie charts showing land change at Wicken Fen. Driving through, and walking around, both Wicken Fen and Banbury, it was clear that things had changed since 1951, but these in-depth studies offered a chance to see things that were not immediately visible.

When she lived in Banbury in the early 1950s, Stacey was aware that the town had recently undergone a period of rapid change. The arrival of the aluminium industry in the 1930s had transformed the market town into the industrial centre that those putting together these tours were so keen for motorists to see. For Stacey, 1930 was the big 'divide'. 'Life in Banbury before then would have been more easily recognizable to a man who had lived a hundred years earlier,' she explained, 'than to one living at the present day, only twenty years after.' Those older residents she spoke to in the 1950s told tales 'of the scores of carriers' carts which came rattling and rumbling in from the villages; of steaming cattle tethered in the streets; of the shouting drovers and the muck on the pavements'. But by the 1950s, it was not only the 'muck on the pavements' that had gone as the market town had become an industrial one. The whole ancient core of this settlement appeared to have been almost swallowed up in the post-First World War building of rows of 'brick, semi-detached, and remarkably uniform' houses along the 'half-dozen main roads' leading in and out of Banbury.[23]

It was the continuing growth of the town that struck sociologists when they returned to Banbury for their follow-up study. 'To a field-worker returning from the first study,' the authors of the second explained, 'the most dramatic change is the many acres of erstwhile fields now covered in new housing estates' with 'the land between the main roads . . . progressively filled in' with a mixture of council and private housing estates connecting the earlier ribbon development of housing along the major roads. The continuing urban growth here had much to do with the 1952 Town Development Act that aimed 'to encourage town development in county districts for the relief of congestion or over-population elsewhere': in particular London. Banbury was one of the towns that approached central government for funding to build the large Bretch Hill council estate on the western edge of the town in the early 1960s.[24]

These new houses coincided with the arrival of a factory that promised new jobs. In the mid-1960s, a company most famous for their custard moved their instant coffee and dessert factory from Birmingham to Banbury. Although Bird's Custard Powder had been made in Birmingham since the late 1830s, it was only after the takeover by the General Foods Corporation and the diversification into other products – especially Maxwell House instant coffee in the late 1950s – that the company began to outgrow its original site in Digbeth. Sales of instant coffee soared in Britain in the late 1950s and early 1960s, so the company looked for a new site for a large, modern factory that could combine the manufacture of desserts with the demands of a growing market for instant coffee. They found their new home along the main road on the northern edge of Banbury that I'd driven up and then back down again in a fruitless search for the aluminium factory.[25] Evidently, they were still making coffee in Banbury, although the factory was now part of the Jacobs Douwe Egberts coffee empire, making Tassimo capsules alongside Kenco instant coffee to sell to a British market whose tastes have shifted to Americanos, lattes and cappuccinos.

Stacey and her team noticed the first period of rapid population growth – from 13,000 in 1931 to 19,000 in 1951 – and then the second when the population reached 25,000 in 1966. Since they were here, Banbury has continued to grow. By 2011, 47,000 were living in Banbury, many of them newcomers in the private housing estates constructed after the motorway was built just to the east of town in the early 1990s. In the middle decades of the twentieth century Stacey had witnessed the transformation of Banbury from market to industrial town. In the last decade of the twentieth century and the early decades of the twenty-first, it became a dormitory town for car-owning commuters driving to work in service-industry jobs further north or south along the M40.

Stacey realized that the population growth in Banbury in the 1930s and 1940s was due to people moving there from elsewhere. Most had not travelled far, coming from the rural hinterland around Banbury or cities just up the road in the Midlands. These newcomers seemed 'foreign' to those already living in the town because they brought what Stacey described as 'non-traditional' ways of thinking and acting with them.[26] Much of the focus of her study was on the tensions that resulted. Banbury has continued to grow as people have made much longer journeys to get here. In this it broadly follows the national trend. While less than 5 per cent of the town had been born outside Britain in 1951, 60 years later that figure was closer to 15 per cent. When they completed their 2011 census returns, 20 per cent living in Banbury identified themselves as members of an ethnic group other than 'white British'.

This market town has long been globally connected. The Banbury cake itself is testament to that, with its inclusion of dried fruit and spices that emerged from the movement of goods and people during the medieval and early modern period. But Banbury – and in particular the poorer, central and western parts of the town – now has a far more diverse population than 70 years ago, as a result of the growth of Polish and South Asian communities.[27] With nowhere selling Banbury cakes, it seemed fitting to eat Polish wafers in a place where Polish is the second language, spoken by around 7 per cent of those living in the central area where I sat before making my way back to the car.

Walking back along the main street I passed the 'handsome' facade of the eighteenth-century parish church. The guidebook's celebration of this church reflected a tendency to privilege the neoclassical architecture of the eighteenth century and modernism of the first half of the twentieth century over the high Victorian in between. It was early evening so I couldn't take a look inside, but I did stop to read the noticeboard. This suggested that although the church was still here, things had changed. In the early 1990s, the building became the shared home of Anglican and United Reformed Church congregations.

This space-sharing arrangement – that was just coming to an end – was not primarily an act of local ecumenism, but rather the result of years of significant decline. Driving through Banbury in the 1950s, 25 per cent of the town would be found in church on a Sunday morning. Six decades later, that figure had dropped to around 10 per cent. The story of decline was particularly marked in the case of Anglican congregations like St Mary's Banbury. When it was first built with a vast gallery, the church could seat 3,000. In 2010, just over 100 attended the separate Anglican and United Reformed Church services there on a Sunday morning.[28]

I found the figures for those attending this church when I discovered that another British sociologist had decided to visit Britain's Middletown. In 2010, Steve Bruce audited church attendance. What he discovered was not a simple story of decline, but a more complex one that varied from church to church. In 1950, Anglicanism had dominated the town's religious scene. However, when Bruce spent time here 60 years later it had declined massively and he found only 250 worshippers spread thinly among the six Anglican churches in town. In contrast, other churches had grown. Close to 1,000 attended the town's two Catholic churches – some of them no doubt members of the town's Polish-born population – and conservative and charismatic Protestant churches were also flourishing. Just across the street from St Mary's, the former Baptist church had been renamed the People's Church and attracted almost as many worshippers as all of the Anglican churches put together, well over double those in the vast building opposite that had been repurposed as part-community arts space, part church.[29] Crossing the street in front of St Mary's, and passing the alley running down to the People's Church, it was clear that this was not a simple story of secularization but a more complex one marked by declining and rising fortunes for different denominations.

Beyond Banbury it felt like the landscape opened up. Perhaps it was the evening sun, but this stretch of road through farmland appeared somehow more expansive than the land I'd driven through the rest of the day. I reached Adderbury too late to stop to admire the carvings in the church that were illustrated in the *About Britain* guide, so kept going, passing London Oxford Airport before entering the 'cycling city' of Oxford past the Begbrook Science Park. Although Oxford is a 'cycling city', it also was, and remains, a car city. On the way out of town, I spotted signs to Cowley, that – much like those in Bournville – were symbols of the happy marriage of industry and tourism. The black sign pointed to the Mini car works. The brown sign directed tourists to Mini Adventure, which included a factory visit with the chance to see robots at work making the most iconic of British cars.

Driving through this university city where robots have replaced humans on the production line, I reflected on a tension that surfaced in the *About Britain* guide. It featured in Hoskins's opening essay, which directed motorists to gaze at the spectacle of industrial, urban Britain from afar. While Hoskins suggested that it was possible to 'admire ugliness on a grand scale' in a city like Birmingham, he was far more dismissive of 'small industrial towns' that he described as 'depressing spectacles' with 'all the aridity and ugliness of the large cities without their titanic vitality and scale to redeem them'.[30] Although he made no specific comment about Banbury, my sense is that he would have been dismissive of the transformation of this ancient market town into a centre of industry.

Hoskins was not alone in remaining distinctly off-message when it came to the wider aims of the *About Britain* guides that modern factories and medieval cathedrals should be visited and celebrated alike. Right at the end of the book, H. G. Stokes couldn't resist informing readers that 'Oxford has, unfortunately, its "base and brickish skirt," especially towards Iffley and the automobile works at Cowley'.[31] Although I was sure that Mini Adventure would be safely on the itinerary of the guide's staff if they were planning these tours today, I was less sure that someone like Stokes would approve.

Just what Britain – and England in particular – is, continues to be contested, just as it was in the 1950s. Whether industrial towns and cities are as 'English' or 'British' as market towns or ancient villages was a question that contemporaries grappled with across the twentieth century and still do in the twenty-first. Although the Festival of Britain office was clear in its answer that Britain was both a nation of modern factories and ancient cathedrals, I did wonder if they unconsciously privileged one over the other by adopting the road trip as the mode of visiting Britain. The motoring age made villages – replete with thatched cottages, ancient churches and cosy inns – accessible and so gave rise to a particular idea of what Britishness – or Englishness – was, as opposed to industrial cities reached by rail and explored on foot. And I feared that by driving through Britain I might be in danger of replicating those partial representations in my own quest to find out where – and what – the country really was, and how it had changed.

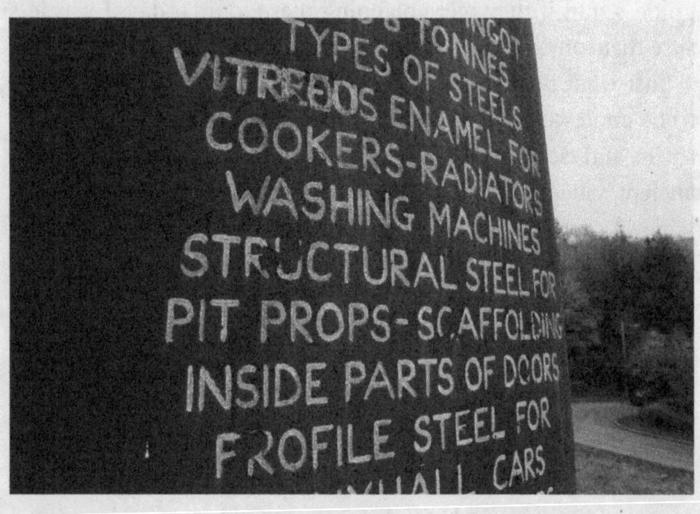

*Hereford–Wormbridge–Pontrilas–Llangua–Pandy–
Llanvihangel Crucorney–Llantilio Pertholey–
Abergavenny–Llanfoist–Gilwern–Blackrock–Brynmawr–
Dukestown–Dowlais–Merthyr Tydfil–Hirwaun–Treherbert–
Treorky–Rhondda–Llywnypia–Tonypandy–Porth–
Trehafod–Pontypridd–Treforest–Nantgarw–Caerphilly–
Thornhill–Cardiff–Rumney–St Mellons–Castleton–
Newport–Caerleon–Christchurch–Penhow–Llanvaches–
Caerwent–Chepstow–St Arvans–Tintern Abbey–Llandogo–
Whitebrook–Redbrook–Monmouth–Welsh Newton–
St Weonards–Much Dewchurch–Callow–Hereford*

6

South Wales and the Marches

Hereford–Merthyr Tydfil–Caerleon–Hereford (147 miles)

At the roundabout with an old cider press in the middle, I followed the signs towards Abergavenny. They still make cider in Hereford: lots of it. A third of all the cider apples grown in the country end up here in the world's largest cider mill, which is now owned by Heineken, but still bears the name of Bulmers, who have been making cider in Hereford for well over a century. This cider mill continues to connect the market town with its rural hinterland. In his gazetteer at the back of the *About Britain* guide, Stokes described Hereford as 'the busy centre of a very prosperous farming and fruit-growing area, with breweries, cider factories and important cattle and fruit markets'.[1] Agriculture still dominates, but the picture of Hereford as 'a busy and comfortable town' didn't fit with my experience driving through the city. Hereford's high streets did not appear to be doing so well. Unprompted, my younger daughter began counting off the number of closed-down shops that we passed. Their demise may have been partly due to online shopping, but also to the building of a multi-million-pound mall on the site of the former cattle market.[2]

I'd ended up in the Old Market mall the night before when the kids had decided we should try burgers made from the beef of Hereford cattle in a local restaurant that claimed to serve the best burger in Britain. Hereford cattle featured in the pages of the guide in a photograph that showed a herd grazing contentedly in a riverside field in high summer, with only a single hefty bull staring directly into the camera lens. As was the case in other volumes, this image was carefully paired with a contrasting photograph. Just to the left of the Herefords, a Welsh upland farmer was shown working his field with horse power. Underneath, and connecting, the two images was a caption that ran from one into the other: 'The uplands are poor and wet' it stated, before adding that, 'The Welsh were driven to them by the invader', a sentence completed under the next image with the words 'who evolved his heavy Hereford cattle on the richer grassland, east of Offa's Dyke'.[3]

The story of contrasts told by this photographic diptych – as well as the one following showing St David's Cathedral 'in a grey village in a low, windy, rocky Pembrokeshire' and 'the milder beauty of Hereford Cathedral, above an English city and fertile river meadows' – was to be experienced by motorists leaving Hereford for Abergavenny and crossing from England into Wales. Working with the wider tradition that painted England and Wales as lands of contrast, the pages of the guidebook prepared visitors to be on the lookout for differences along this border-crossing route. 'The observer, crossing over from the border counties of Hereford or Gloucester,' the opening essay explained, 'finds few of those features which he associates with town and country in England and many features with which he is not familiar.' 'Even' the motorist who 'passes through the country in the fastest of cars' this introduction continued 'will notice that south Wales . . . has few church villages, which are an essential part of the social life of England and the Border', but rather 'small hamlets of humble modern cottages grouped round a box-like Nonconformist chapel'.[4]

In order to reach Wales, I had to drive through the ubiquitous landscape of new housing estates and a large supermarket, complete with weather-vane-topped clock tower. Just beyond the supermarket the city ended abruptly. The sides of the road were now dominated by the rich reddish-brownish soil of freshly ploughed fields on a misty October morning, rather than the reddish-brownish brick of clusters of new-built houses. I'd only been driving for a few miles but decided to turn off to visit the English 'church village' of Kilpeck. Although it lay off the route, it was marked on the map and mentioned in the first caption as home to a 'remarkable Romanesque church'.[5] Seduced by the superlative, I turned off the main road.

I drove past another church before crossing over a railway line and turning onto a narrow road that seemed to lead down a forgotten valley to the hamlet of Kilpeck. The church doorway was a riot of carving: the work of a celebrated Hereford school of Anglo-Norman stonecarvers who also created a rim of gargoyles that graced the roofline of this ancient church. Beyond the churchyard, I clambered up a slippery slope with my kids to find the ruins of the castle. It was clear from the caption and the road signage in tourist-brown, which directed drivers to 'Kilpeck church', that the Romanesque church was the main event and the Norman castle a mere support act. But the castle was a reminder that I was driving through border country.

Once back on the main road, it wasn't long before I reached the border. Driving into Pontrilas, the tree-lined valley was vibrant with the yellows, oranges and reds of late October. Shortly after the village, I crossed the River Monnow or *Afon Mynwg* and was greeted with the traditional signage marking the move from one county – Herefordshire – to another – Monmouthshire. Here, this familiar movement across county lines was freighted with extra significance. Just after passing the sign welcoming me to Monmouthshire – or *Sir Fynwy* – came a second, brown sign welcoming me to Wales with the words *Croeso i Gymru*. But whether Monmouthshire was in England or Wales was an unresolved question asked with particular intensity during the 1960s when roadside signs like this became one of the battlegrounds between those claiming this county as either English or Welsh.[6]

For centuries, the precise location of the border was not a matter for much concern. In the mid sixteenth century, Wales was effectively subsumed within England as a single political state. In many ways those organizing the *About Britain* guides worked with the long-standing assumption that England and Wales were a single administrative unit. Rather than giving Wales its own discrete volume, it was split into two, both of which spanned this historically ambiguous border.

While the Festival of Britain office saw England and Wales as a single unit, they treated Scotland and Northern Ireland differently. In March 1950, they decided that two more volumes should be 'earmarked for Scotland, in case the Scottish Committee desires to be associated with this scheme' and it was 'hoped that funds will be available for a further volume for Northern Ireland'. A few months later, they confirmed that Scotland would be covered by two volumes and Northern Ireland would also have its own guidebook. Including a volume on Northern Ireland in this series of guides called *About Britain* reflected the 'poetic licence' used by the Festival of Britain including all parts of the United Kingdom within a 'Britain' as a single nation with a single story to tell.[7]

Although Wales was not given its own discrete volume, the Festival of Britain's office wanted the opening essay in the guidebook to be written by a Welsh author. This had not been the plan originally. When members of the guidebook committee first put forward names of possible authors, series editor Geoffrey Grigson suggested the artist John Piper for writing the opening portrait to North Wales and the archaeologist and writer Jacquetta Hawkes for South Wales. However, Angwin Penrose 'suggested that it might be desirable to have a Welsh author' for the volume on South Wales and the Marches. By the time of their next meeting, a Welsh author had been identified for both volumes.[8] The man given the job was William Gruffydd, Professor of Welsh and, until 1950, MP for the University of Wales constituency.

The name of the university where he taught – the University College of South Wales and Monmouthshire – and the working title of the guidebook – South Wales with Herefordshire and Monmouthshire – pointed to the ambiguous status of Monmouthshire in the middle of the twentieth century. In 1948 the county had been granted a new coat of arms that sought to codify and make a strength of this ambiguity. Above the text '*utrique fidelis*' – 'faithful to both' – a yellow lion holding a red rose stood side by side with a red dragon holding a green leek. But this attempt at some kind of peacemaking came under increasing pressure.

With the rise of Welsh nationalism in the nineteenth and twentieth centuries the question of whether Monmouthshire was English or Welsh was asked with renewed urgency. This conflict reached a head in the early 1960s when campaigns to 'Make Monmouthshire Welsh' were countered by people seeking to assert its Englishness. When signs were erected welcoming those arriving in the county to Wales, they were painted over by those who wanted to push the boundary much further west. In the end it was the 1972 Local Government Act, whose boundary-making function I saw on other routes, that had the final say. It determined that Monmouthshire would be part of Wales and renamed Gwent in the process, although two decades later yet another act of local government saw the name Monmouthshire return. But these decisions were still some way off when the guidebooks were put together and so the line taken in 1951 was that Abergavenny, some way down the road, was 'the gate of Wales'.[9]

Beyond Abergavenny I crossed into the southern edge of the Brecon Beacons National Park (created in the late 1950s). The 'wooded hills and river dales . . . speckled with cottages' at Gilwern looked striking in the autumn colours. But a little further on, my journey into 'upland Wales' came to an abrupt halt. Ahead of me a long line of traffic was stopped by construction work. On the left was a wooded valley in a variety of shades of yellow, orange and red. On the right, orange-clad men and a yellow JCB hacked the hillside away to widen this road into a dual carriageway. This stretch, between Gilwern and Brynmawr, has proved to be the most challenging section so far of an ambitious scheme to transform the 1960s trunk road running between Abergavenny and Neath into a dual carriageway. Plans developed in the 1990s to complete the work by the end of the 2000s at an estimated cost of just over £250 million proved overly optimistic. The end date was pushed back to 2020 and the estimated cost trebled; when I drove through they were still working and it looked like they would be for a while yet.[10]

I wasn't in a rush, so was happy to follow the instruction to '*Araf*' or 'Slow' down, given by the temporary road signs. I crawled along for a mile or so behind a long stream of very slow-moving traffic navigating its way past rows of cones. Reduced to this slower pace, the world beyond the windscreen seemed to change. Rather than the broad sweep of the landscape, my eye was now drawn to the details within it: a pheasant surrounded by traffic cones here and a single brown plastic chair in a temporary bus shelter there. Moving at a different speed – and one that John Prioleau might have approved of – meant that I viewed things differently. However, once through the roadworks the traffic sped up again and I returned to the more familiar experience of seeing Wales at 60 mph.

The introduction of road signs instructing motorists to '*Araf*' was the result of another spell of road-sign activism in the 1960s and 1970s. In 1967, the Welsh nationalist party Plaid Cymru – formed in 1925, strengthened in the decades before and after the Second World War and which had just picked up its first parliamentary seat at a by-election in 1966 – called for all road signs in Wales to be made bilingual. Their call was echoed by a request from *Cymdeithas yr Iaith Gymraeg* – the Welsh Language Society – that Welsh take precedence over English on bilingual road signs across the country. In 1969, *Cymdeithas yr Iaith Gymraeg* members began painting over or removing monolingual English-language signs that were seen as 'symbols of oppression'. By the early 1970s, they had effectively remodelled Welsh roadsides. Given the ubiquitous and visible nature of these signs their campaign paid off.[11] The recently created Welsh Office asked a committee chaired by the former Liberal MP Roderic Bowen to consider the question of bilingual traffic signs, and broadly accepted its recommendation that they be installed on Welsh roads.

While there was agreement that road signs should be bilingual, there was less consensus over which language should go first. As part of their inquiry, the Bowen committee commissioned research by the Transport and Road Research Laboratory to determine whether it took drivers longer to read a bilingual sign, as well as whether the order of languages made any difference. After a rapid test of only 28 motorists, most of whom were English-speaking, researchers reported that bilingual signs took longer to read and this was particularly the case when Welsh preceded English. This study was not considered robust enough to persuade the Bowen committee that Welsh should follow English on road signs and they recommended precisely the opposite in their final report, which was appropriately published in both English and Welsh. Although the government accepted most of their findings, they were more critical of the recommendation to put Welsh first.[12]

The government's insistence that English go first was challenged by *Cymdeithas yr Iaith Gymraeg* who resumed a campaign of direct action. By the late 1970s, the whole programme of replacing monolingual road signs had started to stall. This was less because of opposition to English first bilingual signs, and more the wider economic situation. When they had undertaken their initial research, the Transport and Road Research Laboratory had recommended against reducing the font size on bilingual signs, and estimated that signs would need to be around 60 to 80 per cent larger to fit those extra words in. As they were well aware, larger signs would cost more. The total cost of replacing or modifying traffic signs across Wales was estimated to be several million pounds, and in the second half of the 1970s this was a low priority in council and government spending. After a decade that saw something of a standoff, the Secretary of State for Wales in effect passed the buck in the early 1980s and told local authorities to decide which order the language would take on bilingual signs.[13]

Entering Monmouthshire and Wales just after leaving Pontrilas, the signs at the county border had listed the English name followed by the name in Welsh, but at the roadworks a few miles further on the sign instructed me to slow down in Welsh first. And later when I travelled into North Wales and the county of Gwynedd, with the highest number of Welsh speakers in the country, I found Welsh trumping English all along the roadside. For now though, the road that climbed up into the low cloud was signposted firstly to Merthyr Tydfil, and only secondly to *Merthyr Tudful*. I climbed the newly completed dual carriageway, clinging to the side of the steep-wooded valley to arrive at the summit. Here a viewpoint was signed, but I couldn't see far along the road ahead, let alone down to the valley far below so kept driving rather than pausing to experience the promised 'exhilarating air'. In the *About Britain* guide, across two short captions, motorists were taken up, over and down to Merthyr through 'Open mountain plateau. Coal tips. A few stunted firs, but exhilarating air' followed by 'Mountain moorland where miners exercise their whippets'. But the cloud was down so low that I couldn't see much to either side of me. There certainly weren't any whippets, but I did spot a sprinkling of ponies grazing close to the side of the road before descending into Merthyr, ringed with post-war housing estates that showed through the gloom.

Entering Merthyr I discovered that the 'monumental archway built of coal' that 1950s motorists passed 'to the left' had gone, along with the industry it represented. The arch was demolished in 1956 and only a single one-tonne block remained in the house now a museum that was once home to the family who owned an ironworks here. Beside this large, chiselled lump of coal, a black-and-white photograph showed the whole arch along with its sister Steel Goat Mill arch, erected for the royal visit in 1912 in order to display locally manufactured steel components. The steel arch had long gone by 1951 and the remaining coal arch was something of an anachronism. When King George V and Queen Mary visited the Dowlais Iron Works in Merthyr in 1912, they witnessed an industry whose heyday was already in the past, and this was even more the case when motorists drove by in 1951. It was a centre for pig iron in the early nineteenth century but the industry began a slow decline as pig iron became outdated in a world discovering steel, a situation compounded when local iron reserves began to run out. At the end of the First World War only one major company was still in business in Merthyr, but this relocated closer to the coast to be nearer imported ore soon after, bringing mass unemployment.[14] Things were so bad that in 1939 there were suggestions that Merthyr simply be abandoned and its population relocated to the coastal plain.

But Merthyr was still there in 1951 and new industries had developed. While 'prosperity ended when the local collieries were worked out and iron and steel works closed down' the *About Britain* guide assured visitors that Merthyr was 'now beginning to return with the establishment of various light industries'. The Hoover factory built here in the 1940s on land where an ironworks had once stood was picked out by Gruffydd in his opening essay as a prominent example of the shift from iron and coal to new industries.[15] New factories making consumer goods were something that the writers of the guidebooks were keen for motorists to take in. And so from Merthyr they were sent to see 'a large post-war trading estate utilizing old ammunition works' at Hirwaun, the 'many new factories' near the 'post-war housing estate' of 'Sweet Abeydare', and then a little further along the road down the valley 'the vast new trading estate, built in the interwar years to deal with the unemployment problem' at Treforest.

In Hirwaun I parked in front of a red-brick building – the aforementioned ammunition works – that now lay abandoned and rotting. But elsewhere on the estate, newer warehouses were busy making everything from metal parts for the automotive and aviation industries to ready meals. Others were distribution hubs for disposable paper plates, greetings cards and specialist civil engineering parts. New industrial estates like this had sprung up as a result of state-sponsored attempts to diversify the economy away from iron and coal and into electronics in the decades either side of the Second World War.[16] Looking around, it was clear there had been further diversification in the last few decades. When motorists visited Hirwaun in 1951, they passed small brick-built, single-storey factories where cameras, radios and televisions were assembled. But consumer electronics are now largely made outside Britain and imported in the containers I'd seen lined up on the dockside in Southampton. The steel-clad units that had replaced the old brick factories were now making more specialist or time-sensitive products, or acting as distribution hubs for imported goods. A similar story had played out at the Hoover factory in Merthyr, which stopped manufacturing in 2009 and now serves as a logistics hub, distributing consumer goods made in Eastern Europe or the Far East along the new dual carriageway leading to the M50 and on to the Midlands.

I left Hirwaun and headed into the Welsh Valleys along roads the guidebook described – like the church in Kilpeck where I'd begun that morning – as 'remarkable'. The impetus for road building came with the decline of mining in the 1920s; it created a large labour force of unemployed miners and a need to shift the economy away from its dependence on coal. One result was the building of the Glamorgan Inter-Valley Road which linked this string of mining villages together and opened the area up for new industries and tourism.

The South Wales coalfield was already declining when motorists drove into the Rhondda Valley in 1951. In his opening essay, Gruffydd explained that the previous decades had seen the closure of some mines and a population decline. However, those planning the volume in London appeared a little removed from the reality on the ground, painting a nostalgic picture that ran from the opening watercolour of a busy pithead through a full-page photograph of singing miners, to another of Cardiff port proudly declaring that 'Coal is the protein of South Wales'. By the 1950s, this was less and less the case. A wave of closures in the 1960s saw the number of pits halved to 50, as the centre of gravity moved from traditional mining areas like South Wales to the mechanized coalfields in Yorkshire, Nottinghamshire and North Derbyshire. Even these coalfields came under threat of closure in the 1980s and 1990s. Across Britain there were close to 200 collieries still working in the early 1980s. After 15 years of industrial disputes less than 20 collieries were offered up for sale when the industry was privatized in 1994.[17] One of those on the market was on the edge of Hirwaun.

Coal mining has taken place at the Tower Colliery for 150 years. For the first century or so, the mine was privately owned. This came to an end in 1947, following the nationalization of the coal industry. State ownership continued for more than 40 years until the privatization campaign of the Thatcher government in the mid-1990s. Originally threatened with closure in 1994, Tower Colliery was bought by the redundant miners and reopened as a workers' cooperative. In the 2010s there was another change when the cooperative brokered a joint venture with a private developer.

The history of employee ownership brought Tower Colliery to national and international attention. Although the idea of workers' buyouts was not popular with the leadership of the National Mineworkers' Union, it was the local union lodge that drove the buyout. When the pit was threatened with closure, they hastily put together a TEBO (Tower Employees Buy-Out) consortia and their winning bid meant they bought the pit for just over £10 million. In the mid 1990s mining restarted and over the next decade the mine bucked the national trend of declining coal production. At Tower Colliery production rose and an average of 3,000 tonnes of high-quality anthracite coal were mined every day for the next 13 years. Much of this coal ended up at Aberthaw Power Station, but the mine also broadened its customer base to generate more income. At the end of the first year there was a post-tax profit of £2 million and Tower Colliery was lauded as a success story, celebrated in an opera and a documentary film, as well as earning a steady stream of visitors eager to learn from this economic experiment.[18]

The deep mine finally closed in 2008, but this was not the end of mining. Rather, attention turned to coal that lay closer to the surface. The opening of Tower Surface Mine followed a shift away from deep pits to open-cast mining. In the mid-2010s, 3.5 million tonnes of coal were extracted. That coal has now gone and so the land is being restored to its 'pre-mining profile' and readied for redevelopment. Alongside the more familiar mix of an industrial estate, shops and housing, there are also plans to transform former mining sites into extreme adventure destinations, an innovation that I was to discover flourishing among the slate-tips of North Wales on my next journey.[19]

I drove through low cloud and mist deeper into the Rhondda Valley. Visibility was down to only a few feet as I went past fish bars, tattoo studios and the offices of Plaid and Labour, through a handful of former mining villages that ran parallel to the river at the bottom of the steep valley. Gruffydd was keen for motorists to see these 'severely utilitarian' villages that made 'no pretence to distinction of architecture' as a contrast with what had been seen earlier in the journey out of Herefordshire and what was to come later as motorists left the Welsh uplands for the wealthy lowlands. There was a politics to these contrasts that he was quick to point out. In part it was the national politics on the two sides of the border. But it was also an internal divide within South Wales framed around capital. As Gruffydd put it, 'the architecture of the upland, plain and often hideous, is the product of wages: that of the lowland the product of profits'.[20]

Little remained of the mines that made those profits. The recently restored Hetty Pit winding engine that I passed in Hopkinstown stood as a memorial to the industry that first brought people to this valley. There were other traces, but you have to dig a little to find them. In Pontypridd – 'the metropolis of the Rhondda' as the *About Britain* guide boasted in 1951 – I passed the buildings of the University of South Wales' Pontypridd campus that was the South Wales and Monmouthshire School of Mines. Just before leaving this route down the Rhondda Valley and heading towards Caerphilly, I passed a large gold-coloured building on the left emblazoned with the name Castle Bingo. I was not sure that the Calvinistic Methodists who built their first chapel in Wales – Groeswen – just around the corner would have approved. What was known as the 'Westminster of Wales' was already in decline in the mid twentieth century as membership of this 600-seater chapel fell from 200 at the end of the First World War to 60 on the eve of the Second. That decline continued in the post-war decades until the number attending could be counted on the fingers of two hands. From a vibrant place of worship in the nineteenth century, the chapel was saved from falling into disrepair by a grant that repurposed it as part museum, part community hall.[21] In the Valleys, both coal mines and chapels have ended up reduced to heritage sites and it was rather depressing to see only the empty shells of both.

Entering Caerphilly, I passed another of the new industries. Now owned by the American firm GE Aviation, the factory stretching along the road originally serviced aircraft engines for British Airways.[22] It was getting late, but I stopped beside the castle in the centre of Caerphilly and walked around the moat to the site where the National Eisteddfod, a celebration of Welsh culture, had been held in 1950. I looked in the visitor centre for Caerphilly cheese, but discovered that it is now made elsewhere. Rather than buying some, my daughters contented themselves with climbing on the large cheese sculpture that jutted across the busy road intersection near the castle. Returning to the car I pressed on towards Cardiff. The guidebook promised a 'magnificent view' of the city 'from the top of Thorn Hill' but the low cloud and rain that I'd hit outside Merthyr earlier had persisted so I couldn't see anything.

Dropping down the hill through acres of new housing, I entered Cardiff, which was busy with early evening commuters. As the economy in South Wales shifted from mining and heavy industry, through light industry, to service sector jobs, so employment has moved down from the Valleys towards the coast, and especially to Cardiff. In 1961, a fifth of those who worked in Cardiff lived elsewhere and commuted in each day. Fifty years later, that figure was around a third.[23] And it seemed that most of them were trying to get out as I made my way into the city. I was reduced to a crawl and slowly made my way past a row of buildings of the expanding university before entering the civic heart of the city.

A photograph of Cardiff's City Hall, 'built in 1904' when Cardiff became a city, featured towards the end of Gruffydd's opening essay. A sketch of its twin, the 'National Museum, Cardiff', was placed alongside the strip map, before reappearing in the gazetteer where H. G. Stokes enthused about the 'very effective group of public buildings' found in the 'Civic Centre' that was 'the first of its kind in Britain'. Those driving by in 1951 might have spotted the Welsh flag flying. In that year the city council in this 'Welsh metropolis' hoisted the Welsh flag above City Hall in a sign of their wish to be Wales' capital. But, as Gruffydd was well aware, Wales did not yet have one.[24]

Whether Wales was to have a capital city was a question that rumbled on through the first half of the twentieth century and picked up pace during the 1950s. In the mid-1920s, a newspaper survey sent to local authorities found that a majority were in favour of a capital, with nearly a half choosing Cardiff and just over a quarter Caernarfon. Although Cardiff had growing support from authorities across Wales, Caernarfon could boast of its Welsh language-speaking credentials. In 1955, Cardiff was finally announced as the Welsh capital. Fifteen years later this new status led to a request from a Welsh MP that 'the name of the capital city of Wales' be 'given equal if not greater prominence than that of Bristol' on the westbound signage on the newly completed M4 leaving London. However his request was rejected on the grounds that 'capital cities are not signposted as such' with all places of equal 'traffic importance' being treated equally.[25]

The decision to name Cardiff the Welsh capital meant that significant changes took place, which were visible as I drove into the city. I made my way around the pedestrianized centre, the steel corner towers of the Millennium Stadium dominating the skyline. All international home rugby union games were played in Cardiff from the mid-1950s onwards in recognition of its new status and in the 1970s Cardiff Arms Park was rebuilt as the National Stadium. This decade was a golden era of Welsh rugby, with the national team either winning or coming runner-up in the Five Nations Championship. The new National Stadium was soon thought to be too small, and so at the turn of the millennium a new stadium seating 70,000 opened a short walk from Cardiff Arms Park. In the 1980s, St David's shopping centre and concert hall opened; 30 years later it was extended southwards.[26] This push southwards took it towards the former docks, which was where I was headed.

It was getting late so I decided to stay in the Welsh capital. As with all the tours, staff in the Festival of Britain office decided the locations where visitors could spend the night, choosing three bases, marked in a white rectangle on the opening map, which acted as departure and end points. Hereford, where I'd stayed the night before, was both start and end point of the first tour, as well as the beginning of the second that took motorists via Builth Wells and Rhayader to Aberystwyth, which was the second base. After a circular tour back here through Trawsgoed, the fourth tour followed the Pembrokeshire coastline to

Carmarthen through Cardigan, Fishguard, St David's and St Clears. After overnighting in Carmarthen, the fifth tour returned there after taking in Swansea, Port Talbot, Llantwit and Neath, before the sixth and final tour returned motorists to Hereford via Llandovery and Brecon. The tours covered most corners of South Wales and Herefordshire. But Cardiff was simply a place to be driven through on this one tour only, not a place to stay.

I left the guidebook's route to pull in to the car park of a hotel built out of former warehouses at Bute East Dock. I'd only glimpsed Birmingham – like other cities – from afar, but this was an opportunity to see Cardiff on foot. That evening I walked with my family past the dockside apartments and hotels, around the back of the County Hall built here in the 1980s and the Millennium Centre – home of the Welsh Assembly – built in the late 1990s, to eat in an Indian restaurant down by the bay.

Since the late 1990s Cardiff has increasing political clout. In 1951, the post of Minister for Welsh Affairs was created, bringing a Welsh voice to the Prime Minister's Cabinet table, and in the mid-1960s the Welsh Office was formed. But the major turning point came in 1997 when Wales voted in favour of devolution and key political decisions were now made in Cardiff not London. This was not the first devolution referendum in Wales. That had come twenty years earlier in 1979 as the Labour government struggled to deal with the rising fortunes of the nationalist parties in Scotland and Wales. However, Wales voted no to devolution in 1979 by a large majority. This was particularly true in Cardiff, where only 10 per cent voted for independence, although there was more support in Welsh-speaking Caernarfon where my next journey began and ended. Twenty years later devolution was once more put to the vote and this time passed, although only narrowly, with Cardiff once more voting against. Originally the City Hall that had flown the Welsh flag in 1951 was identified as a suitable home for the new Welsh Assembly, but in the end a purpose-built Senedd was constructed arising from a plinth of North Welsh slate at the other end of Cardiff.[27]

The Senedd's location here, rather than in the civic centre on the northern edge of Cardiff, speaks of the transformation of this part of the city since the 1990s. Featured in one of the full-page photographs in the guidebook, the southern edge of Cardiff was still an industrial port in 1951. On the eve of the First World War, it was the largest coal port in the world. During the 1950s, coal exports fell, and imports outnumbered exports for the first time in the port's history.[28] Over the following decades, the port fell into decline. By the 1980s most of the docks were becoming derelict and a new future was being imagined for them as waterside homes, offices and leisure facilities. This was something seen elsewhere, with developers seeming to offer a shortcut to urban regeneration in post-industrial Britain. But in Cardiff it was not simply a case of rebadging the former docks as 'Cardiff Bay' and attracting developers to build apartment blocks, hotels and offices. There was a much more ambitious effort to literally beat the tide.

First planned in the late 1980s and built in the later 1990s following years of conflict, the Cardiff Bay Barrage effectively created a freshwater lake at the mouth of the rivers Taff and Ely. Refashioning a muddy, tidal estuary into a large body of water that remained at a constant level was seen to be far more attractive to private developers building waterside apartments and hotels than what the Welsh Office dismissed as 'unsightly' mudflats. But while unsightly to property developers, the mudflats were the preferred feeding ground of a range of overwintering birds. Such was their habitat importance that in 1980 they had been designated a Site of Special Scientific Interest. This presented a problem. There were multiple claims on the same piece of land. Like on Twyford Down and at Pegwell Bay, the battle lines in Cardiff Bay were drawn up between capital and conservation. And just as they did at Twyford Down, campaigners engaged the

European Commission in their attempt to challenge the British state. Ultimately, capital triumphed over conservation. The barrage was built and the size of the mudflats reduced ten-fold, a decline mirrored in the number of birds that fed there.[29]

But the European Commission demanded some kind of compensation. Lost habitat at Cardiff Bay had to be replaced by new habitat. Originally, the plan was to create a new area of mudflats to the east, but this was dropped because there was not enough room at the proposed site on Wentloog Levels to replace the land lost in Cardiff Bay. In the end a larger site was chosen, a little further and another county away. In 2000, the Gwent Levels Wetlands Reserve opened 15 miles along the coast near Newport. While this was compensation of sorts, it was impossible to simply transplant the distinctive habitat. The tidal mudflats in Cardiff Bay had been home to a significant number of birds, most notably the dunlin and redshank. When this overwintering habitat was lost, the replacement reserve 15 miles away was charged with simply becoming a site for 'nationally important numbers' of whatever species they chose, rather than specifically the dunlin and redshank. They opted for two species of duck – wigeon and shoveler duck – most likely to adapt to the habitat on this compensatory reserve.[30]

The following morning I headed east to this new reserve with its population of wigeon and shoveler ducks along the old coastal road that motorists took in 1951 before the parallel motorway was built from London to Swansea from the 1960s to the 1990s. I passed through the industrial edge-land of Cardiff and Newport, with a huge plant processing scrap metal, followed by a steelworks and Airbus factory. Driving through Newport I 'noticed', as the caption urged motorists to, the 'Westgate Hotel, attacked by the Chartists in 1839', which had been turned into apartments. I crossed and re-crossed the River Usk on my way to Caerleon, where I stopped to explore the remains of the Roman amphitheatre mentioned in the *About Britain* guide. Then I headed towards Chepstow through what was described as 'definitely English country, though still in Wales'. On the outskirts of Chepstow I passed a sculpture-filled modern roundabout and the racecourse before driving up the Wye Valley.

I passed a sign informing me that the road ahead was closed but I ignored it and kept going, also ignoring the subsequent signs which said the same thing. But just past St Arvans they became impossible to ignore – a red road closed sign stood in the middle of the road, blocking the way. So I was finally persuaded that the road was well and truly impassable. I turned around and made my way back to St Arvans where I followed the road high on the ridge rather than the one down in the valley. Instead of passing Tintern Abbey, 'famous for its own beauty and its surroundings', I was treated to views of the valleys that tumbled down on both sides of this road. Beyond beech woods in their autumn browns, I found a yellow diversion sign back to the road that I was meant to be on. But I ignored it and kept to this high road that was so lovely. It felt mutinous to stray, intentionally, from the itinerary like this, but also strangely freeing.

I dropped down into Monmouth where I briefly stopped to inspect the gated bridge and the old castle at the top of a road lined with shops and cafes that were abuzz on this Wednesday morning. But I was soon headed back towards Hereford, stopping to let sheep cross the road outside Welsh Newton. This short pause seemed appropriate given that the guidebook promised 'sheep' alongside this 'old road to Hereford'. The weather was very different from the afternoon before and the woods I drove through looked beautiful in the autumn sunshine. Getting closer to Hereford I glimpsed the cathedral tower in the distance, and then again, much closer, as I headed into the city. But rather than stop I kept going. I wanted to make it to Caernarfon, the starting point of one of the tours put together by Gruffydd for the next volume of the *About Britain* guides.

Gruffydd was chosen to write the introductory essay to the guidebook and the next one, because he was a man who knew Wales and the Welsh language. Walking around Caernarfon that night, it was clear that Welsh is the first language of many people who live there. But things have begun to change even in Cardiff. Welsh is now spoken more widely in the capital and especially by young people attending the many Welsh-speaking or bilingual schools in the city.

The Welsh language, as the disputes over road signs in the 1960s and 1970s showed, had an importance for Welsh nationalism that was never quite the case in Scotland. In Scotland from the 1970s, economic arguments were more important in a nationalist movement that proved stronger and in many ways more successful. The Scottish Assembly created in Edinburgh in the wake of the devolution referendum has greater powers than the one that meets on Cardiff Bay, in part because of the different histories of these nations. And it was Scotland, not Wales, that held a referendum for the more decisive move of independence, rather than devolution. Although this was narrowly defeated, post-Brexit things might be different if there is another vote. Driving north through the Marches, I wondered if 70 years hence, motorists might drive across not one country but several with far harder borders.

Indeed, these borders became more significant as my journeying was brought to an abrupt halt in 2020 and the devolved governments responded to the Covid-19 crisis, asserting themselves in relation to Westminster. The language of 'four nations', which was unthinkable in 1951, became commonplace in the press to describe the different ways of managing lockdown emanating from Belfast, Cardiff, Edinburgh and London. Yet at the time of driving through the Welsh Marches the global pandemic was still unimaginable.

Caernarvon–Llanrug–Llanberis–Beddgelert–Gareg–Rhyd–Maentwrog–Blaenau Ffestiniog–Dolwyddelan–Bettws-y-coed–Capel Curig–Bethesda–Llandegai–Bangor–Menai Bridge–Beaumaris–Pentraeth–Menai Bridge–Port Dinorwic–Caernarvon

7

North Wales and the Marches

Caernarvon–Capel Curig–Caernarvon (88 miles)

I left the town spelled as 'Caernarvon' at the bottom of the map in the *About Britain* guide. Its spelling has changed over the course of the twentieth century. In the 1920s, the addition of the Welsh diphthong 'ae' transformed Carnarvon into Caernarvon. Fifty years later, Caernarvon became Caernarfon. Although this final change was some way off, careful readers of the guidebook to North Wales and the Marches might have spotted a hint that the 'v' in Caernarvon was really an 'f'. At the beginning of the volume was a 'Note on Welsh Place-Names' written by William Gruffydd. He offered a short introduction to the Welsh language to help motorists pronounce and decipher the names of the towns and villages they drove through. He explained that 'F is pronounced as English v'.[1] Gruffydd also wanted to make sure that visitors knew that the word 'Llan' in the names of villages meant 'church'. They were thick on the ground at the start of this journey that went through Llanrug and Llanberis.[2]

I reached Llanrug along a road that ran parallel to the River Seiont. The caption beside the map painted a picturesque scene of 'small stony crofts and white-washed cottages dotted among the gorse, heather and rocks'. But these had since been joined, and largely hidden, by modern houses lining the road.

Once through Llanrug, the views opened up and I could see mountains off in the distance. 'Along the valley of the Seiont with the mountains facing us,' the *About Britain* guide informed readers, a 'profusion of birch trees hide old tips from Glyn quarry', before picking out the 'firs among the rocks' on the opposite side of Llyn Padarn, where 'the whole scene looks like an immense rock garden'. I didn't quite know where to look for the 'birch-trees' hiding the 'old tips', but a thin line of silver birches was dotted along the edge of the road off to the left and I came across 'firs among the rocks' as the road reached the shore of the lake. I looked across to what did have something of the look of a 'rock garden' to it.

In 1951 this 'rock garden' was a working quarry. This part of North Wales was an industrial landscape throughout the nineteenth and into much of the twentieth century due to slate production. The peak of the industry came at the end of the nineteenth century when close to half a million tons of slate, most of it destined for roofing, were quarried or mined each year. From this high point, the industry declined as the export market collapsed, cheaper imports increased and slates were replaced with clay roofing tiles. Glyn quarry with its 'old tips' closed in the 1930s and had a more recent wartime history as an ammunition store, as well as a potential future in generating power. But the massive Dinorwig slate works across Llyn Padarn were still in business when motorists drove through here in the early 1950s. Dinorwig closed in 1969, but the terraces hacked out of the hillside, as well as the waste heaps, were still visible on the other side of the lake. Photographs in the opening pages of the guidebook celebrated, rather than hid, this industrial landscape. Indeed, writing in his gazetteer entry on Llanberis, H. G. Stokes suggested that 'more imposing than Snowdon itself from this point are the huge terraced slate quarries on the east side of the valley' a view that not all contemporaries shared.[3]

When slate quarrying ceased, the heritage industry moved in as it did elsewhere in post-industrial Britain. It was a relatively seamless transition with the chief engineer at Dinorwig becoming the first manager of the museum that opened in the quarry's former workshops. In many ways the closure here came at just the right time. As I'd seen elsewhere, the 1970s was something of a golden age when it came to celebrating the industrial past. This was the era of 'industrial archaeology', a term that first appeared in print in the mid-1950s, before gaining traction in the 1960s.[4] In this context, not only were the workshops and waterwheel at Dinorwig seen to be too important to lose, but so was the former quarry railway that had closed in the 1960s but was reopened by a group of rail enthusiasts in the early 1970s.

Dinorwig's was not the only narrow-gauge steam railway that I'd pass on today's journey, let alone the only one in Wales. The first came when the Talyllyn Railway Preservation Society reopened the line that ran for 7 miles between Tywyn and the slate quarry inland in 1951. It attracted thousands of visitors in its first season and over 100,000 passenger journeys by the end of the 1960s. Soon, other lines were being saved. A little further along my route, the Ffestiniog Railway – another former slate railway running from the quarries to a coastal port – was reopened in 1955. From a trickle, rail preservation became a flood. When the Association of Railway Preservation Societies was founded in 1965, it brought together nine societies. Within a decade, this had grown to over 100, with tens of thousands of members. This story of the rapid growth of volunteers saving and then running short sections of track in the late 1960s and early 1970s was particularly concentrated in North Wales. In the late 1960s there were three restored railways in North Wales. By the mid 1970s there were a further four and they joined together to promote the 'Great Little Trains of Wales' as a tourist offer, including six-day bus tours that bore some resemblance to the original plans for the 1951 tours, taking people around the circuit of these restored railways. By the mid 1970s, some were warning that 'the zenith of steam railway preservation cannot be very far off'. However, while the number of new rescue projects did decline, steam trains have remained remarkably popular, with 9 million passenger journeys taken on railways rescued by enthusiasts up and down the country in the early 2010s.[5]

A little further on today's journey, I would see evidence that interest in industrial archaeology has waned. But the former slate landscape on the other side of the lake from where I parked in Llanberis has gained greater significance since the quarries closed. Initially opened as a local museum, in the 1990s the newly renamed National Slate Museum became one of seven national museums funded directly by the new Welsh government and so part of the story that Wales tells about itself. In the 2000s this museum was included as an 'anchor site' on the European Route of Industrial Heritage, linking places associated with the Industrial Revolution across the continent. Slate quarrying in North Wales became part of a shared European past. After gaining both national and European recognition, all eyes are now set on going one step further. In 2020 the 'Slate Landscape of Northwest Wales', which includes the former Dinorwig quarries, was nominated for UNESCO World Heritage Site status.[6] If successful in its bid, the National Slate Museum will join its twin within the National Museum family – the Big Pit National Coal Museum in Blaenafon, just off the previous route I'd taken.

Rather than visiting the National Slate Museum, I decided to board a shuttle bus outside the lakeside Visitor Centre to visit the more recent past of this rocky landscape. When Dinorwig was being repurposed as a heritage site it was also being reimagined as an energy landscape. During the second half of the 1970s and first half of the 1980s, the scarred mountain on the other side of the lake was hollowed out to create what was claimed to be 'one of the wonders of the modern world': a hydroelectric power station hidden in the middle of the mountain. In what was, at the time, the biggest civil engineering project undertaken in Britain, 2 million cubic metres of rock were excavated to create a network of ten miles of tunnels and a large central generating hall deep inside 'Electric Mountain'.[7] My enthusiastic guide led the group I'd joined with my wife and daughters deeper and deeper inside this 'ever ready giant' that generates 'immense power created by nothing more than water'. Walking along miles of tunnels to the viewing gallery that overlooks the generator hall, the words 'huge', 'enormous' and 'massive' spilled from his lips. As well as a story of building bigger, this was also a story of making electricity faster: the power station only takes 12 seconds to reach full generating power as water is released from the upper reservoir on the hilltop high above to rush through the turbines in the mountain and down to the lower reservoir where we had parked up. It was exactly the kind of technological feat that those putting the guidebooks together for 1951 would have loved.

But this is a strange kind of power station. It takes more power to pump the water back up to the upper reservoir than is produced when it rushes down to the lower reservoir, meaning that it only makes economic sense if power is bought cheap and then sold at a high price. This power station was never intended to provide a constant supply of cheap electricity, but rather to meet sudden spikes in power use. In the words of the company that owns and runs it 'it is the National Grid Company's pacemaker . . . ready to step in at a moment's notice to generate the extra power that Britain may need to carry out its business and private activities'.[8] When this was planned and built in the 1970s, those 'private activities' were primarily shaped by shared television-watching rituals. My family and I had taken part in one the night before. Perched on the beds in our hotel room in Caernarfon, we had joined an estimated 14 million others to watch the last final of *The Great British Bake Off* shown on the BBC. But such shared rituals are increasingly few and far between at the end of the television era.

Although invented in the 1930s, it was the 1950s that saw the emergence of the television age in Britain. At the beginning of the decade, televisions were owned or rented by a little over one in ten households. By the end of the decade, this was close to seven in ten. One key milestone in this story of growth was the live broadcast of the coronation of Queen Elizabeth II in 1953, which was the first national mass television event in Britain, watched by an estimated 20 million crowded around sets hastily acquired for the occasion. This growth continued in the 1960s, and by 1970 over 90 per cent of British households had a television, rising to a figure that remained somewhere between 97 and 98 per cent across the 1980s, 1990s and 2000s.

In 1951, the Beveridge Committee recommended the renewal of the BBC charter and the continuation of their broadcasting monopoly. But the new Conservative government had other plans. Although critics were fearful that a second, commercial broadcaster would lead to vulgar Americanization at best, the Television Act was passed in 1954 by a narrow majority and opened the way to commercial television. From 1955 onwards, ITV's programming offered competition to the BBC. In 1964, these two channels were joined by a third with the launch of BBC 2. It took another twenty years before a fourth channel – Channel 4, the same organization that had acquired the rights to *The Great British Bake Off* from the BBC – was added in 1982.[9]

The nature of British television meant that a particular challenge was posed for the nationalized electricity company. The problem lay not in powering the television sets in British living rooms, but powering activities, like putting the kettle on to make a cup of tea, which were concentrated in the few minutes after a popular programme ended or a commercial break began. With just three channels until the early 1980s there were a few moments each evening and at weekends when there was a sudden demand for electricity that the Central Electricity Generating Board dubbed 'TV pick ups'. In the late 1970s and early 1980s, when I watched the FA Cup final at my friend David's house, there was a massive pick up of over 1,000 megawatts when the half-time whistle blew and viewers rushed to their kitchens.[10] To meet the peaks in demand, the electricity industry looked to the post-industrial landscape of North Wales.

A little further along this journey, I drove by the Ffestiniog pumped-storage facility built on the shores of the newly created Tan-y-Grisiau reservoir in the late 1950s and early 1960s. By releasing water from the upper reservoir through shafts and tunnels in the mountain, the turbines here could produce 360 megawatts of power on demand. At the time it was the largest pump-storage project in Europe. But this wasn't sufficient for the kind of 'TV pick ups' that followed national television events. In the 1970s, they decided to go even further. Their attention turned to the site of the former Dinorwig slate quarries where they built a power station that could generate 1,320 megawatts of electricity at the flick of a switch: more than enough to cope with the surge in demand that accompanied the half-time whistle during the FA Cup final.

But by the time Dinorwig power station was opened in the mid-1980s, television was already on the cusp of a change that meant those moments of shared national ritual were becoming increasingly rare. The 1990s saw a dramatic rise in the number of television channels available. Channel 5 began broadcasting in 1997, but more significant was the arrival of satellite television offered by Sky at the end of the 1980s and the digital channels of Freeview in the early 2000s. This multiplication of channels was followed by a revolution in viewing that dispensed with not only television schedules but increasingly with televisions. In 2007, the BBC launched iPlayer, which made programmes available on demand, and as likely to be viewed on the screen of a tablet or laptop as a television. Five years later, Netflix began its streaming service. Television ceased to be a shared national ritual and instead became much more a privatized act of consumption. Not only was the nation less likely to be watching together but also the whole family was less likely to be watching together with the shift from viewing on a single television screen in the living room to individual devices anywhere in the house.[11] The challenge of 'TV pick ups' was a problem of the past and Electric Mountain appeared less an 'ever ready giant' and more of a white elephant that had been built to suit the short-lived television age.

I left Electric Mountain, returned to the car and ascended Llanberis Pass. Just past the station where trains leave for the summit, I entered into Snowdonia National Park. This area had originally been proposed for National Park status by John Dower in 1945, but he had envisioned a relatively modest park confined to the Snowdon mountain range. Two years later, the National Parks Committee proposed a North Wales National Park that was twice the size and extended much further south. This extension was justified, in part at least, on the grounds that as the committee put it, 'to drive from the lake of Trawsfynydd to Dolgelley on a fine winter afternoon with the snowy Rhinogs and the deep romantic cleft of Bwlch drws Ardudwy outlined against the western sky is an unforgettable experience.' Like other large National Parks, the 'scenic grandeur of North Wales' was to be driven through, and so motorists' needs were to be met by 'providing parking and picnic places at suitable points'.[12]

Driving up the Llanberis Pass today it was clear that parking spaces were at a premium. Even though there was low cloud and light rain, every parking space along the road was taken. When

I reached the top, the Pen-y-Pass car park, the starting point for the most popular paths up Snowdon, was full. There were obviously plenty of people heading up Snowdon despite the summit being in low cloud. The weather had put me off climbing to the summit, and besides the *About Britain* guide privileged a day's driving over a day's walking so I dropped down towards Beddgelert along the side of the mountain with low-level views down the valley towards the lake and up to the cloud-topped mountains. Stopping off in a scenic layby, we ate our picnic in the car buffeted by wind and rain.

Snowdonia was among the first National Parks created in 1951. They were all established to marry 'the preservation of landscape beauty' with provision of 'access and facilities for public open-air enjoyment'. But within 20 years these twin aims were becoming harder to reconcile given the number of people accessing National Parks in the age of mass motoring. Explaining that 'all is not well in our National Parks' one contemporary saw the 'conflict . . . between preservation and access' becoming critical in Snowdonia in the early 1970s. In order to address this issue, the government established a National Parks Policy Review Committee, chaired by Lord Sandford. When it reported back in 1974, a key recommendation that became known as the 'Sandford principle' determined that 'where irreconcilable conflicts exist between conservation and public enjoyment, then conservation interest should take priority'. After Sandford, Snowdonia National Park made major changes to how it spent its funding in the late 1970s and early 1980s. The sum spent on recreation was halved, while money committed to conservation rose four-fold and was joined by more investment in those who lived in, rather than simply visited, the National Park.

People living here were a particular concern to Gruffydd. Explaining that Snowdonia was to become one of the first National Parks, he made sure his readers were aware that this decision had won 'almost' rather than complete 'universal approbation'. Writing of 'those who dwell in a National Park', Gruffydd explained that 'some men and women, not only in Wales, seem rather to resent the easy assumption of the word "national", as if this particular area of country was primarily meant by Providence for the enjoyment of others' and urged visitors in 1951 to 'pay the same regard to the people and its history as to the scenery and the non-human aspects of the countryside'.[13]

But I was primarily on the lookout for 'non-human aspects of the countryside' as I made the 'sharp descent to Gwynant Valley'. The guide had promised 'masses of rhododendrons' 'all over the mountainside', but the only ones I spotted were in a garden near Nant Gwynant. It turned out that the lack of these shrubs was not because they had simply died back since 1951. Quite the opposite. There was an 'accelerating . . . rate of spread' in the second half of the twentieth century of this plant introduced as an 'exotic' to British gardens in the eighteenth century and later as moorland pheasant cover in upland areas. This was particularly true in Gwynant Valley where comparison of aerial photographs taken in the late 1960s, mid-1980s and mid-2000s revealed that rhododendron not only covered more land in the valley but also that the density of cover had increased. Five thousand acres were covered in rhododendrons, with somewhere between a quarter and a third of these concentrated along the slopes of the valley that I drove down.[14]

Rather than being seen as a welcome source of colour, the tide turned against *Rhododendron ponticum*. Although Gruffydd was still a fan of the 'wonderful covering of rhododendrons in June' in 1951, the Forestry Commission began trials to control their spread, driven by a concern with the economic impact of a species that crowded out young trees, and by the 1970s rhododendron were seen as a 'major forest weed'. The emerging science of ecology saw them posing a different, and even more serious, threat. In 1957, Charles Elton – who taught animal ecology at Oxford – gave a series of three talks on the radio, popularizing the concept of invasive species. It took some time for Elton's ideas to enter the mainstream, but by the early 2000s *Rhododendron ponticum* had made it into the list of the six most dangerous alien plants in Britain, being described as nothing less than 'a killer, a smotherer, a choker-to-death of native woodland species'. In Snowdonia it was seen as threatening everything from the soil, wetland habitats, and native wildlife – especially pollinators who preferred heather over rhododendron – to the amount of land available for grazing.[15]

In the 1990s, the National Park started uprooting rhododendron from the Gwyant Valley. But the job across Snowdonia was enormous. It was estimated that it would cost somewhere between £40 million and £50 million to rid the park of this pest. After a few years of trying to bring rhododendron under control, the National Park launched a £10 million, five-year programme in the late 2000s to try to eradicate it. A large volunteer army was drawn into the fight. 'Responsible gardeners' were also enlisted. They were given a step-by-step guide on 'how to eradicate Rhododendron bushes' whose seeds could travel vast distances. Even so, driving through Nant Gwynant it was clear that there was at least one gardener who had not yet joined this fight.[16]

Leaving the Gwynant Valley, I followed the River Glaslyn through Beddgelert, before skirting the edge of the National Park and then going back into it just before Rhyd. By the mid-1970s, almost all the houses in this village were second homes. The 1960s had seen a rise in second-home ownership, fuelled by growing wages, a rising gap between the cost of housing in urban and depopulated areas and the opening up of the countryside to a car-owning population. Although the numbers owning a second home never reached levels found elsewhere in Europe – just 3 per cent according to a study in the early 1970s compared to 20 per cent in Sweden – second homes tended to be concentrated in a small number of areas. One of these was North Wales. The decline of the slate quarrying industry and the rural depopulation that followed meant that former slate workers' cottages came up for sale in the 1960s and 1970s and were snapped up by those living a two-hour drive away in areas running from Lancashire to the West Midlands.[17]

This story was repeated in other rural areas, but in Welsh-speaking Snowdonia it was political. Second-home ownership here meant the displacement of Welsh-speakers by English-speaking, foreign incomers. In the early 1970s *Cymdeithas yr Iaith Gymraeg* – the Welsh Language Society – targeted English second-home owners as another battle to be fought alongside their campaign against English-only road signs. While the Society did not engage in violent protest, others did. During the 1980s, around 200 arson attacks were carried out by those claiming to be the 'Sons of Glyndwr' on English-owned holiday homes and the estate agents selling property to incomers, including houses in Snowdonia.[18] This campaign only ended in the early 1990s, the decade that saw the second, and this time successful, Welsh devolution vote.

Just beyond Rhyd the road ran through a conifer plantation, showing the change from 'rather desolate uplands . . . to woodlands' described in the *About Britain* guide. I drove between trees with the dark green of densely planted conifers to the yellows and oranges of the thin line of deciduous trees. After passing beneath a wrought-iron railway bridge carrying the Ffestiniog Railway, I glimpsed one of the stations along the route – Tan-y-Bwlch – which opened in 1958 when this former slate railway was rescued by volunteers.[19] Just before reaching Blaenau Ffestiniog, by road not rail, I left the National Park.

When the National Park boundaries were drawn up, they excluded the industrial landscape of the slate industry. Quarrying and mining had been identified by John Dower in his 1945 report as the cause of 'damage' to some of the upland areas identified for potential National Parks, 'with their trail of waste-heaps and polluted streams'. This was particularly true in Snowdonia, where he wrote of 'the outstanding disfigurement . . . by the vast slate quarries and tips'. It seems that Gruffydd was more accepting, writing that 'the quarry *tomennydd*, the tips [of Snowdonia], do not have that devastating effect which one sees around the coal and metallurgical tips in parts of South Wales'. But in 1947 the National Parks Committee echoed Dower's criticism and declared that 'the quarrying of vast deposits of slate' was 'the most formidable problem of the North Wales National Park'. Focusing on the aesthetic damage wrought by 'enormous', 'dismal' grey-coloured 'waste tips' made up of 'lumps of rock averaging the size of a coffin or mounds and cascades of splintery scree', their solution was simply to 'exclude the whole belt of exploitation through Bethesda, Llanberis and Nantlle' by careful placing of the boundary. In order to hide the 'even worse disfigurement from the Blaenau Ffestiniog quarries, and the unattractive urban development among them' they created a hole in the middle of this doughnut-shaped National Park: a hole that I had just driven into.[20]

Reading these reports from the late 1940s it was clear that aesthetics and the visual landscape were considered important. Since then, there has been greater appreciation and utilization of the towering piles of mono-coloured slates that I saw in Blaenau Ffestiniog. They remain outside the National Park, but their inclusion within the proposed World Heritage Site points to the more recent valuing of these former waste tips as landscapes of industrial heritage. In Blaenau Ffestiniog there were signs that some active quarrying was still taking place. I passed a small yard working slate, although these days it is quarried to make clocks and hearths rather than roofing slates. But on the northern edge of the village, a large sign pointing off to Llechwedd slate mines laid out the range of ways this former industrial area had been repurposed, first as a heritage landscape in the 1970s and 1980s, and then more recently as a destination for extreme sports.

In many ways the story here mirrored that of the Dinorwig quarry. In 1972, when visitors were welcomed to the new museum at Dinorwig, tourists were also taken on trips into the underground caverns at Llechwedd and around the surrounding quarry landscape. Llechwedd Slate Caverns combined a number of elements in the emerging landscapes of industrial archaeological sites and open air museums. Above ground, visitors could see demonstrations of the skills of creating roofing slates in the former workshops, as well as explore a Victorian village. Below ground, they could take the tramway into the former mine workings.

During the 1970s and 1980s visitor figures to this heritage attraction – old trains and old workings – topped 200,000 a year, broadly the same number that visited the other prime heritage attractions in the area: Caernarfon Castle and the nearby Ffestiniog Railway. For a time Llechwedd was one of the top ten attractions in Wales. But visitor numbers began falling and by 2000 they were around half what they had been 20 years earlier. A decade later they had halved again.[21] In order to stay open the mine owners had to reinvent themselves once more. Instead of heritage, they began selling adventure tourism.

First to arrive was a local enterprise that built mountain-bike trails through the former quarry site. Begun in the United States in the 1970s, mountain biking established itself as a mainstream activity. By the early 2000s, one in ten Britons reported cycling off road at least once a year. This growing popularity resulted in the creation of specialist trails in forest and upland areas across Britain, ranging from the more accessible for recreational cyclists to the more extreme downhill runs that attract thrill-seekers to Llechwedd. Next to the site was another local company which had built its first high-ropes course in a forest near Betws-y-Coed. This was one of many treetop adventure courses built worldwide. From forest high-ropes courses, the company expanded and built the fastest zip wire in the world in the former Bethesda slate quarries the other side of the mountain range from where I was. A year later they opened their third site on the edge of Blaenau Ffestiniog, bringing together another zip wire along with an attraction that brought high ropes out of the forest canopy and placed them deep underground in the former slate mine. Such was the novelty of a ropes course set in caverns that it served as the set for an extreme underground escape room called *Y Siambr – The Chamber* – for the Welsh-language television channel S4C.[22]

Heritage and adventure sports represent two distinct waves of tourist attraction on this site in the past 50 years. Snowdonia first emerged as a tourist attraction for climbers and hikers who popularized this mountainous landscape in the late nineteenth century. From the cars parked up Llanberis Pass and the full car park at the top, it was clear that Snowdon continues to attract visitors wanting to ascend Wales' highest peak. But there is something different about the rise of thrill-seeking attractions like the zip wires and mountain-biking trails. With their focus on a combination of speed and height they offer an adrenalin rush that motoring through the National Park or even walking up Snowdon along the popular Miners' Track cannot match. If you are willing to spend £100 you can choose to spend the weekend travelling at 100 mph down the fastest zip wire in the world and get the closest experience to free-falling in the process. These attractions are designed for a post-industrial world. Rather than leisure time being an opportunity for rest from manual labour, it fulfils a different function for those engaged in the new service-sector and knowledge economy who drive to the former slate mines and quarries for a physical and mental challenge that is sold as an antidote to a sedentary working life.

The company that owns these zip wires plans to move south. Instead of a former slate quarry, they have chosen a former coal mine: Tower Colliery just outside Hirwaun, which I'd passed a couple of days before. Announcing these plans, the company explained that their aim was now 'to do for Welsh coal communities in South Wales what we've done for Welsh slate in North Wales and create adventures that bring great tourism opportunities to the local area'. These reinventions of the post-industrial landscapes of slate and coal continue to attract state investment. But there was also something more than economic reworking at play. Zip wires have reinvented these former industrial landscapes of slate and coal extraction not simply as tourist attractions but also, in the words of the company, as 'beautiful Welsh' landscapes.[23]

The idea that former quarries or mines could ever be 'beautiful' was simply unimaginable for those identifying National Parks and those putting the *About Britain* route maps together. It was only once I left Blaenau Ffestiniog and made my way up the hill and back into the National Park and then down the Lledr Valley to Betws-y-Coed that I entered what the guidebook claimed to be 'one of the most beautiful glens in Wales'. It did look attractive with the wooded slopes picked out in their autumn colours. In 1951, this was the heart of a tourist industry that developed in North Wales in the nineteenth century when North Wales was seen as 'a kind of British Switzerland'. Much of the tourist infrastructure referred to in the guidebook was still there. In Betws-y-Coed, I spotted a couple of art galleries on the main street of what the guidebook described as 'a resort of landscape painters, whose work is exhibited and for sale', but these were now outnumbered by shops selling hiking gear. Just beyond Betws-y-Coed I passed the Ugly House Tea Rooms, a Victorian folly built out of large boulders that is now home to the Snowdonia Society, started in 1967 to keep an eye on the conservation of the National Park when rising visitor numbers were seen as a threat to the landscape. A little further on, I stopped off at the Tyn-y-coed Inn. Sitting under cover in the middle of the pub car park was a Royal Mail-red stagecoach that was a replacement of the former film-prop stagecoach bought by the enterprising landlady to attract passing motorists in the 1950s.[24]

I was driving along a road built between London and Holyhead by Thomas Telford in the early nineteenth century. It ensured swift communications between London and Dublin via the port at Holyhead after the 1800 Act of Union, but also opened up the area to tourists. Although the guide explained that the bridge over the Menai Strait – 'a thing of beauty' – 'was built by Telford' it said nothing of the road that crossed over the bridge. But the history of this road was clear. Along its route were large brown signs that directed attention, not to an attraction off to the side of the road, but to the road itself. As the sign made clear, I was driving along a 'historic route' or rather a *Llwybr hanesyddo* as the words at the top of the sign announced. But it seemed that I was driving along it in the wrong direction.

When I'd browsed the shelves of second-hand bookshops looking for copies of the *About Britain* guides, I'd often found other discarded mid-century guidebooks nestling alongside them. I ignored most of them, but I did pick up a distinctive red-covered copy of the popular Ward Lock series of guidebooks to *Caernarvon and North Wales* published just on the eve of the Second World War. Among the handful of drives that this guidebook offered was the journey 'Bangor to Bettws-y-Coed via the Nant Ffrancon Pass and Capel Curig', which followed the stretch of Telford's road I was on, but in reverse. This was intentional. As the Ward Lock guidebook explained 'this road should, if possible, be traversed from north to south rather than in the reverse direction, for the sake of the fine scenery at the top of Nant Ffrancon' adding that while all 'the roads of North Wales contribute to many a notable scene' the ascent of Nant Ffrancon offered 'a supreme example of grandeur'.[25]

Descending Nant Ffrancon Pass, I kept one eye on my rear-view mirror trying to get some sense of what driving in the other direction would be like. I considered driving down, back up again, and then down once more, but decided to press on. I left the National Park again as I approached 'the large quarrying village of Bethesda'. As elsewhere the quarries that 'used to employ over 3,000 workers' at their peak were no longer producing slate.[26] Instead, they now housed the fastest zip wire in the world. The home of the former quarry owner, Penrhyn Park, 'with its high limestone walls' was transferred to the National Trust in 1951 under the auspices of the Land Fund scheme set up by the post-war Labour government. Questions had been raised about whether what H. G. Stokes described in his gazetteer as a 'modern building in Norman style' was of 'sufficient architectural merit' to be saved, but the report compiled for the National Trust recommended acquiring this 'bold impression of romantic intensity' along with 40,000 acres of land.[27] I decided to stop. It was the week before Halloween and almost all of the room stewards and a good many visitors were dressed accordingly; I crept up a spiral staircase with my wife and daughters to the 'forgotten floors' rotting away at the top of the keep, temporarily inhabited by plastic rats and ghosts.

Returning to the car, I drove through Bangor, passing the university that dominates the town, before crossing the old Menai Bridge rather than taking the main road that had been added to the railway bridge in the 1980s. Once in Anglesey, the route took me along the coast to Beaumaris. I missed the turning the first time, so ended up going past the castle before cutting back to the right road that headed inland from the centre of the town. It wasn't entirely clear why the route skipped the castle and instead headed up to Pentraeth before looping back around to the Menai Bridge through farmland and then returning once more to the mainland. Why it did became clearer when I looked again at the piles of receipts paid in the summer of 1950 that I'd discovered in the National Archives in Kew. One had a familiar name on it: William Gruffydd.

On 6 June 1950, Gruffydd was paid £15 for six days' work, along with the cost of the rail fare to Liverpool and a subsistence allowance to 'check on the ground and modification where necessary of provisional tours of North Wales as defined by C.E.O. Tours' as well as to provide 'material for "captions" to flank tour strip maps (roughly 12 captions of about 3 lines each to a route distance of 40 miles)' and 'ideas for "thumbnail sketches" to supplement the captions and suggestions for source of materials'. After driving the routes, he was to submit his suggestions to C.E.O. Tours – Penrose Angwin – within two weeks. It is clear that Gruffydd did as instructed. On 26 June he was promptly paid for his services.

Gruffydd was not the only person in the summer of 1950 checking the tours in the guides. Up and down the country, others were similarly employed. In some cases they were those – like Gruffydd – who had also penned the 'portrait' for the guide. Others – like James Stuart who checked the first route through the West Country I followed – were called into service and £1,000 was set aside in the budget for this undertaking.[28] In most cases, clerks only archived the contracts and details of payment. But there were a few exceptions. Attached to the contract sent to Gruffydd was a typescript of the provisional tours suggested for this volume. None of the other contracts had this, but in the case of North Wales we can see where Gruffydd changed the routes that had been drawn up in London a few weeks earlier.

It seems that Gruffydd decided to change the final few miles of two tours. The second of the six tours through North Wales and the Marches took motorists from Caernarfon through Barmouth and Caersws to the shore of Lake Vyrnwy. He decided to add a minor detour to take in Llanfihangel where, as his caption explained, 'lived Anne Griffiths (1780–1805), famous writer of Welsh hymns, about whom the Welsh are much intrigued', although it would seem that those in the London office were less so.[29] Gruffydd also changed the end of the first tour that I was following. But his alterations were less a matter of including somewhere that the London office did not know about and more missing out somewhere that those in London wanted visitors to see but he did not. That place was 'Llanfair P.G.'.

When they first mapped out this tour in London, the loop onto Anglesey took motorists across the Menai Bridge, immediately left through Llanfair P.G. before heading to the southwestern tip of the island at Newborough – although this was marked with a question mark awaiting Gruffydd's response – before returning to Caernarfon. But Gruffydd didn't want motorists to turn left when they reached Anglesey and so he sent them – and me following his map a lifetime later – to the right. He was no fan of Llanfair P.G. and had referenced the place specifically in the section introducing visitors to those place names beginning with 'Llan'. One example he gave was Llanfair – the church of St Mary – that led to a place name – Llanfair-pwll-gwyngyll – roughly translated as 'of the hazel pit'. Gruffydd added, in parentheses, that, 'It should be unnecessary to point out that the long extension of this name is merely an English tourist's joke and belongs to that class of fun which is expressed in vulgar picture postcards.'[30]

When it came to Llanfair P.G., Gruffydd and Stokes were clearly on the same page. In his gazetteer entry, Stokes translated 'Llanfair Pwll Gwyngyll' as 'Llanfair by the Hazel Pit' before going on to inform readers that this was 'the correct name of a much misnamed village'. But it seemed that the people in the London office were not in accord. They appeared to be those who Gruffydd had criticized in his essay introducing the South Wales and the Marches volume as 'kind, inquisitive and rather uncritical Englishmen who wish to find in Wales something "interesting" and exotic'. While those in the office wanted to send tourists to gawp at Llanfair P.G.'s exoticism, Gruffydd had the final word and bypassed it on the ground and in the text, where he sought to normalize 'these apparently long names' that 'should of course be compared with such English names as "St Mary-within-the-gates", "Moreton-in-the-Marsh" and so on' stating definitively that 'they are not peculiar to Wales'.[31] He skipped Llanfair P.G. and so did I, making my way back to the Menai Bridge after a short detour through Beaumaris and rolling farmland.

Once across the bridge, I headed back towards Caernarfon. I missed the penultimate stop in Port Dinorwig initially, but made my way towards the sea when I could and parked up by a church at the water's edge. I wanted to see what was described in 1951 as 'a cheerful modern port for export of Dinorwig slates' so wandered along the shore to an activity centre where a man was pulling the last boat out of the water at the end of the day. He pointed me in the right direction and I walked towards the abandoned port as three oystercatchers flew low over the water of the straits in the fading early evening light. Once back in the car, I returned to Caernarfon, past what Gruffydd described as 'some good Victorian houses' that made up the 'residential extension of Caernarfon'. The first two had been abandoned and boarded up, their greenhouses overgrown. But I wondered what the office in London would have made of Gruffydd's use of the adjective 'good' before 'Victorian' because this was a question that the starting point of the next route would raise.

Reflecting back on this journey through Snowdonia, one thing that struck me was how there had been important changes in the last 70 years. Working with the geological timescale so beloved in these guidebooks, the underlying bedrock was still the same. It was still a landscape of slate, but its meaning had changed. In 1951, this was a place where slate quarries and mines were seen to clash with the ideals of natural beauty and wildness that shaped thinking about preserving upland landscapes as National Parks. The decision to create a National Park with a hole in the middle to avoid the slate tips at Blaenau Ffestiniog still shaped the landscape. But, as the application for UNESCO World Heritage Site made clear, there are other designations that have included the grey piles of slate that dominate the roadside. This industrial landscape has become a heritage landscape where things other than natural beauty have come to be valued.

But it wasn't only slate that has been seen differently in North Wales. It was also rhododendron. Again the change in thinking reflected a move away from viewing landscapes as visual spectacles where piles of grey slate were bad and clusters of purple flowers were good. The rise of industrial archaeology in the 1960s and 1970s, along with an appreciation of the architecture of the nineteenth and twentieth centuries, meant that slate landscapes were reimagined and reworked. In the case of rhododendron, it was the popularization of ecology that turned an exotic shrub into an invasive species to be eradicated rather than celebrated. Approaching landscapes as sites of biodiversity, rather than working with the aesthetic categories so dominant in the 1950s, meant that there had been changes equally radical as those I'd discovered in the Fens. Driving down Nant Gwynant, the only rhododendron I saw were confined to a single garden.

While the guidebooks I was following set out to introduce a new Britain, one rebuilding after the horrors of war, they also sought to tell a story of how this new nation emerged from the old. The new cathedral rising from the ashes in Coventry was a metaphor of sorts for a country marked primarily by continuities literally anchored in the rock. But, as I'd seen driving through North Wales, even the rock itself had changed when it came to the question of meaning, let alone the stuff growing out of the rocky soil that those researching these routes kept a close eye on. And profound change extended deep inside those rocks: Electric Mountain struck me – for all its apparent slatey permanence – as a strange temple to this fleeting thing called the television age. Everything from how we entertain ourselves, through how we think about the past, to how we understand the world appeared to rest on a much less stable foundation than those working on the *About Britain* guides ever imagined.

Stamford–Ketton–Uppingham–Wardley–Leicester–
Anstey–Newton Linford–Whitwick–Coleorton–
Ashby de la Zouch–Melbourne–Swarkestone–
Chellaston–Thulston–Shardlow–Loughborough–
Shoby–Melton Mowbray–Burton Lazars–
Langham–Oakham–Empingham–Stamford

8

East Midlands and the Peak

Stamford–Ashby-de-la-Zouch–Stamford (108 miles)

The *About Britain* guide instructed motorists to 'leave Stamford by Rutland Terrace' so I did as I was told. Ignoring the signs directing traffic along West Street, I drove past the long row of three-storey stone houses celebrated as 'a notable piece of early 19th-century building' and exactly the kind of architecture that the Festival of Britain so admired. But it was not simply this Georgian terrace that the guidebook wanted motorists to see. It was the whole town. Stamford was described at the end of the strip map as 'perhaps one of the most beautiful towns in England'. W. G. Hoskins was in complete agreement. In his opening essay he introduced Stamford as 'an incomparable town to look at' before adding that 'if there is a more beautiful town in the whole of England I have yet to see it'.[1] It was no surprise then that Stamford was chosen as the beginning and end of today's journey. It was somewhere worth coming back to.

Yet within a few years of the publication of the guides, this 'beautiful' town was threatened by modernization. The clash between the demands of modern mass motoring and the congested narrow streets of a medieval town was navigated not through road-widening but, like in so many other places, by building a bypass. Reporting the opening of this bypass in 1960, a British Pathé newsreel celebrated that 'another Great North Road bottleneck has been uncorked'. I crossed over the same sunken dual carriageway carrying the redirected A1 shortly after leaving Rutland Terrace. However, long lines of traffic were not the only challenge that Stamford faced in the 1950s and 1960s. When the Royal Commission on the Historical Monuments of England visited in the late 1970s, they were aghast that 'several' street-fronts in the town had been 'mutilated by their conversion into shops and the introduction of discordant shopfronts'.[2] While the A1 was rerouted to avoid the narrow streets, and ultimately supplanted by the M1 that steered well clear of all town centres, the redevelopment of the high street with the arrival of chain stores was much harder to bypass.

One solution was to draw on the longer tradition of listing individual historic buildings seen to be of particular value. In the late nineteenth and early twentieth centuries, a number of Acts had been passed to safeguard prehistoric monuments. In order to identify further worthy structures, a series of Royal Commissions were established that began the lengthy process of surveys, starting with Hertfordshire and Buckinghamshire in 1908, before reaching Stamford in the late 1970s.[3] By the time they got there, a host of historic buildings – including Rutland Terrace – had been listed to ensure their survival, yet this did not include all the high street shops that so horrified the commission. It was not only in Stamford that there was a rush to list historic properties. Responding to the situation found in bombed-out cities, 'salvage lists' were drawn up to identify those damaged buildings seen as worth saving, rather than being knocked down. Planning Acts passed in the mid and late 1940s had also identified 'buildings of special architectural or historic interest' in order to protect them from future demolition by developers. A survey was undertaken that highlighted around 120,000 mostly medieval or early modern properties across the country, with sites seen to be worth saving especially concentrated in the ancient heart of Stamford.

However, as critics pointed out, the strategy of listing buildings was an inadequate response to modernization, which threatened not just individual buildings but entire streetscapes. Calls to protect more than isolated buildings grew during the 1960s. The Council for British Archaeology identified 300 towns whose entire 'historic quality' needed protecting. Not surprisingly, Stamford made it onto their shortlist of the top 51 'gem towns'. In order to fill the perceived gap in legislation, Duncan Sandys – who had helped found the Civic Trust in the late 1950s – put forward a private member's bill 'to make further provision for the protection and improvement of buildings of architectural or historic interest' as well as 'the character of areas of such interest'. Designating entire streetscapes as Conservation Areas was to ensure that future developments would preserve the area's historic character. Stamford was in the government's sights when it went on the lookout for pilot schemes and so, in 1967, the historic core of Stamford was designated the first Conservation Area in England. The impact of this was reflected upon by the commissioners in their report, published a decade later, where they noted approvingly that 'Stamford has survived to a large degree undamaged by incongruous modern intrusions' and rather than tower blocks 'the tallest buildings are still the church towers, so preserving a traditional sky-line which is becoming an increasingly rare feature of our towns'.[4]

The number of Conservation Areas grew rapidly during the 1970s, slowed a little in the 1980s and then grew more quickly during the 1990s. There are now more than 10,000 across England. Compared with the larger and more visible areas of protected land – National Parks and Areas of Outstanding Natural Beauty – Conservation Areas tend to be much smaller.

The largest covers two valleys in the Yorkshire Dales National Park. The smallest includes two buildings in a single alleyway in Hampstead. But while they only represent 2 per cent of the land – rather than the 10 per cent covered by National Parks – they include the homes of 10 per cent of the population.

The first Conservation Area in Stamford marked a decisive change in post-war thinking from what one scholar called 'the earlier desire to create entirely new "modern" towns within the image of the second industrial age and compatible with the motor vehicle' to 'a new desire' that 'delights in a sense of historic continuity whenever that is possible'.[5] Rather than sweeping away old buildings as was celebrated in the 1950s, the ancient cores of towns and cities were increasingly preserved, with new building confined to the edges. The end result was that leaving this town I drove through onion-ring-like layers of domestic and commercial architecture that ran from the past to the present: the Georgian stone-built Rutland Terrace morphed into Victorian brick-built villas, followed by a line of interwar pebble-dashed semis with commanding views over the valley to the left of the road, before ending up at the entrance to a new housing estate on the very cusp of the green belt where town gave way to farmland.

Once out of Stamford I entered into Rutland. In 1951 motorists drove into England's smallest county, which had just adopted the motto *Multum in Parvo*, or Much in Little. But in the intervening decades, Rutland officially disappeared for a while when it was included in Leicestershire as a result of the 1972 Local Government Act, before returning in the late 1990s after yet another redrawing of the administrative map. The first village I drove through in Rutland – Tinwell – was one of those made uniformly neat because the houses were built from the same local stone, and I wasn't surprised to discover that it was a Conservation Area. Beyond Tinwell, the road twisted past freshly ploughed fields speckled with scattered oak trees, and before long I reached another neat-looking uniform stone village – Ketton – that also boasted another Conservation Area at its heart.[6]

When motorists drove through Ketton in 1951, the *About Britain* guide drew attention not only to the 'superb church (mainly 13th–14th century)' but also to the cement works that stood 'near the road'. Built in 1928, the works were to be admired as an example of the vibrancy of British industry that drew on longer-standing traditions of an area that 'has one of the famous medieval quarries in the oolitic limestone still working' in the concrete age. Driving past the smoking chimneys, it was clear that they were still making cement in Ketton.

Wartime demand for military construction morphed into the needs of post-war building and especially the slum-clearance programmes of the 1960s. Demand for concrete slowed during the 1980s, and then again after the financial crisis of 2008, but had picked up recently. Over 10 per cent of the cement used in the country is made here, most of it taken by train to London for construction projects. Mirroring the shift away from fossil fuels that I saw on other journeys, this factory had experimented with firing the kilns by something other than coal. In the 1990s, this included burning waste and by the 2010s a large solar farm was built in one of the former quarries adjacent to the works.[7]

The cement works at Ketton were an ongoing concern, rather than an industrial archaeology site like the former slate quarries of North Wales. But this has not precluded thoughts being given to their preservation. The boundaries of the Conservation Area in Ketton were under review when I drove by, with plans to include part of the cement works that lay down a tree-lined drive. What the plans described as the 'structured view along Ketco Avenue towards Hanson cement works' was included in a list of thirty-two 'important views' worth preserving in Ketton, alongside the main interwar office building that lies at the end of the tree-lined drive. Justifying their inclusion of 'this . . . good example of townscape design, associated with the development of the cement works during the early 20th century' the authors of the report reckoned there was 'sufficient architectural and historic interest to be included within the conservation boundary'.[8]

Adding cement works to Conservation Areas is a marked change in ways of thinking about which historical past is worth safeguarding. When the Royal Commissions began their surveys in the early part of the twentieth century, they worked with an assumption that 'historical monuments' predated 1700. By the early 1950s, when they reached Dorset, they had extended the end point to include all notable buildings and monuments built before 1850, meaning that Rutland Terrace made it into their survey of the 'historical monuments in Stamford' as well as featuring in the 1951 *About Britain* guide. But in the decades since, the past has come closer. In Stamford, subsequent waves of listing in the 1970s and 1980s saw attention paid not only to the retaining wall, railings and gates at Rutland Terrace, but also to three telephone boxes from the mid 1930s. This chronological shift also led to the Conservation Area in Stamford being expanded to include the brick-built Victorian houses of the Northfields district in the mid 2000s, followed by further expansion that brought more nineteenth- and early twentieth-century developments into the fold.[9]

Across the twentieth century then, the age of what is worth saving has moved closer to the present. It would be impossible to imagine anyone in 1951 thinking of a building from 1921 as historic, let alone anyone in 1910 thinking the same of something built in the 1880s. But in the late 1980s it was decided to get rid of the date of 1939 as the cut-off for listing historic buildings and work instead with a rolling period of three decades. By the 1990s, history ended 30 years ago, at least when it came to safeguarding the material past. It is not only the case that the Victorian age has been belatedly embraced, but we have also come to appreciate mid twentieth-century industrial architecture in places like Ketton.

The move from coal to solar at the cement works I passed on my way into Ketton was mirrored by another greenwards shift as I left the village. On the edge of Ketton, I passed a sign pointing to one of three cemeteries in the village of 2,000 inhabitants. The first, in the churchyard around Ketton's 'superb' medieval church, was full towards the end of the nineteenth century, so a new cemetery opened in 1881 just off the road heading north out of town. Over a century later, in 2001, two enterprising local farmers created a third. But Ketton Park Green Burial Ground was not built because its forerunner was now full. Instead, it offered a self-conscious 'natural alternative to traditional graveyard or crematorium burials', providing 'a peaceful final resting place in a manner friendly towards nature, wildlife and the environment'.[10]

The Green Burial Ground is one of more than 250 green cemeteries established across the country in the decades after the first 'Woodland Burial Area' was created in a cemetery in Carlisle in the early 1990s.[11] This marks a change of thinking about death. In the nineteenth century, burial, often accompanied by an elaborate gravestone, was the norm. But during the twentieth century, cremation began to replace it. Although the first legal cremation took place in the 1880s and the 1902 Cremation Act regulated the construction of crematoria, the big boom in crematorium building came in the 1950s and 1960s when over half of those built were constructed. By the end of the 1960s, more people chose cremation over burial for the first time. By the century's end, more had become most, with roughly 70 per cent choosing to be cremated. But the sharp rise of the natural death movement in the 1990s and 2000s marked the beginnings of a return to burial, or rather green burial. Key to this change has been growing concerns with the environmental impact of death.

The rise of green burial has been stimulated by an attempt to minimize environmental harm by lessening the use of fossil-fuel-powered crematoria furnaces, and to offer a positive environmental contribution. In green burial, the corpse is reimagined as an environmental asset for 'fertilising the soil', one that sustains either a woodland or, in the case of Ketton, a wildflower-rich meadow. Over at the late nineteenth-century cemetery in Ketton 'no trees, bushes or shrubs may be planted on any grave as these prevent the cemetery being maintained'. In direct contrast, in many green burial sites, a tree is not simply planted on the grave, but grows out of and is sustained by it. As a number of scholars have pointed out, this marks an important change in thinking from the 'disposal' to the 'dispersal' of human remains that are reimagined 'as a gift to the living and to the planet'.[12]

There is also something else going on. Green burial sites tend to have either no permanent gravestone or a very simple and small marker. The corpse not only sustains the trees or meadowland that grow from it, but is also overgrown and hidden by them. In this way green burial represents a growing awareness of environmental concerns as well as an increased mobility in modern life. Over at the late nineteenth-century cemetery in Ketton, the dead require ongoing care from the living. 'All gravestones, monuments, kerbs and other memorials are to be kept in good repair by the owners,' the bereaved are advised, before being instructed that 'if not repaired after due notice, the memorial may be removed by the Parish Council'. By contrast, the green burial ground reassures the bereaved that 'a Green Burial needs no maintenance from family or friends to secure an everlasting dignified field of rest'. Nature is left to take care of the dead. The decision to create a woodland cemetery in the cemetery in Carlisle was motivated in part by the challenge of managing a place where graves were no longer visited or maintained. This lessening of the ties between the dead and the bereaved could soon reach its epitome in proposals to utilize the inaccessible spaces of miles of motorway verges as flower-strewn, green burial sites.[13]

Past Ketton, the road followed the contours through rolling agricultural land. Even in the car I was conscious of the rise and fall of the road, although no doubt far less than the two cyclists I overtook: one wearing a red jersey, the other bright yellow. I passed a windmill just before reaching South Luffenham where a grand manor house – listed in 1955 – stood alongside the road. RAF North Luffenham, signposted to the right, is home to another more recently listed building. In 2011, the Thor missile site on the edge of this airfield was listed as the most complete of the 20 sites in Britain that were home to American Thor nuclear missiles in the late 1950s and early 1960s – those quite hot decades of the Cold War. Reaching the junction with the main road, I made my way towards Leicester.

I drove along the ridge with views to the left over the valley, where a huge viaduct stretched into the distance. Built in the 1870s, it is over three-quarters of a mile long. When motorists drove this road in 1951, they may well have seen trains crossing, but when I drove by it was empty. After the Beeching cuts of roughly a third of all passenger services in the mid-1960s, only freight trains crossed the Welland Valley on this impressive feat of Victorian engineering, which through listing in the late 1980s had become a heritage site.[14] More recently a small number of passenger services have been reintroduced, bringing Melton Mowbray within the ever-expanding London commuter belt. However, the train had departed with its load of Leicestershire commuters at six that morning and wasn't due to return until seven-thirty that evening. So the viaduct remained train-less as I drove on to Glaston, where the village inn was not only still open but had been listed in the mid-1950s because of its mid eighteenth-century pedigree. In Glaston the underlying geology was made visible in houses built from stone that looked very different from the pale limestone used to build Tinwell less than a 20-minute drive away.

Approaching Uppingham, I decided to drive into town rather than continue on the bypass built in the early 1980s. It was busy on the shop-lined high street that morning, but it was busier still when I headed west past Uppingham School whose main gateway was featured as the first image alongside the strip map for this journey. Checking the clock in the car it seemed that 9.45 must be the time when students head to their lessons. Uniformed teenagers wearing striped ties in their house colours of blue, green, red, pink and yellow spilled off the pavements and onto the road. All 800 students, both boys and – since the 1970s – girls, appeared to be on the move. Originally founded as a grammar school in the late sixteenth century, it expanded in the mid nineteenth century when it became part of the rebirth of the English public school. It has continued to grow; as I passed by I noticed the mass of new buildings flanking the Leicester Road.

Uppingham is towards the top end of a private education system that has grown, rather than diminished, in the post-war era. Numbers attending private schools remained more or less constant from the 1970s through to the 2000s at just over 600,000 at any one time. What has changed is a decline in boarding schools in rural locations and small towns like Uppingham and the rise of day schools in the cities. Eight out of nine in private education now attend day schools, and so the boarders at Uppingham represent something of an anomaly: an expensive anomaly costing over £40,000 a year per pupil. With declining numbers of British students attending boarding schools, there has been a consequent rise in foreign students. At schools like Uppingham, roughly 25 per cent of boarders are from overseas and pay in excess of £50,000 a year for the privilege.[15]

Back on the main road, I left Rutland behind and entered into Leicestershire: the 'heart of rural England' as the fox-topped sign spelled out. Leicestershire has only recently claimed this title for itself since the Ordnance Survey moved the centre of England from the traditional holder of the title, Meriden, a little further east. Driving through 'the rolling grasslands of east Leicestershire' motorists in 1951 were provided with a geology lesson. 'The route drops off the marlstone escarpment into the clay country and leaves predominantly arable country for a mainly pastoral landscape,' the caption noted. Entering first Tugby and then Skeffington, I did pass fields of sheep among a much smaller number of arable farms. The patterns of settlement seemed quite different from the first part of my journey. There were far fewer villages along the main road. As W. G. Hoskins explained in his opening essay, these changes came with the enclosures in the eighteenth century, which saw 'the old village arable fields . . . enclosed and turned over to grass' in 'High Leicestershire in the east of the county'.[16] This changed landscape became, the strip map asserted, 'the best fox-hunting country in England', hence the fox on the top of the road sign welcoming me and the nickname of Leicester City Football Club, 'the Foxes', although attitudes towards fox hunting have altered since the 1950s.

I soon caught my first glimpse of Leicester in the distance, dominated by a tall chimney pumping out smoke. Following the Uppingham Road into the city, I went through the outer suburbs with their rows of interwar, semi-detached houses on either side of the street. Getting closer to the city centre, rows of houses were replaced by rows of shops. As in Uppingham, the pavements were busy with mid-morning shoppers. It was chilly out, so one lady sported a khaki parka over her shalwar kameez. Coming from the east brought me into the city centre through areas where non-white communities are in the majority; this is a city where over a quarter of residents in the last census identified themselves as being of Indian ethnicity.

In Leicester the street scene was both similar to, and radically different from, that in the small market town of Uppingham less than a half-hour drive away. In both, shoppers thronged the independent shops on the high street. But those shopping on the Uppingham Road in Leicester were far more diverse. According to the Office for National Statistics, Leicester was one of five cities in Britain – the others were London, Birmingham, Luton and Slough – where two strangers bumping into each other on the street were more likely to be of different ethnic groups than the same. On the high street in Uppingham, like most of rural and market-town Britain, the chances of that are negligible, international students at the boarding school aside, given that the population of Rutland is 97 per cent white.[17] Twenty-first-century Britain may be multi-ethnic, but as Uppingham and Leicester show this is far from uniform, even in places a few miles apart.

Once I reached the inevitable inner ring road, I looked for signs to my next destination – Anstey – but there weren't any. Instead the plethora of signs directed drivers to the places where Leicester's planners assumed they wanted to go: the historic centre, the King Power Stadium parking, the National Space Centre and the airport. I plumped for the one simply stating 'King Richard III', whose remains were discovered buried under a car park in central Leicester and reinterred in Leicester Cathedral in the first half of the 2010s, and followed that. After briefly tunnelling under the city and then bypassing it on a short stretch of the M1 motorway, I finally found a sign marked to Anstey and made it back onto the road so clearly marked on the strip map in my *About Britain* guide. Once more, the building of new roads in and around cities was not only one of the biggest changes since 1951, but also made trying to retrace these routes a challenge.

Entering Anstey, I reached the self-proclaimed 'Gateway to Charnwood Forest'. Those putting this itinerary together were quick to point out that 'Charnwood Forest, through which the route passes for several miles . . . is well wooded' but explained that there was more to see than the trees in 'a completely uncovered tertiary landscape, of great interest to geologists'. It was certainly an unusual landscape. A little further along the road, a field's width of green farmland abruptly gave way to bracken-brown moorland topped with a row of pale exposed rocks. It felt like chancing upon the landscape of upland Britain inserted one field up from the road in 'the rural heart of England'. Crossing the M1, I reached Whitwick where large plastic red poppies had been attached to signposts and lamp posts ahead of Remembrance Sunday, and which also adorned the huge black cast-iron winding wheel that was a monument to the former colliery in this small town.

When motorists drove through here in 1951, coal mining was thriving in 'one of the smallest but most highly mechanized and efficient coal fields in England'. Mechanization was seen as particularly well suited to the coal seams that lay around Ashby-de-la-Zouch, so there was heavy investment in this region after the post-war nationalization of the industry. In his introductory essay, Hoskins noted that 'the collieries are larger, more up to date' in the East Midlands and pointed to coal as a growing rather than declining industry in the region. The Leicestershire coalfield reached peak production during the 1950s, but a number of mines closed in the late 1960s followed by more closures – including Whitwick Colliery – in the late 1980s. With the deep pits gone, some open-cast mining continued at

Coleorton, which I passed a few miles down the road, but this colliery also closed in the mid-1990s. There were 20 collieries in this coalfield in 1947; by the end of the 1990s none remained.

This was a familiar story repeated across former mining areas, but the rapid decline was particularly striking in Leicestershire given the optimism that pervaded in the early 1950s as mechanization offered new opportunities to exploit the rich seams of coal. Even at that moment, Hoskins could imagine a different future 'when all the coal and iron are exhausted and forgotten'. But I think he would have been surprised at how quickly that future without coal would come, with mines closed down three decades later and coal-burning power stations, like the one at Rugeley, being erased from the landscape.[18]

I made my way through farmland, as the old road twisted and turned through the ancient field boundaries. In Coleorton, a wind turbine on the left marked the shift away from coal-fired power. To the right a small industrial estate signalled a changing economy not based around coal-fired heavy industry. Traversing a large roundabout that had attracted the warehouses of the logistics industry, I drove into Ashby-de-la-Zouch and down the wide high street, which was just as busy as the one in Uppingham. From here I followed a sunken and tunnel-like road and drove semi-submerged through farmland hemmed in by hedges to Ticknall: another neat village that was also a Conservation Area. It was getting close to lunchtime and I was about halfway through my journey, so I pulled into the driveway of Calke Abbey, owned by the National Trust since the mid-1980s. A sign welcomed me to an 'Unstately Home', and the woman on the front gate warned me, 'It's a bit weird our house, but it's good.' After lunch I found out just what she meant.

Rather than restoring Calke Abbey to its eighteenth- or early nineteenth-century heyday, the National Trust have maintained the house in a state of twentieth-century decay. From the 1920s, the house had 'slowly shut down'. When motorists passed this secluded property in 1951, Charles Harpur-Crewe was living in an ever-diminishing set of rooms, with most of the main house simply used for storage. Thirty years later he died and the estate was inherited by his brother Henry, along with a massive bill for death duties. It passed into the hands of the National Trust and was opened to the public in 1989 after work to stabilize the decay. Walking the long corridors I passed from one shuttered and darkened room to another, where dusty furniture was piled up in the middle, and paint flakes and wallpaper had peeled off the walls.[19]

That all was not well with the English country house in 1951 was hinted at in captions below two of the photographs in the volume covering the East Midlands and the Peak. The first showed family tombs in Bottesford Church; the second an aerial view of Belvoir Castle. While the images suggested historic continuity, the text underneath hinted at dramatic changes taking place. 'According to the Gowers Report, the passing of the great houses is the most important social change since the dissolution of the monasteries' stated the caption below the interior shot of Bottesford Church, thereby radically reinterpreting this image. The choice of a family crypt was apposite for what was seen to be 'memorials of a dead civilization'. Things were not quite as bad at Belvoir Castle, 'seat of the Dukes of Rutland', which was described as 'one of the historic country houses in which the East Midlands abound'. However, the caption noted that 'despite the enforced break-up of its art collections they are still magnificent, including many fine sporting pictures'.[20] It was clear that the challenges facing stately homes were something that those putting the guidebooks together wanted to bring to the attention of visitors. In the archives in Kew, the surviving 'Specimen Rough outline of a "Steering Script"' for the opening essay in each of the *About Britain* guides included the keywords:

'The passing of the Great House. National Trust Property, Nature Reserves' at the end of a long, chronological list of 'Historical Transformations'.[21]

These warnings about 'the passing of the Great House' were repeated in the National Trust's 1951 annual report, which claimed that stately homes 'are today literally falling down; their irreplaceable contents, brought together by successive generations, are being dispersed; their gardens are overgrown; and the surrounding parklands of which they form the central and essential feature are becoming derelict.' This bold statement was borne out by the statistics showing a rise in the number of country houses demolished from the early 1950s through to the mid-1960s. In 1951 alone, at least 23 were demolished.

Given this situation, Sir Ernest Gowers was appointed to chair a committee to explore the role of the state in 'the preservation, maintenance and use of houses of outstanding historic or architectural interest which might otherwise not be preserved'. The committee reported back in 1950 and recommended that tax relief be granted to owners of 'designated' houses to enable the necessary maintenance to take place. Failing this, they called upon the government to fund the maintenance or the purchase of 'designated' houses. These recommendations were never fully implemented when Labour lost the 1951 general election. By the mid-1970s the tide was turning, and the decades of demolition were halted with the celebrated exhibition shown at the Victoria and Albert Museum on 'The Destruction of the English Country House'.[22]

Leaving the 'unstately' home at Calke Abbey, I drove through farmland, with wind-turbines off in the distance, and then into Melbourne. A heron stood still, reflected in a large puddle in the field to my right as I entered the village, which looked very smart, complete with high-end independent shops and restaurants. This was the first of yet another run of Conservation Areas from the late 1960s and 1970s: first Melbourne, then Stanton by Bridge, and then Swarkestone. The fields on either side of the ancient Swarkestone causeway were flooded. At the bridge the Trent was in spate. I pulled in and walked down to the swollen banks through an empty and sodden riverside pub garden. Back in the car, I made my way through Chellaston, highlighted for the motorist in 1951 because of its 'famous gypsum quarries which gave rise to the schools of alabaster carvers at Nottingham and Burton on Trent in the Middle Ages'. From the signs pointing towards the Aerospace Campus, it was clear that transport technologies have replaced gypsum quarrying, with Airbus, Rolls-Royce engines and the companies in their extensive supply chain all located here. Taking the dual carriageway, I crossed over the raging River Trent, back into Leicestershire and on to Loughborough.

When motorists followed this route in 1951, Loughborough was described as 'a rising engineering town with an important engineering college'. That college is now Loughborough University. I could see the tops of the buildings of the main campus in the distance. But in 1951, the only university in the region was not here but, as Hoskins explained in his introduction, in Nottingham, which had been awarded its charter in 1948 and was 'the newest of the Universities'.[23] But Leicester and Loughborough were not far behind. University College, Leicester became Leicester University in 1957. Loughborough University of Technology became the first technological university in the country in 1966: a category invented by the 1963 Robbins Report that planned for significant growth in the numbers of students going to university.

The massive expansion of British universities that I saw elsewhere took place in stages. The first, in the late 1950s and early 1960s, saw former university colleges like Leicester granted independent university status, as well as the building of seven new universities: East Anglia, Essex, Kent, Lancaster, Sussex, Warwick and York. The second, following the publication of the Robbins Report, which addressed the 'educational emergency' as the post-war baby boomers reached the age of eighteen, proposed a further six new universities and a doubling of student numbers within 20 years. This growth was not to be uniform across subjects but rather focused on 'a growth in the proportion of students taking science and, particularly, technology'. By the late 1960s, degrees in science and technology had gone from a minority in the pre-war years to a post-war majority. Although Robbins had considered the suggestion that students pay for higher education by taking out loans, he decided that the state would continue to pay not only fees, but also a maintenance grant to cover the cost of living in university accommodation.[24] In what became known as the 'Robbins' principle', those with the aptitude were to be enabled to study wherever they could gain admission through the support of their local authority.

A third wave of expansion came in the late 1960s and 1970s as the Labour government invested heavily in expanding higher education by developing a binary system. The first of the new 'polytechnics' was established in 1969, with a total of 30 rapidly added by 1973. Twenty years later all of these became universities. In the early 1990s the Conservative government announced plans to increase student numbers from a fifth to a third of all school leavers. The assumption was that this growth would be evolutionary and take place, slowly, over three generations. In reality, growth was revolutionary and occurred within a decade marked by high levels of unemployment. Perhaps not surprisingly, the massive growth of students was not matched by increasing numbers of academics. Instead, class sizes rose – from a one-to-nine staff–student ratio in 1980 to double that 20 years later. This was the era of mass higher education. Once the goal of a third of school leavers in higher education was reached, the New Labour government pushed for even higher numbers, setting a target of half of school leavers by 2010. That goal was never reached and has recently been shelved, but the late 2000s saw a new high point of over 40 per cent of 18–30-year-olds in higher education, although they tended to come overwhelmingly from the middle classes. Those kind of figures simply could not have been imagined in 1951 when a little over 3 per cent were studying at university.[25]

This expansion in higher education can be seen in Loughborough where there were 1,500 students at this 'important engineering college' when motorists first followed the routes. By 1970, 4,000 students studied at the recently established Loughborough University of Technology, rising a little to 6,000 by the end of the 1980s. But it was the 1990s that had the most marked expansion. Student numbers doubled within a decade, reaching 12,000 in 2000 at what was now simply called Loughborough University, before peaking at 17,000 in the mid-2000s. They have since dropped slightly, and there were around 14,000 students studying here when I drove through. In a small market town like Loughborough they are highly visible. Students make up close to a quarter of the population and the university is the main employer in the town and a key contributor to the local economy.[26] Rather than visiting 'a rising engineering town with an important engineering college', I drove through Loughborough at a time when the university and the so-called knowledge economy had trumped manufacturing as the main business in town.

The rise in the number of students in towns and cities has not been welcomed by all. During the 2000s, there was 'town' versus 'gown' conflict over where Loughborough's students were choosing to live. While the Robbins Report had called for the expansion of student accommodation on campuses so that two-thirds of students would live in university residences, the lack of investment during the Thatcher period meant that the pace of residence building failed to keep up with student numbers. By the late 1990s and early 2000s, there were only enough places in university halls for a third of Loughborough's students, meaning that students turned to the private rental market for somewhere to live. Student housing became a lucrative business, with landlords carving up Victorian terraced houses into multi-occupancy premises that could squeeze in four, five or more students. In Loughborough, students became concentrated in a handful of streets that landlords dubbed the 'Golden Triangle' close to the main university campus. Journalists visited the area in the early 2000s and found students living in well over half the terraced houses on one street.[27]

Local residents mobilized to fight the influx of student houses, seizing on the legislative tool of Conservation Areas. In 2002, they gained Conservation Area status for the streets of Victorian and Edwardian houses. However, while Conservation Area status could limit the building of new extensions and the dumping of litter in front gardens, it could do little about noisy neighbours. But this particular tide was starting to turn as student expectations rose during the era of fee-paying for education. From the mid-2000s, a number of privately built, larger student residences were developed, often in former industrial premises. This was a picture repeated nationally, with the building of high-rise and high-end student accommodation blocks – often including a gym or cinema room – in gentrifying city centres, partly driven by the limits placed on houses of multiple occupancy by local authorities. In the 2010s, purpose-built student accommodation emerged as a highly lucrative multi-billion-pound business, controlled by a small number of key players backed by institutional investors, rather than the buy-to-let landlords of the 1990s and early 2000s.[28]

The building boom of private halls in Loughborough and elsewhere bore witness to the fact that the majority of British students continue to leave home. Four out of five continue the tradition imagined in the Robbins Report that students would attend the university best suited to their needs, rather than the one closest to their home as is the case elsewhere in Europe. Each autumn sees the mass migration of a large number of young people, mainly drawn from middle-class southern England to a number of northern cities with large universities, before they return to the south once they graduate.[29] But the growth in higher education means that there are not only lots of British students on the move each year, there is also a large number of young people from across the world as higher education has become a global market. Just under 500,000 international students study in British universities, with China accounting for more than 20 per cent of these.[30] To attract even more of this lucrative market, Loughborough opened a second campus, 100 miles to the south, in East London in the mid-2010s. The location, in the area developed to host the 2012 Olympic Games, was carefully chosen given Loughborough's reputation as the pre-eminent home of elite sport, and the taught masters courses offered, in sport business for example, were aimed primarily at international students who preferred the lifestyle of the capital over that found in a small East Midland town.

Leaving Loughborough, at the end of the school day, I passed streams of uniformed children walking home, lacking the multicoloured house ties I'd seen in Uppingham. I passed through the layered landscape of a small industrial town: canals, new housing, ring roads, the Silbey Fabrications factory and the Brush electrical factory. Here was continuity with the names reeled off by Hoskins in 1951 as he informed readers that 'most of the larger East Midland towns have important engineering industries with firms of household names – notably Rolls-Royce at Derby, Raleigh at Nottingham, Imperial typewriters at Leicester, Brush electrical equipment at Loughborough . . .' Imperial closed in the mid-1970s, but the rest remain open for business in their long-standing hometowns in the heart of what is not quite entirely post-industrial Britain.

Entering farmland once more, I saw bales piled high in the fields and a little further on a farm advertising sacks of potatoes for sale. The road ran parallel to an estate wall for a stretch. The old house on the other side was now, inevitably perhaps, a wedding venue that promised couples that they would 'feel like you are marrying "At Home, at Prestwold Hall"'. Away from the hall and gardens, another part of the estate had been turned into a green burial site, offering interment in a setting that will 'eventually create wildlife-rich natural woodland with wildflower glades' filled with 'primroses, cowslips and oxeye daisy'.[31] The greening of burial was mirrored by the greening of energy with a cluster of wind turbines to the left before I crossed the old Fosse Way and drove down to Melton Mowbray.

The *About Britain* guide informed motorists that 'the busy little market town of Melton Mowbray' was 'famous for fox-hunting and pork pies'. There was no mention of fox hunting as I drove into the town, and it seemed that more than pork pies were now on offer in this place that boasted being the 'rural capital of food'. I decided that the high street was probably where to go to taste the town's delights, so headed past the cattle market and parked up at the end of the pedestrianized high street where the market traders were just pulling in with their white vans to pack up their stalls. Finding a sign pointing towards the 'pork pie shoppe' I followed it. Halfway down the street Ye Olde Pork Pie Shoppe, listed since 1950, and home to Dickinson & Morris's Melton Mowbray pork pies, was still open, so I went inside to try one.

While those drawing up the tours in the London office sent motorists to Melton Mowbray for pork pies, Hoskins seems to have cared more for cheese, with a particular fondness for Red Leicester. 'If it were not for the fame of Stilton,' he wrote, 'the red cheese of South Leicestershire would be much more widely known than it is.'[32] I don't know what he would have made of Dickinson & Morris's Stilton-topped pork pie, which tried to offer the best of both worlds, but he would no doubt have been pleased to see that the Tuxford & Tebbutt creamery that I passed on my way out of town advertised both Stilton and Leicester cheese in black lettering on their whitewashed facade.

Just who could make Stilton cheese and Melton Mowbray pork pies became a point of contention in the 1990s and 2000s. The appeal by cheese- and pie-makers to European regulators to protect the integrity of products resembled the later successful attempt by watercress growers in Hampshire to create clear water between chalk-stream-grown watercress and polytunnel land cress. Both Stilton cheese-makers and Melton Mowbray pie-makers were successful in their campaigns. After gaining Protected Designation of Origin (PDO) status, Stilton could only be produced in the counties of Leicestershire, Nottinghamshire and Derbyshire. Following the awarding of Protected Geographical Indication (PGI) status, Melton Mowbray pork pies could only be made in Leicestershire and parts of Lincolnshire, Nottinghamshire and Northamptonshire. The protection offered by two different three-letter designations, pointed not only to the differences between cheese and pies, but also to a typically European, Franco-German compromise. Rather than adopting one designation, the European Union created two that drew on French and German traditions respectively.

The Protected Designation of Origin status given to Stilton owed much to the French system of Appellation of Origin introduced in the early twentieth century to safeguard the French wine industry. It drew on ideas of *terroir*, a distinctively

French term that combined a sense of soil, topography and climate as well as local traditions of winemaking. The physical link with the soil meant that PDO status was not simply about where something was produced, but a more material connection with a 'particular geographical environment with its inherent natural and human factors'.

Such a link was easier to make when it came to cheese made from milk produced by cows grazing the grasslands of east Leicestershire than with pies whose multiple ingredients came from much further afield. This is where the other designation came in, which was adopted from an early twentieth-century German tradition of place-based protection that lacked the material link with the soil. This looser connection focused on where production took place and the link between product and place being 'based on a specific quality, reputation or other characteristics attributable to that geographical origin'. It was that reputational, rather than more direct material, link with place that the Melton Mowbray Pie Association successfully argued for. However, it left more room for interpretation, and in the last decade or so a long-running legal challenge has rumbled on involving Northern Foods, a company that manufactured a 'Melton Mowbray pork pie' at factories in Shropshire and Wiltshire well outside the newly adopted PGI region. They were ultimately unsuccessful and were given five years to move their factories in order to keep the name.[33]

I left Melton Mowbray behind, heading towards Oakham with views of a patchwork of fields in the distance. I re-entered Rutland, passing a stretch of fenced horse-racing track running parallel to the road. I was hoping to catch a glimpse of 'the hill-top mansion, built 1694–1702 by Daniel Finch, Earl of Winchelsea and Nottingham (now a hospital)'. The house at Burley on the Hill was still there, but it had come full circle from home to hospital to homes again having been carved up into luxury apartments in the 1990s.[34] But more obvious changes had taken place. The view from the hill had changed dramatically, as it had from the road. After bypassing Oakham, I saw Rutland Water stretching away to the right. Since the mid-1970s, the route sketched out in the *About Britain* guide 20 years earlier has paralleled the shore of the newly created reservoir. As with the creation of numerous other reservoirs, two villages were demolished when the valley was flooded and Hambleton, signposted to the right, now clung on to a hilly peninsular jutting out into the lake.

Making my way back to Stamford, I drove through another of the attractive stone-built villages that had peppered today's route. Entering Whitwell, I glanced at the sign welcoming me to the village. Like other places, it had been twinned with another location. But this wasn't merely a similar-sized European village but France's capital city, Paris. After gaining Conservation Area status in 1979, it seems that there was no stopping Whitwell's inhabitants, who decided to send a letter to the then mayor of Paris, and later French president, Jacques Chirac, 'indicating that unless anything was heard to the contrary before 20.30 hours on the 13 June in 1980, a state of *jumelage* (twinning) would exist between Whitwell sur l'Eau and Paris'.[35] Chirac failed to reply and the sign I passed at the village edge was the end result.

The guide was keen for motorists to have a second look at what was 'perhaps one of the most beautiful towns in England'. Driving into Stamford once more, I made my way back in time through the concentric circles of buildings that ring the town: housing estates from the 2000s on the very edge, then developments from the 1980s, before reaching the 1930s suburbs and finally the ancient core. In the corner of Red Lion Square, Nelsons butchers was offering 'authentic' Melton Mowbray pork pies: those safely made within the boundaries of the Protected Geographical Indication. But I'd eaten enough pies for one day and so looked for dinner elsewhere.

Setting out from, and then returning to, Stamford I was struck by the creep of what is perhaps best described as preservationism in post-war Britain. From 1967, when entire streetscapes in this town were included in the first Conservation Area, the desire to preserve the past has spread spatially and chronologically. From this initial Conservation Area, there are now over 10,000 in Britain. Driving this route, it seemed that more or less every village I drove through had acquired this status between the 1970s and 1990s. But I was struck not only by the way that this new designation had been seized upon, but also by the way the sense of which past was worth conserving had crept ever closer to the present.

I saw the subtle, but significant, changes that have taken place over the course of a century in ways of thinking about what constitutes the past. When William Morris set up the Society for the Protection of Ancient Buildings (SPAB) in the 1870s, his sights were trained on the insensitive 'restoration' of medieval buildings being undertaken by his Victorian contemporaries. In the 1930s, the Georgian Group was founded to protect threatened Georgian architecture from demolition, picking up where SPAB left off, and including buildings constructed between 1714 and 1830. Twenty years later, the Victorian Society was founded and pushed the chronology closer to the present, looking to safeguard what they saw as architectural gems built between 1830 and 1914. Another twenty years later, the Twentieth Century Society picked up where the Victorian Society left off and lobbied for the protection of post-1914 buildings, including the 1951 Royal Festival Hall.

Following these guidebooks, I found myself immersed in a historical moment in time that came well after the founding of the Georgian Group but prior to the creation of the Victorian Society, when most agreed that the past ended, roughly speaking, in the 1850s. This conception of historical value led to Rutland

Terrace being chosen for my exit from Stamford. W. G. Hoskins was the author of both the opening essays in the volumes in the *About Britain* guide focused on the Midlands, and he articulated his dislike of industrial towns and cities in the middle of England, not only because they were industrial, but also because they had grown during the late nineteenth century – a period the authors dismissed. While he loved Stamford, Hoskins could not even bear to name those towns scattered across the East Midlands that had grown 'with increasing speed in late Victorian and Edwardian days, street after street of shiny new brick, with shiny new Welsh slates'. Far from being places to visit, Hoskins advised his readers, 'let us steer quietly away from any little boot-and-shoe town or hosiery town and leave it alone to its monumental Victorian dullness'.[36]

These guidebooks were themselves a product of history when it came to the way they approached the past. They weren't only interested in past history of course, they were also interested in Britain's present and future. Yet the distance between the past and present has shrunk dramatically since 1951 from a period of around a century to one of only thirty years. There was, in a sense, far more of the 'past' to see when I drove these routes than when they were first followed by motorists a lifetime earlier. But I wondered whether in this rush to expand and preserve the past, the present – and future – celebrated in 1951 had sometimes been lost sight of.

Southport–Tarleton–Much Hoole–Longton–Hutton–Preston–Samlesbury–Blackburn–Accrington–Burnley–Brierfield–Nelson–Colne–Cowling–Glusburn–Steeton–Keighley–Bingley–Shipley–Apperley Bridge–Calverley–Rodley–Leeds–Monk Fryston–Hambleton–Thorpe Willoughby–Selby–Barlby–Riccall–Escrick Park–Crockey Hill–York

9

Lancashire and Yorkshire

Southport–Glusburn–York (108 miles)

As the *About Britain* guides moved north, the country narrowed. The ninth volume covering Lancashire and Yorkshire was the first to introduce a region that, as Yorkshire-born author Leo Walmsley wrote in his opening portrait, was '"washed", as we used to say in our school geography lesson, by two seas'. The idea of travelling from coast to coast was one that appealed to Walmsley. 'Between and including these coasts' he claimed that Lancashire and Yorkshire afforded 'some of the loveliest natural scenery in Great Britain'. He explained to sceptical visitors that 'you could drive from one coast to another, say from the ancient red-roofed fishing port of Whitby to the very modern holiday resort of Morecambe, without seeing on your journey any "mechanical" industrial towns or areas: any coal mines, blast furnaces, mills.' On the next four pages, he painted a detailed picture of this imaginary journey from east to west 'over moors which in the summer are a sea of purple . . . whose only inhabitants are the black-faced sheep, the grouse and the curlew', 'through villages and quiet little market towns, almost every one with a parish church dating back at least from the fifteenth century', past 'ruined castles, and monasteries', through 'rich' farmland, with glimpses of trout-filled pools and 'tiny becks of clear sparkling water'. Making his point clear, he asserted that 'visually, at least, you have completed one authentic cross-section of the North Country without seeing a single manufacturing town, or coal-mine, or smelling any other smoke than the delicious one of peat and wood from farm or cottage fires'.[1]

Then came a 'but' as Walmsley imagined, but could not bring himself to describe, another coast-to-coast journey from Hull to Preston through Pontefract, Halifax, Burnley and Blackburn, exclaiming 'what a different picture you would get!'.[2] It was precisely that 'different picture' that those organizing the tour itineraries – in this case the geographer Norman Pye – were interested in introducing visitors to. Rather than taking roads further north as Walmsley did in his imaginary journey, thus avoiding the industrial towns and cities of eastern Lancashire and western Yorkshire, the guide sent motorists right through them. And so, leaving Southport, the strip map sent me towards the first of a string of what were then cotton and woollen towns: Preston, the place where I was born and grew up.

I followed the signs to Preston along Marine Drive. To my right lay more than a century of the accrued townscape of leisure: the Victorian South Marine Gardens and Marine Lake, what remained of the Edwardian 'Pleasureland' amusement park and the twenty-first century shops, chain restaurants and multiplex cinema of Ocean Plaza Retail and Leisure Park. To my left was marshland, sand and sea. I should perhaps have stopped to explore the beach given that the gazetteer at the back of *About Britain* rated the sands here as 'excellent'. This was a rare accolade given only to Southport and Clacton-on-Sea while H. G. Stokes saw that most places had merely 'good sands'. But it was not the sand but the sky that caught my attention on this summer morning. Walmsley commented on the flatness of Lancashire's coast in his introduction, and it was this that drew my gaze as I drove up the river.[3] With the land reduced to a flat plain, the sky looked huge and its dominance was magnified by the way the shadows of the clouds appeared projected onto the salt marshes. It seemed that the sky was literally everywhere as I drove from Marine Drive onto Water Lane running parallel with the tidal River Ribble.

Back in 1951, Southport was firmly in Lancashire, and therefore one of the three centres chosen for the guide. But as I'd found elsewhere, county boundaries have shifted and Lancashire lost almost two-fifths of its county following the 1972 Local Government Act. Parts of northern Lancashire became Cumbria and parts of the south – including Southport – were included in the two new metropolitan counties of Merseyside and Greater Manchester. These emerged from the 1969 Redcliffe-Maud Report that recommended making Birmingham, Liverpool and Manchester into distinct 'metropolitan areas'. It was a case of catching up with well over a century of growth in England's industrial cities. Over the next few years, and surviving a change in government from Labour to Conservative, the new metropolitan counties expanded to include West Yorkshire, South Yorkshire and Tyne and Wear.

The seemingly innocuous sign welcoming 'careful drivers' leaving Merseyside to Lancashire has been a source of conflict. In 2005, CountyWatch activists removed dozens of 'Welcome to Lancashire' signs from the borders of the smaller county and dumped them along the roadside close to the Boundary Mill factory outlet on the outskirts of Colne. One activist explained to the press that 'the sign says "Welcome to Lancashire", it doesn't say "Welcome to the administrative unit of Lancashire County Council" – that would be all right'. Drawing this distinction between the original county and the post-1974 administrative unit was important to the Friends of Real Lancashire, a pressure group founded a decade earlier. But CountyWatch were also clearly interested in other borders. They had the European

Union in their sights, articulating fears that it wasn't only historic counties that were threatened by bureaucrats and eurocrats, but also the nation state.[4] Road signs were a battleground in populist nationalism.

In 2014, the Conservative–Liberal Democrat coalition government offered the sign removers an olive branch by allowing councils and pressure groups to erect new signs marking 'traditional' county borders. In doing so, the government accepted the underlying Eurosceptic logic of CountyWatch. Announcing the decision symbolically on St George's Day in April 2014, Eric Pickles, Minister for Communities and Local Government, framed this as an act of English nationalism. 'The tapestry of England's counties', Pickles asserted, 'binds our nation together, and is interwoven with our cultural fabric – from our cricket to our ales.' He saw traditions to be under threat. 'Previous governments', he warned, 'have tried to wipe the counties off the map, imposing bland administrative structures or alien euro-regions.' Erecting signs marking traditional counties was represented not only as a strategy to 'free councils from Whitehall red tape' but also a way of turning back the clock to the more mythical English past stretching back to the Anglo-Saxons, which I'd found echoes of in some of the *About Britain* guides.[5]

I was welcomed not only into Lancashire but also into West Lancashire with the jaunty boast: 'We've got it all in West Lancashire'. West Lancashire had been created in the 1970s move to rationalize not simply counties, but also the administrative districts that lay beneath the county structure. The number of districts across the country were reduced from around 1,000 to 300, with four earlier districts now becoming West Lancashire. What West Lancashire meant when they claimed to have 'it all' wasn't entirely clear, but the first few miles certainly had plenty of farmland. Driving over the coastal plain, the farm stalls advertising new potatoes and nurseries selling summer bedding plants were evidence that this fertile landscape was dominated by market gardening.

My concerns began to focus on the more parochial question on all these journeys of where the original road lay in 1951. Just before Much Hoole, I spotted a turning to the left onto the Liverpool Old Road. Assuming this was the original route, I turned off and went through an avenue of horse-chestnut trees with candles of flower in full bloom before rounding a bend and finding myself back on the main road again. A few yards later, the Liverpool Old Road reappeared, this time heading off to my right for a short stretch, before wending its way left. This criss-crossing continued. Over the course of the twentieth century the original road was straightened out by a new road that curved, rather than twisted, across the coastal plain, before being superseded by the Longton By-Pass which not only ironed out the kinks resulting from centuries of patterns of land ownership, but went round smaller towns that might slow down the journey.[6]

Ignoring the bypass built in the late 1950s, I drove through Longton, passing rows of shops, the local supermarket chain Booths – the Waitrose of Lancashire – and Longton Hall, before reaching Hutton, where a faded warning sign told me to watch out for ducks crossing the road. There were more children than ducks, or at least the sound of boys enjoying a few minutes of freedom in the grounds of the grammar school that has been here since the mid eighteenth century. It changed from a selective grammar school to a comprehensive in the 1970s. When I rejoined the main road, I saw a boy in a school uniform riding towards me on the cycle path that runs alongside this stretch. In the late 1930s the Ministry of Transport insisted that local authorities include nine-foot-wide cycleways on each side of planned roads.[7] Separate cycle paths for Hutton Grammar School boys were intentionally integrated into the bypass design implemented two decades later.

A little further on I slowed down as two lanes became one. There were roadworks due to the construction of a new Penwortham Bypass to improve 'access between local and motorway networks' in this area where thousands of new homes were being built for commuters who wished to skirt, rather than drive through, any towns that stood between them and the M6.[8] But this morning it wasn't only the traffic lights in Penwortham that slowed my progress. As I crested the hill and went down into Preston, I braked behind a hearse and the procession of cars following. The hearse was going at the customary 20 mph. I was on a dual carriageway and etiquette suggested it could be overtaken respectfully, but no one else passed and I didn't want to be the first person to do so. I was saved from my dilemma by the turn-off to Preston and drove parallel to the former port.

Preston was described in the guide as 'the lowest bridging point of the Ribble, an inland port and the administrative centre for the county of Lancaster'.[9] Although it is still an administrative centre, the port now lies off to the left where overgrown rails snaked beneath the fence and continued into the rewilded space of post-industrial edgelands. In 1951 things were very different. When it opened in the 1890s, Preston's Albert Edward was the largest single dock in Europe with a basin stretching 3,000 feet long and 600 feet wide. The first ship to unload here was chartered by the Preston-based grocer E. H. Booth. But the port's prime trade was not in foodstuffs but cotton, and when motorists drove to Preston on the *About Britain* tours the port was still in business.

In the post-war years, Preston saw the emergence of commercial roll-on/roll-off ferry services. Like the repurposing of military transport planes laden with the cars of upper-middle-class motorists to France from Kent that I'd seen on an earlier journey, the Atlantic Steam Navigation Company used military ships to carry cars and lorries. In 1948 the SS *Empire Cedric* began a twice-weekly commercial service between Preston and Larne in Northern Ireland, taking lorries laden with raw materials and finished goods. During the late 1940s and into the early 1950s the company ran four ferries between Preston and Larne, as well as three on the southern route between Tilbury and Antwerp. Throughout the 1960s it was Preston, rather than Tilbury, that was the most important hub for ferry traffic, with up to 1.5 million tonnes of goods passing through the docks each year.

From this high point the docks entered into rapid decline. The development of Britain's road network was part of the story. Motorways meant that it became quicker and cheaper to move goods on land. But in the case of Preston, the inland docks, which were 20 miles from the open sea, could also no longer cope with larger ships, nor the costs of dredging the channel. In 1981 the final ship – appropriately perhaps, a dredger – left the port. In the mid-1980s, the port was renamed and reimagined as 'Riversway', which is now home to a marina, blocks of ubiquitous waterside apartments, as well as the familiar out-of-town landscape of car showrooms, call centres, office buildings, supermarkets, multiplex cinemas and chain restaurants. In turn, the reimagining of the former port also provided the stimulus for rebuilding the pre-motorway networks of canal and rail, although this time for leisure rather than trade.

In 2002, a new canal was opened here. Connecting the Lancaster Canal via the rivers Ribble and Douglas with the Leeds and Liverpool Canal, the Millennium Ribble Link was the first new stretch of canal built since the Manchester Ship Canal in the nineteenth century. As well as linking up the landlocked Lancaster Canal, its towpath forms a 'linear water park'. Then there was a revival of rail. In 2005, the Ribble Steam Railway and Museum opened up a new station – Preston Riverside – to service steam trains running along the former docks. Canals and railways have been repurposed here, like elsewhere, as a kind of nostalgic slow leisure travel. But the business of fast land travel takes place on trunk roads and motorways, which are more about the efficiency of getting there as quickly as possible.

I left Riversway and made my way through the city centre. I caught a glimpse of the infamous late-1960s brutalist concrete of Preston Bus Station. It was a building of a particular moment not only architecturally, but also conceptually, given that it celebrated the road as the pre-eminent transport network. When it was built, it was the largest bus station in Europe. On the ground floor was room for 40 double-decker buses. Above that were row upon row of parking spaces, spread over five floors, where my dad would park the car if we came into the town at the weekend. Its vast size came at a moment when travel by road – whether by bus or car – was imagined as the only way of moving around with little thought given to the train, let alone the canal boat.

The building of the bus station spoke of an optimistic vision for this town, which was slated for dramatic population growth. However, that growth was never realized. Instead, like the other cotton towns that I passed through later on that day, Preston suffered from the collapse of the domestic cotton industry and the 1970s and 1980s were decades of decline. Yet it was not all bad – in the 1990s and 2000s it bucked the trend of other Lancashire cotton towns and had the third highest growth in private-sector jobs of any English town or city. During this period Preston also gained coveted 'city' status when it became England's fiftieth city, winning a hard-fought competition with more than 20 towns, including its near-neighbour and bitter rival, Blackburn. In this mood of buoyancy, the centre of this city was reimagined as somewhere to attract all those private-sector wage-earners to come to live and spend their money. Thirty-two acres of the eastern part of the city centre were slated for redevelopment as part of the £700 million Tithebarn project. In the words of one of the developers, this was 'not just about shopping – it is to deliver wholesale City Centre regeneration, offering a more cosmopolitan city-based working and living culture . . . creating a destination for living, working and recreation.'[10] This rebuilding of Preston's city centre had no place for the largest bus station in Europe, which was to be demolished to make way for a mall that would be accessed on foot or by private car.

Yet, driving through Preston on a grey Monday morning, it was clear that the bus station was still there and the promised Tithebarn was not. This was largely due to the wrangling that delayed this ambitious redevelopment project. Opposition to the scheme came from the neighbouring towns of Blackpool to the west and Blackburn to the east. Both feared that building a massive mall in Preston would destroy their already struggling commercial centres. Their concerns were serious enough to lead to a public inquiry into the proposed development. By the time that planning permission was finally approved, the economic situation had changed for the worse. Ultimately it was not the fears of their neighbours that put an end to Preston's ambitions, but the 2008 global financial crisis. In its aftermath, one of the two developers pulled out and John Lewis announced that they were withdrawing. With its anchor department store gone, the whole scheme collapsed.[11]

In the wake of the 2008 global financial crisis Preston was forced to look for alternative, and more home-grown, solutions. It has become known for experiments with economic localism dubbed 'the Preston model'. Rather than looking to investment from developers the council has focused attention closer to home. In 2013, a group of institutions in the city – Lancashire County Council, the University of Central Lancashire, Lancashire Constabulary among others – drawing on the 2012 Social Value Act, which determined that tendering could focus on things other than simply cost, decided to spend more in the city region. Within four years, the amount spent on businesses in Preston had tripled and the sum spent in Lancashire had doubled. This experiment in community wealth-building drew on earlier experiments in another post-industrial city – Cleveland, Ohio – and stimulated attempts at re-energizing local economies elsewhere in Britain.[12]

While the bus station was spared by the collapse of the Tithebarn redevelopment, it was only a temporary reprieve. New plans for its demolition were now being driven by a cash-strapped council that wanted to replace it with a more modest bus station that was cheaper to run. As had been the case earlier, plans to level a building that was seen as iconic beyond Preston met with more than local opposition. The Twentieth Century Society lent their support to the campaign. As a result Preston Bus Station was listed as 'a remarkably good example of integrated 1960s traffic planning'. No longer able to demolish it, Preston Council offloaded this dubious asset, and 'sold' the building to Lancashire County Council for a pound, who set about restoring it to its former glory.[13] As I drove by the freshly painted concrete fins on the multistorey car park gleamed proudly amid the surrounding muted greys of generic city-centre buildings.

Although they had invested in restoring the bus station, it was clear that all was not well with Lancashire County Council in post-2008 austerity Britain. I passed the Museum of Lancashire, housed in the building I'd visited on a primary school trip to the Lancashire Regimental Museum. I wanted to take a look at what story of Lancashire this museum told, but it had closed to the public in 2015 as the county council sought to cut costs to balance the budget. This was only the first of a number of museums I passed in Lancashire that were closed because of cost-cutting.

Preston is where I grew up and so should be a place that I know well. Despite this I found myself driving south out of Preston rather than east. Crossing the Ribble, I realized my error. I could simply have taken the M65 motorway signposted to Blackburn but I didn't want to miss Samlesbury Hall, which had earned a lengthy paragraph alongside the strip map. So, at Walton-le-Dale I followed the lovely road perched on the river cliff above the Ribble that I knew would reconnect with the main road at Samlesbury.

Before reaching the village, I crossed over the M6 motorway on a minor road that ran through farmland. The bridge had been built to ensure that there was no interference with the smooth and rapid movement of a steady stream of cars and lorries passing at 70 mph underneath in a new era of fast travel. When Prime Minister Harold Macmillan opened the Preston Bypass in 1958, he unveiled the first eight and a quarter miles of a planned network of more than 1,000 miles of motorway criss-crossing Britain. Plans for the motorways had emerged in the late 1930s, but were delayed, first by the war and then the post-war economic situation; it was only in the mid-1950s that major investment in building these became possible.

Just after crossing over the motorway I drove through Samlesbury and joined the road that I should have left Preston on. My eyes were drawn to two large restaurants built along the main road. The first, Bukhara, offered two floors of Indian and Pakistani dining. Just a little further along was Mezzo, equally spacious with two levels of Italian eating and drinking. This was something I had seen elsewhere on other routes: large roadside restaurants seemingly in the middle of nowhere. But they were also restaurants in the middle of somewhere: halfway between Preston and Blackburn, along this transport corridor, with large car parks that were empty when I passed in the middle of a weekday, but they were no doubt packed on Friday and Saturday nights.

These restaurants build on a longer history of roadside eateries. Bukhara occupies a building that was previously a Little Chef that opened in the early 1970s. The first Little

Chef – transplanting roadside diner-culture from America to Britain – was a modest, caravan-like offering with seating for just eleven, located along the Oxford Road on the edge of Reading in 1958. During the 1960s and 1970s the number – and size – of restaurants grew. By the mid-1970s, when the restaurant opened here, there were 150 Little Chefs along Britain's main roads. The company rapidly expanded to 300 restaurants by the end of the 1980s and over 400 by the end of the 1990s, making Little Chef the largest restaurant chain in the country.[14]

However, these restaurants – like the one in Samlesbury – were increasingly located on the wrong roads. Long distance journeys had switched from A-roads to the growing motorway network. To try to keep up with these changes, Little Chef began opening outlets at motorway service areas or closer to the motorway network. The Little Chef in Samlesbury closed in 2001 and relocated to the junction of the nearby and recently completed M65. After a string of new owners and initiatives aimed at rebranding – including a made-for-television makeover of the Popham restaurant by the chef Heston Blumenthal – Little Chef was sold to Euro Garages in 2017. They turned the remaining sites into Starbucks coffee or Greggs' bakery franchises catering for on-the-go snacks, rather than to diners sitting down for my childhood favourite of a plate of pancakes with cherry sauce. This change also brought with it the importing of the American 'drive-thru' that I'd already seen on urban edges. The first was opened by McDonald's in south Manchester in the mid-1980s, a decade after the chain opened its first restaurant in Britain in Woolwich. Since then, McDonald's has 1,300 restaurants, with over half of these Drive-thrus.[15] Indeed, McDonald's growth was, in part, responsible for Little Chef's decline as roadside eating shifted from drive-bys to drive-thrus.

But rather than a drive-by or drive-thru, it seems that Bukhara is something of a drive-to. Writing in the 'Road Hog' column that flagged decent places to eat close to main roads, the *Sunday Times*'s restaurant critic Hilary Armstrong picked Bukhara out as a place where 'an impromptu detour will enliven a dull day on the M6 with a feast of whole stuffed sea bass (£40), boned chicken (£30), or a leg of lamb (£50) to feed a (hungry) party of four.' But, as well as the hungry family of four making a detour off the motorway, the car park serves motoring diners who are happy to drive sometimes considerable distances for the northern Indian cuisine. Most come from neighbouring Preston and Blackburn, but according to Armstrong the food 'is so good some of its regulars think nothing of driving 30 miles from Manchester to pick up a takeaway' and that 'other diners have been known to travel from as far afield as Leicester – about 130 miles'.[16] Bukhara is a destination restaurant in a way that the Salmesbury Little Chef never was.

Destination dining was intimately linked with the early years of motoring, the most striking example being the *Michelin Guide*. First published in France in 1900, these guides began starring notable restaurants in the 1920s and added the now familiar hierarchy of one, two and three stars in the 1930s. According to the *Michelin Guide*, a two-starred restaurant was 'worth a detour' and a three-starred restaurant was 'worth a special journey'. The interests of the publishers – a tyre manufacturer – were clear. Michelin wanted motorists to drive further for leisure so that they had to change their tyres more frequently; one way to do this was by encouraging them to make journeys to historic sites and restaurants across rural France. Michelin were not alone in seeing the value of publishing guides. Dunlop, another tyre manufacturer, also sold guidebooks to British motorists that aimed to increase the use of cars as leisure vehicles.

Just after passing the Bukhara restaurant, I left the road and drove along the tree-lined drive that led down to Samlesbury

Hall. My window was down, so I was greeted by the pungent smell of the wild garlic that carpeted the ground beneath the avenue of beech trees. There were two large car parks, but in the middle of a weekday I easily found a space and got out to explore a 'lovely example of 14th century and Tudor domestic architecture'. This was, as the guide explained, the higher of two halls. The one lower down, close to the riverbank, 'was destroyed by the Scots after Bannockburn' and was reduced to a 'ruin'.[17] The surviving hall was threatened with demolition in the 1920s to make way for new housing but rescued by a trust that has run the hall ever since.

It was now a visitor attraction and wedding venue. Signs were tacked on trees and benches with a warning: 'Hello visitors. No picknicking please! We are a registered charity and charge no entry or parking fees, instead we rely on income from our fabulous restaurant and wafflery.' Just as the Brewers' Society was keen to send people about for a day's motoring knowing they would need to stop somewhere to eat and drink, Samlesbury Hall welcomes day trippers banking on the fact that at some point they will become hungry and thirsty and make use of these amenities.

Samlesbury Hall also caters to wedding parties like so many of the former stately homes. Entering into the black-and-white timber hall, a framed certificate by the entrance informed me that Samlesbury Hall was 'approved by Lancashire County Council' for the 'solemnization of marriages . . . and the formation of civil partnerships'. On the welcome desk, a large sign urged me to vote for the Hall, which had made it to the Final Three of the Great Northern Wedding Awards 2019 in the 'Best Heritage/ Historical Wedding Venue' category. It turned out that there are plenty of sub-categories within the term Wedding Venue: Barn/Farm, Boutique/Intimate, By the Water, Country House, Countryside, Creative Space, Hotel, Hotel and Spa, Town or

City as well as the Heritage/Historical sub-category which Samlesbury Hall had been shortlisted for. Inside, rooms were dressed for marriages, civil ceremonies and post-ceremony dining. Across the lawn, a marquee stood looking forlorn with the remnants of the last wedding held there. Chalked up on boards was the order of ceremony and where to sit at tables named after the many houses and streets where the groom had lived.

I surreptitiously ate a few crisps in the car, hoping this did not constitute a picnic, before driving past the bees, chickens, shepherds' huts, miniature golf and Bluebird golf course that all ensure a longer dwell-time and therefore the purchasing of more food and drink. After reaching the second and larger car park, passing the nursery and shop, I continued on to Blackburn. It was another lovely stretch of road, that gently twisted and turned, dropping up and down through an undulating landscape of farmland and woods blanketed with bluebells. Once I reached Blackburn, I drove through the 'good suburbs' that the guidebook offered up at the western entrance to this cotton town. As was the case with Leicester on my previous journey, the prevailing wind blew smoke from the mill chimneys from west to east, identifying the western suburbs as the 'posh end'. I descended into Blackburn past large, Victorian villas and the grand entrance gates to the Corporation Park and onto the inner ring road before taking the Accrington Road further east underneath the M65 motorway.

The M65 was built two decades after the Preston Bypass as part of an investment in infrastructure in the 1980s and 1990s in an attempt to kickstart this post-industrial region. It connected this string of Lancashire cotton towns – Blackburn, Accrington, Burnley, Nelson – that motorists were directed through in 1951. Although all shared a single industry, they had distinct specialities. As Walmsley explained to the uninitiated in his opening essay, Preston specialized 'in shirting and high quality cloths; Blackburn and Accrington in cheap thin cloth for India and China and tropical Africa; Burnley in narrow lengths for printing; Nelson and Colne in various sorts of patterned cloth, and fancy fabrics such as satin, poplin and brocade.' He emphasized that 'employment *is* good in the cotton mills today' but he was aware this had not been the case 20 years earlier when the 1930s trade slump coincided with the rise of competitors – especially the Japanese, and later the Indian, cotton industry – the Indian boycott and the introduction of tariff barriers. However, he was relatively optimistic about the immediate future, suggesting that 'Hitler's war brought life to the mills again with an insatiable demand for cotton fabrics for military use' and in the post-war years the cotton industry was 'regaining the old markets against fierce competition'. He was half right. The end of the Second World War did see a short-lived revival in the British textile industry, with around a million workers employed in this sector: most of them in Lancashire and Yorkshire.[18] But the resurgence prompted by the manufacture of wartime uniforms proved to be a temporary blip in the story of decline.

The post-war downturn was most marked in those towns – like Blackburn – producing lower quality cloth. There were already hints of this when motorists armed with their *About Britain* guide drove through. In September 1951 there was an extended shutdown in some of Blackburn's mills because of the declining market. The following year saw further periods of extended closure, and over the course of the 1950s, two-fifths of Blackburn's mills closed. In 1958 the unimaginable happened as Britain imported more cotton goods than it exported. There was an attempt to manage decline and kickstart a new modern industry through the 1959 Cotton Industry Act, which paid out for redundancies on the one hand and invested in a new wave of mechanization on the other. The response to the decline of King Cotton was a shift to new 'man-made' fibres and fabrics. As motorists drove through Blackburn in 1951, the Ealing comedy *The Man in the White Suit* was playing to cinema audiences. It told the story of a young chemist, Sidney Stratton, who succeeded in inventing a miracle fibre that offered the promise of clothes that will never wear out. It was very much a film of its time: a time when it seemed that the future of the British textile industry lay in the hands of chemists such as those working at ICI who developed Terylene.[19]

Another artificial fibre, rayon, first developed by Courtaulds from wood pulp, was being spun and woven in Blackburn. In the *About Britain* guide Blackburn was described as a 'cotton town formerly engaged almost exclusively in making cheap Indian garments but now making a wider range of goods, including rayon'. As rayon began to replace cotton in Blackburn, the workforce changed. The new 'more capital-intensive' textile industry manufacturing artificial fibres 'required . . . continuous operation' and so new ways of working, with low-paid, unskilled, shift-working became the norm. These jobs were unpopular, especially those requiring night shifts spent in hot mills, and so during the 1960s and 1970s men from post-independence Pakistan and India were recruited to work in Blackburn and elsewhere in Lancashire and Yorkshire. As I drove around the hills on the east of Blackburn in search of the road to Accrington, I could see the minarets of mosques alongside the few remaining mill chimneys in a town where a quarter of the population identify themselves as either Asian, British Indian or Pakistani.[20]

As well as shifting to rayon, Blackburn was the birthplace of the new fibres and fabrics of Netlon and Tensar. Both were developed by the Mercer family business based at Pioneer Mill, Blackburn. In the late 1950s, the company developed Netlon, making plastic netting from polymer. As well as being produced by the company in Blackburn, it was also made globally under licence and was used for, among other things, the mesh netting that fruit and vegetables were packaged in as greengrocers were replaced by supermarkets. In the 1980s, Mercer developed a new high-strength, polymer mesh – Tensar – that became a staple in the construction industry. It was particularly important in road-building schemes, where it was used to hold up embankments. This new product demanded new premises and production moved to a new industrial estate on the south-east edge of Blackburn. The old mills in the centre of the town closed down and the manufacturing that remains has clustered in industrial estates located by the motorway network.[21]

Although some new industries grew out of the ashes of the old, the decline of the cotton industry hit east Lancashire hard. This was the case at both ends of the M65 – Blackburn and Burnley – where more than a third of the workforce had been employed in the textile industry at the beginning of the twentieth century. As cotton manufacturing declined, so did the population. This was less marked at the western end of the M65. The population of Blackburn and its neighbour Darwen peaked at just over 180,000 in 1911, falling to just over 150,000 in 1951, shrinking further in the post-war decades before returning to its 1951 levels in 2011. But, at the eastern end of the M65 in Burnley, the decline in population over the last 70 years has been more marked. Changes in borough boundaries make it hard to measure like with like, so comparing census data gets tricky. However, I visited a town that has almost halved in size since 1951.

The picture of dramatic population decline in Burnley is the opposite of a place like Banbury or Cambridge, which have grown so dramatically since 1951. They represent in miniature the broader shift in population at a national scale across the last 70 years or so, as population has moved from the north to the south-east in post-industrial, service-sector Britain. The decline in population in Burnley was so dramatic that by 2013 an anonymous article in the *Economist* called for 'decaying towns' like Burnley to simply be abandoned, rather than the state continuing to invest in their future, echoing earlier suggestions over what to do with post-industrial Merthyr Tydfil. As can be imagined, this provocation met with considerable pushback. Just as in Preston, Burnley has focused on economic localism in the shape of the 'Burnley Bondholders' scheme.[22] This town has not simply been left to die.

Coming into Burnley a sign announced that far from being abandoned Burnley was 'Open for business' and a 'Top 16 UK tech town'. This claim followed the publishing of the 2018 Tech Nation report that flagged Burnley as one of a handful of British towns with a higher than average number of digital businesses. The only one in Lancashire, Burnley came fourth after towns such as Newbury, Reading and Basingstoke. The 'narrow lengths' of cotton for 'printing' that Walmsley identified as Burnley's manufacturing strength in 1951 have been replaced by 3D printing as a new 'swarm' of high-tech businesses build everything from sound desks for music and film production to making parts for the aerospace, automotive and medical industries.[23]

But driving through its cotton past was more immediately visible than its high-tech present. Plenty of mill chimneys were still there. One was being offered for redevelopment. Others were signposted with brown and yellow signs that spoke of new futures as tourist destinations and housing developments respectively. Although still signposted from the main road, Barden Mill had closed as a factory shop, and the museum at Queen Street Mill had gone the way of other Lancashire museums; closed to the public because of funding cuts. But the future is not necessarily gloomy since its status as the 'last surviving steam-powered weaving mill in the world' has piqued the attention of national heritage bodies.[24]

It was far easier to drive through the town centre in Burnley than Blackburn, and I made my way along the main street past the Burnley Mechanics theatre, the bus station and then out along the Colne Road where the halal butchers advertised spring lamb. With views over the moors to the left, I passed the Prairie Sports Village where one of the teams playing football were kitted out in the claret and blue of Burnley Football Club. In some ways, the changing fortunes of Burnley FC reflect those of this recently reborn town. During the 1980s the club fell through the lower divisions of the Football League and came one game away from crashing out altogether. By the 2000s however, their fortunes had changed and in 2009 they made it into the Premier League.

Making my way towards Nelson and then on to Colne, I passed terraced streets that sloped off, often steeply, to the left or right, at regular intervals. The main road was lined with shops that included a mix of Polish groceries and halal butchers doing a brisk, mid-afternoon business. At Colne, the *About Britain* route map directed me towards Keighley, but I was distracted by the brown sign pointing to the Boundary Mill Stores. Founded in the early 1980s, this was one of the first factory outlets in Britain. Like the Mercer family, the Bannisters who owned Boundary Mill successfully made the move from cotton weaving. However, rather than manufacturing new fabrics, they transformed their mill into what became the first of a network of so-called 'factory stores'.

As elsewhere, former industrial premises – mills in particular – were repurposed as shopping centres, during a decade when shopping became a leading leisure activity, focused in particular on out-of-town destinations. Not wanting to miss out, I parked up and headed inside. Past racks of clothes on the ground floor, I went to the first floor, which smelled strongly of scented candles, in search of homewares. A few minutes later, I left clutching a newly purchased frying pan via the large, slowly revolving doors where a woman told me that she hoped to make it home before it started to rain because she had left the washing out. The sky was darkening but I reassured her that I thought she'd make it back in time. But I was proved wrong. Just as we left the revolving doors, a few large drops of rain quickly turned to a torrential shower that sent her scurrying one way and me the other across the huge car park.

I got caught in traffic on the way out of Colne through the pouring rain and crawled along towards Keighley. Here the *About Britain* guide explained that 'the mills of the cotton industry are left behind' and 'the A6068 follows the valley of the Colne Water to the moors'. I could see the moors off to my right and after Laneshawbridge I entered them proper. It was a jarringly different landscape from both the salt marshes of the coastal plain in West Lancashire and the string of former mill towns that I'd just about managed to navigate my way through. It was a landscape of greens fading to browns, as grass gave way to bracken. Here, in the hilly spine of northern England, I left Lancashire and entered North Yorkshire through scattered sheep farms and smart, stone-clad, barn conversions. Going through Cowling, the stuff that the houses were built from changed so visibly from red brick to pale stone. I had returned to agricultural land once more, and followed a tractor pulling a trailer stacked high with bales of straw, which brushed a confetti of cherry blossom down onto my car.

But I was soon back into a mill town. Entering Glusburn, I saw a mill chimney off to the right. When motorists were sent across Lancashire and Yorkshire, this point on the journey was flagged up as significant, since it was here that the mill owned by 'Hayfield Knitting Wools at Glusburn provides the first evidence of the shift of interest from cotton to wool'. However, as Walmsley was well aware, this momentous shift in industries was not immediately apparent to the outsider. 'There is, to the casual observer', he wrote, 'very little to distinguish the cotton towns from the woollen ones. They are nearly all situated in the river or stream valleys, with the mills of the "coal" age, independent of water power, built higher up and even on the top of the hills. A cotton mill looks very much like a woollen mill.' But while all mills might look alike, this journey across country was designed to take motorists from the world of cotton to the world of wool. It was the moorlands that I had just driven through that marked the divide.

Answering his own question, 'Why then these great, and in many senses rival, industries divided east and west of the Pennines, to make Manchester the "capital" of cotton, Leeds and Bradford "capitals" of wool?', Walmsley pointed out that 'the answer is that there is the physical barrier of the hills themselves, depriving Yorkshire of quick and consequently cheap communication with the Lancashire coast and the Atlantic sea-board' as well as the clouds that dumped rain on the west coast and offered humidity that 'favoured the spinning and weaving of the more brittle cotton' thread.[25] However, passing the first woollen mill along this journey from 1951, it became clear that wool was no longer being spun or woven here. Like the cotton industry to the west, the woollen industry had also declined. Most woollen mills had closed or been repurposed like their cotton counterparts. In some cases, new industries have taken over. In the mid-1990s the mill in Glusburn stopped working with wool and began manufacturing car parts.

From Glusburn, I drove along a stretch that clung high to the ridge line, passing swathes of bluebells in Hawcliffe Woods amid the vibrant green of new-growth beech. On through Utley, I passed Keighley Cricket Club, skirted the town, and entered Bingley past a mill chimney with the word DAMART spelled out in capitals up its length, which has been home to this mail-order catalogue company since the late 1960s. In the *About Britain* guide, Bingley was described as a 'typical Yorkshire industrial town: textile machinery, cotton and woollen manufactures'. In the 1970s and 1980s it became better known for the set of Bingley Rise Five lock gates on the canal. I saw them signposted by yet another brown tourist sign, but there was no mention made of the lock gates in my guidebook and so I kept going towards Leeds. In 1951, canals were very much seen as transport technology of the past, rather than the present or future.

Another omission came a short way along the road in Saltaire. Not only did Saltaire not make it into the *About Britain* gazetteer or warrant a sentence alongside the strip map, it didn't even make it onto the map. In 1853, Titus Salt built the largest factory in the world at the time, one that combined all processes from spinning raw wool through dyeing and weaving to produce a mile of cloth each day in one vast mill.[26] He surrounded it with rows of 800 Italianate stone-terraced houses for his workers on streets that he named after family members, in a town he named after himself.

As was the case with so many other cotton and woollen mills, Salt's Mill closed in the mid-1980s. Rather than being demolished, its renaissance came at the hands of entrepreneur Jonathan Silver who had bought, regenerated and then sold on another former mill in Halifax a few years earlier. In the 1980s, mills were going cheap and Salt's Mill cost him less than £1 million. He quickly set about regenerating and reinventing part of it as a gallery showcasing the work of his friend, the Bradford-born artist David Hockney. Alongside displaying the largest collection of Hockney's art anywhere in the world, the huge mill was repurposed bit by bit, partly as a new workspace for 1,000 employees – hosting companies that make everything from television top boxes to software – and partly as a leisure space that combined theatre, shops and restaurants visited by hundreds of thousands each year.

While those in the Festival of Britain office had no interest in Saltaire in 1951, by the mid-to-late-1990s it was the fastest-growing tourist destination in post-industrial Yorkshire. It attracted over 750,000 visitors a year and became a UNESCO World Heritage Site in 2010, because the 'layout and architecture of Saltaire admirably reflect mid-nineteenth century philanthropic paternalism, as well as the important role played by the textile industry in economic and social development'.[27] At the turn-off to Shipley, I passed the stone marking the entry of Saltaire into the UNESCO World Heritage Site register – it looked somewhat out of place in the middle of the pavement at this busy road junction of shop-lined streets.

The transformation of Saltaire is one example of what the director of the Victoria and Albert Museum, Tristram Hunt, describes as the process of creating 'manufactories of culture' out of former industrial sites. But the transformation of Saltaire has been driven not only by cultural policy focused on the mill, but also by transport policy focused on the surrounding model village. Prior to Silver's purchase of the derelict mill, things had already begun to change in Saltaire. In the mid-1980s, the Saltaire Village Society was formed to fight plans to build a stretch of the planned Bingley Relief Road through Robert's Park, created by Titus Salt across the River Aire from his mill. Saltaire had been designated a Conservation Area in 1971, but opponents to the proposed road sought a more robust designation to safeguard the park and village. They succeeded in gaining listed building status for all the buildings in this former model village. The defeat of plans to build a road through Saltaire in the mid-1980s coincided with the reopening of the railway station that connected commuters living in this gentrified dormitory village with Leeds, where I was headed next.[28]

Stopping for petrol as I entered Claverley, I watched the long line of commuters leaving Leeds on the opposite side of the road. Beyond Bramley I got my first glimpse of Leeds city centre down below in the middle distance. The skyline was framed by the tall buildings in the city centre; cranes that towered above these were building yet more. Passing Kirkstall Abbey among the trees, I crossed over the Leeds and Liverpool Canal and River Aire and headed into the city past ITV's *Emmerdale* studios. First shown on British television in October 1972 as *Emmerdale Farm*, the show was renamed *Emmerdale* in 1989 as the original farming family were increasingly replaced by wealthy, non-farming incomers to the fictional village. This long-running show is still filmed at the studios on the Kirkstall Road that I drove past. Round the corner, fans can immerse themselves in the '*Emmerdale* Studio experience' in this city that lies at the heart of Screen Yorkshire, one of the fastest-growing and most important centres of television and film production in the country. In Leeds, as in Manchester, the former regional capitals of textile industries have been reborn as the heart of creative industry. This has led to the suggestion that the binary 'north–south' division in Britain is more complex and there are just as many divisions within the 'north'.[29]

Leaving Leeds, I looked out for what the guide described as the 'city's large blocks of flats built to rehouse people affected by slum clearance'. Following the 1930 Housing Act, local authorities were empowered to clear slums and rehouse those affected in council housing. After the Second World War, the pace of slum clearance quickened. Between 1955 and 1974, over a million houses were demolished and over 3 million people moved into new housing. One in seven of the houses that stood in large cities in England and Wales in the 1950s had been demolished by the mid-1980s.[30] But I was not sure which of the post-war housing I passed was highlighted by the guide and so I kept going, over the M1, towards Selby.

Driving through Garforth, I saw some yellow-painted children's bikes hanging up at the side of the road, along with some yellow and blue bunting, but thought little of it. Then climbing up out of Garforth there were expansive views of wind turbines to the left beyond a field of oil-seed rape in full flowering vivid yellow that I could smell as well as see, and to the right a power station in the distance as the land flattened out. The closer I got to Selby, it seemed, the more yellow and blue flags and bunting I saw. It was only then that I realized that the road I was on would be closed the next day for the first stage of the Tour de Yorkshire. I'd made it just in time.

The first Tour de Yorkshire took place in 2015. It followed the decision to begin the first stage of the 2014 Tour de France, the *grand depart*, in Leeds rather than in France. The race traversed Yorkshire for two days, before the peloton took to the roads of France. Originally started by the French newspaper *L'Auto* in 1903, the Tour de France is intimately linked to the French countryside. It connects the different *départements* in a performance of national identity through cycling. The inclusion of Yorkshire on the Tour route therefore appears rather strange. In the same year that Eric Pickles was permitting councils to erect historic county boundary signs the expansion of the Tour could be read as a counterpunch in the battle over Britain's European identity. But this export was also about the global business of sport. Owned by the French media company EPA, the Tour de France and its offshoot Tour de Yorkshire are global brands.

The arrival of professional cyclists was still a day away, so the only thing halting my progress was a passing train that I stopped for at a railway crossing. The land around was pancake flat, with the only verticals the lines of trees forming windbreaks. Entering Selby, I saw police bollards readied for the road closure the next day. Yellow and blue bunting and tiny jerseys knitted in a range of colours bedecked railings including those around the beautiful abbey at the end of the high street. Crews were constructing a grandstand and setting up TV cameras in front of the finish line by the abbey. After crossing the former toll bridge over the River Ouse I walked over to see what the guidebook said was 'Selby's greatest feature'. The vast church would look impressive anywhere, but perhaps particularly here incongruously placed at the end of a very ordinary looking high street.

Leaving Selby, I passed mills for flour and animal feed on the edge of town – the riverside 'silos and other buildings of large oil-seed crushing mills' referenced by the *About Britain* gazetteer – before driving through flat land, where raised banks guarded the river to the left.[31] After Barlby I passed a sign advertising a new egg-vending machine and, at Crockey Hill, a roadside farm shop. I was reminded of the landscape of market gardening that I'd driven through that morning. But the chimneys and cooling towers of the power stations I had seen a little earlier, and a sign pointing off to the North Selby Mine, indicated that there was more to this land than met the eye. Now being reimagined as a potential glamping site, North Selby Mine marked the northernmost edge of a coalfield that opened in 1991.[32] The Selby coalfield formed the centrepiece of expansion of the coal industry in the early 1970s, framed around the Labour government's 1974 'Plan for Coal' that came at the time of the oil crisis. Mining got underway in the 1980s, and by the early 1990s 10 million tons of coal were being extracted each year to service the needs of the power stations built in the Aire valley. However, by the early 2000s, this now privatized coalfield was being closed down. Mining stopped in 2004.

I pressed on towards York, stopping only when a young deer ran into and then off the road before darting through the hedge. The road bisected the attractive market town of Fulford, before depositing me on the outskirts of York. I first saw the tower of York Minister, then Clifford's Tower, and finally the remains of the city walls reflecting the light of the setting sun. I had not quite made it to the east coast. The sea lay some distance away, but in Selby I had come close to the estuarial River Humber. While I hadn't made it to Bridlington, this final stretch of the journey had felt like a mirror image of the agricultural coastal plain where I had started off that morning over on the west coast. Walmsley may not have approved of the more industrial route that the guidebook had sent me on through the mill towns of Lancashire and Yorkshire, but he would no doubt have been glad to see me travel from marshland through moorland and then back to marshland again across the spine of northern England.

Driving through the string of former mill towns along this route that rose up through the Pennines, it was clear that Britain is now predominantly a post-industrial economy. The change in the nature of employment is one of the most significant differences that has taken place over the human lifespan. The year 1950 was the zenith of industrial manufacturing. It was when the highest percentage of the population was engaged in industrial occupations. In the early 1950s, over half of the British workforce were employed in industrial manufacturing; 50 years later this had dropped to just over one in ten.[33] This dramatic shift in the jobs that Britons do was nowhere more marked than in these towns in east Lancashire where the cotton industry had more or less disappeared. In Blackburn, there were 100 mills in the industry's heyday. By the early 1990s, the number of working mills could be counted on the fingers of one hand.

One result of this deindustrialization is the movement of wealth and people. The second half of the nineteenth century was a boom period in the cotton and woollen industries in Lancashire and Yorkshire, just as it was for coal in South Wales. The grand municipal buildings in the towns along the way spoke of not only pride but also money. But with the decline of these dominant industries, the towns hit hard times, and in the case of Burnley the result was depopulation on a scale like Merthyr Tydfil in the wake of the collapse of the iron industry. Merthyr, Coventry, Burnley were all places that had seen once-dominant industries rise and fall, and the later years were marked by attempts to prevent them remaining 'ghost towns'. Driving through Burnley, which was in the early stages of rebuilding around high-tech manufacturing, things looked very different than in Banbury. In the south, the post-war years had seen a massive population rise rather than depopulation. Banbury was fuelled by the growth of food manufacturing, as well as its emergence as a commuter town node on the motorway network. I'd seen evidence of rapid population growth elsewhere in southern England too, most visibly among the science parks of Cambridgeshire.

As historians suggest, the so-called 'North–South divide' could begin to be seen as early as the mid nineteenth century, if not before.[34] Yet driving through Leeds it was clear that the divide is more complex than the cliché. Wealth and opportunity are distributed unevenly in Britain, and there is a geography to that, which reflects in large part the dramatic economic shifts that have taken place over the course of the twentieth century. Driving along the valley road through a string of former mill towns, I wondered how far England – let alone Britain – could really be imagined as a single nation in the way that those putting the Festival of Britain and these guidebooks together were so keen to affirm.

Newcastle–Ponteland–Higham Dykes–Belsay–
Cross Roads–Wallington Hall–Hartington–
Forestburn Gate–Rothbury–Thropton–Hepple–Otterburn–
Rochester–Elishaw–Bellingham–Wark–Humshaugh–
Low Brunton–Wall–Hexham–Dilston–Riding–
Shotley Bridge–Leadgate–Lanchester–
Witton Gilbert–Durham

10

The Lakes to Tyneside

Newcastle on Tyne–Otterburn–Durham (108 miles)

I left Newcastle by Metro rather than car. After watching the services to Monkseaton and then St James via Whitley Bay come and go, the train to the airport approached and I found a seat among teenagers making their way to school. A group of girls wearing uniforms emblazoned with the name Gosforth Academy got off at Regent Centre. Three sixth-form boys left at Callerton Parkway, wearing their own unofficial uniform of trainers, tracksuit bottoms and hoodies in a muted palette running from black to dark blue. I stayed in the now-almost empty carriage until the final stop. Once through the station barriers, I walked up the passageway to the airport, picked up my keys from the car-hire desk in the arrivals hall and battled against the wind to find my car for the day.

Although the Metro tracks ran more or less parallel to the route in the *About Britain* guide, the first stretch travelled through tunnels and so I missed out on seeing the city centre. According to the people who planned this tour there was plenty to see. In a lengthy caption alongside the strip map, motorists were informed that their first mile or so out of the city took them past 'Newcastle United Football ground, the Barracks (early 19th century) and

Leases Park – "When Mayses breezes shake the treeses The cowses hooves go on the Leazes" – and Nuns Moor, separated from the Great Town Moor, and the Lesser Dukes Moor, by the grandstand' through 'the green heart of modern Newcastle'.[1] In the subterranean world of the Metro, there were no 'treeses' or 'cowses', and it was only when I headed back into the city and then out to the airport again by car that I passed through this wedge of parkland with views of the new stadium at St James' Park looming up, cathedral-like, above the city.

Making use of pre-existing, largely industrial freight railway tracks, the Metro followed a sunken path north-west along the backs of rows of housing that evolved from nineteenth-century terraces through interwar council housing and a field of post-war prefabs before running through uniform red-bricked domestic architecture. Rather than the backs of houses the road offered a more respectable view of their fronts. Both the Metro and road followed a vein through the historic layers of housing that have accrued as this city has grown. These layers were dismissed by former miner turned author Sid Chaplin in his introductory essay as 'the industrial suburbs, products of a later unimaginative industrialism' compared to the 'great streets and distinctive buildings' of the early nineteenth-century city that I'd left by car.

Just how to get in and out of Newcastle was a lively issue in the post-war decades. Shortly after the *About Britain* guides were published, Newcastle City Council drew up plans to build new ring roads around the heart of the city. A decade later, these plans were revisited and proposals to build a series of interconnected urban motorways around, underneath and through the city were considered. These new roads would link directly to large multistorey car parks that would provide thousands of parking spaces around the city's core. In the words of the 1963 plan that promised to remake Newcastle the 'Brasilia of the North', the city 'cannot be successful unless the increasing numbers of moving and parked vehicles are adequately catered for'.[2] However, only a tiny fraction of this network of urban motorways was ever built, with a mere two miles of Central Motorway East completed in the early 1970s.

By the time that motorway building began in Newcastle, the high point of urban modernism was beginning to wane as the creation of the first Conservation Area in Stamford in 1967 suggested. In Newcastle the council's road-building plans were challenged by the emphatically named SOC'EM! – Save Our City from Environmental Mess! – adding environmental concerns to the earlier focus on historic conservation. Reading their campaigning literature from the early 1970s, SOC'EM!'s concerns with issues such as air and noise pollution, which drew on studies of earlier urban motorways in Birmingham, appear strangely prescient.[3] They were supported in their fight by the national lobbying group Transport 2000, which had been created in 1972 by a broad church of railway workers' unions, conservation and environmental groups that shared a post-Beeching pro-train and anti-car outlook. A move away from roads was beginning to be seen in the pronouncements of national government in the early 1970s, especially in the midst of the Oil Crisis in 1973 and 1974, which saw shortages of petrol and a dramatic rise in prices.

But there was also a more prosaic reason for the adoption of the Metro in Newcastle in the 1970s, one that came in the wake of the reorganization of local government in 1972. Just as Liverpool became the core of the larger unit of Merseyside, so Newcastle became part of the newly created Tyne and Wear Metropolitan County Council. It was this new entity that assumed responsibility for transport policy, and it was more interested in requesting central government's financial support for a Metro system than city-centre urban motorways.[4]

While car ownership had increased in this region like others across Britain, it had not been to anything like the same extent as, for example, cities in the Midlands. The number of cars on the roads rose five-fold nationally between 1950 and 1970, but in 1970 in Newcastle 70 per cent of people did not own a car.[5] Public, rather than private, transport therefore remained the primary concern of regional planners. As they planned how to move people to new jobs in new kinds of workplaces they chose the cheaper option of developing a metro system.

Construction began in the mid-1970s on Britain's first urban light rail transit system, which would make use of 25 miles of existing railway lines alongside 7 miles of new track, much of it in tunnels running under the heart of Newcastle and Gateshead. The Metro opened in the early 1980s, although the 2-mile extension to the airport that I travelled along wasn't added until 1991. More recently, plans have been put forward to gauge whether the Metro could be used to transport goods as well as people around the region, with the 'last mile' from station to front door completed by bicycle couriers or electric vans.[6]

The extension of the Metro to the airport came during expansion of Newcastle International Airport. There has been an airfield here for some time. First built as Woolsington Aerodrome in 1935, this grass runway serviced the needs of the Newcastle Aero Club as well as being used in the late 1930s by Aberdeen Airways for their service to Stavanger in Norway and North Eastern Airways for a hop up and down the east coast from Croydon, via Doncaster and Newcastle, to Perth or Aberdeen. The airfield was requisitioned during the war and used for pilot training and aircraft maintenance, before being handed back to the city in 1946. By the 1950s it was back in business with Hunting-Clan Air Transport offering flights to London, Manchester and Glasgow, as well as further afield to Paris, Amsterdam, Düsseldorf, Hamburg, Copenhagen, Oslo and Stockholm.[7] In 1954, when the grass runway was replaced by concrete, 5,000 passengers were travelling through the airport each year.

Leafing through Hunting-Clan's timetables the post-war rise in air travel can clearly be seen. Nationally, there was a six-fold increase in passenger numbers at British airports during the 1950s from 1 million at the beginning of the decade to 6 million by the end. This was partly due to the emergence of package holidays at the end of the 1950s. In 1958, the first charter flights took tourists to the Costa Brava and Costa del Sol in Spain. Over the course of the 1960s, the number of charter flights grew. Sid Chaplin's 'steelworker', who stayed at the seaside resorts along the North-East coast for 'one holiday week in the year' in the early 1950s, was now starting to travel further afield.[8] A new terminal was opened at the airport by Prime Minister Harold Wilson in 1967 to accommodate the rise in passenger numbers during what he called the 'air age'. By 1980, Newcastle Airport reached the milestone of 1 million passengers a year. Just over a decade later there were 2 million, then 4 million by 2005, and 5 million by the mid-2010s. A 1,000 per cent rise in air travel from here over 70 years signals one major change in post-war Britain.

One of the most successful of the low-cost carriers in Europe, easyJet, arrived in Newcastle in 2003. They operate flights to a range of British and European destinations from here, and I myself had flown up on one of their daily flights from Bristol a couple of days earlier to speak at a workshop, planning to return on the last flight of the day. Following the creation of a single market in air transport by the European Union in the 1990s, low-cost airlines in Europe successfully adopted the business model pioneered by companies such as Southwest Airlines in the United States. Ryanair – who also fly from Newcastle – began operating from Stansted in 1991 and easyJet from Luton in 1995. Both made use of new aircraft at high occupancy rates to fly short-haul routes between the less popular airports in Europe with quick turnarounds to keep costs – and ticket prices – low.[9] From two leased planes, easyJet grew to a fleet of 100 aircraft a decade later and 300 when I flew from Bristol. In the pre Covid-19 era of budget air travel, driving around the country felt strangely quaint when people take multiple annual European city-breaks and cities like Barcelona and Venice have reached the point of tourist oversaturation.

It was not only the European airlines that were subject to deregulation. British airports were included in the Thatcher government's privatization drive during the 1980s. The 1986 Airports Act resulted in the sale of the state-owned British Airports Authority, which operated seven British airports including the big two, Heathrow and Gatwick. The situation was a little different for those regional airports – like Newcastle – owned by local authorities. After 1986, these could no longer receive any public subsidy, and so local authorities were encouraged to sell all or part of them off to raise the capital needed for growth. Since 2001, Newcastle airport has been part-owned by Newcastle City Council, and part-owned by first Copenhagen Airport, and then a decade later, Australian investment firm APM.[10] British airports became private businesses that made money not from servicing the airlines landing and taking off, but selling things to the millions of passengers passing through.

Just after driving past this regional airport I crossed into 'England's border county' of Northumberland. The other side of the busy commuter village of Ponteland, I saw that I was only 97 miles from the Scottish capital. I could see hills, lightly dusted with snow, off in the distance from the road that undulated through a mixture of pastoral and arable farmland, with a scattering of snowdrops on the verge between road and leaf-less hedge. Straw blew along in front of me, picked out by the low winter sun against the black tarmac. A little further on I caught up with the slow-moving source of this dancing straw, passing a tractor pulling a trailer piled high with round bales. The scene could not have been more of a contrast with the view from the window of the Metro train that took me from central Newcastle to the airport earlier that morning. Rather than layers of high density housing, there were only a few houses and a couple of pubs – one up for sale – strung along this road to Scotland.

It was busier in Belsay. It was school drop-off time and clusters of parents stood talking on the pavement behind a row of parked cars in front of the school and nursery. A little further on, where the road made a sharp turn to the right, a lane led off to Belsay Hall. This early nineteenth-century hall and the entire estate village were, architecturally, just the kind of place that the Festival of Britain favoured, and so motorists were informed that 'Belsay is a fine Italian arcaded village with a Grecian mansion, designed by Monck and John Dobson'. However, as elsewhere, this house was on the cusp of decline in 1951 following its wartime requisition. Although the family moved back in, they soon abandoned their 'Grecian mansion' in the early 1960s and moved into a smaller house on the estate. The hall was left empty and rotting, and was only saved when it was taken over by the state and listed in the mid-1980s.

A few miles later, I passed another former country house. The 'grotesque figures overlooking the road' that 'keep guard over Wallington Hall', which motorists passed in 1951 were still there, staring out on the road that twisted and turned its way past the estate boundaries. Just beyond the row of four gargoyles, a gardener armed with a leaf blower was preparing the gardens for the day. But the car park, with its patches of snow, was empty at this early hour and I kept on to Hartington where the guide warned motorists that 'the road turns sharply due east to catch the lower slopes of the Simonside Hills'.

This wasn't the only sharp turn that morning. There had been plenty of others since leaving the main road after Belsay. Rather than driving the kind of roads that wander through the landscape, I had adjusted to a rhythm of driving straight stretches, before making a sharp turn, followed by another long straight. The zigzags became more compressed as I approached Wallington and navigated a succession of right angles around straight-edged fields. No doubt my attention had been drawn to this rectangular landscape by something that a colleague had said. Once he heard where I was going, he remarked on the straight roads that were evidence of the early enclosure of land here, as well as – he wondered out loud – perhaps an uncanny aping of the road-building norms of the Romans. What was clear was that I was driving through a landscape dominated by great estates.

This was something that Chaplin remarked upon in his opening essay as 'a land little changed since feudal times' where 'most of the fields are large, and the survival of the great landowning families has kept intact most of the great parks and country houses'.[11] In Belsay and Wallington those families have gone, but the contours of their estates remain intact and enforce an order on this landscape that can be seen from the road. Elsewhere, there has been a remarkable persistence in private land ownership. A recent study suggests that two-thirds of land in Britain is owned by less than half a per cent of the population, with established landowning families still dominant.[12]

On the slopes of the Simonside Hills, I drove through a mixture of farmland and game estates. I could see scattered farmhouses in the middle distance with fields – mainly of sheep but some of conifers, one hiding a mobile phone mast – closer to the hedge-fringed road. But farmland turned to moorland as the road climbed up and the dominant roadside colour turned from pale green to brown. I disturbed a bird of prey feeding along the road, drove by a dead pheasant and slowed down for a grouse that was making its way very cautiously across the road. Climbing up to the moor the views to the right over the plain were matched by those to the left of the ridgeline of the distant hills. The guide's authors were keen to draw attention to these same visions of the landscape: 'From Garleigh Moor, there's a view worth stopping to see, of Rothbury beside the Coquet, the Simonside Hills to the west, and north-west the Cheviots' a caption explained, and I came upon that same view looking over Rothbury and to the snow-covered hills in the distance as the road dropped steeply down from the moors into the valley.

Descending into Rothbury, I caught a glimpse of the Gothic fantasy of Cragside house and gardens on the opposite slope. It was exactly the kind of architecture that the *About Britain* guides steered well clear of, given their bias towards the clean lines of early nineteenth-century Georgian design seen at Belsay. But as I'd noticed on earlier journeys, by the 1970s Victoriana such as that seen at Cragside was seen to be worth saving. The building topped the list of Victorian great houses drawn up by Mark Girouard, former architectural editor of *Country Life*, for the National Trust. In the 1970s it came up for sale. Not all the Trust's leadership were keen on this house which some saw as 'a Victorian monstrosity'.[13] But rather than being turned into apartments, it was transferred into the hands of the National Trust in 1977 as one of the final purchases made by the Land Fund, and opened to the public in 1979 in the same year that Girouard's book *The Victorian Country House* was published.

Instead of following the National Trust signs off to the right towards Cragside, I headed left down through a village built on both sides of the valley. It is still being built. On the way in, I passed new housing at 'Cragside Gardens' – named after the estate that could be viewed on the other side of the steep valley. The new red brick looked out of place in this village built, as the gazetteer explained, from the 'grey stone' that lies beneath this part of Northumberland.[14] The road dropped down to the bridge that crosses the river, before heading back up the steep valley on the other side where it ran into Rothbury's grey-stone main street. The caption alongside the map in the guide pointed out that 'the medieval four-arched bridge over the Coquet has been reconstructed in concrete'. In 1951, sleek grey concrete was not seen to be out of place. However, parking up to have a closer look, I discovered that most of the concrete has now gone.

The bridge was widened in the late 1920s with concrete parapets replacing the original stone. In the early 1970s, parts of these concrete parapets were falling off and had to be replaced, this time by metal railings. In 2010, a three-year-long restoration project reinstalled stone parapets in a kind of undoing of the restoration work of the twentieth century. When it reopened to motorists at the end of 2012, the bridge was given a Victorian finishing touch, with the introduction of six black cast-iron lamp posts that echo the Gothic architecture of nearby Cragside. I imagined that those putting together the *About Britain* guides would not have been impressed. If returning to stone was not backward-looking enough, dressing the bridge with reproduction Victorian lamp posts was surely a case of adding insult to injury.

Beyond Rothbury, the road followed the River Coquet along the edge of the river cliff. Unlike the straight roads around the rectangular field boundaries earlier, this road meandered like the river below. I drove along it through a string of small grey-stone villages. After the last of these, Hepple, the road went down to the river and crossed over it. Just before the bridge, a stone and metal marker signalled the boundary of the Northumberland National Park. Just where to draw the boundaries of this National Park created in 1956 was a vexed question. In Dower's original 1945 list of possible National

Parks, 'the Roman Wall' had featured in his suggested second wave of designations. It survived the initial cut, and 'the Roman Wall' was there in the legislation developed in the Report of the National Parks Committee published in 1947. But I was still a long way from Hadrian's Wall here in the middle of Coquetdale.

At a national level, the National Parks Commission was keen on Dower's original focus on the area immediately around Hadrian's Wall. Locally however, Northumberland County Council wanted to include the Cheviot Hills and the border region in the north of the county. The 'North-east Cheviots (Till and Coquet) (300m2)' did feature on Dower's reserve list for 'Possible Future National Parks', although the 'South-west Cheviots (Kielder and Kershope Forests)' were excluded as they were in the hands of the Forestry Commission and, as in the case of the New Forest, Dower was of the opinion that commercial forestry and National Parks made for uneasy bedfellows.[15] In the end, both national and local authorities got to include their preferred areas in this National Park that runs from the stretch of Hadrian's Wall in the south up to the Cheviot Hills and the Scottish borders in the north. What had originally been imagined by Dower as two potentially separate National Parks were brought together.

I hadn't been in the National Park long before I reached a familiar sight: a riverside car park and picnic area. I pulled in to stretch my legs and looked out across the river to the sheep-speckled and bracken-covered moorland rising up from the opposite, non-National-Park side of the river. But back on the road, I soon came across something that suggested that access is severely limited here. A number of identical signs appeared at regular intervals. After the third or fourth, I pulled over to read what they said. A familiar circular red No Entry sign explained that this was a 'Military Firing Range. Keep out when red flags or lights are displayed or barriers closed'. On the right, what is perhaps best described as a yellow exploding triangle announced 'Danger. Do not touch any military debris. It may explode and kill you'.

I drove on a little further and stopped at the next car park. There were lovely views over the valley to the left, and an information board, footpath sign, and stile over the fence all invited me to explore Darden Lough. But on the right, there seemed to be less of an invitation to wander. The track leading into the hills was flanked by three warning signs that transformed what appeared to be very ordinary fields stretching up to the moors into something more threatening. The first was a small triangular warning sign tacked up by the tenant farmer on a fence post next to a cattle grid announcing that there was a 'Bull in Field'. The second was another of the signs that had dominated the right-hand side of the road for the last few miles announcing that this was a 'Military Firing Range'. The third was a red-edged military sign warning of the presence of 'slow moving military vehicles' on this 'narrow road . . . with passing places'. The information board in the car park did tell me that I should 'feel welcome to travel on some of the most remote roads in the country' if there wasn't a red flag flying. There was no red flag, but I'd checked online the night before and discovered that today was a day when live firing was taking place so I decided against venturing any further up the track.

The road I was following did not just cross through the middle of the Northumberland National Park but skirted the edge of the Otterburn Ranges. The presence of the country's second-largest military training area in the middle of a National Park was something of a surprise, but it is not the only National Park where this is the case. The planners of both National Parks and military training areas have historically tended to gravitate to the relatively un-peopled areas of upland Britain from Dartmoor to Northumberland. The Ministry of Defence is the second-largest landowner in the country, owning over 1 per cent of Britain, a figure roughly parallel to the land owned by the militaries of other Western nations. But its landownings are proportionally much larger in National Parks, where it owns 3 per cent of all National Park land and over 20 per cent of the land in the National Park I was driving through.[16]

Here, as elsewhere, the military arrived first. Redesdale Camp was established in 1911 just outside Otterburn and during the First World War, training trenches – traces of which still remain – were dug into the soil of upland Northumberland. In the Second World War, the camp and training area expanded considerably. Rather than being closed in 1945, this large area of land continued to be used for military training as one conflict gave way to the threat of another during the era of the Cold War.[17]

The presence of other occupants is something that distinguishes National Parks in Britain from those created in America. In America, people were cleared off the land as National Parks were demarcated as wilderness and the land came under state ownership. By contrast, in England and Wales people lived and worked on this land that remained in the hands of public and private owners. Dower knew that the American model would not work in England and Wales, which were on a different scale and with 'relatively wild country' in contrast to America's wilderness.[18] But while public and private land ownership was assumed to continue as the norm within National Parks, from Dower onwards there was a consensus that the twin aims of preservation and access would not be an easy fit with the demands of military training. In the words of the 1977 Sharp Report on military training on Dartmoor, there was something 'discordant, incongruous and inconsistent' about military use of land designated for preservation and public access.[19]

But while there was a growing consensus that military training should take place away from National Park land, successive governments did little to act on this. Instead, the 'dilemma' posed by the 1973 Nugent Report was that 'the very factors of remoteness and freedom from human interference that make areas one of great natural beauty, also make them suitable for the Armed Forces, who need space and freedom to carry out their activities.'[20]

With the end of the Cold War and the withdrawal of British troops from Germany, Otterburn was identified for further development. The British Army had bought a range of new weapons – the Multiple Launch Rocket System and Artillery System 90 – that operated at a far greater scale than previous technologies. Otterburn was seen as the only place, given its size, that was big enough for troops to train with these larger artillery systems. But this meant that miles of military roads needed widening and new roads needed building alongside a vast amount of other infrastructure to house both weapons and increased numbers of troops. As with any proposed development within the National Park, these plans had to be submitted for approval. Unsurprisingly, they met with multiple objections and in the end two public inquiries were held in the late 1990s. During these, it was clear that much local opinion was in favour of the military presence and the jobs it brought to the area, but there was also considerable opposition to the planned expansion of the base because of the damage that would result and the greater restrictions on access. Ultimately the military won, received planning permission and began constructing new artillery firing facilities in the early 2000s. It was clear whose interests were pre-eminent. When it came to multiple claims to the same piece of land, the interests of the military overrode those of preservation and access. While the claims of the National Park to this land were 'very important' the claims of the military were 'absolute'.[21]

I left the edge of the training area as the road went down through Elsdon, another attractive grey-stone village with a large house and pub-lined triangular village green dominating a small settlement of perhaps 50 or so houses. This is the only village of any size in the Northumberland National Park. In 1956 the boundaries were drawn up to exclude villages like Rothbury, as well as Otterburn and Bellingham where I was headed. The result is that this National Park has an unusually low population density. A little over 2,000 live within the park boundaries. In another park of similar size – Dartmoor – there are close to 30,000 inhabitants. But, while Northumberland National Park has few permanent residents, it does have a sizeable military presence. I passed the signpost in MoD red to Otterburn Camp as I left Elsdon, which can house 1,000 troops at a time in an area used by 40,000 troops a year.[22]

Shortly after passing the sign to Otterburn Camp I rejoined the main road that I'd taken out of Newcastle earlier, pulling out just ahead of a car transporter with a long line of cars trailing after it. Another mileage sign confirmed that Scotland was getting closer: Edinburgh was now 75 miles away. I drove into Otterburn, before pulling off when I saw the woollen mills signposted. I wanted to see this place that had 'welcomed' 'visitors' in 1951 to buy the 'excellent tweeds, blankets, etc. . . . produced' there. As the heritage signage inside showed, this 'traditional' 'industry' had modernized through the post-war period, but production had stopped in 1976. Visitors are now welcomed to the 'heritage and visitor facilities' opened in the late 1990s that combine a coffee shop with the 'Otterburn Life Shop', which sells outdoor clothing produced on another continent. I visited both, before going back to the main road that I followed out of Otterburn with the River Rede to my left.

Just before re-entering the National Park on the edge of Otterburn, I passed the road to Bellingham. But those putting these drives together did not want motorists to go there just yet. First they wanted to take them to the 'Redesdale Inn', which 'is the last in England' along this ancient route through 'the Debatable Lands of the border'. They didn't quite take visitors into Scotland but they took them pretty close: from the inn the border was 10 miles away. I came upon the last pub in England – now named the Redesdale Arms – and pulled in to the car park. It was still too early for lunch, although I was sure that these Brewers' Society sponsored guides sent people up here halfway through their journey for something to eat and drink. They didn't start serving until midday, and besides I'd been tempted into buying a mid-morning snack at Otterburn Woollen Mill where a tray of pasties had just come out of the oven and smelled too enticing to miss. The Redesdale Arms was still trading on its reputation as the '"First and Last" Inn en route to Scotland' but they now make more of their location near another more recently established galactic rather than national boundary. And as it turned out, this was not the only roadside pub that I passed cashing in on being 'beautifully situated on the edge of the "Northumberland International Dark Sky Park".'[23]

Leaving the Redesdale Arms, I headed south, turning onto the road to Bellingham, which dropped down to cross over the River Rede. I passed a sign warning me not only of sharp bends and hidden summits but also that there had been 75 accidents on the A68 in the last three years. These signs appeared after this road was included in a list of the top 50 accident blackspots in the country. The number of accidents here is almost double the national average, which sees over 1,700 killed on British roads each year.[24] I slowed down a little, but I wasn't on this deadly road for long. I turned off onto a route flanked by black-and-white snow poles that took me up, onto, and over the moors. There wasn't any snow on the road but there were melting piles off to the sides. From the summit I could see the road stretching off into the distance, with most of the limited traffic heading to the right, over the moor, signed towards Kielder.

The Forestry Commission started planting trees at Kielder a few years after those pioneering trees I'd visited on the first of my journeys. From small beginnings in 1926, Kielder Forest has grown to be one of the largest in Europe at around 50,000 hectares, complete with its own new village – Byrness – built for forestry workers and their families in 1950. In the early 1980s, one of Europe's largest forests also became home to the largest lake in northern Europe when a reservoir was created in Kielder to supply water to the industries and workers of the North-East after a run of public inquiries in the early 1970s.[25] It was the kind of scheme the people organizing these guidebooks would have approved of, but I headed south towards Bellingham with lovely views on the left.

According to the *About Britain* guide 'Bellingham is a quiet village with a church of considerable interest' so I decided to stop and take a closer look. Bellingham – the self-proclaimed 'Capital of North Tyne' – was busy so it took a while to find somewhere to park among the late-morning shoppers. The Parish Church of St Cuthbert was open so I stepped inside. According to a leaflet introducing today's visitors to all the churches in the area, Bellingham is 'a straightforward and honest church in which you can be yourself'. Spurred on by these words, I explored a little and found a list of the long line of rectors of this twelfth-century church hanging on the wall. Those who paused here in 1951 did so when William John Flower was rector and had been for a long time: serving here from 1919 to 1956. The present team rector was Dr Susan Ramsaran who was ordained in 1994: the year when as the front page article in the *New York Times* put it 'After 460 years, the Anglicans ordain women'. Since then the rate of change in the Anglican church has been more rapid. From just 30 women ordained in Bristol Cathedral in spring 1994, two decades later there were 5,000, and that figure looks likely to grow. While women make up around a third of all clergy, they are expected to soon be in the majority.[26]

I left the ancient church where 'you can be yourself' and returned to the car. Just on the edge of the village, past the entrance to a Forestry Commission yard, I spotted a wooden sign marking a footpath that ran across the field to the right. It was marked with a black acorn and made clear that this wasn't simply any old footpath, but the Pennine Way. What this sign also made clear was that I had just driven along a stretch of the Pennine Way on its route along the backbone of England from the Scottish border down to the Peak District. When it officially opened in 1965, the Pennine Way was celebrated as the first of what has been an ever-growing number of long-distance footpaths created in Britain. But it took a long time for this first path to be completed, and one of the reasons for that delay lay with this short stretch of path that I had just driven, rather than walked, along.

The idea of 'a Pennine Way from the Peak to the Cheviot' had first been raised in the pages of the *Daily Herald* by their Rambling Correspondent, Tom Stephenson, in 1935. The fact that a mass publication workers' paper had a 'rambling correspondent' in the mid-1930s was testimony to the popularity of hiking. However, as Stephenson pointed out in his article, Britain did not have a national footpath akin to the Appalachian Trail in America, and so issued the call for one to be created. It was to be 'a meandering way' rather than a 'Euclidean line' and 'a faint line on the Ordnance maps, which the feet of grateful pilgrims would . . . engrave on the face of the land' rather than a 'concrete or asphalt track'.[27] It took thirty years from this initial article before the Pennine Way was completed, and as I'd just experienced this tarmacked stretch along the road through Bellingham was one that did not quite fit with Stephenson's initial vision.

In 1938 the Pennine Way Association sketched out a potential route. The outbreak of war put things on hold, but the idea of this and other long-distance footpaths appeared in the wartime and immediate post-war discussion of plans to create National Parks. In 1951 they started planning the Pennine Way, which they hoped to open the following year. In the end, it took well over a decade because of the problem of securing additional rights of way on privately owned land. One critical pinch point was the six miles over Blakehope Fell north of Bellingham. By 1962, the National Parks Commission had decided that the only way to secure access rights for this stretch of the path was to suggest an alternative route from that originally planned. In 1964 a public inquiry was held to consider the options. For the Ramblers Association the proposed new route that included stretches on both roads and forest tracks was 'totally out of keeping with the conception of the Pennine Way'.[28] However, their appeal to purity of vision was rejected in favour of the pragmatic compromise of getting this final stretch of the path finished as quickly as possible.

I continued on to Wark. I passed a few yellow Road Ahead Closed signs but the place where the road was closed – Nunwick – wasn't marked on the strip map I was following so I decided to keep going anyway along this beautiful stretch of road that hugged the bank of the Tyne on the way into and out of Wark. 'Wark-on-Tyne is just another village' the caption alongside the map told motorists in 1951 before letting them in on the secret that there was more to Wark than meets the eye: 'but when Tynedale was a possession of the Scottish King his courts of justice were held here'. There is now even more to Wark. Leaving the village I passed the Battlesteads Dark Sky Observatory signed off in tourist brown. It opened at the back of the Battlesteads Hotel, shortly after the nearby area was designated the Northumberland International Dark Sky Park at the end of 2013. Quick to see the potential for attracting visitors during the long dark nights of the winter off-season, the owners of the Battlesteads Hotel arranged nightly stargazing events in their newly built observatory where it was possible to view 'the Ring of Saturn with a pint of English Ale in your hand'.[29] That night they had two hours of 'Aurora Hunting' on offer but it didn't start until 9 p.m. so I kept driving.

This village pub turned 'astro-tourist' destination is offered up as a place 'where the twinkling stars of the milky way can be seen with the naked eye in all their glory' given its 'Bortle Dark Skies rating of 1' and 'an SQM reading of 21.77'. These attempts to measure just how dark the night sky is have a relatively recent history. John Bortle only introduced his nine-point 'Bortle Dark-Sky Scale' in 2001. A few years later, a Canadian company developed a Sky Quality Metre to test the darkness of the night skies from a score of 22 for pitch-black skies through to 16 for the bright lights of the night-time inner-city. Both were targeted at growing numbers of amateur astronomers and responded to concerns with 'light trespass' that emerged in the 1970s and 1980s.

In 1990, the British body of amateur astronomers (the British Astronomical Association) started a 'Campaign for Dark Skies', which sought to highlight the spread of 'light pollution' and take action against it. They publicized the problem of 'light pollution', worked with lighting manufacturers and lobbied local and central government to minimize and limit artificial lighting.[30] But they also wanted to safeguard areas where major light pollution had not yet reached. And this part of Northumberland was one of those.

In the early 2000s, the Campaign for Rural England joined the fight of amateur astronomers and launched their own campaign against what they termed 'Night Blight!'. They published a series of maps using satellite images captured by the

US Air Force's Defense Meteorological Satellite Program since the 1960s. A sequence of two images of Britain at night in 1993 and 2003 showing that only 20 per cent of England lay under 'pristine skies' caught the public imagination. In the mid-2010s, they published another image from space showing the hotspots of light generated by cities, major towns and busiest motorways. As those putting these maps together recognized, these images had their limits given that they adopted the perspective from space, rather than seeing what light was visible on the ground. But what all these maps suggested was that Northumberland was the area of darkest skies in England, with 'pristine dark skies' covering almost three-quarters of the county.[31]

It is no surprise then that Northumberland has tried to cash in on this natural asset. In 2013, the National Park and adjacent Kielder Water and Forest Park successfully applied to the International Dark-Sky Association for 'Dark Sky Park' status. Established in the late 1980s when the idea of 'light pollution' was gaining currency, the International Dark-Sky Association began awarding 'International Dark Sky Place' status in the late 2000s. From the designation of Natural Bridges National Monument in Utah as the first Dark Sky Park in 2007, there are now 130 worldwide. Galloway Forest Park across the border in Scotland became the first Dark Sky Park in Britain in 2009. In 2013, Northumberland National Park and Kielder Water and Forest Park became the second in Britain – and the largest in Europe – with the stated aim of creating what they dubbed in their application to the International Dark-Sky Association 'a dark sky "collar" between the border of England and Scotland' that would run from Northumberland westwards into Galloway.[32] Since the creation of this 'dark sky "collar"' on the English–Scottish borders, a number of other spots of dark sky across the country have been recognized with prized Dark Sky Park status – the Elan Valley Estate in

Wales, Bodmin Moor and Tomintoul and Glenlivet estates in the Cairngorms – or the lesser Dark Sky Reserve status: Exmoor, the Brecon Beacons, Snowdonia, part of the South Downs and Cranborne Chase.

Following the award of Dark Sky Park status, space-loving visitors were targeted. Northumberland launched a national marketing campaign that sold the area as 'the land that's just as good with the lights off'. By their reckoning 'astro tourism' was big business, bringing £25 million into the region, much of it during the dark winter nights of what is traditionally the off-season. Flagging Northumberland National Park's initiative as an example for others to follow, the British government recently picked out Battlesteads Hotel's winter occupancy rates of above 70 per cent as inspiration for their strategy for exploiting the economic potential of having almost 10 per cent of land devoted to National Parks.[33]

Shortly after passing the Battlesteads Hotel and observatory I came to a halt. The yellow signs warning of road closures changed abruptly into a red sign that simply said Road Closed. I didn't want to return all the way to Bellingham but the strip map was no help. All it showed was this road that was now closed, not any others. There was a hint of a road at Wark crossing over the Tyne, but that soon literally faded out to either side of the single route that the guide chose for motorists to follow. With the 1951 road closed, and the diversion route miles away, I decided to head back to Wark and try my luck with the road that crossed over the Tyne and see if it continued on the opposite bank of the river. I went across a very narrow bridge and onto a road that wasn't quite single track, but nor was it wide enough for white lines to be painted down the middle. It was the kind of road that was far too narrow to send motorists along, whether instructed by a mass-publication guidebook or a yellow road diversion sign.

Rejoining the road on the strip map again after this unofficial diversion I was tempted to stop at the layby where a footpath sign pointed towards Brunton Turret on Hadrian's Wall, but I kept going. This particular tour merely passed by, or literally over, Hadrian's Wall: as the caption explained 'the road passes over Hadrian's Wall' between Low Brunton and Wall. Those wanting to see more, could take tour two from Penrith through Brampton to Newcastle, or stop off in Hexham which was 'the best centre for exploring the Wall'. But I simply drove into and around Hexham rather than staying there a while. Instead of taking the bypass along the north bank of the Tyne to Corbridge, I crossed the river into Hexham, in 1951 a place 'famed for its orchards and market gardens', past a factory belching out smoke on the left and the edge of the compact old town on the right. The factory looked somewhat out of place given the predominantly agricultural, estate and forestry land I'd driven through. But it was very much connected with that hinterland. Since the mid-1980s, Austrian firm Egger have been making chipboard for flat-pack furniture and wood-effect flooring at this factory with the largest single concentration of manufacturing jobs in the county. Their other British factory is in Scotland, sited like this one close to the raw materials of upland forest.[34]

Leaving Hexham, I followed the Tyne to Riding Mill before heading from this valley over to the next through a landscape of sheep and conifers. At the top of the river cliff above the Derwent, the view changed abruptly with glimpses of Consett arranged in dense rows of houses on the opposite slope. I went down into Shotley Bridge, leaving Northumberland behind. Shotley Bridge was described as a place that by 1951 had already changed from 'a centre for flour milling, paper-works and cutlery-making' into 'a suburb for the industrial town of Consett'. That story of change has continued here as well as along the next few miles of the journey to Durham. When motorists drove through in 1951

Consett was a steel town; just beyond it lay the string of collieries that provided the coking coal for the steelworks. 'Along the valley', the final caption on the route map noted, 'are collieries with interconnecting aerial ropeways spaced so infrequently that they do not spoil the effect of well-wooded pastoral land.' But the collieries and their ropeways had gone, and so had the coal-hungry steelworks in Consett.

I drove past new industrial estates and then on towards Durham; there were few clues of what was here during the 1950s, 1960s and 1970s. I saw rows of housing to the right on the other side of the river as I drove out of Consett. The neat lines of rooftops looked as if they had been dropped into this rural setting. But all evidence of the mining industry, whose workers these homes were built to house, had gone. Scholars have noted the irony that more remains of the Roman occupation of this region 1,500 years ago than of the industries that dominated here from the mid nineteenth century until the 1980s.[35] Where steel was made in Consett for 150 years, there is now a huge Tesco Extra supermarket adjacent to the chainstores and restaurants like in any out-of-town shopping area. Only a hint of these former industries can be seen in a couple of sculptures placed on the route of the popular long-distance coast-to-coast cycle path opened in the mid-1990s that journeys from the Cumbrian coast through Consett on its way to either Sunderland or Tynemouth.[36]

Consett was a town that grew up around the steel industry. Originally built by and around the privately owned Consett Iron Company, the town experienced two waves of post-war nationalization – first of the neighbouring coal mines supplying the works in 1947 and then the steelworks in 1967, which became part of British Steel. After nationalization, decisions about Consett's future were made in London rather than locally. In the late 1960s its future looked bleak given that it was in a sense, like Merthyr Tydfil, in the wrong place. It was inland, rather than on the coast, and this began to matter as raw materials and coal were brought from further afield rather than just down the road. By the 1960s, the Durham coalfield was in sharp decline. Between the summer of 1968 and 1969, twelve pits closed across the coalfield as a whole. By the early 1990s, the last pit had been closed and the industry that had once numbered close to 150 pits was no more. The result was both high levels of unemployment, and also population decline.[37]

A similar story of decline, closure and ensuing mass unemployment can be seen in the steel industry, which reflected the fate of coal. In 1979, British Steel announced that they were closing Consett. Despite local opposition, the factory shut its doors in 1980. The results were catastrophic in this place built around a single industry. Around a third of jobs in the town were lost and the local economy collapsed. In the early 1980s, roughly a quarter of those living in Consett were unemployed, making it one of the towns with the highest unemployment levels within a region – the North-East – that already had the highest unemployment in Britain. As was the case elsewhere in post-industrial Britain in the 1980s, the Thatcher government tried to stimulate new high-tech and small manufacturing industries through the creation of enterprise zones. The results were mixed. In the end, most new jobs in Consett came in the service sector. In what I saw of these attempts to encourage new investment to the area, the recent industrial past was just as absent from the promotional literature as it was from the roadside.[38] That past has been quite literally relocated to the industrial museum at Beamish that I saw signposted in tourist brown off the road I took from the former steel town of Consett through the former colliery towns of the Durham coalfield.

I was nearing journey's end. I avoided the bypass to drive briefly into and through Witton Gilbert, before reaching the outskirts of Durham, ringed by an older hospital, Park and Ride and a newer hospital. I got the first glimpse of the cathedral as I began the descent into the city. Past County Hall and under the bridge, where there was a train paused at the station before heading down the East Coast line to London, I dropped into Durham proper. The cathedral loomed up ahead of me, huge and dominating the city.

Driving back to the airport to return my hire car and head home I was struck by the way that this route had drawn my attention to not only the land but also the skies above Britain: both the dramatic rise in air travel but also the rise of popular astronomy. Reading more on the dark skies movement once back in the light glow of Bristol, I discovered that as well as claiming to have England's darkest skies Northumberland also professes to be one of the most tranquil places in the country. Not content with mapping out 'Night Blight' in the 1990s, the Campaign for Rural England was also busy 'Mapping Tranquillity'. Working with what they acknowledged was a rather rough and ready methodology that measured distance from certain key features, they offered up a picture of England as a patchwork of noisy and tranquil places. They claimed that noise stretched two and a half miles from large power stations; two miles each side of the 'most highly trafficked roads', major industrial areas and large towns the size of Leicester or above; one and a quarter miles from other major roads and smaller towns; 1,000 yards from main railway lines and roads that were 'difficult to cross in peak hours'; as well as within the 'noise lozenges' of airports. By contrast, tranquillity was only found in the 'peace, quiet and calm' of 'nature'.[39]

Given this methodology it was no surprise that 'tranquillity' and 'dark skies' had shrunk from the 1960s to the 1990s. Clearly visible in the maps produced to show these changes was the growing motorway network developed during this period, which was not only a mesh of blue veins but also the harbinger of artificial light, traffic noise and visual intrusion. However, this mapping worked with a set of long-established, if problematic, ways of thinking about England, seen at times in the pages of the opening essays in some of the *About Britain* guides, which also fought to keep the urban at bay. In privileging the rural, the Campaign for Rural England failed to consider the possibility that 'tranquillity' might be found within the city.

But while problematic, the mapping of both tranquillity and dark skies do offer a visual shortcut to some of the things that have changed in the last 70 years. Just as the series of pie charts that I'd found about land use at Wicken Fen suggested changes there that were not immediately visible on the ground, these maps highlight the impacts of suburban spread and growth in transport, which I'd seen from the windows of the Metro train on its way to Newcastle airport. Looking through these maps it was clear that Britain had become both lighter and noisier in 70 years, although these changes were ones that some at least were seeking to undo. But within a month of completing this trip through England's darkest and most tranquil county it was another unseen threat that stopped my journeying in its tracks.

*Edinburgh–Blackhall–Barnton–Cramond Bridge–
Forth Bridge–Crossgates–Cowdenbeath–Lochgelly–
Bowhill–Kinglassie–Markinch–Windygates–Craigrothie–
Ceres–St Andrews–Guard Bridge–Leuchars–
Newport–Dundee–Longforgan–Inchture–Glencarse–
Kinfauns–Perth–Bridge of Earn–Aberargie–
Glenfarg–Milnathort–Kinross–Drum–Powmill–
Blairingone–Kilbagie–Kincardine–Grahamston–
Falkirk–Kilsyth–Milton–Lennoxtown–Torrance–
Cadder–Bishopbriggs–Glasgow*

11

Lowlands of Scotland

Edinburgh–Perth–Glasgow (146 miles)

The *About Britain* guide instructed motorists to 'leave Edinburgh by the Queensferry road, crossing the Dean Bridge'.[1] But in the spring of 2020 that was a lot easier said than done. My wife was going to be travelling with work over the Easter school holidays, and I'd planned to take the kids with me to drive the final road trips through the Lowlands and Highlands and Islands of Scotland. But a global pandemic meant that the furthest anyone could get from their homes for weeks was to the nearest supermarket. Our car remained parked outside the house, and we took to our bikes, cycling around the deserted streets of Bristol for an hour of exercise each day. As the emails arrived informing me of the cancellation of my Scottish hotel bookings, I briefly considered trying to make it to Edinburgh to drive the remaining road trips, finding somewhere quiet to sleep in the car in between. But I decided against it and instead did something unimaginable in 1951: I set out to follow the journey from Edinburgh to Glasgow from the laptop screen on my makeshift writing desk – the kitchen table.

Driving about England and Wales, I'd often reflected on those changes which were less immediately visible. The digital transformations that have taken place since the Festival of

Britain are some of the most ubiquitous and yet also the most invisible. While it was impossible to miss the motorway network built in Britain from the late 1950s onwards – driving down the Roman Road of Stone Street from Canterbury, the M20 literally stopped me in my tracks – the more recent digital network lay buried underground. The 'cloud' was both everywhere and nowhere, although it takes energy-intensive concrete form in a network of server farms that tend to be located in drier climates beyond Britain.

Being restricted by the lockdown, I decided that there was nothing else to do but to try to complete the route between Edinburgh and Glasgow on Google Street View given its claim to 'enable people everywhere to virtually explore the world'.[2] I was intrigued to see whether this was possible, and if so, what the experience would be like. So I sat down with the guidebook next to my laptop, pulled Google Maps up on the browser, entered 'Dean Bridge, Edinburgh' into the search bar and began my virtual journey to Glasgow via Perth.

I found myself in the middle of Dean Street on a rainy day in July 2019. Pedestrians strode along the pavements to each side, sheltering under their umbrellas. In many ways the view from Google Street View offered more possibilities than the one from the driver's seat, with a 360-degree perspective that even a car's many windows and mirrors could not match. I was able to look all around me from the middle of Dean Bridge. But while I could look up into the threatening sky, I couldn't look down to what the *About Britain* guide described was the 'pretty village of Dean hundreds of feet below on the Water of Leith'. I wanted to stand on the pavement and peer over the edge as the pedestrians with their faces blurred were doing. I wished I could join them. So I briefly left Google's roadscape, pulled up the photo-sharing site Flickr and typed Dean Bridge, Edinburgh into the search bar. Within seconds a gallery of heavily photoshopped images came up. I chose Kev Walker's 'Dean Village From Above' taken in May 2018, clicked on it and vicariously enjoyed the panoramic view over the parapet with him.

Back on Google Street View, I left Edinburgh along the tree-lined Queensferry road. The trees were in full leaf and largely hid the familiar Edinburgh streetscape of Georgian grey-stone terraces that lay beyond them. Toggling back through the years of footage provided, most came from the early and mid-summer. But October 2012 offered a starkly different colour scheme to the deep greens of high summer and so I decided to leave Edinburgh in the autumn just as the leaves were starting to turn. I followed the road, clicking on the arrow in front of me, through the different decades of roadside housing, before reaching a high-rise hotel that looked incongruous both in scale and building material. It was clear that the road rose up a hill here, but it was hard to gauge just how steep it was on the screen. At the top, I joined the dual carriageway signed to the Forth Bridge, and moved from October 2012 back to the mid-summer foliage of June 2019.

This involuntary movement through time was a little disconcerting. On some stretches of road I moved almost frame to frame through time as I navigated contiguous space, with the algorithm stitching together an ever-changing selection of the most recent, or clearest images. The effect was less visible in the city and when the images were taken during a single season: the foliage in June and July more or less merged together. But it was far more visible beyond Edinburgh's suburbs where the road ran through tree-edged fields rather than gardens. Off to the side of the road bare fields ploughed ready for planting transformed from brown earth to pale-yellow corn with the click of a button. Journeying with Google Street View is an experience where space is fixed – rigidly so as crossing Dean Bridge had shown – but time is, as one scholar puts it, 'fractured'.[3] This is mapping that privileges a continuous geography, rather than history, as we move virtually through the world.

Superficially, travelling virtually was quicker. I wasn't slowed down by the red traffic lights that I came upon, or by the relatively heavy traffic – each car with its number plate blurred automatically along with the pedestrians' faces – that I encountered leaving Edinburgh. But beyond the traffic jams, it seemed slower as I moved along at the speed of my broadband connection. Clicking along the road frame by frame was not a smooth journey through the landscape, but a much more jerky experience that felt more like travelling on a pogo stick than in a car. This slow, staccato movement involved a surprising amount of concentration. It took me some time to adjust to 'driving' along the dual carriageway that curved through farmland. I had to get used to focusing on the arrow on the road surface in front of me and clicking directly on that, because it seemed far too easy to stray over onto the other carriageway with the cars bearing down on me alarmingly, or end up on a bridge overlooking the road.

This road grew from two to three lanes as I got closer to Queensferry. I kept – or rather the camera car kept – in the middle lane. But this didn't mean that I stayed on the straight and narrow. Just before the bridge, one wrong click meant that I ended up in a cul-de-sac of 1990s detached houses on what was obviously the day when recycling had just been collected. It was hard to extricate myself. I simply ended up in another cul-de-sac where the upturned red recycling boxes lay scattered on the driveways or patches of scorched-grass lawns in July 2014. I used the inset map on the bottom left-hand corner of the screen to make my way back to the main road, which was clear in July 2014 but the scene of a lengthy traffic jam in September 2016. I stuck with the free-flowing traffic and continued on to and over the Forth Road Bridge with its sister structure the rust-red Forth Bridge carrying the railway north from Edinburgh to my right.

Built in the late nineteenth century, the railway bridge was the only one here in 1951. Its distinctive three-arched silhouette was captured against the setting sun in a rare colour photograph in the *About Britain* guide to the Lowlands of Scotland above a caption that gave its vital dimensions (three miles long, built from 38,000 tons of steel) as an object of engineering prowess.[4] But motorists following this route north from Edinburgh in the 1950s had to make do with an older transport technology and take one of the ferries across the Forth. Plans for a road bridge had been discussed in the late 1920s and throughout the 1930s, but these had been put on hold during the war when metal was needed for armaments. Soon after the end of the war, these plans were revived. When it was finally opened by the Queen on a dreary day in September 1964, it was the longest suspension bridge built anywhere outside the United States.

However, the reason for this bridge being built across the Firth of Forth – the rise in road traffic in the twentieth century – was ultimately its undoing. When plans were first discussed in the mid-1930s, it was estimated that around 5,000 vehicles might use the bridge each day. Three decades later it was designed to cope with 30,000 vehicles crossing in each direction, every day. But by the end of the twentieth century this capacity was not only exceeded, but often doubled. In its first full year, close to 5 million cars crossed over the new bridge. Forty years later this had quadrupled. The result was not simply congestion but also frequent repairs to the carriageway and most seriously the weakening of the cable core. By the 1990s, plans for a second bridge were being considered. Before this was built, there was a short-lived experiment with the wonder technology that had been and gone in Pegwell Bay, the hovercraft, to take cars across the estuary and so bypass the congested bridge.[5]

From my Google view in July 2014, off to the left they were still constructing the new Queensferry Crossing. Only the base of the piers and a short stretch of deck extended from the southern shore of the estuary. But toggling through the images the bridge gradually took shape. The central piers had grown in height by May 2015 and it seemed that the deck stretched just a little further over the water. By September 2016, it was clear that there was still some work left to do, with a missing stretch of deck midway along the section to my left. I kept 'driving' across the old road bridge during September 2016 as the last work was being completed, before ending up in May 2017 with the new bridge more or less complete.

The last image from a Google camera car crossing the Forth Road Bridge came from May 2017 for a reason. In that year, the second finally opened. While initial plans were to build a new bridge and repair the old and so have two road crossings to double capacity, by the time the Queensferry Crossing was completed thinking had shifted and the decision was made to 'replace . . . but . . . not increase the road provision for general traffic across the Firth of Forth'. In contrast to Thatcher's policy in the 1980s and early 1990s of simply building more roads to try to keep pace with the rising numbers of cars – as I'd seen when I drove through Twyford Down – the new Scottish government was explicit in stating that it was not their 'policy to provide unconstrained growth in vehicle traffic and to attempt to do so would be unsustainable'. As a result, cars and lorries were directed to take the new Queensferry Crossing from 2018, and the Forth Road Bridge was repurposed for 'sustainable travel'. It became part of a 'dedicated Public Transport Corridor' that stretches south to Edinburgh, and a route across the Forth for walkers, cyclists and motorcyclists.[6] The motorists of 1951 were not alone in not being able to drive across this suspension bridge that only opened in 1964: I wouldn't have been able to either if I had made it to Edinburgh in the spring of 2020.

I decided to retrace my steps and take the new Queensferry Crossing. Driving over the new bridge I had a choice of days to choose from: either the brooding grey of low cloud and drizzle in March 2019 or the spring sunshine of April the year before with the dramatic clouds reflected in the water. I chose the sunshine, settling in behind a bright yellow van and vivid purple car that both gleamed in the light. But as I came close to the end of the bridge, I lost both these colourful vehicles and the bright sunshine as April gave way to cloudy May. What the range of dates on offer allowed was not only the opportunity to cross the Forth in different weather conditions, but also different traffic conditions and I could either cross over at 50 or 70 mph. It wasn't only sunny in April 2018; there was also a lot less traffic meaning the variable speed limit signs on the overhead gantries were switched off.

The development of these mandatory variable speed limits is the latest advance in the history of the speed of driving that I'd first thought about as I left Barnstaple on my first journey. The twentieth century saw the shift from fixed speed limits, to no speed limits – aside from the kind of self-policing urged on the driver by the writers I'd read – to fixed speed limits encircled in red along the side of the road. The first two decades of the twenty-first century have seen the introduction of digital variable speed limit signs on so-called 'smart motorways' making use of the same digital infrastructure that allowed me to virtually cross the Firth of Forth from my laptop. Deploying a digitally connected battery of sensors and cameras – traffic flow detectors, CCTV, journey-time cameras, automatic number-plate recognition – real-time data of road usage travels from the Queensferry Crossing to Traffic Scotland's National Control Centre on the Edinburgh side of the estuary at South Queensferry where it is displayed on a bank of 40 screens. These show images from the more than 400 CCTV cameras along the main Scottish motorways and trunk roads.[7] This big data triggers the raising or lowering of the speed limits displayed on the road signs above the carriageway in order 'to reduce traffic build up' and the accidents that can result. Rather than fixing speed limits by type of road, these smart highways are dynamic and adjust to the volume of traffic.

The next logical step from smart roads and bridges is to dispense entirely with the driver who has to read and respond to these variable speed limit signs, and simply connect the vehicle directly with all the available data on road and traffic conditions. Indeed, this was being trialled on the neighbouring bridge following the unveiling of Europe's first full-size autonomous bus in 2019, which is planned to be part of an initial fleet of five taking 500,000 commuters and shoppers across the Forth Road Bridge each year. Rather than relying on a driver using their windscreen and mirrors to spot and react to pedestrians, cyclists and traffic ahead, these buses are equipped with a raft of cameras and sensors as well as GPS. According to the government minister introducing the project, this vehicle would not simply get people into Edinburgh safely but offer them the chance 'to experience the future for themselves'.[8] These words echoed those used to describe the arrival of hovercraft over forty years earlier and I wondered if they were similarly over-optimistic.

The transport of the future is predicted to include not only autonomous buses, but also lorries and cars. This will spell a radical reworking of the relationship between humans and the road that developed in the early years of motoring. In the interwar years, the car was offered up as a tool of freedom giving motorists the chance to travel where they wanted, when they wanted and at their own pace in contrast to the confines of railway tracks and timetables. Autonomy was the watchword of motoring and continued to be so through Thatcher's road-building binge and short-lived hopes for a motorway under the Channel in the 1990s. Those notions of independence and freedom were vested in a new persona: the car driver. This was not the professional identity of the chauffeur who came with the earliest elite car ownership, but rather the amateur and embodied identity of, initially, upper-middle-class motorists. But while the twentieth century saw the rise of the driver as a modern identity, the twenty-first may see its fall as driverless cars render us all passengers.

Navigating from my laptop, I was neither driver nor passenger. I felt more like a voyeur accessing the visual traces that remained of a series of journeys made by Google camera cars over the last decade or so. I accompanied one as it left the new bridge and headed towards North Queensferry and Rosyth, crossing underneath a rust-red bridge of cast iron carrying train tracks to the original Forth Bridge. The motorway was signed to points further along my route in Dundee and Perth, but I wanted to follow the old, downgraded, road through what the guidebook promised as a journey 'from farming to industry'. Once 'across the river' the *About Britain* guide offered up 'pleasantly arable' land 'with herds of dairy cattle, mortared stone walls and red-roofed cottages'. I passed through a landscape that shifted screen by screen between the high summer and early autumn of 2009 with the roadside palate changing from green to brown accordingly. The road twisted through woods before re-emerging into the June sunlight and ran through open fields with what the guide identified as a 'mortared stone wall' marking an estate boundary to the right, but there seemed little sign of the 'herds of dairy cattle' in what appeared to be a solidly arable landscape, one field of grazing beef cattle in October 2009 aside.

I paused at the field of cattle, where a track led to the right. I was just outside Crossgates, the point in their journey where motorists in 1951 were told that 'the nature of the countryside changes from farming to industry' as they made their way through a string of 'typical mining towns surrounded by colliery workings', and the *About Britain* guide celebrated the 'clean layout' of the new pits in Fife with a photograph of Comrie Colliery that had opened in 1939.[9] As if on cue, the large signs to either side of the track declared that this was the entrance to ATH Resources' Muir Dean surface coal mine in both of the available images from May and October 2009. I switched to satellite view and hovered above the landscape on a clear day in 2020. By then it was apparent that this mine had almost entirely disappeared, with just fragments of coal workings showing amid restored rolling fields. This story of decline and erasure of the Fife coalfield mirrored what I'd found elsewhere. Most pits on this coalfield closed in the 1960s and 1970s, during a period when coal's share of electricity generation fell dramatically from around 75 per cent to 50 per cent with the rising importance of other new fuels: oil, gas and nuclear. In the 1980s the last pits closed. But there was a last gasp for the mining industry here as in other places. With the end of deep mining, a number of surface mines were opened. In the 2000s Muir Dean supplied coal to the nearby Longannet power station, Europe's biggest coal-fired plant when it opened in the early 1970s. But Longannet – the last coal-fired power station in Scotland – and Muir Head had both closed within the last decade.[10]

This change from coal to other forms of energy could be seen just down the road in Crossgates, which I entered past a sign instructing me curtly to 'drive carefully' through 'Fife's first energy efficient village'. Past the petrol station in the middle of the village, I saw another sign, this time for 'MRS Training and Rescue' on the grass bank to my right in front of a nondescript-looking building. Originally named Mine Rescue Service, this started off life at the turn of the last century as a specialist disaster response team for deep mines. MRS navigated the nationalization and subsequent privatization of the coal industry, before adapting to the closure of the last deep mines. Rather than offering training in rescuing miners from deep underground, these days they have shifted to the new technology of energy: wind power. Out the back a wind turbine offers up training for safe working on the 5,000 onshore and offshore wind turbines that have been erected across Scotland.[11]

Soon after leaving Crossgates, I clicked my way to Cowdenbeath through industrial estates, a new housing estate and older grey, pebble-dashed houses. I carefully navigated around the roundabout in the shopfronted centre of town and followed a long, thin strip of semi-detached houses that ran all the way to the next settlement marked on the route map: Lochgelly. Progress was slow, one click at a time. Past the cemetery, I was once more back in the farmland of the earlier part of my journey. I kept an eye out for what the caption running alongside this part of the route described as 'some dairy cattle on this stretch and a good view of the twin peaks of the Lomonds – the "Paps o' Fife"'. Rounding a bend, I could see the twin peaks in the distance, wind turbines in the middle distance and cattle in the field beside the road. I toggled back from 2016 to 2009 when both the cows and wind turbines disappeared. I drove 'safely' through Kinglassie, before traversing farmland on a cycle-path-edged dual carriageway on my way to Markinch.

In his opening portrait, the Scottish journalist John Allan was eager to point out to visitors that 'the people of Fife do not live in the past' but that 'the future is very much at their door'. Evidence lay near at hand, with both the new pit at Comrie and plans for 'a new town near Markinch for the miners' that 'will be as different from the older mining towns as Comrie pit is from the older ones'.[12] Glenrothes was one of the two first new towns – the other was East Kilbride – planned for Scotland in the late 1940s after the 1946 New Towns Act. This legislation had sought to channel post-war reconstruction into the planned building of new towns from scratch rather than allowing existing cities to spread. Stevenage was the first to be built in the early 1950s, with Milton Keynes perhaps the most famous following a decade later.

None of my routes had taken me through any of these New Towns, so I was eager to take a closer look at this place that had literally appeared on the map since the *About Britain* guide was published. In the Festival year, initial plans for Glenrothes were published that made clear that this would not be a new town for miners from the new Rothes 'superpit' alone. Miners would only make up roughly 10 per cent of the population in order to avoid over-reliance on one industry. Although it took some time to attract new light industries, by the 1960s new factories, office blocks and the first airfield at any British New Town had been built, and it was projected that the population in Glenrothes would reach 55,000, rather than the original figure of 30,000. By the mid-1970s, 30,000 lived in this town and it had gained a reputation as a place with one of the highest concentrations of electronics firms anywhere in Europe.[13] It was a good job that it wasn't simply a mining town, given the embarrassing and expensive failure of the new Rothes 'superpit' that was originally Glenrothes' raison d'être, but closed within four years of opening.

I faced something of a dilemma. Glenrothes was simply not here in 1951, therefore the route on the strip map ran to the south, before heading north to the old 'mining town' of Markinch. If it had been here, I was sure that tourists would have been directed to this new town given the guidebooks' love of the new. But I had chosen to be constrained by the route laid out and had consistently attempted to follow it faithfully. I decided upon a compromise. I made my way via a series of roundabouts along the tree-lined parkways that ringed this town built for the car age. But I also strayed every now and then into a few of the post-war streets that lay within this forested outer ring and looked quite different from my next destination: the house-lined main street of Coaltown of Balgonie that replicated the mining towns I'd gone through earlier on.

After another stretch of farmland, I reached Markinch, a coal and whisky town in 1951. It now lays claim to neither. When motorists drove through here it was 'the headquarters of the whisky firm of John Haig', whose blended Scotch was the best-selling whisky in Britain on the eve of the Second World War. I could see the large 1930s red-brick factory that dominated the town, but they don't bottle whisky here any more. The plant closed in the 1980s during the downturn in the market that spelled the end of a number of distilleries.[14] Only the name remained emblazoned on the building and in the Haig Business Park that now occupies the vast space. The Haig name is now one of among 40 other Scotch whisky brands owned by the large holding company Diageo, whose Cameronbridge distillery, originally owned by Haig, lay just south of the road that I took from Markinch to Windygates. Along this stretch a brown tourist sign instructed those heading to 'Scotland's Secret Bunker' to follow the A915, but this Cold War-era Nuclear Command Centre hidden beneath an ordinary-looking farmhouse lay off my route, so I headed north instead towards 'the pretty little farming town of Ceres' described by the caption writers as a 'contrast . . . with the colliery towns of the earlier part of the tour'.

The route passed through a string of small settlements with rolling farmland in between, before reaching a long line of holiday lodges peering over the road to the fields that stretched off in the distance. A little further on, a grey-stone gateway by a grey-stone lodge was enlivened by a mass of purple rhododendrons in full bloom. I ran alongside the estate wall for what seemed like for ever, but it was hard to judge distances on this virtual navigation. It was a beautiful road that emerged from a tunnel of trees and snaked its way through a patchwork of gently undulating fields. For the first time on this virtual journey I could almost feel the gentle movement of driving this road to Craigrothie where I turned off towards St Andrews.

I reached Ceres, winner of Gold in the Beautiful Fife Awards. Instead of the utilitarian pebble-dash of the earlier mining towns, the cottages on either side were built of large blocks of dark stone, their windows picked out with a lighter, finer stone surround. After the village, the road went through the 'good farming land' of the coastal plain to St Andrews. The land was flat and so I looked out for the 'wonderful view of the grey houses and spires of St Andrews, four miles distant'. I passed a sign informing me that St Andrews lay six miles away, so kept clicking. On Google Street View I thought I glimpsed the sea off in the distance, but I couldn't see St Andrews until I came upon it.

I followed South Street past a group of tourists, clad in colourful cagoules and each wearing a backpack, clustering around their guide on their way down to the harbour. The tide was out in the first two time-stamped images – an overcast May day in 2009 and 2015. But in June 2018, the deep-blue sky was studded with clouds and the tide was in. I meandered through this city that H. G. Stokes raved about in his short gazetteer entry, where he boasted that 'proportionate to its size (population 8,500) St Andrews has more ancient buildings and a more eventful and important history than almost any other town in Scotland' before listing the cathedral, university, castle, the Royal and Ancient Golf Club – the oldest gold club in the world – as notable features. The university here, like elsewhere in Britain, has grown considerably and now has 9,000 students, swelling the population of St Andrews to around double what it was in 1951. I left the city past the St Andrews Links, where a coachload of tourists had just finished being photographed in front of the sign welcoming them to 'the home of golf'. Although this was as close as they could get to the Old Course where tee times are snapped up months in advance, Google Street View offered a chance to go off road and follow the gravel paths travelled by golf carts past greens where clumps of golfers were dressed up warm on a cold, crisp day.

I meandered through the farmland of the flat coastal plain towards Leuchars, crossing over the river at Guard Bridge. I missed the turn and ended up following a red car to Dairsie. It was, it seemed, just as easy to get lost on Google Street View as it was on the ground. But getting back to where I wanted to go was far easier. I simply flicked over to Google Maps, clicked on the road that I was meant to be on and followed that. Leaving Guard Bridge on the right road now, I passed the whitewashed facade of a factory that had come full circle from whisky distillery to paper mill and within the last year or so back to distillery again during a recent renaissance in the making of whisky and other spirits. Clicking on Eden Mill's website through the sidebar in Google Maps I discovered that I was just a couple of days late for their 'Virtual Home Gin Tasting Experience' that they'd held online at the weekend. Unable to host their usual distillery tours, their 'wonderful Brand Ambassadors' were ready at their computers on a Saturday evening in early June to guide me through six different gins that I could order online ahead of time and have ready to quaff.[15]

But innovation at this site was not restricted to the gins, which run the full range of flavours from Passionfruit and Coconut through Spiced Rhubarb and Vanilla to Chocolate and Chilli. Most of the former paper mill is slated to become home to the University of St Andrews' new Eden Campus. This will not simply offer space for an expanding university to grow, it is one key plank in St Andrews' ambitious vision to become the first carbon neutral university in Britain. In part, the site will house a wood-fuelled biomass boiler that will heat the halls of residence down the road in the city. But this former paper mill on the banks of the River Eden will also be home to the appropriately named GENESIS centre which aims to bring academics and businesses together to research new ways of storing and converting energy.[16]

Past Guard Bridge I followed the signs for military traffic and went through a tunnel with military perimeter fencing either side because I wanted to see the medieval church of St Athernase set in an elevated churchyard, which was shown in the drawing beside the strip map in the *About Britain* guide. I headed north through the flat farm- and heathland of the coastal plain towards Newport which, as the guidebook explained, 'though on the opposite side of the Firth of Tay' was 'largely a residential suburb of Dundee to which it is linked by a half-hourly ferry service'. This was another point on this journey in 1951 when motorists had to wait for the ferry to take them across the estuary where the only bridge carried the railway, not the road.

There was now a road bridge over the estuary that is the twin of the bridge I had taken that morning. Planned as part of the extension of the Great North Road, it was opened by the Queen Mother in 1966, just two years after her daughter had opened the Forth Road Bridge. But the opening did not pass without incident. The police had received a phone call shortly before the official party crossed the bridge informing them that a bomb had been planted on the structure. It turned out to be a hoax, and what the press described as 'six youths' were arrested, tried and fined for posting up protest signs along the route taken by the royal car, calling not simply for the end to tolls on this bridge – like the Forth Road Bridge when it opened – but also for a 'Free Scotland'.[17] They would have been pleased to see that tolls were abolished here in 2008, but their calls for a 'Free Scotland' have not been fully realized, at least not just yet.

Scottish nationalism was something John Allan commented on in the guidebook. As he explained to readers 'a feeling has begun to grow up in the arts and in politics against English standards and the centralizing of authority in London', although he was quick to assert that 'there are very few who wish to break the long association with England'. Writing in 1951, he remained unsure about whether this 'feeling' would amount to 'the appearance of yet one more nationalism' or 'not'.[18] In some ways the post-war story in Scotland has been like that in Wales, with an unsuccessful referendum for devolution in 1979, followed by a successful referendum in 1997 and the establishment of a Scottish Parliament. But the story here also differed. Language was never the focal point in the way that it was in Wales. Instead, the discovery and exploitation of North Sea oil from the mid-1970s meant that the argument for Scottish devolution and independence was framed more around economics than culture alone, and attracted greater support. The 1979 vote only failed on a constitutional nicety and was resoundingly passed in 1997. In 2014, a referendum calling for fully fledged independence came close to being successful, with just under half voting for and just over half voting against. The results of a future – post-Brexit referendum – may well be rather different.

I left the bridge and headed along the waterfront. Here the option to move through different slices of time came into its own. Between July 2008 and March 2019, this sliver of land between the river and the road had been dramatically transformed. In 2008, the road ran past the Hilton hotel and underneath the concreted overhang of a leisure centre, as the tiled murals of swimmers and water-polo players in the waves on the outside revealed. This was opened in the early 1970s to replace the Victorian baths that had been located where the hotel now stood. But in the early 2010s the Olympia leisure centre closed and a New Olympia pool opened a short distance away behind the former docks.[19] The site was cleared, as the images from 2014 showed, and its new occupant slowly began to take shape over the following years. By 2018 it was complete and opened to the public. Rather than leisure centre, this site was now home to the Scottish offshoot of the Victoria and Albert Museum – a striking building clad in concrete ledges that rose up to represent Scottish cliffs.

The insertion of the museum here is another act of regeneration framed around investing in cultural infrastructure following the path first trodden by building the Guggenheim Museum on the dock front of deindustrializing Bilbao in northern Spain. It is something many have sought to emulate since. On an earlier journey, I had driven by the Turner Contemporary on the seafront of the declining seaside resort of Margate. In Dundee, the Victoria and Albert Museum is the latest attempt to regenerate the former docks by undoing the earlier wave of post-war redevelopment that the leisure centre was part of. Nestling next door to the museum lies another cultural object relocated from London. The triple-masted sailing ship RRS *Discovery* was used by Scott and Shackleton on their Antarctic expedition at the beginning of the twentieth century, before winding up as a visitor attraction in London. In the mid-1980s it returned to its birthplace, where it reopened as Discovery Point museum in the early 1990s under the slogan 'Made in Dundee. Designed for Adventure'.

The *Discovery* was not the only thing made in Dundee in the twentieth century. When motorists were sent there in 1951, this was an industrial town founded on jute manufacture, which had diversified to include jam- and marmalade-making as well as a thriving publishing industry. Explaining that Dundee was home to 'coloured comics for small children . . . heart-throbs for young women, and comfortable tales for those too tired to throb any longer', John Allan – himself a journalist and author – felt confident that publishing had a brighter future than jute, given that 'few people can resist a story'.[20] The publishing giant DC Thomson continues to have its base in Dundee, and still produces paper copies of its most famous comic – the *Beano* – among a reduced range of newspapers, magazines and comics. In the company's pursuit of stories, it has sought to transition from print to digital.

One foray that proved unsuccessful was its purchase of the first British social networking site, Friends Reunited. Originally started in 2000, this site's brief history mirrors the fate of other technology businesses that succumbed to the 'dot com bubble'. Initially this start-up subscription service grew rapidly and attracted millions of members keen to reconnect with their high school friends. It was acquired by ITV for £120 million. However, despite a shift from subscription to advertising the site failed to attract new users who were turning instead to the dominant player in the social media market, Facebook. When DC Thomson bought the site in the early 2010s they paid around 20 per cent of what ITV had paid a few years earlier. In retrospect it was still too much, with the relaunched site quietly shelved in the mid-2010s.

But Friends Reunited was not the Dundee company's only venture into the digital. DC Thomson has been much more successful in its foray into digital archives and family history. It bought an early web-based platform for genealogists in the mid-2000s that it relaunched as Findmypast. It is a good example of the shrinking of time and space that the World Wide Web has enabled. By digitizing and making searchable literally billions of census returns and administrative records – records of births, marriages and deaths – Findmypast connects individuals to the archives in a fast and virtual way that Google Street View enabled for my travels as I clicked my way along the banks of the Tay out of Dundee. With the development of high performance computing, it is possible not only to store billions of scanned records but also to rapidly search through them for an individual name. That comes at a cost. Would-be family historians have to pay to virtually travel to archives from their armchair. On the surface, Google Street View – like Facebook, or Friends Reunited in its final stages – seemingly offers the same kind of rapid connectivity for free. But I was not naive to the fact that Google were harvesting what has been termed the new oil: my data.

While Google offers the chance to travel anywhere, including out of Dundee along the Tay, the experience privileges the sense of sight. Describing 'the last zoom layer on the map', Google Maps' vice president of engineering explained the company's Street View function as offering up 'what a place looks like as if you were there in person'. However, sense of place is about so much more than optical experience.[21] As I proceeded on Street View, I was left wondering what the landscapes I drove through felt, sounded or smelled like – whether driving over the Forth Road Bridge buffeted by the wind on a dreary day or past fields of freshly harvested corn with the window down on a summer's evening. There are limits to what can be experienced through the windscreen of the car and it has, rightly, been criticized as a technology that removes us from the world within an individualized, hermetically sealed bubble. Yet in a car it is still possible to roll the window down and sniff the air, which was precisely what Allan encouraged motorists to do on this next stretch of road through the Carse of Gowrie. 'On a hot day in the berry time,' he explained, 'by the ripeness in the air you might think the gods were making jam all over Gowrie.'[22]

Looking around at the polytunnel-fringed dual carriageway it was clear that this was still 'good agricultural land'. Around midway along the busy road leading to Perth, a sign pointed to the Cairn O'Mohr winery. They first started making fruit wines – Strawberry, Raspberry, Bramble – here in the late 1980s. But it wasn't just the sign to a winery that suggested a connection with the Devon landscape I'd driven through on my first journey. Like Devon, this area has also seen the rapid decline of orchards alongside more recent attempts to halt that decline. Developed here in the eighteenth and nineteenth century, commercial orchards were already diminishing in the first part of the twentieth century. As the faster railways replaced the river and canal age, Tayside orchards could not compete with cheaper imported fruit. This history of decline before 1951 became more rapid in subsequent decades as orchards were torn up not only to make way for housing, but also to grow other crops to be transported further afield by road. However, as in Devon, new efforts are being made to turn back this history of decline, spearheaded by the Heritage Orchard Forum who meet up at the Winery, no doubt with a bottle or two of Scottish cider in their hands.[23]

I continued towards Perth. Whatever time-stamped image I chose, it seemed that this stretch of road was always busy. The camera car changed lanes on the dual carriageway to pass slower moving lorries. The result was that I jumped from lane to lane in a series of jerky sideways movements alongside the forward leaps that I'd begun to get used to. As I got closer to Perth I realized that the road had turned into motorway. Rather than continuing on to the next junction and heading back the way I'd come, I simply had to click onto the slip road that I'd just missed and leap across the barrier and head down the slope. I passed underneath the bridge carrying motorway traffic both over my head and across the River Tay which, the

About Britain guide poetically described, had 'narrowed from a firth with treacherous mudbanks to a charming swift-flowing, winding river'.

The road followed the river into what H. G. Stokes described in his gazetteer entry as 'a city of sedate stone buildings giving little hint of its antiquity or its ancient importance as Scotland's capital'.[24] But rather than advertising its former status as national capital, the sign welcoming motorists to Perth boasted instead of its current role as a 'University City', spelling out underneath that it was home to the Perth campus of the University of the Highlands and Islands. In Perth, I was clearly in danger of straying into the Highlands rather than staying in the Lowlands, but this was as far north as this route went. I turned onto the appropriately named South Street and crossed over the river, before heading through parkland and passing what the caption along the map identified as 'Perth Prison, the general prison for Scotland, on the left'. The camera car had clearly driven into and around the prison car park. But to breach the high walls required switching over to satellite view and hovering above the recently modernized site that clocks up its share – as other prisons have – of tongue-in-cheek Google reviews complaining about the beds and service.

Behind these walls lies a history of changing attitudes to punishment across the course of a century or so. This prison was the site in 1870 of the first execution inside a British prison following the decision to end executions in public two years earlier. Executions took place in private for much of the next century. When motorists drove by here in 1951, Viscount Templewood had just published a book that joined calls for the end to capital punishment. However he was pessimistic about the pace of change, recognizing that his views were 'not shared by many' of his 'fellow countrymen'.[25] In the end the abolition of capital punishment came more quickly than he imagined in the mid-1960s. It was not only Templewood who was taken by surprise at the speed of change. The new 'hanging shed' built at Perth jail had only just been completed, and the gallows remained unused here for a further three decades before its removal.[26]

Beyond Perth the road returned to farmland as it curved through 'the rich, arable plain of Strathearn to Bridge of Earn'. It ran alongside the River Earn, the water in the river and the puddles to the side of the road both catching the light of the setting sun on a clear evening after rain in March 2019. It was a beautiful stretch of road and a charming evening, so I was sorry to be sitting at my laptop rather than in the car. Making my way virtually across the river and into the village, I was on the lookout for the 'one-storey modern hospital with 1,200 beds' that the caption drew attention to. Originally opened in 1940 as one of seven Emergency Medical Scheme hospitals across Scotland designed to take in civilian casualties of the aerial war, the hospital became part of the nationwide infrastructure of the post-war National Health Service, before closing in the early 1990s, and being transformed into a housing estate.[27]

The Google camera car was soon on another lovely stretch of road, on the same beautiful clear evening in March 2019. The sun cast shadows on the road surface as it descended through a wooded valley with glimpses of the river to the right. The weather wasn't quite as perfect in April 2010 but the road following this river was exactly the kind of road that those putting these tours together liked to send motorists along. It was the nicest stretch so far and I wished that I'd been able to drive to Glenfarg in April 2020, rather than witnessing the journey made by someone else a decade earlier. Passing under the motorway, the road lost some of its charm as it ran next to the M90, built in the late 1970s. I was relieved that I couldn't hear the sound of the traffic's roar. Reduced to the sense of sight alone, I looked beyond the motorway to mountains covered in snow in April 2010, the year when Google announced their plans to photograph 238,000 miles of public roads across rural Britain.[28]

Just after passing the motorway junction in Kinross, I saw what seemed to be a large white 'golf ball' off in the distance. Getting closer, I discovered that it was for sale. Built in the mid-1980s on a former wartime airfield, this NATO Communications Facility was on the market for just under £1 million. Given its proximity to the motorway, the estate agents boasted that this was 'prime development land suitable for a variety of uses' ranging from 'retirement village' through 'high-end residential log cabins' to a 'data centre' and 'secure storage', but it seemed to have been up for sale for a while with the sign visible in all the photographs from 2015 to 2018, and the estate agent's details still up on the web. This wasn't the only 'golf ball' – or radome – built in Britain. Its more famous family members included three larger 'golf balls' found at Fylingdales in North Yorkshire that were home to radar systems in the US ballistic missile early warning network. Created as fibreglass and plastic protective housing for the radar systems inside, these radomes are now old technology replaced at Fylingdales, not just with new protective material – steel and aluminium – but also a new shape – the pyramid.[29] I headed off the main road to find the track leading to the 'golf ball' but the camera car hadn't gone past the red gate. The estate agents' website offered a better view, taking me not only inside the gated complex, but also inside the now empty radome.

For a period between the later 1990s and early 2010s, this site had lots of noisy neighbours each summer when the surrounding landscape was transformed into the temporary home of Scotland's Glastonbury, T in the Park, bringing the road I was following to a standstill for one weekend each July.[30] But there was relatively little traffic on the days that the camera car had driven along here. As the algorithm flicked through the cache of images, there were moments when I realized that I was, in effect, making the journey in reverse and seeing images captured by the rear-facing camera of a car in the other lane. It felt a little disconcerting so I toggled through to an older set of images when the car was making the journey in the same direction as that suggested by this linear tour. Driving through Blairingone, one property in the centre of the village was blurred on all three camera images. I'd got used to seeing the faces of pedestrians and the number plates of cars coming towards me blurred out, which occasionally mistook part of a sign for a number plate. But the blurring of a whole property facade does not happen automatically; rather it is something intentionally requested by the owners and I was left wondering what it was about this house that demanded such invisibility.

Just beyond Blairingone lay a new county. I must have passed other county boundary signs as I'd travelled from Edinburgh, but somehow I had missed spotting them on Street View which surprised me given they'd been such important markers on the other journeys that I'd undertaken. This sign welcomed me to Clackmannanshire, a place I'd never heard of before. The tagline – 'more than you imagine' – seemed apposite for Scotland's smallest county. Given the small size, I was curious as to how long it would take to drive from one side of the county to the other. I pulled Blairingone up on Google Maps and searched for Kincardine Bridge. It offered the A977 – the road marked on the *About Britain* route map – as the fastest route, and informed me that it would take 14 minutes to cover the just under eight miles in 'the usual traffic'.

Before the Forth Road Bridge opened, Kincardine Bridge was the lowest crossing point by road. When motorists crossed it in 1951 it was still relatively new. Opened 15 years earlier, the central '300-ft. swing span, enabling ships to pass up the Forth to Alloa' was the longest such bridge in the world.[31] I dipped underneath the art deco concrete gateways at either end of this middle section and returned once more to the southern bank of the Forth. Here, this route that 'runs south through land that is gradually turning from farming to industry' was seen to fully embrace the industrial. After crossing the river, motorists were warned as much, being informed that 'the route enters the heavy industrial belt of mid-Scotland, the Clyde Forth strip, crowded with factories and people'. From the frequent signs that appeared once I left mudflats and salt marsh, it was clear that this strip is now also crowded with motorways. I was instructed to follow the M876 for both my next and final destination: Falkirk and Glasgow. But rather than take this short stretch of motorway that opened in the early 1980s to connect the bridge with motorways further east, I pretended to be 'Local Traffic' in order to find and follow the old road to Falkirk. The first few times it was impossible to exit, but toggling back to March 2009 I managed to leave the motorway and follow the agricultural floodplain between estuary and motorway, crossing over an inlet running down to the Forth.

Looking upstream, I was able to go through the images available, starting in March 2009 and October 2010 when the camera car crossed here during high tide, the sun reflecting off the water. It was low tide on a dreary day in August 2016, with the river reduced to a narrow channel running between muddy banks. But that was not the only change in the view upstream. Two large, silver horse-head sculptures, one rearing up, had arrived in the field to the left. It was exactly the kind of place I'd be tempted to stop off, park up, and get out of the car to take a closer look, so I followed a Google Street View camera operator who had walked around the sculptures, looking up at the artwork rising 30 metres above.

Opened to the public in 2014, *The Kelpies* was the latest in a series of large-scale, roadside public art commissions. In the 1990s, Antony Gormley's *Angel of the North* was placed alongside the A1 just outside Gateshead. Like the *Angel of the North*, these two oversized horse-heads were sited to be seen from the road. I shifted over to the neighbouring M9 and passed them where they reared up above the low fence that separated them from the motorway. Their sculptor, Andy Scott, was no stranger to large-scale horse sculptures. He was one of a handful commissioned for work to enliven the M8 – which runs between Edinburgh and Glasgow – in the 1990s. Leaping over to the eastern edge of Glasgow on Google Maps, I passed by the skeleton-like mesh of a Clydesdale horse standing tall above the sign to Glasgow Business Park. Scott's transformation of what 'was once a working beast' into 'just a show horse' was symbolic of the shift from heavy industry to service industries that he saw taking place in Glasgow, and could also be seen on the roadsides of Falkirk.[32] However, *The Kelpies* gestured to a much older, watery transport network.

As I'd discovered on a previous journey, the *About Britain* guides didn't care much for canals. The Bingley Five Rise lock gates were not seen to be worth a mention, let alone stopping for. It was the rise of industrial archaeology in the 1970s that brought them to the attention of tourists, alongside other aspects of a rapidly disappearing industrial past. Following Google Street View around the base of the *The Kelpies*, it became clear that they stood either side of a newly built lock gate welcoming boat-borne tourists crossing Scotland from the Forth to the Clyde through this new cut. Like the new stretch of canal that I'd discovered in Preston, this was a product of an investment in Britain's canal network, not as a place for work but for leisure. A little further along the canal from *The Kelpies* lay a dramatic sign of that investment where the Falkirk Wheel moves boats from one canal network to another, thereby linking the cities of Edinburgh and Glasgow lying at either end of this journey taken by the preferred technology of 1951: the car.[33]

Heading into Falkirk, with the Wheel signed in tourist brown not industrial black, I passed through a newly regenerated landscape of leisure. To the right, the parkland of the Helix stretched to the canal and *The Kelpies*. On the left was the new football stadium, built in the early 2000s, which hosts not only games played by Falkirk Football Club but also a regular roster of concerts. Just before the stadium, a fenced-off piece of land destined for redevelopment was advertised between March 2009 and August 2016 as a site where 'the future is coming' as Falkirk was 'changing for the better'. By April 2017, that future had crept a little closer and the sign now announced that 'development sites' were 'coming soon' at the 'Falkirk Gateway'. Those sites were still 'coming soon' in the latest image as I headed into what the guidebook described in 1951 as the 'centres of Scottish iron casting and oil refining, with chemical by-products'.

There was still oil refining here: a little further east of my route at the sprawling Grangemouth refinery on the banks of the Forth. Indeed, this business grew in importance following the discovery of North Sea oil in the mid-1970s, which is piped here from the platform through a 100-mile-long underground pipeline that I'd crossed – unawares – close to the 'golf ball'. But iron-casting has largely been and gone. The decline of the nearby shipbuilding industry on the Clyde and competition from overseas producers meant that the industry began faltering in the 1970s, and the most famous firm – the huge Carron works – closed in the 1980s. A few small companies continue, and they manufacture stainless-steel kitchen sinks at part of the Carron works site, but driving into Falkirk it was clear that the former landscapes of heavy industry have been, and continue to be, supplanted by leisure and light-engineering industrial estates.[34]

I tried to navigate my way around the one-way system, realizing that this was as – if not more – difficult to do on Google Street View as it was on the ground. I only made it because the 360-degree photography allowed me to go the wrong way down a one-way street. I finally found the Glasgow Road and followed it westwards past the large factory of bus-builders Alexander Dennis whose autonomous buses were shortly to begin running across the Forth Road Bridge. The roadscape quickly changed from rows of out-of-town supermarkets and car showrooms to hedge-lined fields. Nestled in the fields lay a forest of concrete and wire towers: one node in an electricity generating network that ran off in all directions along regularly spaced out pylons, as well as less visibly in underground cables powering the trains running between Edinburgh and Glasgow.[35] Back out in predominantly agricultural land, the frequent movement in time behind images became visible again as I clicked my way through a changing palate of browns, greens and yellows. Leaving Bonnybridge, I passed a tree-lined entrance sporting a familiar name: Diageo. The road leading down to Bonnybridge Bond was, as the sign spelled out, a Private No Through Road. It was out of bounds for the camera car, but not the satellite that offered me a bird's-eye view of the uniform rooftops of metal warehouses where Scotch whisky is aged in oak, close to the motorway junction that I crossed over a short while later.

I moved from Falkirk, through North Lanarkshire and then on into East Dunbartonshire passing farmland punctuated by towns and villages. Looking on the route map, it was clear that the road ran parallel to a canal that, like me, was also headed towards Glasgow. But the canal was invisible on Google Street View until I reached Kirkintilloch. In 1951, Kirkintilloch was picked out as a place of 'iron foundries, collieries, chemical works and a famous children's choir' but the old industries and the children's choir that was at the height of its popularity in the 1940s and 1950s have gone. Instead, Kirkintilloch has dug deeper back in time to celebrate the old transport network that these industries first relied upon. The sign on the edge of town welcomed me to the self-proclaimed 'Canal Capital of Scotland' as well as offering as something of an afterthought that it was also 'A Walkers are Welcome Town'.

The Forth and Clyde Canal that runs through the town has something of a chequered recent history. Nationalized in 1948, it was little used in the 1950s and closed in the early 1960s. The canal was a means of transport that had been twice supplanted, first by rail in the nineteenth century and then by road in the twentieth. In the case of the Forth and Clyde Canal it was ultimately road building that led to its closure. Rather than build a new bridge to span the canal as part of an urban expansion project, it was decided that it would be cheaper to simply dispense with a canal that was superfluous. The remaining stretches of canal fell into disrepair, but by the mid-1990s things had changed and canals were starting to be seen as an asset rather than liability. British Waterways unveiled plans to reopen the Forth and Clyde Canal, which became a reality after attracting funding from the National Lottery Millennium Fund. Over £80 million later, the canal reopened for business. As well as offering a coast-to-coast link by boat, the towpath could accommodate cross-country walkers and cyclists as well as the network cables that digital connectivity depended upon.[36]

It would have seemed foolhardy in 1951 to invest so much in what was seen as a long-dead technology. But it wasn't simply in the lowlands of Scotland that canals were reopening. As I'd discovered in Preston, the first few years of the new century saw a burst of canal building. Around 300 miles of canal were either reopened or dug anew. This investment was seen to make economic sense with the prospect of the outlay being paid back many times over by the tourist economy. But there were also bigger ambitions for canals that included their role in flood management and moving water around the country from areas of plenty to those of drought. Cashing in on this revival of canals, Kirkintilloch started an annual canal festival in the early 2000s, which draws thousands to the town, and claimed the title 'canal capital' for itself, much to the bemusement of some locals who saw Falkirk with its dramatic new wheel as offering a better claim. The sign I passed hadn't been altered, or at least if it had it had been changed back. But on Flickr I found an image where the first 'c' was erased on the sign welcoming motorists to Scotland's self-proclaimed '(c)anal capital'.[37]

It wasn't long before I approached the edges of Glasgow and passed, as the *About Britain* guide instructed, through 'the suburb of Bishopsriggs' before making my way into the 'Proud Host City of the Glasgow 2018 European Championships'. I could see a cluster of tall tower blocks to the left, before the road became the dual carriageway of post-war road widening that led on to the urban motorway. I kept going on the old route as far as I could into Scotland's 'Second City' which H. G. Stokes seemed to be both enthralled and appalled by in equal measure. Gazetteer entries were supposed to be confined to describing the mere essentials, but Stokes could not resist giving his prejudices free reign as he described a 'place of energy and purpose . . . a place of continual noise and appalling slums . . . a place where the cosmopolitanism of a seaport is aggravated by largescale immigration from Ireland.' I very much wanted to explore Glasgow on foot, but from my kitchen in Bristol I was only able to get virtually lost in its streets on Google Street View.

It was one of a number of times along this digital journey where I'd longed for more than the screen-based experience. I'd wanted to smell the air in the Carse of Gowrie, and feel the wind crossing over the Firth of Forth and River Tay. And on the beautiful stretch of road that meandered through a wooded valley along the River Earn, I'd wished that I'd been, literally, in the driving seat, feeling the twists and turns of the road. At virtual journey's end, I reflected that it had been possible to retrace the entire length of this guidebook route online because the Google Street View camera car had been there before me, in most cases multiple times. Google had delivered on their promise to photograph 250,000 miles of Britain's road network. Not only was it possible to retrace the route virtually, but as I discovered in Clackmannanshire, following these roads on Google Street View took about the same amount of time as driving them in 'normal traffic conditions', even if the constant, rapid clicking left me feeling that I'd just taken part in a slightly nausea-inducing pogo-stick race.

That it was possible to retrace this entire route from Edinburgh through St Andrews, Dundee and Perth, to Glasgow, was evidence of one of the most dramatic and ubiquitous changes that has taken place since 1951. The development of computers and the digital infrastructure of the World Wide Web offered not only the raw processing power that meant that millions of images could be stored, stitched together and summoned at the click of a mouse, but also the connectivity that meant I could access all this from my lightweight laptop in Bristol. This technology meant I didn't need to leave my kitchen. As I'd discovered when crossing the Firth of Forth, a future is being enacted that sees autonomous vehicles as the answer to getting commuters and shoppers in and out of Edinburgh. With plans to roll this out in buses, lorries and cars, the digital revolution amounts not only to a radical reimagining of our relationship with place, but also to cars and the road. Autonomous vehicles make drivers into passengers. I've never really thought of myself as anything like a 'petrol head'. I tend to buy incredibly functional, second-hand cars that I then run into the ground and replace with another, suitably sensible and reliable, model. But following the Google camera car along the twisting road in the wooded valley of the River Earn, I found myself itching to get back on the road.

Perth–Huntingtower–Methven–Braegrum–Gilmerton–Crieff–Comrie–St Fillans–Lochearnhead–Luib–Crianlarich–Ardlui–Tarbet–Arrochar–Rest and Be Thankful–Cairndow–Clachan–Inveraray–Cladich–Dalmally–Taynuilt–Connel Ferry–Oban

12

Highlands and Islands of Scotland

Perth–Crianlarich–Oban (128 miles)

In the summer of 2020 Scotland opened up a little after four months of lockdown. In the narrow window between the dip in the first wave and the rise of the second that winter, I drove north. I considered retracing my earlier virtual journey from Edinburgh to Glasgow by road, but decided to leave that as my sole screen-based experience. Heading into south-east Scotland I was careful to avoid all the roads from that previous journey, but there was one moment when I saw something that looked familiar. Off to the right, I spotted a large, white 'golf ball' as I drove on a road that ran parallel to the one I'd followed on my laptop. I was struck not only by the difference in driving past this scene rather than clicking along online, but also by the wider view of the 'golf ball', and particularly its setting, which was afforded by actually being there. I took the motorway that I'd virtually criss-crossed from my kitchen table into Perth where I stopped to fill up with petrol. With a mask covering my nose and mouth, I went inside to pay. The shop door was emblazoned with a sobering sign warning drivers that 'over half of all road deaths happen on country roads' like the ones that I was about to embark on. Perhaps virtual journeys were safer after all.

I'd chosen to drive from Perth to Oban for my final journey because of the symmetry with the first that I'd taken across Devon a couple of years earlier. In most of the *About Britain* guides six tours were chosen to provide a taste of the region. But there were exceptions. Two volumes – to the West Country and the Home Counties – offered double the number of tours. And the volume to the Highlands and Islands of Scotland that I'd brought with me also included more than six. There was a seventh slipped in as a kind of bonus tour. It seemed fitting to follow the seventh tour for my first and final drives, more or less coast to coast and once more accompanied by my wife and daughters. So after a few days holidaying in the Neuk of Fife, I headed to Perth and embarked on this final journey.

I followed the guidebook's instruction to leave 'by the Crieff Road'.[1] As I'd discovered elsewhere, this was easier said than done. After navigating the one-way system through the centre of Perth, and then the inevitable inner ring road around it, I headed west past the familiar signs of strip-mall chain stores and restaurants. Just beyond these lay the entrance to Perth College, set back from the road in walled, wooded grounds. Originally established as Perth Technical College in the early 1960s, these buildings were transformed into the south-easternmost point in Scotland's newest university, which I'd glimpsed a reference to on the sign on the outskirts of Perth on my screen-based journey. Granted university status in the early 2010s, the University of the Highlands and Islands includes thirteen colleges that run from Perth and Dunoon in the south, up to Stornoway and Lerwick in the north. Driving into Perth, I'd been welcomed into 'a University city', and when I reached Oban at journey's end I was once more welcomed into 'a University town'.

Perth's place on the southernmost edge of this 'Highland' university reflects its ambiguous position somewhere along the boundary between Scotland's Lowlands and Highlands.

In his opening essay in the guidebook, the author, journalist and newspaper editor Alastair Dunnett explained that the Highlands lay north of a line 'drawn between Dumbarton on the Clyde, and Stonehaven, south of Aberdeen, on the east coast': a line replicated in red ink on the guidebook cover. As a result, 'by a freak of' what he saw as 'this too rigid geography' Perth was 'abandoned to the Lowlands'. This did not prevent it being chosen as one of the three centres, along with Oban and Inverness, for the seven tours that took motorists through the Highlands and Islands. But while the starting point for this tour, Perth, was missing from the gazetteer at the end of the guidebook; given that 'freak of . . . geography' it had been located instead at the back of the guidebook to the Lowlands.[2]

Beyond the entrance to this south-easterly spur of the University of the Highlands and Islands, I passed a string of businesses spaced out along the road. On the left, a car showroom was paired with a crash repair centre. With the rather ominous sign that I'd seen at the petrol station still in the forefront of my mind, I gripped the wheel a little tighter. On the other side of the road lay St Johnstone's football ground. The Scottish Premiership had just restarted and the sign out front advertised the next home game against Aberdeen. Scheduled for the Saturday a few days before I drove by, it had been postponed at the last minute after a local spike in Covid-19 infections in Aberdeen had also included some of the squad in its number. When it was finally played, fans would not be in attendance but reduced to sitting on their sofa watching live on 'Saints TV' while digging into a snack pack containing McDiarmid Park staples: Scotch pies and empire biscuits all washed down with a mug of Bovril. Just past the stadium, I stopped for masked shoppers crossing from the DIY superstore on one side of the road to the grocery superstore on the other, before leaving the urban edges behind.

I drove through undulating arable land on a road whose tight turns followed the historic field boundaries. From the ridge, I looked down on fields that ran the full gamut from freshly ploughed to freshly harvested and offered up a patchwork of colours ranging from browns, through greens, to yellows. In one field, the farmer was midway through ploughing, turning it from golden to dark brown strip by strip, and I wondered if he'd bought his tractor and plough from the large, roadside showroom I'd passed with a row of shiny agricultural equipment parked out the front. In the distance another field appeared almost spotlit by the sun gleaming on ripe barley. But my focus quickly shifted from the colours in the middle distance to matters much closer to hand when a pigeon flew straight at the windscreen, making me instinctively duck my head.

Following this road from Perth to Crieff in 1951, motorists were instructed to look out for the 'ruined Huntingtower Castle, formerly called Ruthven Castle'. I passed the ruins, now safeguarded by Historic Scotland, to the right, but it was closed to visitors like other heritage attractions along the route. It was the first of a number of castles visible from the road. The next, perched up on a low ridge and standing out from the surrounding green in its creamy-white render on the edge of Methven, had been restored and was normally busy offering 'fairytale' castle homestays and hosting weddings, but now lay empty.[3] Driving through Methven, I passed a Scottish flag proudly flying outside a house to the right, and a life-sized model of a deer standing to attention by the front door of one of the row of houses on the left. Just beyond the village I turned off to the right, drawn by a brown tourist sign pointing up the hillside that simply said 'Pictish Stone'. I found the etched red-sandstone slab, or at least a replica of it, surrounded by an ornate, black, iron fence, in the tiny hamlet of Fowlis Wester. The original lay a short distance away in the squat church, but this was locked so I had to peek in through the window. But there was also another way to take a look. A sign hanging on the fence explained that 'the stone is currently inaccessible for your safety. Scan this QR code for a glimpse inside.' My older daughter pulled her phone out, and the Pictish Stone appeared, rotating, on the screen, but I decided to stick with the physical replica in front of me and the sight of the original through ancient glass.

Back on the main road, I continued towards Crieff along the ridge. Motorists driving along here in 1951 were told to look out for the 'Abercairny market gardens' that 'lie to the left in this fertile and richly wooded part of Strathearn'. I passed a lonely polytunnel along the road, and a little further on there was a house with a decent-sized steading for sale. Heading into Crieff – the 'heart of Strathearn' as the sign informed me – it seemed that this was also the beginning of the Highlands. 'Coming into Crieff there is a good view of the Knock of Crieff (911 feet) and of Ben Chonzie (3,048 feet)' the caption by the map in the *About Britain* guide explained, and it was here that I saw the first high mountains in the distance. It was clear I was entering a tourist landscape. Both sides of the road were liberally sprinkled with large Victorian villas that had been remodelled as B&Bs and small hotels and the shops that lined either side of the main road in Crieff offered up crystals and kilts alongside loaves and fishes.

On the far edge of this tourist town, I passed another brown tourist sign pointing down to the Glenturret Distillery. I'd seen the first one advertising 'The Famous Grouse Experience' beside the road a few miles back. It reminded me of similar signs advertising Bombay Sapphire when I'd driven along the River Test, and I was tempted to pull in. First opened in the early 2000s, 'The Famous Grouse Experience' cashed in on the rise in whisky tourism. But its location here owed more to the fact that this distillery lay on the southern edge of the

Highlands than it did to any idea of *terroir* that I'd reflected upon before. Given that this blended whisky was made from tens of different kinds, in a sense 'The Famous Grouse Experience' could be sited anywhere. But it was the well-established and conveniently located tourist landscape of the Trossachs that was chosen to take the visitor on a virtual tour of Scotland, followed by a tasting and shopping 'experience'. Even if I had pulled in, I was a couple of years too late for the Famous Grouse because the distillery had since changed hands. It now offered a tasting of Glenturret single malts that I imagined the motorists in 1951 might have enjoyed as much as the modern-day traveller.[4] They had just reopened for business after being closed since the spring, but I had a long day of driving on country roads ahead of me, so kept going towards Comrie.

When they directed motorists along these routes in 1951, those planning the *About Britain* guides were aware that they sent them into a tourist landscape. The Trossachs had drawn visitors since its celebration by nineteenth-century romantics and the guidebook described it as 'bristling' with people and 'some of the most famed scenery in the world'. Dunnett was conscious that the post-war years marked the growth of mass tourism, with 'a Highland . . . holiday' no longer 'an elaborately simple life for the wealthy in a shooting lodge' but rather the experience of 'visitors who neither shoot, fish, nor climb, and are content with country and people' and stayed in 'the small remote hotel and the wayside cottage which have rooms to let to ordinary folk'. Since 1951, tourism has grown here from cottage industry to big business. The last fifty years have seen a tripling in visitor numbers to over 15 million a year – with most coming, like me, in August – and a five-fold rise in the numbers that come from overseas. Tourism has grown to become a big part of the Scottish economy, mirroring the global trend, although there were signs along my route of the impact of a global pandemic on this industry.[5]

It was perhaps not surprising that the former 'Lawer's Agricultural School' between Crieff and Comrie that the guidebook mentioned now offered up the former lodge as a holiday cottage. The Agricultural School had been developed just a few years before motorists drove past. It responded to the increased mechanization of agriculture that the *About Britain* guides celebrated, and offered a year of training to 30 or so local boys to prepare them for the changing world of farming.[6] The lodge was not the only place to stay along a road peppered with a hostel, caravan park, holiday cottages and lodges, B&Bs and small hotels.

On the southern edge of Comrie, five Nissen huts in a former POW camp were being renovated as holiday cottages that 'retain the "look" of the Nissen hut, but with quality fittings and furnishings'. Elsewhere on this site bought by a local trust when military use ended in the mid-2000s, other Nissen huts have been developed to house small businesses as well as a heritage exhibition. 'Due to the Covid-19 outbreak' the 'visitor attraction' was 'closed until further notice' so I wandered around at my 'own risk'. The camp was one of a network of labour camps rapidly constructed in the early years of the war for Italian prisoners, before housing captured German soldiers after the D-Day landings. In the late 1940s, the last German prisoners of war left and the camp was repurposed to house British soldiers who trained here. In the far corner, a nuclear bunker was built at the very end of the Cold War; it had recently been bought to be repurposed for server and data storage in the digital age.[7]

I left this former military landscape turned community asset and made my way back to the main road and out of Comrie. The road ran along the side of the river for a while, before turning away and then returning to run parallel to it again. It was another of those tree-lined tunnels of a road that ran through a familiar landscape of estates I'd seen on my journeys through Northumberland and Scotland. The uniform stone walls of one estate after another ran alongside the road, punctuated by stone lodge houses. Mixed deciduous and coniferous woods the other side of the wall were wreathed in young green ferns. Dropping down to Loch Earn, I entered into the Loch Lomond and Trossachs National Park. Once inside the park I stopped in a lochside layby and sat with my family on a bench looking out across the water eating the Scotch pies, which we'd bought at the red double-fronted bakery in Comrie, before scurrying back to the car during a sudden heavy rain shower.

This National Park was a relative latecomer compared to many of the others. Although it was the first one created in Scotland, the Loch Lomond and Trossachs National Park was not established until 2002. The second, in the Cairngorms, followed quickly in 2003. Both were a long time coming. At the time that National Parks were being planned in England and Wales in the 1940s, the same process was taking place for Scotland. In their 1947 report, the Scottish National Parks Committee recommended that five National Parks 'be established in Scotland as soon as possible' and certainly within ten years. Top of their list was 'Loch-Lomond – Trossachs' with 'The Cairngorms' also included, along with three others: 'Glen Affric – Glen Cannich – Strath Farrar', 'Ben Nevis – Glen Coe – Black Mount' and 'Loch Torridon – Loch Maree – Little Loch Broom'. As they confessed, choosing only these areas proved difficult 'since so much of the whole area of Scotland is of National Park quality'.[8]

In the end it took more than half a century before the first Scottish National Park was finally created in Loch Lomond and the Trossachs. In part this delay was because Scotland and

England faced different problems in the post-war years. While in England, the growth of urban and industrial areas were seen as forces to be kept at bay through preservation of 'wild' land, in Scotland the situation was seen to be the opposite. Rather than preservation being the priority, rural depopulation and economic decline were more pressing concerns. This was a view clearly shared by Dunnett. In his opening essay he referenced what he termed 'the Highland problem' as well as offering up the kind of large-scale infrastructure investment like hydroelectric power schemes as the 'solution', one that sat uneasily with the wilderness of National Parks.[9]

But there was another economic issue at play. While the Scottish National Parks Committee's report shared much with the reports in England and Wales, it differed significantly in one important way. It assumed that the creation of National Parks would involve the purchase of large areas of uncultivated land, owing more to the model developed in the United States. In the case of Loch Lomond and the Trossachs, they estimated that this was likely to cost £300,000 (over £9 million today). A second inquiry was initiated to consider financing National Parks given that it would involve the compulsory purchase of large tracts of land. Not only did the costs involved present a challenge, but these plans also clashed with the interests of a powerful group of landowners in a country where landownership was – and still is from the frequent sight of estate walls running alongside the road – highly concentrated: just under 1,300 landowners own two-thirds of Scotland. Rather than becoming National Parks, the five areas identified by the committee in the late 1940s ended up receiving something of a consolation prize and were made into 'National Park Direction Areas'. In the 1980s, they became part of a wider group of 'National Scenic Areas'. It was only after Scottish devolution that legislation was finally enacted to create National Parks that were charged with promoting sustainable social and economic development alongside the more familiar twin aims of preservation and access.[10]

I drove along Loch Earn on a stretch of road that the *About Britain* guide described as 'one of the most pleasant in Scotland'. The route clung to the shore of the loch and turned out to be the first of many such roads shaped by the water's edge. This middle section followed a regular rhythm: tracking the full length of the loch shore, turning up into the hills and then driving up and over a mountain pass before descending down to drive alongside another loch and repeating the same. The first mountain pass took me from Lochearnhead and over to Crianlarich 'up wild, boulder-strewn Glen Ogle'. Although ascending by car, the guidebook drew attention to the 'marvel of railroad engineering' that could be seen 'high on the opposite side of the glen' where 'the railway cuts its way through sheer rock'. Once in Crianlarich, H. G. Stokes also favoured rail over road, describing the station here as 'one of the pleasantest spots in which to await a rail connection'.[11] I didn't stop at the still-functioning station, but admired the Glen Ogle Viaduct, which now carries a cycle path, rather than the Callander to Oban railway.

Making my way towards Crianlarich with its scenic station I spotted something more normally seen on British motorways. An average speed camera system had recently been installed to deter the estimated third of drivers who race along this flat and gently twisting stretch of road that goes along the valley floor at something well above 60 mph. It was not the first such deterrent to speeding. Alongside the familiar sight of yellow rectangular speed cameras introduced in the early 1990s, I encountered a variety of speed-reducing technologies, ranging from a policeman pointing a speed camera at the road, through police-jacketed scarecrows on the edge of villages, to what can best be described as a stern-looking welcoming committee of four women with their arms crossed standing alongside the road where drivers were meant to slow from 60 to 30 mph. These actions represent an attempt to reduce, or eliminate, road deaths in Scotland. The trend in Scotland has been downward, from around 700–900 a year in the 1970s to around 200 in the 2010s. This mirrors the wider picture on British roads where fatalities fell during this period, levelling out at somewhere around 1,700 a year during the 2010s, making Britain's roads, per head of population, some of the safest in Europe.[12]

At Crianlarich the road climbed up over another pass. From the bilingual road signs it was clear that this was no longer simply the way from Crianlarich to Tarbet, but also from A'Chrìon-Làraich to An Tairbeirt. The first bilingual road signs had been placed alongside the A87 through Skye in the mid-1980s and some roads in the Highlands in the mid-1990s. But after devolution there was more widespread adoption. In the early 2000s, Transport Scotland decided to put them along the main trunk roads that ran through the more Gaelic-speaking areas of Highland and Argyll. The road I was driving on was included in this scheme, and in the late 2000s bilingual road signs were erected on this stretch as part of a £2-million initiative to support the new Scottish government's Gaelic Language Plan which sought to safeguard a language spoken by less than 2 per cent of the population. As was the case in Wales, questions were raised over the impact of bilingual signage on road safety, as well as the cost. Although a Transport Research Laboratory report in the early 2010s recognized that bilingual signs 'increased the demand' placed on drivers in Scotland, they concluded that 'this increase can be absorbed, and managed'.[13]

The bilingual direction signs weren't the only ones that caught my eye as I drove 'into wooded Glen Falloch with 3,000 feet mountains towering on the left'. I'd read in the guide that 'some

4 miles from the head of Loch Lomond the untamed Falls of Falloch cascade down the mountain into the glen' and wondered about stopping off there for a quick look. But the brown tourist sign had been painted over and the car park closed during the pandemic. I'd hoped to stop and walk a short stretch of the West Highland Way that crossed the road just before the falls and then ran parallel to me along the riverbank. Created in 1980 as Scotland's first long-distance footpath, the West Highland Way runs for close to 100 miles from just north of Glasgow up to Fort William. But those mountainous 100 miles or so could be simply the start of many miles more. In the 2010s, the creation of the International Appalachian Way linked this stretch of long-distance footpath with others in Europe in an act of reversing the separation of the continents and returning to the kind of geological timescales that the guides were so attuned to.

Instead of braving the August midges on a stretch of the West Highland Way, I stopped on the shores of Loch Lomond. Driving into the valley, I could see layers of peaks in a greyish-blue haze in the distance. I was reminded of the words of an earlier guidebook that wrote of the 'capacity' of the 'rugged' 'Highland hill' 'to take on at a distance a wistful, cerulean blue'.[14] But this wasn't merely a National Park landscape of romantic 'wistful' mountains and lakes. As the caption that ran alongside this stretch of the route map proudly explained, the more than 3,000-foot-high Munroe of 'Ben Vorlich (3,092 feet) dominates the first few miles of the drive down Loch Lomond' before 'suddenly scenery combines with utility where the Loch Sloy hydro-electric scheme commences at the Invereagles power station'. When motorists passed by here in 1951, the lochside power station and pipes running down the steep hillside from the top reservoir at Loch Sloy had just been completed. Planned in the early 1940s and constructed later that decade, this vast hydroelectric power station was opened in 1950.

Invereagles shared much with the technology deployed inside Electric Mountain in North Wales, but here the 10,000-foot tunnel carrying water released from Loch Sloy down to the turbine hall on the banks of Loch Lomond was all clearly visible. There was no hiding this transformative technology in the 1950s. Rather, the coming of concrete hydroelectric power-station buildings and miles of pipelines to the Highlands were cause for celebration. The author of the commemorative booklet produced to celebrate its official opening wrote that this was not simply about bringing electricity to the Highlands but a 'new spirit . . . where before there was only depopulation and despair'. And it was merely the beginning of a much greater transformation. The closing pages offered up a long list of other sites either completed, under construction or due to be built, along with the optimistic boast that 'the story of Loch Sloy is being repeated in other Highland glens where turbulent waters are being diverted and controlled to produce electricity'.[15]

Hydroelectricity was celebrated by Dunnett, so it was no surprise that he drew the passing motorist to the wonder of this new technology and the mountain scenery in equal measure. He referenced the scheme at Loch Sloy in his opening essay, seeing it as a worthy transformation of this landscape of tourism. While he was sure that 'a day's sample' of the Trossachs would 'more than satisfy anyone who has not been to the far north' he was critical of the way that this area had been 'so resoundingly romanticized by Sir Walter Scott that history has tended to hang round Highland necks' before adding as a more hopeful aside 'not entirely, however'. His hopes lay on 'the newly completed power house of the Loch Sloy hydroelectric scheme'. While 'before work started on the dam in 1946 there had not been for years any soul living within miles of it' its appearance had brought jobs in its wake. Just a few pages on in the guide, a photograph of the Loch Sloy Dam was paired with one of a mountain range, with a shared caption running underneath the two that explained that 'distilling and the other small local industries of the Highland zone cannot solve the Problem. But perhaps it can be solved by the production of power in this land of lochs and high rainfall. Here is Loch Sloy Dam, one of the projects giving new hope to the Highlanders – who cannot live by the superb scenery' alone. Dunnett chose to close his opening essay with a celebration of this technology that was 'giving the Highlands the chance of a well-balanced economic life' and proving 'that the Highlands and Islands are not to be left behind or left bankrupt in the modern world'.[16]

I stopped to take a closer look at this power station, pulling into the car park of the National Park visitor centre. Walking out along the jetty stretching into the loch, I gazed across the water to the power station and the miles of pipes running up the hillside behind it. 'It's an unmistakable sight on the shores of Loch Lomond' announced the National Park signage but it was clearly a sight that the architects who had created the first of a series of 'Scottish Scenic Routes' viewing platforms in the mid-2010s had chosen to eschew. I found, and clambered up, the wooden pyramid of An Ceann Mòr among the trees behind the visitor centre. Standing at the top offered a different view along the length of the loch, the water framed by the mountains that tumbled down on either side. It was a view purposefully composed to omit the concrete of the power station from the vantage point of a wood-clad structure designed to blend in with the landscape. Not for the first time did I discover a turn away from the concrete so beloved of the 1950s.

Shortly after leaving the visitor centre I entered another designated landscape that partly overlaps with the National Park. Argyll National Forest Park was created in 1935. This 'vast area of about 60,000 acres, heaving with hills and pierced by sea and inland lochs' as Dunnett described it, was 'the first

. . . state forest park . . . to be established' in Britain. As I'd discovered on my first journey through Eggesford, mass afforestation was originally envisioned as a means of ensuring a steady supply of home-grown timber during future conflicts. But by the 1930s, there was a concern to also develop forests as recreational areas. The first National Forest Park here was quickly followed by National Forests in the Forest of Dean, Snowdonia and elsewhere in Scotland.[17] That this was a landscape of both arborial production and recreation was clear from the road. I passed trucks coming in the opposite direction laden with freshly felled timber, as well as the turn-off to Argyll Forest Cabins offering timber-built accommodation in a woodland setting beside the loch, complete with bike hire for those who wanted to follow the forest roads.

At Tarbet, I left the shore of Loch Lomond that I'd followed for the last few miles. 'The route turns off to the right at Tarbet Hotel for a 2-mile run to Arrochar, but not before some fine views of Ben Lomond looming above the far shore of the loch' the *About Britain* guide informed me. Turning at the Tarbet Hotel it was clear that not all was well. From the paper sign tacked to the doors, it was apparent that it had just closed. The company – which owned a string of hotel chains and coach tours – had collapsed as tourism became one of the industries hardest hit by a global pandemic that kept both overseas and domestic visitors at home.[18] It was not the only large hotel I passed where the empty car park and signs pasted up on the front door were evidence that they were 'closed until further notice'.

This stretch of road – from Tarbet, through Arrochar, and then along the side of Loch Long – was recommended to motorists following a tour from the sister *About Britain* guide to the Lowlands, which took them from Glasgow around Loch Lomond and then along the full stretch of Loch Long before returning to Glasgow. As they drove along this loch, those motorists were informed that 'Loch Long is an attractive sea loch, fringed by trees and with a torpedo-testing range'. Although Dunnett checked the tours for both volumes in September 1950, and wrote the captions alongside the editorial team in London, there was no mention of the weaponry below the surface in the guidebook I followed.[19]

First created in 1912 to test and range torpedoes manufactured at the new munitions factory built in Greenock, RNTR Arrochar only closed in the mid-1980s and the buildings were finally demolished in the late 2000s. It was, perhaps not surprisingly, at its busiest during the Second World War, when around 50 torpedoes were tested each day. By the 1980s, the loch was no longer suitable for testing new, guided torpedoes. I saw what little was left of the former Loch Long Torpedo Range buildings just beyond Arrochar, where fishermen perched on the remains of the pier stretching out into the water. In place of torpedo testing, grand plans have been drawn up to build a resort complex of hotel, housing, timeshare apartments and a marina on the shore. But when, and whether, these will be built remains unclear. Planning permission has lapsed, and if the recent closure of the Tarbet Hotel is anything to go by, this site may remain fenced off and derelict for quite some time.[20]

The closure of the torpedo testing site did not spell the end for the military-industrial complex. Far from it. Another part of Loch Long closer to the sea was reworked during the Cold War as a home for Britain's nuclear weapons: first Polaris in the 1960s and then Trident in the 1980s. The spot chosen lay over 10 miles away on the other side of the loch. Millions were spent in the 1960s building storage and maintenance facilities for the new Polaris warheads, carried aboard navy submarines. A few decades later, far more was spent on an engineering project, which rivalled the cost of the Channel Tunnel, to construct a series of deep bunkers to house Trident missiles.[21] While the missiles are housed along this loch, the submarines that carry them are based a short sail away on the neighbouring Gare Loch. The warheads are manufactured much further away in Aldermaston, and are taken a few times a year by road in a tightly guarded convoy. Where they'd be moved to in England or Wales if Scotland voted in favour of independence was much debated in the run-up to the 2014 referendum, and no doubt will be again if another independence vote is held.

But I didn't follow the shores of Loch Long very far before turning up Glen Croe, where the guide explained that the 'route turns right from Loch Long and skirts the majestic Cobbler (2,891 feet), a favourite climb with the Clydeside workers' and then 'after a steep ascent from sea level the road reaches Rest and Be Thankful, marked by a stone (860 feet)'. In the end the road turned out to be particularly steep. Earlier I'd passed digital road signs warning me that the A83 was 'open via Old Military Road' built in the eighteenth century in the wake of the Jacobite rebellion. What this meant became clear as signs directed me off the main road, which rises more steadily up the glen, and onto a narrow single-track road that followed the valley before making a final steep ascent. I waited while a long line of cars and lorries descended. Once they were down it was my turn. From the stop–start progress the line of vehicles made, it was clear that there were some sections particularly challenging for the large trucks and coaches. One came a little over halfway up, where the lorry a few cars ahead of us was guided through a tight left-hand corner leading to a narrow stone bridge by two men in high vis tops. Another came at the final steep hairpin that climbed to the car park at the top, which had been commandeered by the construction crew working to clear the landslip blocking the main road and repair the embankment above it.

The steep and twisting single-track road that I slowly made my way up following a convoy car was one well known to motor-racing enthusiasts in the post-war period. H. G. Stokes drew attention to it in his gazetteer when describing the Cobbler, whose 'lower slopes are the grandstand during the Glen Croe motor hill climb races'. From 1949 until 1970, an annual hill climb was raced here each summer and on a wet July in 1951 Dennis Poore made it to the top of this steep, mile-long track in his Alfa Romeo in well under a minute.[22] He would have been disappointed with my slow crawl up this rough track that avoided a long detour around to the next valley. I had planned on stopping at the top to take a look at the stone placed up here at the head of the pass, but was waved through by the convoy car as they prepared to escort the long line of waiting traffic down the narrow road in low gear. So, instead of resting and being thankful on the summit, I went down to Loch Fyne.

Making my way around the loch, I looked back across to Cairndow, where a cluster of warehouses with refrigerated lorries out the front spoke of what was going on alongside and underneath the water. Sitting cheek by jowl were a pair of factories owned by two of the big five companies that dominate fish farming in Scotland and whose activities lie at either end of the aquaculture business that has redefined fishing from an activity of harvesting to one of intensive farming. At the Cairndow hatchery, genetically selected fish are reared from eggs in freshwater tanks, before being transferred or sold on to fish farms where they are fattened in large cages that can hold over 500,000 salmon. These are found scattered around sea lochs like Loch Fyne or just offshore on Scotland's Atlantic coastline. Automated feeders regularly dispense pellets made from a mix of so-called 'trash fish' – fish too small to be sold – oil and meal. The tidal flow ensures that waste is washed away. Once the right size, the fish are stunned, gutted and cut up into fillets to be packaged at processing plants like the one in front of me, before ending up at smokehouses or on supermarket shelves. Their cycle is controlled from birth to death to ensure that consistently uniform fish are continuously produced for a market that demands both.

It is the piscine equivalent of Thanet Earth where the same processes of controlled and intensive production are applied to ensure year round high yields of salad vegetables. Like the greenhouses in Kent that do not rely on the inconsistencies of rainfall and sunshine, the hatcheries, sea cages, and processing plants along Loch Fyne and beyond are not dependent on the inefficient vagaries of natural processes such as migration. Confined to hatchery and sea cage, there is no need for farmed salmon to stray on to land, and head up river to spawn. The factories were a world away from the fly-fishing, trout-filled River Test I had visited on an earlier journey, and the photograph of a hatted gentleman 'gaffing a salmon in the Dee' towards the front of the guidebook. Scottish salmon production had come a long way from 1951 when Dunnett had reminded readers that 'Salmon, by the way, is something more than a sportsman's fish', and pointed out that 'every year a thousand tons or so are commercially netted on east- and west-coast rivers'. Seventy years later, the output of a large multinational industry was 200 times that in the 1950s, and it had shifted from using the fishing technology of the net to the intensive-farming technology of the cage.[23]

Intensive factory farming of Atlantic salmon was pioneered in Norway's fjords in the 1960s and 1970s, and the industry quickly developed in Scotland after the first fish farm was started in 1969. During the second half of the 1980s, salmon farming intensified here. Looking through the statistics from these early years the rate of growth is striking. In the mid-1980s, 7,000 tons of caged salmon was produced. Within two years, this had doubled. Another two years later it had doubled again. By the early 1990s, over 40,000 tons of salmon were being farmed in Scottish waters. While Norway remained the world leader, Scotland quickly established itself as the second major player in a rapidly growing global business that included Canada and Chile's west coast. In the mid-1980s, 500,000 tons of farmed salmon was produced worldwide. By 2010, this had risen five-fold. Aquaculture transformed fresh salmon from occasional treat to dinner-table staple, with farmed Atlantic salmon replacing tinned Pacific salmon in British supermarkets. Much came from Scotland, where well over 100,000 tons of salmon were produced each year in the 1990s and close to double that by the end of the 2010s. Like other regional foods that I'd come across, Scottish Farmed and Scottish Wild Salmon both received European Union protected (PGI) status in the mid-2000s.[24]

The industry created thousands of new jobs. By the early 2000s, 10,000 employees were involved in farming salmon at 200 sites across western Scotland, bringing in well over £500 million for the nation's economy. Reading Dunnett's opening essay, my sense is that he would have approved of this much-needed injection of cash into a region that he saw as having a 'problem' in the 1950s. In particular, he would have been pleasantly surprised at the growth of a new successor to replace the 'herring fishing industry' whose demise he discussed at length over the course of four pages. But as well as its supporters who heralded it as much needed diversification of the rural economy, the salmon farming industry also attracted its critics. Fears were expressed after every large escape that farmed salmon would overwhelm native, wild salmon. Animal rights campaigners flagged up the high numbers of deaths at hatcheries and farms. The industry reports 'mortality information' to the Scottish government on a regular basis, and the figures from the hatchery here at Cairndow over the last few years as a result of 'suffocation', 'fungus' and 'poor water quality and high water temperatures' make for rather grim reading. A particular challenge given the overcrowded conditions farmed fish live in has been managing disease, leading to the widespread use of antibiotics and pesticides, ending up in the oceans. Higher traces of toxins were found in farmed salmon by the authors of an article published in *Science* in the mid-2000s than wild salmon: an account that was quickly picked up by the press and led to a food scare over the safety of Scottish farmed salmon. It has therefore variously been seen as economic saviour or toxic danger.[25]

Continuing along the edge of the loch, I came upon another seafood being farmed in these waters. Just off the road was Loch Fyne Oyster Bar. It has been here since the late 1980s, when the owners of Loch Fyne Oysters converted old farm buildings to serve up Pacific oysters that they'd been rearing in the loch since the late 1970s. They have since diversified. Not only did the company move into smoking farmed salmon, but also set up a chain of restaurants across Britain during the 1990s.[26] Just like the salmon being hatched and dispatched, this was another story of 1970s aquaculture. The oysters farmed here in the waters of Loch Fyne were not the native, flat oysters that had dominated the domestic market in the nineteenth century but the non-native Pacific oyster brought to Britain to boost declining numbers of native oysters in the twentieth century. Like other non-native species, questions have been asked more recently about the long-term impact of introducing Pacific oysters to British waters. I pulled in to see if I could book a table for later that evening, but they were fully booked and it seemed a bit too early to pause for a mid-afternoon take-away snack of half-a-dozen Loch Fyne oysters. So I kept going along the side of the loch into Inveraray.

A sketch of Inveraray as seen from the other side of the loch lay alongside the strip map I was following. That view

– from afar – was the one also favoured by H. G. Stokes, who described Inveraray in his gazetteer as an 'intriguing village, looking like a town when viewed from across the water and preserving a remarkable medieval air'. Inveraray was pictured, but it was not picked out as a place to stop off, being in the eyes of the *About Britain* guide simply a place to drive through on the way to more 'attractive' spots to come. It was perhaps not surprising that Inveraray was overlooked on this 1951 itinerary. At the time it was a town belonging to the landed estate of the dukes of Argyll that had seen better days. In the 1950s, many of the houses in the old town were 'rapidly deteriorating'. Unable to maintain them, the estate sold them off to the Ministry of Works, which set about restoring them. This came after the death of the 10th Duke of Argyll in 1949 brought costly death duties. Parts of the estate were sold off, and the castle was opened up to paying visitors seven days a week for the summer season. By the 1970s, a period that has been described as the 'rise of the stately home', over 100,000 visited each year and the Duke of Argyll joined forces with a number of other great houses still in private ownership to attract overseas tourists. Following restoration after a fire in the mid-1970s, the castle continued to draw large numbers of visitors in the 1980s. It was the familiar story of the growth of the heritage industry, including the opening of the town jail to ghoulish visitors who flocked here in the early 1990s.[27] Reinvigorated by the heritage industry, Inveraray went from decaying estate town to popular historic attraction.

After a quick discussion with my fellow travellers, we decided to stop for the night. It was lovely to get out of the car, pull on our walking boots and head up a hill. We chose the Dun Na Cuaiche walk up the steep woodland path in the Inveraray Castle grounds to the castellated folly at the top. It was a beautiful early summer evening and the views from the top over Loch Fyne were wonderful. So much so that I half ran, half walked back up there first thing the next morning as the mist rose from the lake and the sun appeared behind the hills to the east. Looking out from the summit both times, I was conscious of the traffic noise coming from the lochside road that seemed to be funnelled up the steep slope. Standing there alone the next morning I was thinking about the whole motoring venture that was coming to an end. I enjoy driving and there were some roads that I'd driven that were a delight. But I realized from the top of Dun Na Cuaiche that I much prefer pulling on a pair of walking boots or running shoes and making my way up a hill.

After a breakfast of eggs and smoked salmon, I returned to the car for the last few miles over to the coast at Oban. The road passed beneath the central arch in this walled town before ascending steeply past the shinty club – a sport that Dunnett warned 'the tourist will rarely see . . . as it is a winter event' – and up the glen that I'd looked over and into on my way up and down Dun Na Cuaiche just a few hours earlier. Like so many other places along this route, the hillsides were covered in conifers that ran from light to dark green and were of different heights, reflecting decades of planting. Snow poles lined the road, but there was no need for them in mid-August, although the early morning sunshine had given way to cloud that rested on the mountain peaks. Off to the right, a herd of woolly brown Highland cattle grazed contentedly. Dropping down from the summit of this pass, I glimpsed the 'gaunt ruins of Kilchurn Castle' on the left jutting out into Loch Awe.[28]

Around, and then along, the other side of the loch I passed Cruachan Power Station. Opened in 1965, this was another of the hydroelectricity projects on which the pro-industry Dunnett pinned his hopes. But this was a little different from the earlier power station on the shores of Loch Lomond. The pipes weren't visible. Like in Dinorwig miles of tunnels were dug out of the mountain in the 1960s to create the first pumped-storage hydro-power station. As in North Wales, here visitors can board a bus at the visitor centre to take a guided tour into 'The Hollow Mountain'. But Covid-19 had put a stop to that, and I did wonder rather if the inside of one hollow mountain looked quite like the inside of another.[29]

At what the guide described as 'the majestic narrow gorge of the Pass of Brander, where the loch is narrowed to the River Awe', it felt as if the road too narrowed as the mountains closed in on this restricted corridor carrying road and river. The landscape opened out again as I entered into Taynuilt, where the cloud-covered high mountains were now visible only in the rear-view mirror rather than the windscreen as I drove towards the sea at Connel Ferry. Along the coast, I passed a marina and another of the waterside hotels – this time with the car park full – and entered the 'University town' of Oban. I passed the Furan Gaelic centre opened in the mid-2010s as part of the council's response to the wider desire to safeguard and promote the language that I had seen on the road signs along much of this route. Descending to the bay I pulled in and wandered down to the water's edge. A ferry was just leaving from what Dunnett explained was the 'Charing Cross of the Highlands', hinting that the journey by car could be continued further west to the Islands.[30] But my driving was done. I headed back to the car, fixed magnetic L plates to the front and back and handed the keys over to my older daughter who had just started taking driving lessons. She drove along the coast road, underneath the 'ruins of Dunollie Castle guarding the entrance to Oban' to where the road met its end and turned into a path heading through bracken and brambles along to a deserted bay. Abandoning the car for walking boots once more, I made my way along the coast path as far as I could go.

It was good to be off the road and walking along a muddy path again. This was a journey that had made me think more about roads themselves as a technology. Slowly ascending Glen Croe, I had advanced up a landscape that had been criss-crossed with military roads to reassert control after the Jacobite rising. It reminded me of driving the ten straight miles of Stone Street from Canterbury and Telford's road into Bangor. Both had also been built to ensure state power over territory: one during the Roman occupation, the other to connect the colonial metropole in London with its periphery in Ireland. Roads continue to serve military purposes. In the case of the nuclear submarine base on Loch Long, warheads make their way from Aldermaston to Coulport by road, not water or air.

It was these landscapes that the state had already opened up that were ripe for the early decades of road-borne tourists. But in the early 1950s there were places, as Dunnett explained, where metalled roads had still not been built to connect isolated communities. In those places with rough tracks, Dunnett cautioned that 'the motorist needs a slight adjustment of mind when he comes to this countryside. It is not speed country, but there is reward in learning to take side roads or lesser tracks at twelve miles an hour.'[31]

The only 'lesser track' that I'd taken at 'twelve miles an hour' was the old military road up Glen Croe following a convoy car at a maximum speed of 15 mph. It was a speed – like crawling along through roadworks in South Wales – where it was possible to see differently. I wondered what I'd actually seen driving *About Britain*, along rural A and B roads generally at somewhere between 40 to 60 mph. I wondered if there was much that I'd missed. Walking up the steep hill just outside Inveraray, or along the coast path from Oban, I was aware of the different kind of experience of journeying through the landscape at 3 mph. I didn't simply glimpse the flash of colour of the roadside pink of rosebay willow herb as I climbed Dun Na Cuaiche, but picked and ate the wild raspberries growing along the wooded track. Following Google Street View I'd been itching to get back on the road again, with the window down. Driving again, I'd found myself longing to walk along muddy paths rather than follow shiny tarmac. I'd driven *About Britain*, but I wondered if I'd really managed to scratch the surface. In one sense the journey was over. In another sense, it felt like I'd only just begun.

Back About Britain

Sitting on a rock with my feet dangling in the water in Oban, I thought back to the dozen journeys I'd taken. I was reminded of something the guy who owned the chip shop in Inveraray had told me the day before when I'd met him on the street as I was having a late evening stroll and he was preparing to close for the night. We got talking and conversation turned, as it tended to in the summer of 2020, to the global pandemic that had closed his takeaway, and more or less the whole country, down for several months. With nothing to do, he told me that he'd decided to walk up Dun Na Cuaiche, the hill I'd headed up earlier that evening, for the first time in his life.

Like him, this series of guidebooks that I'd chanced upon in a charity bookshop had taken me places that I had never been to despite growing up and living in Britain for most of my life, a few years in Hungary and America aside. Although the strip maps that I followed felt at times impossible to navigate through the one-way systems and inner ring roads of British towns and cities transformed by the automobile age, they forced a kind of straitjacket discipline on me that took me places where someone else had decided I should go. That opened up roads that I had never travelled, places that I had never been and stories that I hadn't even thought of.

Setting out on the first journey, I'd been curious about how far things had really changed. Those putting the *About Britain* guides together were quick to celebrate the new, but they also had a strong sense that the new grew from the old and was evolutionary rather than revolutionary. 'On the Downs in

Wiltshire we can stand on a minute plot of ground on which the Iron Age farmer reaped his corn with a sickle' the series preface that opened each volume explained, before adding 'and watch a few yards away a combine harvester steadily devouring ripe acres of wheat'.[1] But I was less sure that this sense that change was limited by the underlying bedrock still rang true. Perched on a rock at the end of the final journey, it seemed that so much had changed. Not simply the bigger and more obvious stuff I'd expected to find like the decline of manufacturing industry and the closure of coal mines, but also the more subtle and yet critically important things like the ways that we think about the past, present and future, or about the land and what grows on it. Ways of imagining the world had changed just as much as infrastructure in something as seemingly short and fleeting as the course of a human lifespan.

That things have changed – and that things do change – felt like the single overarching and overwhelming experience that I took away from this journey of 1,345 miles. And that matters in all sorts of ways. One thing that histories of change suggest is a need for humility in the present. Revisiting places 70 years on, it was easy to be dismissive of the false hopes of those putting these guides together in the early 1950s. But one thing that being a historian has convinced me of is that we do well to be aware of our own blind spots that will be so obvious to future generations, but remain stubbornly hidden from us. Walking along the weed-covered tarmac at Pegwell Bay, it was almost laughable to imagine a moment in the 1960s when the hovercraft was lauded as the transport technology of the future, with visions of nuclear-powered hovercraft crossing the oceans. History has a way of being the pin that bursts the hyperbole of bubbles in the past. But it does this not so that we can laugh at those in the past who thought that way, but to hold up a mirror in the present to encourage us, if not to laugh at ourselves, then certainly to exercise a little more humility.

But there is more to histories of change than simply urging humility in the present. There is also the potential for imagining different futures. One of the things that draws me time and again to history is that understanding that things haven't always been this way means also realizing that things won't, and don't, always need to be like this. Stories of change in the landscape offer the potential for imagining and implementing new futures. At times those futures may well draw on the past, and those potential futures found discarded in history. Driving through the Fens I was struck by the ways that the future imagined for the landscape drew on a pre-seventeenth-century past that would seem to those sending motorists across Britain in 1951 as a reactionary turning back of the clock to a period before this area was drained for productive agriculture. The rewilding of the Fens offers a very different future from that of ever-increasing mechanization of agriculture that the *About Britain* guides both imagined and celebrated.

Despite this talk of change being potentially emancipatory, that is not how it always feels when you are living in the midst of it. I finished driving, and writing, this book during a global pandemic that led to the coining of the phrase 'the new normal', a phenomenon that suggested change was something very much here to stay. But change is something that has been mourned and fought, just as much as it has been celebrated. Driving through Britain I found plenty of stories of attempts to halt change. So many of the regulated spaces, whose boundaries I crossed, were created with an eye to preservation. There were plenty of buildings or landscapes that I passed by and through that I was only able to see because of the actions of those who set out to save them from the developer's bulldozer. And I was thankful for that.

But, I was also left troubled by a certain conservatism underlying some of these attempts to preserve. There is a long-standing critique that post-industrial and post-imperial Britain has been enamoured with the past rather than the future, and there was certainly evidence of this along these routes.[2] It was shockingly refreshing to read the celebration of the new in the *About Britain* guides, which thought nothing of lauding the application of concrete to a medieval bridge. Although naive in hindsight (and I, for one, was pleased to see the bridge over the Coquet restored to stone) there was also something attractive about reading the guidebooks that immersed me in a moment of optimism about building a new future from the past. Driving home after the last of the journeys, I wondered whether something had been lost since motorists were sent *About Britain* in 1951 in a year that seemed to promise the start of something new.

Back in Bristol, I tried to imagine what this experience might be like in another 70 years. I most likely won't be around in 2091, but I hope my children will be and I wondered what they would notice if they retraced these 12 routes put together in the middle of the twentieth century at the end of the twenty-first. Historians are notoriously bad at guessing what the future holds. Our specialism is the past. Following these guidebooks from 1951 it was clear that Britain has changed in many unexpected, as well as more predictable, ways over the three score years and ten of a human lifespan. And I was sure that this would also be the case in another 70 years.

Notes

ABOUT BRITAIN

1 *About Britain* (London: Collins, 1951) dustjacket blurb; Ruari McLean, *True to Type: A Typographical Autobiography* (London: Werner Shaw, 2000), p. 89; The National Archives, Kew (hereafter TNA), Works 25/57/A5/Q1, Confidential FB.C. (50) 8, 'Memorandum from the Director General to Council' (3 March 1950).

2 Ian Cox, 'The South Bank Exhibition. A Guide to the Story it Tells,' in *South Bank Exhibition. Festival of Britain Guide* (London: HM Stationery Office, 1951), p. 5.

3 TNA, Works 25/57/A5/Q1, Tours Advisory Panel, FB/Tours (49) 1, Ian Cox, Chairman 'Tours of Britain 1951', 'Festival of Britain 1951. Tours of Britain. Memorandum prepared by the Chairman as a basis for discussion at first meeting of the Tours Panel' (7 September, 1949).

4 TNA, Works 25/57/A5/Q1, FB Tours (49) 2, 'Memorandum from Angwin to Tours Panel' (7 October, 1949); TNA, Works 25/57/A5/Q1, Confidential FBC (50) 8, 'Memorandum from the Director General to Council' (3 March, 1950); TNA, Works 25/44/A5/A3, 12th meeting of the Festival of Britain Council (15 March, 1950).

5 TNA, Works 25/57/A5/Q2, 'Minutes of Meeting held in the Director-General's Office'. Becky Connekin, 'The Autobiography of a Nation', p. 129 sees the inexpensive pricing as evidence of the 'democratic approach to knowledge' that characterized the Festival's aims 'to distribute knowledge across class lines as well as the geographical areas of the United Kingdom' but my sense is that the pricing and production was more determined by the wishes of the Brewers' Society and their editorial team; TNA, Works 25/57/A5/Q2, 26/9/49, 'Notes on Financial and Other Implications of "Happy Travellers" Guides for the Festival of Britain' (26 September, 1949); TNA, Works 25/57/A5/Q1, FB Tours (49) 2, 'Memorandum from Angwin to Tours Panel' (7 October, 1949); TNA, Works 25/57/A5/Q1, FB Tours (49) 1st Meeting, 'Minutes of the First Meeting of the Tours Advisory Panel' (12 October, 1949);

TNA, Works 25/57/A5/Q1, 'Minutes of Second Meeting of the Guide Books Editorial Committee' (15 December, 1949).

6 TNA, Works 25/256/G1/C2/425, Letter from Penrose Angwin to Colonel James Stuart (19 May, 1950).

7 Tim Cole, *Traces of the Holocaust: Journeying in and out of the Ghettos* (London: Continuum, 2011); Robert Bickers, Tim Cole, Marianna Dudley, Erika Hanna, Josie McLellan, William G. Pooley and Beth Williamson, 'Creative Dislocation: An Experiment in Collaborative Historical Research', *History Workshop Journal* (forthcoming 2021).

8 TNA, Works C/2/457, 'Letter from H. O. Aldhous to Norman Pye' (12 July, 1950); 'Letter from Norman Pye to the Director' (20 July, 1950); 'Letter from Norman Pye to Contracts' (8 August, 1950).

9 William Balchin, 'Obituary: Professor Norman Pye, 1919–2007', *Geography* 92, 3 (2007), pp. 299–301.

10 *About Britain No. 1*, West Country. A New Guide Book with a Portrait by Geoffrey Grigson (London: Collins, 1951), p. 59. Hereafter, I simply reference the guidebooks as *About Britain No. 1*, *About Britain No. 2* etc.

11 Simon Schama, *Landscape and Memory* (London: HarperCollins, 1995), p. 26.

CHAPTER 1: WEST COUNTRY

1 *About Britain No. 1*, p. 80.

2 https://historicengland.org.uk/listing/the-list/list-entry/1385202

3 TNA, Works C/2/425, 'Letter to Colonel James Stuart from Penrose Angwin' (19 May, 1950).

4 TNA, Works 25/57/A5/Q2, 'Specimen Rough outline of a "Steering Script"' (16 November, 1949).

5 Robert Hewison, *Culture and Consensus: England, Art and Politics since 1940* (London: Methuen, 1995), p. 59; Becky E. Conekin, *'The Autobiography of a Nation': The 1951 Festival of Britain* (Manchester: Manchester University Press, 2003), p. 80.

6 TNA, Works C/2/425, 'Letter to Colonel James Stuart' (8 June, 1950).

7 John Prioleau, *Car and Country: Week-End Signposts to the Open Road* (London: J. M. Dent and Sons Ltd., 1929), p. 109.

8 Harold Perkin, *The Age of the Automobile* (London: Quartet Books, 1976); Sean O'Connell, *The Car in British Society: Class, Gender and Motoring 1896–1939* (Manchester: Manchester University Press, 1998),

p. 19; John Sheail, *An Environmental History of Twentieth-Century Britain* (Houndmills: Palgrave, 2002), p. 185; Trevor Rowley, *The English Landscape in the Twentieth Century* (London: Hambledon Continuum, 2006), p. 36.

9 'UK motorists facing busiest spring holiday in three years', *Guardian* (21 May, 2016).

10 N. D. G. James, *A History of English Forestry* (Oxford: Basil Blackwell, 1981), pp. 216–17.

11 J. D. U. Ward, 'Forest Birthday', *Daily Telegraph* (28 March, 1953), p. 6.

12 *Journal of the Forestry Commission* 23 (1952–1954), p. viii.

13 James, *A History of English Forestry*, pp. 207–10; Sheail, *An Environmental History*, pp. 82–3, 86.

14 J. D. U. Ward, 'An Oak to Mark a Million', *Daily Telegraph* (5 May, 1956), p. 6.

15 *Journal of the Forestry Commission* 25 (1956), p. v; Forestry Commission England News Release No: 14051 (28 September, 2010).

16 James, *A History of English Forestry*, pp. 233–6, 266.

17 Ward, 'Forest Birthday'; Ward, 'An Oak to Mark a Million'.

18 Fifty-First Annual Report, cited in James, *A History of English Forestry*, p. 257.

19 W. Gore Allen, *John Heathcoat and his Heritage* (London: Christopher Johnson, 1958), p. 191, plate opposite pp. 192, 201–3, 208–9.

20 https://www.bickleighmill.com

21 Roger Cary, 'Country Houses Open to the Public', *Burlington Magazine* 92, No. 568 (July 1950), pp. 209–13; 'Old Castle For Sale', *The Singapore Free Press* (22 October, 1953), p. 11; Curtis and Henson advertisement, *The Times* (30 June, 1955), p. 20; Property Market Correspondent, 'Bickleigh Castle Sold', *The Times* (13 February, 1957), p. 5; 'Sale of a Devon Castle', *Daily Telegraph* (18 February, 1957), p. 2; 'Bickleigh Castle Paintings Sold', *The Times* (16 April, 1957), p. 12; Hugh Montgomery-Massingberd, 'A House in Tune with the Past', *Daily Telegraph* (1 April, 1988); 'Top Six Castles', *Daily Telegraph* (15 July, 1989), p. ix; Hugh Montgomery-Massingberd, 'Thrills that Thunder down the Ages', *Daily Telegraph* (15 July, 1989), p. ix; John Armstrong, 'Petrol Crisis Cuts Visitors to Stately Homes', *Daily Telegraph* (19 November, 1979), p. 10; 'Two Big Successes', *Daily Telegraph* (24 November 1980), p. 8; Graham Norwood, 'How Can a Castle Earn its Keep?', *Daily Telegraph* (12 May, 2003).

22 Norwood, 'How Can a Castle Earn its Keep?'; Graham Norwood, 'Take me to the Tower', *Independent* (13 September, 2005).

23 Elizabeth Williamson, 'Growing Grapes of Success', *Daily Telegraph* (11 June, 1985), p. 9; Diana Wildman, 'A Vintage Crop of Vineyards', *Daily Mail* (29 October, 1993), p. 63; Hugh Clout, 'An Overview of the Fluctuating Fortunes of Viticulture in England and Wales', *EchoGeo* 23 (2013), pp. 7–9.

24 Anton Massel, *The Wine Pioneers*, p. 102; Gillian Pearkes, *Vinegrowing in Britain* (London: J. M. Dent and Sons, 1989), p. 12.

25 George Ordish, *Vineyards in England and Wales* (London: Faber and Faber, 1977), pp. 49–51; 'Maj.–Gen. Sir Guy Salisbury-Jones, inspecting the grapes . . .', *Sunday Telegraph* (5 November, 1961), p. 21; 'Grapes being gathered on the Hambledon vineyard of Maj.-Gen. Sir Guy Salisbury-Jones . . .', *Daily Telegraph* (7 November 1966), p. 20; Clout, 'An Overview of the Fluctuating Fortunes of Viticulture in England and Wales', p. 5; Prue Leith, 'Bacchus Brought to British Shores', *Daily Telegraph* (14 April, 1976), pp. 18–19.

26 'Off-Licence for Vineyard', *Daily Telegraph* (10 February, 1961), p. 17; 'Hopeful Vintner', *Daily Telegraph* (16 May, 1966), p. 14; John Morrell, 'A Winner for Shellfish', *Sunday Telegraph* (14 October, 1973), p. 10; Guy Salisbury-Jones, 'Burden on the British Wine-Grower', *Daily Telegraph* (13 July, 1977), p. 16; 'Wine Growers "Hampered by Prejudice"', *Daily Telegraph* (15 March, 1973), p. 9; Guy Rais, 'Bumper Year for *le vin* Hambledon', *Daily Telegraph* (11 October, 1976), p. 3; Leith, 'Bacchus Brought to British Shores'.

27 Estimates vary. See Leith, 'Bacchus Brought to British Shores'; Ordish, *Vineyards in England and Wales*, p. 15; Clout, 'An Overview of the Fluctuating Fortunes of Viticulture in England and Wales', pp. 1–14.

28 '£50,000 Cider Apples Rot', *Daily Telegraph* (24 September, 1951), p. 5; A. E. Burroughs, C. M. Ones, S. P. Oram and H. J. Robertson, *Traditional Orchard Project in England – The Creation of an Inventory to Support the UK Habitat Action Plan* (Natural England Commissioned Reports 77, 2010); Steven Morris, 'Orchards May Vanish by the End of Century, Conservationists Warn', *Guardian* (24 April, 2009).

29 'Apple Day a Public Holiday?', *Orchard Link News* 1, 13 (Autumn 2001), p. 2; Common Ground, *Orchards: A Guide to Local Conservation* (London: Common Ground, 1989).

30 'English Gardens' Part in 1951 Exhibition', *The Times* (21 January, 1950), p. 3; 'Spring Blossom in Devon', *The Times* (16 May, 1951), p. 10.

31 Francis Williams, *Journey into Adventure: The Story of the Workers Travel Association* (London: Odhams Press Limited, 1960), p. 113.

32 'Trust Opens House', *The Times* (8 June, 1978), p. 18.
33 'Killerton and Holnicote', *The Times* (26 February, 1943), p. 5;
34 'Killerton and Holnicote', *The Times* (26 February, 1943), p. 5; '17,000 Acres for Nation', *Daily Mail* (26 February, 1943), p. 3.
35 Alun Howkins, 'From Diggers to Dongas: the Land in English Radicalism, 1649–2000', *History Workshop Journal* 54 (2002), p. 19.
36 'Private Ownership of Large Estates', *The Times* (31 January, 1944), p. 2.
37 Valerie R. Belsey, *British Roads: Devon: Past and Present. A nostalgic look at the county's highways and byways* (Peterborough: Past and Present Publishing, 1993), p. 26; 'Motorway "Scar" on Estate', *Daily Telegraph* (21 July, 1971), p. 15; 'National Trust Profits From M5 Defeat', *Daily Telegraph* (28 February, 1973), p. 6.
38 Belsey, *British Roads: Devon*, pp. 15, 18, 20–21.
39 Cited in Phil Macnaghten and John Urry, *Contested Natures* (London: Sage, 1998), p. 170.
40 'Buy Locally, Act Globally', *Orchard Link News* 1, 2 (Autumn 1998), p. 2; 2007 UK Biodiversity Action Plan (2007).

CHAPTER 2: WESSEX

1 *About Britain No. 2*, pp. 75–6. Unless noted, other references to the guidebook in this chapter come from these pages.
2 *About Britain No. 2*, pp. 37; 55.
3 Simon Scott Plummer, 'Lost at sea but found in the Channel', *The Times* (13 October, 1976), p. iv.
4 Jean-Paul Rodrigue and Theo Notteboom, 'The Geography of Cruises: Itineraries, not destinations', *Applied Geography* 38 (2013), pp. 31–42.
5 https://www.mayflysound.com
6 'Roads for Prosperity' White Paper (1989). See launch of this White Paper in House of Commons Debate (18 May, 1989), *Hansard*, Volume 153, cc 482–96.
7 John Schofield, 'Discordant Landscapes: Managing Modern Heritage at Twyford Down, Hampshire (England)', *International Journal of Heritage Studies*, 11, 2 (2005), pp. 154–6.
8 House of Lords Debate (7 August, 1980), *Hansard*, Volume 412, cc 1586–7; Barbara Bryant, *Twyford Down: Roads, Campaigning and Environmental Law* (London: E & FN Spon, 1996), pp. 115; 181–2.
9 Martin Biddle, cited in Bryant, *Twyford Down*, p. vii.
10 Bryant, *Twyford Down*, p. 157.
11 Bryant, *Twyford Down*, pp. 193–206; Brian Doherty, 'Opposition to Road-Building', *Parliamentary Affairs*, 51, 3 (1998), pp. 370–83; Derek

Wall, 'Mobilising Earth First! in Britain', *Environmental Politics*, 8, 1 (1999), p. 82; Schofield, 'Discordant Landscapes', p. 152.

12 Cited in George McKay, *Senseless Acts of Beauty: Cultures of Resistance since the Sixties* (London 1996), p. 146.

13 Doherty, 'Opposition to Road-Building', p. 370; Wall, 'Mobilising Earth First!', p. 95.

14 See comments of Jonathon Porritt in Bryant, *Twyford Down*, p. 299; House of Commons Debate (18 May, 1989), *Hansard*, Volume 153, cc 482–96; 'Gloom on the M3', *Southern Daily Echo* (8 January, 2001).

15 Sally Eden, 'Faking it? The multiple meanings of environmental restoration near Twyford Down', *Cultural Geographies* 9 (2002), p. 324.

16 East Hampshire District Council, Planning Committee. Report of the Head of Planning, PS 491/2017 (7 December, 2017); https://www.bbc.co.uk/news/business-45086080

17 *The Dunlop Guide* (n.d. 1924?), p. 804.

18 http://www.alresfordheritage.co.uk/around-the-villages/ropley/ropley-032.html

19 'The Motorway Code', p. 2.

20 *About Britain No. 2*, p. 82.

21 Gilbert White, *The Natural History and Antiquities of Selborne, in the County of Southampton* (London: White, Cochrane and Co, 1813), p. 69.

22 Charles Lewis, *The Mid-Hants 'Watercress' Line: A brief history* (A Mid-Hants Railway Preservation Society Publication, 1980); https://www.watercressline.co.uk/product.php?xProd=139

23 P. N. Grimshaw, 'Steam Railways: Growth Points for Leisure and Recreation', *Geography*, 61, 2 (1976), p. 83; Simon Bradley, *The Railways. Nation, Network and People* (London: Profile Books, 2016), pp. 535–6.

24 *About Britain No. 2*, p. 81.

25 https://www.winchesterdistillery.co.uk/pages/our-story

26 *About Britain No. 2*, p. 44.

27 Paul Clayton and Judith Rowbotham, 'How the Mid-Victorians Worked, Ate and Died', *International Journal of Environmental Research and Public Health*, 6 (2009), p. 1242; Lewis, *The Mid-Hants 'Watercress' Line*, p. 12; Graeme John Down, 'Crook root disease of watercress: investigations into zoospore attraction, diagnostics and phlogeny', University of Bath PhD (2000), p. 4; https://www.watercress.co.uk/historical-facts; Overton Parish, 'Biodiversity Action Plan 2009 to 2014' (Overton Biodiversity Society, 2010), p. 14.

28 Anthea Gerrie, 'Watercress: Best of the Bunch', *Independent* (5 May, 2010).

29 EU No. TSG-GB-0062 'Watercress', *Official Journal of the European Union* C401/8 (2019).
30 *About Britain No. 2*, p. 65.
31 'Grosvenor Hotel, Stockbridge', plaque in hotel lobby; 'Obituary, Mick Lunn, river keeper', *Telegraph* (27 February, 2015); 'Clubs you cannot join', *Country Life* (30 October, 2008); James Gillespie and Graham Mole, 'Aristocracy of fishing turn to EU to save river', *Sunday Times* (9 December, 2012); *About Britain No. 2*, p. 65; Ian Katz, 'Come fly with me', *Guardian* (19 May, 2007); 'Unaudited Financial Statements for the Year ended 31 December 2018 for the Houghton Club Limited' submitted to Companies House (12 June, 2019).
32 http://www.users.waitrose.com/~horsebridge/about.htm
33 'Introduction' in Forestry Commission Guide, *New Forest* (London: HMSO, 1951), p. 2.
34 John Dower, *National Parks in England and Wales* (London: HMSO, 1945), p. 6.
35 *About Britain No. 3*, pp. 57–8.
36 Dower, *National Parks*, pp. 7–10.
37 Lord Robinson, 'Foreword' in Forestry Commission Guide, *New Forest* (London: HMSO, 1951), p. v; D. W. Young, 'The Forester's Task' in Forestry Commission Guide, *New Forest*, pp. 50–2.
38 Robinson, 'Foreword', p. v ; Young, 'The Forester's Task', pp. 48–52.
39 D. W. Young, 'The Commoners' Animals and the Court of Verderers', in Forestry Commission Guide, *New Forest*, p. 64.

CHAPTER 3: HOME COUNTIES

1 *About Britain No. 3*, pp. 62–3. Unless noted, other references to the guidebook in this chapter come from these pages.
2 *About Britain No. 3*, p. 1.
3 *About Britain No 3*, p. 34.
4 *About Britain No. 3*, pp. 60–79.
5 See for example Traffic Team and Highway Team, North Lincolnshire Council, 'Traffic signs, road markings and road studs on the public highway' (Version 2, October 2012), p. 28; 'UK Statutory Instruments, 2016 No. 362', 'The Traffic Signs Regulations and General Directions 2016', Schedule 11, 37.4.
6 'Operation Stack/Lorry Parking in Kent' (25 October, 2017), *Hansard*, Volume 630, Column 172WH.
7 Anthony J. Moor, *Lympne Airfield at War and Peace* (Fonthill, 2014), pp. 218–55; Keith J. Dagwell, *Silver City Airways: Pioneers of the Skies*

(Stroud: The History Press, 2010); 'Silver City Airways Car Ferry Service' brochure (1952); '*Skyways* Coach-Air' brochure (1969).

8 Dennis Barker, 'Sidney De Haan', Obituary, *Guardian* (23 February, 2002); John Carter, 'The little man's package', *The Times* (7 September, 1974), p. 11; Ray Maughan, '£6m Saga Holidays group is first on new issues market this year', *The Times* (19 March, 1978), p. 21; Robin Young, 'Old people are the "most adventurous travellers"', *The Times* (25 April, 1984), p. 3.

9 Office for National Statistics, 'Period expectation of life, England and Wales, 1910–12 to 2010-12'; https://www.ons.gov.uk/peoplepopulationandcommunity/birthsdeathsandmarriages/lifeexpectancies/bulletins/englishlifetablesno17/2015-09-01

10 Russell Wareing, 'Economic Power: Ignore the "Grey Pound" at your peril!', *Teaching Business and Economics*, 19, 3 (2015), p. 23.

11 Royal Voluntary Service, 'Older people gift 1.4 billion hours a year to volunteering' (27 September, 2016); https://www.royalvoluntaryservice.org.uk/news-and-events/news/older-people-gift-14-billion-hours-a-year-to-volunteering

12 The Battle of Britain Memorial Trust, '25 Years Anniversary' (n.d.).

13 Eve Darian-Smith, *Bridging Divides: The Channel Tunnel and English Legal Identity in the New Europe* (Berkeley: University of California Press, 1999), p. 100; R. A. Gibb, 'The Impact of the Channel Tunnel Rail Link on South East England', *Geographical Journal*, 152, 3 (1986), p. 335; Michael R. Bonavia, 'Europe's Missing Link: The Channel Tunnel', *Transportation Journal*, 23, 4 (1984), pp. 20–4; Ricard Anguera, 'The Channel Tunnel – an ex post economic evaluation', *Transportation Research Part A* 40 (2006), pp. 291–315.

14 http://www.doverferryphotosforums.co.uk/ts-lord-warden-past-and-present/; Michael Baily, 'There's money in Channel ships', *The Times* (10 July, 1967), p. vi; 'Car Travellers Go Free', *The Times* (2 April, 1969), p. 11; R. A. Gibb, 'The Impact of the Channel Tunnel Rail Link on South East England', *The Geographical Journal*, 152, 3 (1986), pp. 337–9; Ricard Anguera, 'The Channel Tunnel – an ex post economic evaluation', *Transportation Research Part A* 40 (2006), pp. 291–315; 'Number of passengers using the Channel Tunnel and international short sea routes in the United Kingdom from 1994 to 2018'; https://www.statista.com/statistics/315456/channel-tunnel-and-short-sea-passengers-in-the-united-kingdom/

15 Michael Evans, 'Defiant Deal loses fight to keep Marines', *The Times* (26 May, 1995).

16 Lynne Greenwood, 'A cash crop from farm shops', *The Times* (14 December, 1991), p. 6.

17 *About Britain No. 3*, pp. 38–9.

18 Tom Peterkin, 'Viagra the most popular pill on Saga cruises', *Daily Telegraph* (9 May, 2008).

19 Jill Sherman, '2,400 join the dole queue in area where jobs are hard to find', *The Times* (3 February, 2011), p. 17.

20 Gordon Young, 'Vikings Sail Again For Kent Shores', *Daily Mail* (19 July, 1949), p. 5; Jorgen Rojel, *The 1949-Cruise of the Viking Ship Hugin* (Copenhagen: Samlerens Forlag, 1949), pp. 6; 14–15; 21–22; 35–6; '"Vikings" Set Out. Cheers, Sirens – and an Orchestra', *Manchester Guardian* (19 July, 1949), p. 7.

21 'Girls mob the invaders at midnight' and 'Picture Gallery', *Daily Mail* (29 July, 1949), p. 5; Rojel, *The 1949-Cruise*, pp. 51, 59–60; '"Vikings" to Row to Richmond', *Manchester Guardian* (30 July, 1949), p. 4; '"Vikings" Land at Broadstairs', *Manchester Guardian* (29 July, 1949), p. 5; '"Viking" Ship To Be Sold. For Exhibition in U.S.?', *Manchester Guardian* (3 August, 1949), p. 6; 'Sale of the Hugin. Claims by Rival Kent Towns', *Daily Mail* (4 August, 1949), p. 2; 'Daily Mail Buys The Viking Ship', *Daily Mail* (5 August, 1949), p. 1.

22 'Picture Gallery', *Daily Mail* (9 August, 1949), p. 5; 'Hugin Tops Bill', *Daily Mail* (10 August, 1949), p. 5; 'Hugin will head river pirates', *Daily Mail* (10 September, 1949), p. 5; F. G. Prince White, 'The Hugin dodges land hazards', *Daily Mail* (13 September, 1949), p. 5; 'School ends for Hugin', *Daily Mail* (15 September, 1945); 'Hugin road trip ends', *Daily Mail* (16 September, 1949), p. 5; 'Blackpool lit up again', *Daily Mail* (17 September, 1949), p. 5; '800, 000 see Hugin', *Daily Mail* (19 September, 1949), p. 3; 'The Hugin queue', *Daily Mail* (20 September, 1949), p. 5; 'All lights on the Hugin', *Daily Mail* (21 September, 1949), p. 5; 'Hugin's visitor', *Daily Mail* (27 October, 1949), p. 5; 'Hugin lies up', *Daily Mail* (12 November, 1949), p. 5; 'By Hugin, £500', *Daily Mail* (14 November, 1949), p. 5; F. G. Prince White, 'Jensen of the Hugin goes home', *Daily Mail* (22 November, 1949), p. 4; F. G. Prince-White, 'Two towns take over Hugin', *Daily Mail* (29 July, 1950), p. 3; 'Ramsgate' and 'Broadstairs' advertisements in *Daily Mail* (28 July, 1950), p. 3.

23 White, 'Jensen of the Hugin goes home'.

24 'Comment: Two Men in a Boat', *Daily Mail* (18 August, 1949), p. 1.

25 Cyril Frank, 'The Longship Voyages', *Observer* (31 July, 1949), p. 4.

26 F. G. Prince-White, 'Two towns take over Hugin', *Daily Mail* (29 July, 1950), p. 3.

27 *About Britain No. 3*, p. 7.

28 'News Review', *Official Architecture and Planning*, 31, 2 (1968), p. 221; 'News Review', *Official Architecture and Planning*, 31, 5 (1968), p. 687; 'Cross-Channel Hovercraft Under Way', *The Times* (7 April, 1966), p. 8; 'History in the Making', *The Times* (24 August, 1967), p. 6; Michael Baily, 'Take-off for the Champion Stakes', *The Times* (2 April, 1969), p. l; 'The Pegwell Terminus', *The Times* (11 January, 1968), p. 9.

29 Robin Paine and Roger Syms, *On a Cushion of Air: The Story of Hoverlloyd and the Cross Channel Hovercraft* (Woodstock: Writersworld, 2012), p. 140; 'Ocean Hovercraft in 20 Years', *The Times* (18 July, 1968), p. 2; Hoverlloyd adverts, *The Times* (28 December, 1968), p. 24; (4 January, 1969), p. 25; 'Car Travellers Go Free', *The Times* (2 April, 1969), p. 11.

30 Michael Baily, 'Expansion for Swedish Hoverlloyd', *The Times* (16 December, 1975), p. 16; Simon Scott Plummer, 'Lost at sea but found in the Channel', *The Times* (13 October, 1976), p. iv; Michael Baily, 'Swedes may end cross-Channel hover service', *The Times* (6 October, 1969), p. 4; Michael Baily, 'BR and Hoverlloyd may combine Channel hovercraft operations', *The Times* (10 May, 1973), p. 22; Michael Baily, 'Seaspeed may be sold as part of joint hovercraft operation', *The Times* (17 December 1979), p. 3; Peter Hill, 'Merger of hovercraft operations approved', *The Times* (27 June, 1981), p. 17; Paine and Syms, *On a Cushion of Air*, pp. 14–17.

31 https://www.english-heritage.org.uk/visit/places/st-augustines-cross/history/

32 Robin Pagnamenta, 'Review to put turbines on level playing field', *The Times* (23 September 2010), p. 45.

33 *About Britain No. 3*, pp. 63; 88.

34 Alice Thomson, 'Cucumbers grown in giant greenhouses . . . that sucks', *The Times* (5 March, 2009), pp. 16, 28; Martin Fletcher, 'Thanet Earth: the farm of the future', *Daily Telegraph* (20 September, 2013); 'Sixth Thanet Earth greenhouse completed' (22 June, 2018); http://www.fruitnet.com/fpj/article/173821/sixth-thanet-earth-greenhouse-completed

35 *About Britain No. 3*, pp. 50; 8; Canterbury Archaeological Trust, 'Thanet Earth 2007–2008'.

CHAPTER 4: EAST ANGLIA

1 S. H. Steinberg (ed.), *The Statesman's Year-Book: Statistical and Historical Annual of the States of the World for the Year 1951* (London: Macmillan and Co. Ltd., 1951), p. 70; David M. Adamson, *An Era of*

Expansion: Construction at Cambridge University 1996–2006 (London: Routledge, 2015), pp. 29–30.

2 *About Britain No. 4*, pp. 75–6. Unless noted, other references to the guidebook in this chapter come from these pages.

3 American Battle Monuments Commission, 'Cambridge American Cemetery and Memorial' (November 2018), p. 6.

4 Beacon Planning, 'New Interpretive Centre: Cambridge American Cemetery. Heritage Statement' (June 2011).

5 Department for Transport, 'Traffic Signs Manual', chapter 4, p. 54; David Millward, 'Britain's toads get new protection from the Department for Transport', *Daily Telegraph* (18 September, 2009); https://www.froglife.org/what-we-do/toads-on-roads/

6 William Seale, 'Horny Toads!'; http://www.bbc.co.uk/cambridgeshire/content/articles/2007/06/14/toad_patrol_feature.shtml; Arnold Cooke, 'The role of road traffic in the near extinction of Common Toads (Bufo bufo) in Ramsey and Bury', *Nature in Cambridgeshire*, 53 (2011), pp. 45–50.

7 Department for Transport, 'New road sign to improve road safety and protect animals', (17 June, 2019); https://www.gov.uk/government/news/new-road-sign-to-improve-road-safety-and-protect-animals

8 Steven Swinford, 'End of the Road for Cats eyes?', *Daily Telegraph* (4 September, 2015).

9 Samantha Subramanian, 'How our home delivery habit reshaped the world', *Guardian* (21 November 2019), citing a report by the Society of Motor Manufacturers and Traders.

10 Cotswold Archaeology, 'Caxton Gibbet. Caxton, Cambridgeshire. Archaeological Evaluation' (March 2013), pp. 6–7; https://yimwahexpress.co.uk

11 *Papworth Village Settlement* (1946), directed by James Carr; http://papwortheverardpc.org.uk/the-village/

12 https://www.enterifyoudare.co.uk/about-us

13 J. F. Pickering, 'The Abolition of Resale Price Maintenance in Great Britain', *Oxford Economic Papers*, 26, 1 (1974), pp. 120–46.

14 Helen Mercer, 'The Abolition of Resale Price Maintenance in Britain in 1964. A Turning Point for British Manufacturers?', *London School of Economics and Political Science Working Papers in Economic History*, 39/98 (January 1998), pp. 18–31.

15 B. S. Yamey, 'The Net Book Agreement', *The Modern Law Review*, 26, 6 (1963), pp. 691–9.

16 TNA, Works 25/57/A5/Q2, 'Confidential Guide Books' (49) 2. General Remarks from Prof Taylor and Wooldridge 'Guide Books – Scope and arrangement' (16 November 1949).
17 *About Britain No. 4*, pp. 91, 23–5.
18 National Trust, 'Wicken Fen Vision Newsletter', Issue 2 (May 2019).
19 E. Duffey, 'The re-establishment of the large copper butterfly Lycaena dispar batava obth on Woodwalton Fen National Nature Reserve, Cambridgeshire, England, 1969–73', *Biological Conservation*, 12 (1977), pp. 143–58; S. A. Corbet et al., 'Insects and their Conservation' in Laurie Friday (ed.), *Wicken Fen: The Making of a Wetland Nature Reserve* (Colchester: Harley Books, 1997), pp. 123–7; Timothy Richard New, *Insect Species Conservation* (Cambridge: Cambridge University Press, 2009), pp. 188–9; N. Mark Collins et al., 'Ecology and conservation of the British Swallowtail butterfly Papilio Machaon britannicus: Old questions, new challenges and potential opportunities', *Insect Conservation and Diversity*, 13 (2020), pp. 1–9; Richard Fox et al., 'A new Red List of British butterflies', *Insect Conservation and Diversity*, 4, 3 (2011), pp. 159–72.
20 T. A. Rowell and H. J. Harvey, 'The Recent History of Wicken Fen, Cambridgeshire, England: A Guide to Ecological Development', *Journal of Ecology*, 76, 1 (1988), pp. 73–90; T. A. Rowell, 'The History of Wicken Fen', in Laurie Friday (ed.), *Wicken Fen: The Making of a Wetland Nature Reserve* (Colchester: Harley Books, 1997), p. 211.
21 *About Britain No. 4*, p. 36.
22 Report of the Wild Life Conservation Special Committee, *Conservation of Nature in England and Wales* (London: HSMO, 1947), p. 100.
23 Isabel Sedgwick, *Wicken Fen, Cambridgeshire: A souvenir guide* (Corsham: Park Lane Press, 2016), pp. 14; 25.
24 *Biodiversity: The UK Action Plan* (London: HMSO, 1994).
25 National Trust, 'Wicken Fen Vision' (2008), pp. 3–5; Francine M. R. Hughes et al., 'The challenges of integrating biodiversity and ecosystem services monitoring and evaluation at a landscape-scale wetland restoration project in the UK', *Ecology and Society*, 21, 3 (2016).
26 *About Britain No. 4*, pp. 36–7.
27 TNA, Works 25/57/A5/Q2, 'Minutes of Fifth Meeting of the Guidebook Editorial Committee' (8 May, 1950).
28 *About Britain No. 4*, pp. 54; 35; 1 (for a similar watercolour by Jones in the V&A's collection see, http://collections.vam.ac.uk/item/O1105374/farm-carts-near-wisbech-watercolour-jones-barbara/); 33; 37; 34.

29 Hughes et al., 'The challenges of integrating biodiversity and ecosystem services'.

30 David J. T. Douglas, Peter S. Jones, Ian Crosher, Iain Diack and Nick Littlewood, 'Peatland Biodiversity' (September 2019). Review commissioned by the IUCN UK Peatland Programme's Commission of Inquiry on Peatlands; https://www.rspb.org.uk/reserves-and-events/reserves-a-z/lakenheath-fen/

31 *About Britain No. 4*, pp. 40–41; Marianna Dudley, 'Limits of Power: Wind, Energy, Orkney and the Post-war British State', *Twentieth Century British History*, 31, 3 (2020), pp. 316–39.

32 *About Britain No. 4*, pp. 36–7; 47.

33 Defence Estates, 'DTE East. Public Information Leaflet' (n.d.); Mark Nicholls, 'Touring the Stanta ghost villages', *Eastern Daily Press* (17 June, 2006).

34 House of Commons Debate (20 December, 1945), *Hansard*, Volume 417, c1659W; House of Commons Debate (18 October, 1946), *Hansard*, Volume 427, c269W; Richard Hobbs, 'The Secret History of the Mildenhall Treasure', *The Antiquities Journal* 88 (2008), pp. 376–420.

35 House of Commons Debate (5 July, 1960), *Hansard*, Volume 626, cc227–30; House of Commons Debate (5 July, 1960), *Hansard*, Volume 626, cc227–30; House of Commons Debate (21 June, 1960), *Hansard*, Volume 625, c29W; House of Commons Debate (13 July, 1960), *Hansard*, Volume 626, cc1389–91.

36 House of Commons Debate (7 April, 1998), *Hansard*, Volume 310, cc219–20W; HQ USAFE/FMAO, 'USAFE-AFAFRICA Economic Impact Analysis 2017' (May 2018). See also House of Commons Debate (7 July, 2000), *Hansard*, Volume 353 c337W.

37 Peter M. Jones, 'British Defence Policy; The Breakdown of Inter-Party Consensus', *Review of International Studies*, 13, 2 (1987) pp. 111-131.

38 William Wallace and Christopher Phillips, 'Reassessing the special relationship,' *International Affairs* 85, 2 (2009), p. 279.

39 P. W. J. Bartrip, 'Myxomatosis in 1950s Britain', *Twentieth Century British History*, 19, 1 (2008), pp. 83–105.

40 http://news.bbc.co.uk/1/hi/england/norfolk/3880249.stm; Malcolm Macalister Hall, 'Bernard Matthews: Life with all the trimmings', *Independent* (22 December, 2004); John Plunkett, 'Children keep gobbling Turkey Twizzlers', *Guardian* (22 March, 2005); Afua Hirsch, 'Toppling statues? Here's why Nelson's column should be next', *Guardian* (22 August, 2017).

CHAPTER 5: CHILTERNS TO BLACK COUNTRY

1 *About Britain No. 5*, p. 5.

2 *About Britain No. 5*, pp. 79–80. Unless noted, other references to the guidebook in this chapter come from these pages.

3 Dower, *National Parks*, pp. 6–13; Ministry of Town and Country Planning, *Report of the National Parks Committee (England and Wales)* (London: HMSO, 1947), pp. 121–2.

4 Kenneth Summerfield, 'Worboys Report', *Traffic Engineering and Control* (July 1963), p. 152; Phil Baines, 'A design (to sign roads by)', *Eye* 34,9 (1999).

5 Ray Crowther, 'New Deer Deterrent planned for busy Cannock Chase Road', *Stafford FM Local News Online* (21 September 2017); The British Deer Society, 'First UK Trial of Electronic Deer Deterrent Devices in Staffordshire'; https://www.bds.org.uk/index.php/news-events/332-first-uk-trial-of-electronic-deer-deterrent-devices-in-staffordshire

6 Historic England, *20th-Century Coal- and Oil-Fired Electric Power Generation: Introduction to Heritage Assets* (Historic England, 2015), p. 16.

7 'Rugeley Power Station first blowdown event' (7 February 2019); 'Completion of first explosive demolition at Rugeley Power Station (14 February, 2019); www.engie.co.uk/about-engie/news

8 Adam Vaughan, 'Rugeley coal plant to be transformed into a sustainable village', *Guardian* (19 November 2018); Mike Parker, *Mapping the Roads. Building Modern Britain* (Basingstoke: AA Publishing, 2013), p. 214.

9 Department of Education, 'National Curriculum in England: history programmes of study'; https://www.gov.uk/government/publications/national-curriculum-in-england-history-programmes-of-study

10 https://www.m6toll.co.uk/about-us/

11 *About Britain No. 5*, pp. 26; 66.

12 'The "Straight Mile"', *Daily Mail* (22 August, 1929), p. 7.

13 *About Britain No. 5*, p. 87; Paul Bewsher, 'In England's Centre they said this . . .', *Daily Mail* (14 November, 1938), p. 7; Brady Haran, 'A tale of two centres', *BBC News Online* (22 October, 2002).

14 Bewsher, 'In England's Centre', p. 7; 'The Centre of England is to be Moved', *Daily Mail* (7 January, 1952), p. 3; Rhona Churchill, 'The Heart of England is Coming to Town', *Daily Mail* (1 February, 1952), p. 2; John Hall, 'In Economy Village', *Daily Mail* (26 February, 1952), p. 6; Charles W. V. Truefitt, 'The Show that Puts the Accent on Value',

Daily Mail (3 March, 1952), p. 2; Rhona Churchill, 'A Band Struck Up (High Up!)', *Daily Mail* (4 March, 1952), p. 6.

15 'Beating the Clock', *Daily Mail* (16 September, 1958), p. 5; *Daily Mail* (14 October, 1958), p. 7; *Hansard*, House of Commons Debates (19 November, 1958), Vol. 595, cc 166–7W.

16 'Motor bike plant is closed', *Daily Mail* (15 September, 1973), p. 14; Thomson Prentice, 'Chrysler: "It is Very Grave"', *Daily Mail* (3 October, 1973), p. 1.

17 Piers Brendon, *The Motoring Century: The Story of the Royal Automobile Club* (London: Bloomsbury, 1997), p. 250.

18 *About Britain No. 5*, pp. 50; 39.

19 Coventry Transport Museum, *Your Journey Starts Here . . .* (n.d), pp. 28–30.

20 https://historicengland.org.uk/listing/the-list/list-entry/1392653

21 Margaret Stacey, Eric Batstone, Colin Bell and Anne Murcott, *Power, Resistance and Change: A Second Study of Banbury* (London: Routledge, 1975), pp. 9; 114; Philip Brown, 'Letter: Cake battle', *Independent* (4 November, 1998); Andrew Webb, *Food Britannia* (London: Random House, 2011), pp. 328–9; http://www.banburycakes.co.uk/index.html

22 Robert S. and Helen M. Lynd, *Middletown: A Study in Contemporary American Culture* (New York: Harcourt, Brace, and Company, 1929); Robert S. and Helen M. Lynd, *Middletown in Transition: A Study in Cultural Conflicts* (New York: Harcourt, Brace, and Company, 1937).

23 Margaret Stacey, *Tradition and Change: A Study of Banbury* (Oxford: Oxford University Press, 1960), pp. 10; 91.

24 Margaret Stacey, Eric Batstone, Colin Bell, and Anne Murcott, *Power, Persistence and Change: A Second Study of Banbury* (London: Routledge & Kegan Paul, 1975), pp. 9–10; Alice Eaton, 'Why did Banbury Borough Council decide to expand between 1952 and 1974?' (MA thesis, Leiden University, 2014).

25 Michael Mann, *Workers on the Move: The Sociology of Relocation* (Cambridge: Cambridge University Press, 1973), pp. 68–9.

26 Stacey, *Tradition and Change*, pp. 12–19.

27 https://www.nomisweb.co.uk/sources/census_2011_ks/report?compare=1170217759

28 Steve Bruce, 'A sociology classic revisited: religion in Banbury', *Sociological Review*, 59:2 (2011), pp. 201–22.

29 Bruce, 'A sociology classic revisited', pp. 210, 219.

30 *About Britain No. 5*, pp. 40–41.

31 *About Britain No. 5*, p. 88.

CHAPTER 6: SOUTH WALES AND THE MARCHES

1 *About Britain No. 6*, p. 86.

2 Robin Eveleigh, 'Orchards face being bulldozed as Heineken ends cider-apple deals', *Guardian* (23 July, 2018); *About Britain No. 6*, pp. 86; 17; https://www.bbc.co.uk/news/uk-england-hereford-worcester-18536486

3 *About Britain No. 6*, pp. 36–7.

4 *About Britain No. 6*, pp. 38–9; 9; 7; 48; Pyrs Gruffudd, David T. Herbert and Angela Piccini, 'In Search of Wales: Travel Writing and Narratives of Difference, 1918–50', *Journal of Historical Geography* 26, No. 4 (2000), pp. 589–604.

5 *About Britain No. 6*, pp. 68–70. Unless noted, other references to the guidebook in this chapter come from these pages.

6 Chris Williams, 'Who talks of my nation?' in Chris Williams and Andy Croll (eds.), *The Gwent County History Volume 5: The Twentieth Century* (Cardiff: University of Wales Press, 2013), pp. 342–62; Chris Williams, 'The Monmouthshire Myth', BBC Wales (31 July, 2016); https://www.bbc.co.uk/cymrufyw/36747027

7 TNA, Confidential FBC (50) 8, 'Memorandum from the Director General to Council' (3 March, 1950); TNA, Works 25/57/A5/Q2, 'Memorandum from Penrose Angwin to all members of the Guide Book Committee' (23 June, 1950); Atkinson, *The Festival of Britain*, pp. 12, 15, 28.

8 TNA, Works 25/57/A5/Q1, Minutes of the Fourth Meeting of the Guide Book Editorial Committee (3 February, 1950); TNA, Works 25/57/A5/Q1, Minutes of the Fifth Meeting of the Guidebook Editorial Committee (8 May, 1950).

9 *About Britain No. 6*, p. 82.

10 Anna Lewis and Martin Shipton, 'New 8km stretch of A465 Heads of the Valleys road is £100 m over budget and three years late', Wales Online (20 February, 2020); https://www.walesonline.co.uk/news/wales-news/a465-heads-valley-dual-carriageway-17779356

11 Pyrs Gruffudd, 'Remaking Wales: nation-building and the geographical imagination, 1925-50', *Political Geography*, 14, 3 (1995); Peter Merriman, 'Archaeologies of Automobility' in Paul Graves-Brown, Rodney Harrison and Angela Piccini (eds.), *The Oxford Handbook of the Archaeology of the Contemporary World* (Oxford: Oxford University Press, 2013), pp. 445–7.

12 K. S. Rutley, 'An Investigation into Bilingual (Welsh/English) Traffic Signs. Transport and Road Research Laboratory Report LR475' (Crowthorne, Berkshire, 1972); Peter Merriman and Rhys Jones, '"Symbols of Justice": The Welsh Language Society's campaign

for bilingual road signs in Wales, 1967–1980', *Journal of Historical Geography*, 35 (2009), pp. 350–75; Rhys Jones and Peter Merriman, 'Hot, banal and everyday nationalism: Bilingual road signs in Wales', *Political Geography*, 28 (2009), pp. 164–73.

13 Merriman and Jones, ' "Symbols of Justice"', pp. 370–72; Rutley, 'An Investigation into Bilingual (Welsh/English) Traffic Signs', p. 8; Jones and Merriman, 'Hot, banal and everyday nationalism', p. 168.

14 Teresa L. Rees, 'Population and Industrial Decline in the South Wales Coalfield', *Regional Studies*, 12, 1 (1978), pp. 69–70.

15 *About Britain No. 6*, pp. 88; 63.

16 Edgar C. Conkling, 'South Wales: A Case Study in Industrial Diversification', *Economic Geography*, 39, 3 (1963), p. 258.

17 *About Britain No. 6*, pp. 61; 90; 1; 33; 35; Rees, 'Population and Industrial Decline,', p. 70; Christina Beatty and Stephen Fothergill, 'Labour Market Adjustments in Areas of Chronic Industrial Decline: The Case of the UK Coalfields', *Regional Studies*, 30, 7 (1996), pp. 627–40.

18 Ian Herbert, 'Filmmakers mine rich seam of stories from the colliery that took on the Government', *Independent* (17 January, 2004).

19 'Land Reclamation. Surface Coal Mining and Restoration at the Former Tower Colliery Site. Environment Statement' (2010); Rhondda Cynon Taf, Planning and Development Committee, 'Report of the Service Director Planning' (8 March, 2018); https://www.hargreavesland.com/project/tower/

20 *About Britain No. 6*, pp. 14–15.

21 *About Britain No. 6*, p. 62; David Parry, *Capel* 24: The Chapels Heritage Society Local Information Sheet, Caerphilly (n.d.), p. 5; 'Information further to OAQ0698 (CWS) issued by Alan Pugh, the Minister for Culture, Language and Sport' (29 March 2006), Welsh Assembly.

22 Chris Kelsey, 'GE Aviation celebrates 75 years at Nantgarw overhauling engines for some of the world's most iconic aircraft', *Wales Online* (23 October, 2015).

23 Martin Johnes, 'Cardiff: The Making and Development of the Capital City of Wales', *Contemporary British History*, 26, 4 (2012), p. 522.

24 *About Britain No. 6*, pp. 63, 69, 84; 60; Johnes, 'Cardiff', p. 513.

25 See for example, Sir D. Maxwell Fyfe, Oral Answers to Questions (6 December, 1951), *Hansard*, 494; Johnes, 'Cardiff', pp. 509–28; Question from Mr William Edwards (25 May 1971), *Hansard*, 818.

26 Johnes, 'Cardiff', pp. 516–18; Martin Johnes, 'A Prince, a King, and a Referendum: Rugby, Politics, and Nationhood in Wales, 1969-1979', *Journal of British Studies*, 47 (2008), pp. 129–48.

27 Johnes, 'Cardiff', pp. 509–28.

28 *About Britain No. 6*, p. 35; Richard Cowell, 'Substitution and Scalar Politics: Negotiating Environmental Compensation in Cardiff Bay', *Geoforum*, 34 (2003), p. 348; Mr George Thomas (16 July, 1958), *Hansard*, Volume 591, 1394.

29 Peter N. Ferns and James P. Reed, 'Effects of the Cardiff Bay Tidal Barrage on the Abundance, Ecology and Behaviour of Shelducks *Tadorna tadorna*', *Aquatic Conservation: Marine and Freshwater Ecosystems*, 19 (2009), pp. 466–73.

30 Cowell, 'Substitution and Scalar Politics', pp. 343–58.

CHAPTER 7: NORTH WALES AND THE MARCHES

1 *About Britain No. 7*, p. 4.

2 *About Britain No. 7*, pp. 66–7. Unless noted, other references to the guidebook in this chapter come from these pages.

3 https://www.quarrybattery.com; Trevor M. Thomas, 'Wales: Land of Mines and Quarries', *Geographical Review*, 46, 1 (1956), p. 70; *About Britain No. 7*, pp. 22; 36; 86.

4 https://museum.wales/slate/history/; Barrie Trinder, 'Industrial Archaeology in Britain', *Archaeology* 34, 1 (1981), pp. 8–16.

5 J. G. Berry, 'Railway Preservation and the Planner', *The Town Planning Review* 40, 2 (1969), pp. 190–3; Bradley, *The Railways*, pp. 511; 539; Grimshaw, 'Steam Railways', pp. 83; 86–7.

6 https://www.erih.net/about-erih/erihs-history-and-goals/; Steven Morris, 'Welsh slate mining landscape nominated as world heritage site', *Guardian* (24 January, 2020).

7 Elaine Williams, *Dinorwig: The Electric Mountain* (Irvine, CA: Edison Mission Energy, 1999), pp. 7; 31.

8 Williams, *Dinorwig*, p. 31.

9 Alan Burton, 'Moral Objection of Trading Imperative? The British Consumer Co-operative Movement Responds to Commercial Television in the 1950s', *Arbeiten aus Anglistik und Amerikanistik*, 32, 2 (2007), pp. 241–56; Robert Silvey, 'Television Viewing in Britain', *Public Opinion Quarterly*, 14, 1 (1956), pp. 148–50; https://www.closer.ac.uk/data/television-ownership-in-domestic-households/

10 Derek W. Bann and Jeremy P. Seigal, 'Forecasting the Effects of Television Programming upon Electricity Loads', *The Journal of the Operational Research Society*, 34, 1 (1983), pp. 17–25.

11 Ben Dowell, 'TV ownership in the UK falls for the first time', *Radio Times* (9 December 2014).

12 Dower, *National Parks*, p. 8; *Report of the National Parks Committee*, pp. 10; 88–91.

13 *Report of the National Parks Committee*, p. 8; J. W. Gittins, 'Conservation and Capacity: A Case Study of the Snowdonia National Park', *Geographical Journal*, 139, 3 (1973), p. 482; https://www.nationalparks.uk/students/whatisanationalpark/aimsandpurposesofnationalparks/sandfordprinciple; D. Anne Dennier, 'National Park Plans: A Review Article', *The Town Planning Review*, 49, 2 (1978), p. 181; *About Britain No. 7*, p. 8.

14 Katharina Dehnen-Schmutz and Mark Williamson, '*Rhododendron ponticum* in Britain and Ireland: Social, Economic and Ecological Factors in its Successful Invasion', *Environment and History*, 12, 3 (2006), pp. 325–50; Snowdonia National Park Authority, 'Rhododendron in Snowdonia and a strategy for its control' (2008), p.7; Snowdonia Rhododendron Partnership, 'The Ecosystem Benefits of managing the invasive non-native plant *Rhododendron ponticum* in Snowdonia' (2015).

15 *About Britain No. 7*, p. 58; Dehnen-Schmutz and Williamson, '*Rhododendron ponticum*', pp. 340–41; J. R. Cross, '*Rhododendron ponticum L.*', *Journal of Ecology*, 63, 1 (1975), p. 363; David M. Richardson and Petr Pyšek, 'Classics in Physical Geography Revisited. Elton, C. S. 1958: The Ecology of Invasions by Animals and Plants. London: Methuen', *Progress in Physical Geography*, 31, 6 (2007), pp. 659–66; Chris Smout, 'The Alien Species in 20th Century Britain: Constructing a New Vermin', *Landscape Research*, 28, 1 (2003), pp. 11–20; M. Campbell-Culver cited in Dehnen-Schmutz and Williamson, '*Rhododendron ponticum*', p. 341; Snowdonia National Park Authority, 'Rhododendron in Snowdonia', p. 2; Snowdonia Rhododendron Partnership, 'The Ecosystem Benefits.'

16 R. H. Gritten, 'The Spread of *Rhododendron ponticum* – a national problem. Report of discussion conference held in Snowdonia. 26–27 March 1987' (1987); Snowdonia National Park Authority, 'Rhododendron in Snowdonia', pp. 20; 7; Sarah J. Manchester and James M. Bullock, 'The Impacts of Non-Native Species on UK Biodiversity and the Effectiveness of Control', *Journal of Applied Ecology*, 37, 5 (2000), p. 858; '£10 m to rid Snowdonia National Park of rhododendron', BBC News (16 April, 2014); https://www.bbc.co.uk/news/uk-wales-north-west-wales-27050336; https://www.snowdonia-society.org.uk/event/rhododendron-clearance-4/; https://www.snowdonia.gov.wales/looking-after/invasive-species/rhododendron

17 Peter Ashby, Graham Birch and Martin Haslett, 'Second Homes in North Wales', *Town Planning Review*, 46, 3 (1975), pp. 327; 325; Madhu

Satsangi, Nick Gallent and Mark Beran, *The Rural Housing Question: Community and Planning in Britain's Countryside* (Bristol: Bristol University Press Policy Press, 2010), p. 80.

18 Satsangi, Gallent and Beran, *The Rural Housing Question*, p. 81; 'Thirty years since the first Welsh holiday home arson', BBC News (12 December, 2009); http://news.bbc.co.uk/1/hi/wales/north_west/8408447.stm; 'Meibion Glyndwr: Home Office papers released about holiday home attacks', BBC News (16 March, 2017); https://www.bbc.co.uk/news/uk-wales-39281345

19 Brian Hollingsworth, *Ffestiniog Adventure: The Festiniog Railway's Deviation Project* (Newton Abbot: David & Charles, 1981), pp. 11–14; 44–140; 143–57.

20 Dower, *National Parks*, pp. 15–16, 18; *About Britain No. 7*, p. 8; *Report of the National Parks Committee*, p. 90.

21 J. Arwel Edwards and Joan Carles Llurdés i Coit, 'Mines and Quarries. Industrial Heritage Tourism', *Annals of Tourism Research*, 23, 2 (1996), pp. 348–56; Marston Planning Consultancy, 'Planning Statement' (August 2013), p. 3.

22 http://www.anturstiniog.com; Shelley Burgin and Nigel Hardiman, 'Extreme sports in natural areas: looming disaster or a catalyst for a paradigm shift in land use planning?', *Journal of Environmental Planning and Management*, 55, 7 (2012), pp. 925–6; 'The Top Line: Zip World's Co-founder Sean Taylor' (23 January, 2017), Blooloop.com; https://www.dailypost.co.uk/news/tv/behind-scenes-look-zip-world-15726492

23 Rhondda Cynon Taf Press Release, 'Planning permission granted for Zip World attraction in Hirwaun' (20 December, 2019); https://www.rctcbc.gov.uk/EN/Newsroom/PressReleases/2019/December/PlanningpermissiongrantedforZipWorldattractioninHirwaun.aspx; 'Zip World to open first South Wales adventure park', BBC News (20 December, 2019); https://www.bbc.co.uk/news/uk-wales-50864640; Tyler Mears, 'Plans for Zip World adventure park in Rhigo are revealed – and they include three zip wire course', *Wales Online* (17 February, 2019); https://www.zipworld.co.uk/press/view/zip-world-planning

24 *About Britain No. 7*, p. 7; https://historypoints.org/index.php?page=horse-drawn-coach-capel-curig; Mari Jones, 'Famous Capel Curig stagecoach gets new lease of life', *North Wales Live* (14 April 2016).

25 *Ward Lock & Co's Illustrated Guide Books: Caernarvon and North Wales* (London: Ward, Lock and Co.: 1939), p. 187.

26 *About Britain No. 7*, p. 81.
27 *About Britain No. 7*, p. 81; Jenkins and James, *From Acorn to Oak Tree*, pp. 136–7; 178.
28 TNA, Works 25/256/G1/C2/424, letter to Prof. W. G. Gruffydd from Director, Finance and Establishments (6 June, 1950); TNA, Works 25/256/G1/C2/454, letter from Colonel Penrose Angwin to Finance (22 June, 1950).
29 *About Britain No. 7*, p. 70; TNA, Works 25/256/G1/C2/424, F.B. 1951 Provisional Tours for the North Wales Area. Tour No. 2.
30 TNA, Works 25/256/G1/C2/424, letter to Prof. W. G. Gruffydd from Director, Finance and Establishments (6 June, 1950); *About Britain No. 7*, p. 4.
31 *About Britain No. 7*, p. 86, 4; *About Britain No. 6*, p. 10.

CHAPTER 8: EAST MIDLANDS AND THE PEAK

1 *About Britain No. 8*, pp. 72–3. Unless noted, other references to the guidebook in this chapter come from these pages; *About Britain No. 8*, p. 55. See also p. 19.
2 British Pathé, 'Stamford Gets New By-Pass' (1960); The Royal Commission on the Historical Monuments of England, *An Inventory of the Historical Monuments in the Town of Stamford* (London: HMSO, 1977), pp. ix–xi.
3 Giles Worsley, *England's Lost Houses: From the Archives of Country Life* (London: Aurum Press, 2002), p. 9; The Royal Commission on the Historical Monuments of England, *An Inventory of the Historical Monuments in Hertfordshire* (London: HMSO, 1910), pp. ix–xvi; The Royal Commission on the Historical Monuments of England, *An Inventory of the Historical Monuments in Buckinghamshire, Volume 1, South* (London: HMSO, 1912), pp. xvii–xx; The Royal Commission on the Historical Monuments of England, *An Inventory of the Historical Monuments in Buckinghamshire, Volume 2, North* (London: HMSO, 1913) pp. xvii–xix; The Royal Commission on the Historical Monuments of England, *An Inventory of the Historical Monuments in the Town of Stamford*, pp. ix–xi.
4 https://www.civictrust.org.uk; The Royal Commission on the Historical Monuments of England, *An Inventory of the Historical Monuments in the Town of Stamford*, pp. ix–xi.
5 Tarn, 'Urban Regeneration', p. 259.
6 Ketton Conservation Area, 'Ketton Conservation Area Appraisal and Management Plan' (August 2019), p. 5.

7 *About Britain No. 8*, p. 5; https://www.solarpowerportal.co.uk/news/rutland_cement_works_powered_by_9mw_solar_farm_2356

8 Ketton Conservation Area, 'Ketton Conservation Area Appraisal and Management Plan' (August 2019), p. 24; 'Important Views Index'.

9 The Royal Commission on the Historical Monuments of England, *An Inventory of the Historical Monuments in Dorset, Volume 1, West* (London: HMSO, 1952) pp. xix–xx; Ketton Conservation Area, 'Ketton Conservation Area Appraisal and Management Plan' (August 2019), p. 21.

10 https://beta.companieshouse.gov.uk/company/04146968/officers; http://www.greenburial.co.uk/about.htm

11 R. Yarwood, J. Sidaway, C. Kelly and S. Stillwell, 'Sustainable deathstyles? The geography of green burial in Britain', *Geographical Journal* 181, 2 (2015), pp. 173, 183; Hannah Rumble, John Troyer, Tony Walter and Kate Woodthorpe, 'Disposal or dispersal? Environmentalism and final treatment of the British dead', *Mortality*, 19, 3 (2014), p. 257.

12 Hannah Rumble, John Troyer, Tony Walter and Kate Woodthorpe, 'Disposal or dispersal? Environmentalism and final treatment of the British dead', *Mortality*, 19, 3 (2014), p. 247, 244; Andrew Clayton and Katie Dixon, 'Woodland burial: Memorial arboretum versus natural native woodland?', *Mortality*, 12, 3 (2007), pp. 256–7; Ketton Parish Council, 'Cemetery Rules for the Guidance of the Bereaved' (Amended January 2014); D. J. Davies, *A Brief History of Death* (Oxford: Blackwell, 2005).

13 Ketton Parish Council, 'Cemetery Rules for the Guidance of the Bereaved' (Amended January 2014); http://www.greenburial.co.uk/about.htm; Clayton and Dixon, 'Woodland burial', pp. 240–1; Rumble, Troyer, Walter and Woodthorpe, 'Disposal or dispersal?', p. 254; Nicola Davis, 'Bury bodies along UK's motorways to ease burial crisis, expert suggests', *Guardian* (5 July 2019). https://www.theguardian.com/science/2019/jul/05/bury-bodies-along-uks-motorway-to-ease-burial-crisis-expert-suggests

14 https://historicengland.org.uk/listing/the-list/list-entry/1400806; Daniel J. Codd, *Secret Rutland* (Stroud: Amberley Publishing, 2018); https://historicengland.org.uk/listing/the-list/list-entry/1264288

15 Alan Rogers, 'The Making of Uppingham as illustrated in its topography and buildings' (Uppingham Local History Study Group, 2003), p. 25; Rosen, *The transformation of British Life*, p. 75.

16 *About Britain No. 8*, pp. 52–3.

17 John Carvel, 'Analysts name Britain's most racially diverse areas', *Guardian* (6 October, 2006); Strategic Business Intelligence Team,

Leicestershire County Council, 'Rutland Joint Strategic Needs Assessment 2018. Rutland's Population' (December 2018), p. 18.

18 *About Britain No. 8*, pp. 57, 68.

19 Lydia Greeves, *Houses of the National Trust* (London: National Trust Books, 2013), pp. 67–9.

20 *About Britain No. 8*, pp. 38–9.

21 TNA, Works 25/57/A5/Q2, 'Specimen Rough Outline of a "Steering Script". East Anglia' (16 November, 1949).

22 National Trust Annual Report 1951–2, cited in Jennifer Jenkins and Patrick James, *From Acorn to Oak Tree: The Growth of the National Trust 1895–1994* (London: Macmillan, 1994), pp. 151–5; Worsley, *England's Lost Houses*, p. 19–20; Peter Mandler, *The Fall and Rise of the Stately House* (New Haven: Yale University Press, 1998).

23 *About Britain No. 8*, p. 21.

24 Rosen, *The transformation of British Life*, p. 78; *Report of the Committee appointed by the Prime Minister under the Chairmanship of Lord Robbins, 1961–63* [hereafter *Robbins Committee Report*] (London: HMSO, 1963), pp. 271–6, 287; Edgerton, *The Rise and Fall of the British Nation*, p. 341.

25 Adamson, *An Era of Expansion*, p. 28; Kathleen Burk, 'Conclusion: fin de siècle', in Kathleen Burk (ed.), *The British Isles Since 1945* (Oxford: Oxford University Press, 2009), pp. 231–2; Paul Chatterton, 'Commentary. The student city: an ongoing story of neoliberalism, gentrification, and commodification', *Environment and Planning A* 42 (2010), p. 509; Phil Hubbard, 'Geographies of studentification and purpose-built student accommodation: leading separate lives?', *Environment and Planning A* 41 (2009), p. 1904; William Whyte, *Redbrick. A Social and Architectural History of Britain's Civic Universities* (Oxford: Oxford University Press, 2015), pp. 332–3.

26 *Robbins Committee Report*, p. 271; Hubbard, 'Geographies of studentification', p. 1910.

27 Phil Hubbard, 'Regulating the social impacts of studentification: a Loughborough case study', *Environment and Planning A*, 40 (2008), pp. 323–41; Brian Oliver, 'Town v gown: is the student boom wrecking communities', *Observer* (23 September 2018); https://www.charnwood.gov.uk/files/documents/appendix_6_the_student_housing_market/Appendix%206%20-%20The%20Student%20Housing%20Market.pdf, p. 2; Tony Tysome, 'Town and gown: The biggest employer but its customers "are revolting"', *Times Higher*

Education Supplement (1 August, 2003), p. 5; Hubbard, 'Geographies of studentification', p. 1905.

28 'Ashby Road Conservation Area Loughborough. Conservation Area Character Statement. Adopted November 2005', p. 4. https://www.charnwood.gov.uk/files/documents/ashby_road_conservation_area_appraisal/ashbyroadconservationareaapprais.pdf; Chatterton, 'Commentary', p. 513; Hubbard, 'Geographies of studentification', pp. 1906–12.

29 Chatterton, 'Commentary', p. 510.

30 UKCISA, 'International Student Statistics: UK Higher Education' (2019); https://www.ukcisa.org.uk/Research--Policy/Statistics/International-student-statistics-UK-higher-education

31 *About Britain No. 8*, p. 58; https://prestwold-hall.com; https://www.thenaturalburialcompany.co.uk/site-locations/prestwold/

32 *About Britain No. 8*, pp. 53–4.

33 Dev Gangjee, 'Melton Mowbray and the GI Pie in the Sky: Exploring Cartographies of Protection', *Intellectual Property Quarterly*, 291 (2006), pp. 291–309.

34 'Eye in the Sky: Burley on the Hill', *Rutland Pride* (20 March, 2019). The developer, Kit Martin, was co-author of the 1980s bible for those looking to buy and renovate their own country house, *The Country House: To Be or Not to Be* (1982).

35 Letter from Chris Olney, 'How Whitwell got its French Connection', *Guardian* (11 August 2004).

36 *About Britain No. 8*, pp. 59–60.

CHAPTER 9: LANCASHIRE AND YORKSHIRE

1 *About Britain No. 9*, pp. 7–12.

2 *About Britain No. 9*, pp. 12–13.

3 *About Britain No. 9*, pp. 89; 7. For more on this see Tim Cole, 'Sands, Good Sands, Excellent Sands: Writing and Ranking the British Coastline in the Middle of the Twentieth Century' in Jo Carruthers and Nour Dakkak (eds.), *Sandscapes: Writing the British Seaside* (Houndmills: Palgrave Macmillan, 2020).

4 'Boundary protest "to be reported"', BBC News online (14 November 2005); 'County signs dumped after protest', BBC News online (15 November 2005); www.forl.co.uk; https://en.wikipedia.org/wiki/Talk:CountyWatch

5 'By George! England's traditional counties can return to England's roads', Ministry of Housing, Communities and Local Government press release (23 April, 2014). www.gov.uk

6 https://api.parliament.uk/historic-hansard/written-answers/1957/mar/14/programme See question to Minister of Transport. The sum represents circa £12 million today.

7 Carlton Reid, *Bike Boom* (Island Press, 2017). http://www.bikeboom.info/cycletracks1930s/ https://www.theguardian.com/environment/bike-blog/2017/may/09/how-80-forgotten-1930s-cycleways-could-transform-uk-cycling

8 'City deal clears way for £200m Preston road schemes', *The Construction Index* (13 September, 2013).

9 *About Britain No. 9*, p. 74.

10 Paul Swinney and Zach Wilcox, 'Strength from within: Supporting economic growth in Preston. An independent report by Centre for Cities.' (December 2011).

11 Owen Hatherley, 'Preston bus station: a sublime choice for grade II listing', *Guardian* (24 September, 2013).

12 Hazel Sheffield, 'A British Town's Novel Solution to Austerity', *The Atlantic* (13 May, 2019).

13 Haroon Siddique, 'Preston bus station demolition approved by council', *Guardian* (18 December, 2012); Mark Brown, 'Preston's brutalist bus station gets a reprieve from culture minister', *Guardian* (23 September, 2013); Rowan Moore, 'Preston bus station review – a glorious reprieve', *Observer* (10 June, 2018).

14 Kathryn A. Morrison and John Minnis, *Carscapes: The Motor Car, Architecture and Landscapes in England* (New Haven: Yale University Press, 2012), pp. 309–10.

15 'Little chef move brings more jobs', *Lancashire Telegraph* (9 August, 2001); Morrison and Minnis, *Carscapes*, pp. 310–11.

16 Hilary Armstrong, 'Road Hog. Bukhara, near Preston', *Sunday Times* (18 November, 2007).

17 *About Britain No. 9*, pp. 77–8. Unless noted, other references to the guidebook in this chapter come from these pages.

18 *About Britain No. 9*, pp. 17, 20–21; Edgerton, *The Rise and Fall of the British Nation*, p. 133.

19 Edgerton, *The Rise and Fall of the British Nation*, pp. 135; 316.

20 *About Britain No. 9*, p. 80; https://www.blackburn.gov.uk/facts-and-figures/people-and-demography-facts-and-figures

21 Hugh Ford, 'Frank Brian Mercer, OBE Obituary', *Biog, Mems. Fell. R. Soc. Lond.* 46 (2000), pp. 345–63.

22 https://www.centreforcities.org/wp-content/uploads/2014/08/12-07-11-Cities-Outlook-1901.pdf; GB Historical GIS/University of

Portsmouth, Blackburn with Darwen UA through time/Population Statistics/Total Population, A Vision of Britain through Time; https://www.clitheroeadvertiser.co.uk/news/population-of-burnley-has-been-halved-1-6180433; 'City Sicker. Britain's decaying towns', *Economist* (12 October 2013); https://burnley.co.uk/business/about-the-bondholder-scheme/

23 https://technation.io/insights/report-2018/

24 https://www.lancashiretelegraph.co.uk/news/10213553.burnley-mill-shop-to-move-as-marina-grows/; https://www.pendletoday.co.uk/business/barden-mill-and-pendle-village-mill-merger-takes-place-1-5624807; https://www.nationaltrust.org.uk/features/finding-a-future-for-lancashires-historic-mills

25 *About Britain No. 9*, pp. 21–2, 17.

26 *About Britain No. 9*, p. 80; Catherine Dormor, 'Cloth and Memory', *Textile: The Journal of Cloth and Culture*, 11, 1 (2013), pp. 88–93.

27 Stephen Daniels, 'Hockney Country', *Journal of Historical Geography*, 38 (2012), pp. 458–64; David Hockney, 'King of Salt's Mill', *Telegraph* (22 November, 1997); Anthea Gerrie, 'How my dad came to fill a mill with David Hockneys', *Jewish Chronicle* (15 July, 2010); Rhodri Thomas and Huw Thomas, 'Micro politics and micro firms: a case study of tourism policy formation and change', *Journal of Small Business and Enterprise Development*, 13, 1 (2006), pp. 100–14.

28 Tristram Hunt, *Building Jerusalem: The Rise and Fall of the Victorian City* (London: Penguin Books, 2019), p. 471; Thomas and Thomas, 'Micro politics and micro firms', pp. 100–14; Emma Wood and Rhodri Thomas, '*Research note*: Measuring cultural values – the case of residents' attitudes to the Saltaire Festival', *Tourism Economics*, 12, 1 (2006), pp. 137–45; John Minnery, 'Model industrial settlements and their continuing governance', *Planning Perspectives*, 27, 2 (2012), pp. 309–21.

29 http://theconversation.com/englands-north-south-divide-is-history-but-the-nations-rifts-are-deepening-99044

30 S. Ward, *Planning and Urban Change* (London: 1994), p. 153.

31 *About Britain No. 9*, p. 89.

32 https://www.yorkpress.co.uk/news/17410398.former-north-selby-mine-near-york-could-become-glamping-site/

33 Edgerton, *The Rise and Fall of the British Nation*, p. 132; Rhys Herbert, 'Economic Trends: The First Fifty Years', Economic Trends 600. Office for National Statistics.

34 K. Schürer & Joe Day (2019), Migration to London and the development of the north–south divide, 1851–1911, *Social History*, 44:1, 26–56.

CHAPTER 10: THE LAKES TO TYNESIDE

1 *About Britain No. 10*, pp. 78–9. Unless noted, other references to the guidebook in this chapter come from these pages.

2 John Pendlebury, 'Alas Smith and Burns? Conservation in Newcastle upon Tyne city centre, 1959–1968', *Planning Perspectives*, 16 (2001), pp. 115–41.

3 Mary Cooper, 'Motorways and transport planning in Newcastle upon Tyne. A report commissioned by the Chairman and Committee of SOC'EM Newcastle upon Tyne, and sponsored by TRANSPORT 2000 (North East)' (SOC'EM, 1974).

4 The Chartered Institution of Highways and Transportation, 'The Newcastle Central Motorway East and Other Plans' (2012).

5 *About Britain No. 10*, pp. 15; 67–8; Simon Gunn, 'The history of transport systems in the UK' (2018), p. 21.

6 D. F. Howard, 'Tyne and Wear Metro – A Modern Rapid Transit System', *Proceedings of the Institution of Mechanical Engineers*, 190, No. 18 (1976), pp. 1–26; N. L. Heslop, 'Newcastle International Airport: an overview of the Metro link and aircraft safety considerations', *Proceedings of the Institution of Civil Engineers Transport*, 117 (1996), pp. 291–5; Alex Dampier and Marin Marinor, 'A Study of the Feasibility and Potential Implementation of Metro-based Freight Transportation in Newcastle upon Tyne', *Urban Rail Transit*, 1 (2015), pp. 164–82.

7 Air Ministry, *Report of the Committee of Inquiry into Civil Aviation and the observation of H.M. Government thereon* (London: HMSO, 1938), pp. 68–9; https://www.nelsam.org.uk/NEAR/Airfields/Histories/Woolsington.htm; Hunting Air Transport, 'Fly Between Newcastle and London. Timetable and Information' (October 1953); Hunting-Clan Air Transport, 'Timetable and Fares. UK and Continental Services' (April 1954).

8 Gunn, 'The history of transport systems in the UK', p. 12; Mark E. Casey, 'Low Cost Air Travel: Welcome Aboard?', *Tourist Studies*, 10, No. 2 (2010), p. 175; *About Britain No. 10*, p. 44.

9 Casey, 'Low Cost Air Travel', p. 181.

10 Ian Humphreys and Graham Francis, 'Policy issues and planning of UK regional airports', *Journal of Transport Geography*, 10 (2002), p. 251.

11 *About Britain No. 10*, p. 61.

12 Gary Shrubsole, *Who Owns England? How we Lost our Green and Pleasant Land and How to Take it Back* (London: HarperCollins, 2019).

13 Jenkins and James, *From Acorn to Oak Tree*, p. 277.

14 *About Britain No. 10*, pp. 90; 56.

15 Dower, *National Parks*, pp. 7–9, 10; Ray Woolmore, 'Designation History Series. Northumberland Coast A.O.N.B.' (2004).

16 David Doxford and Tony Hill, 'Land Use for Military Training in the UK: The Current Situation, Likely Developments and Possible Alternatives', *Journal of Environmental Planning and Management*, 41, No. 3 (1998), pp. 279–97; Andrew Cattermole and Rachel Woodward, 'Public Access Restrictions and Environmental Conservation on the Otterburn Training Area', University of Newcastle Centre for Rural Economy Research Report (1999), p. 7; Rachel Woodward, 'Gunning for Rural England: the Politics of the Promotion of Military Land Use in the Northumberland National Park', *Journal of Rural Studies*, 15, No. 1 (1999), p. 18.

17 Revitalizing Redesdale Landscape Partnership, 'Revitalizing Redesdale: Landscape Conservation Action Plan' (2017), p. 22; Chris Pearson, Peter Coates and Tim Cole (eds.,), *Militarized Landscapes* (London: Continuum, 2010).

18 Dower, *National Parks*, pp. 6–7.

19 Sharp Report (1977) cited in Woodward, 'Gunning for Rural England', p. 18.

20 Doxford and Hill, 'Land Use for Military Training', p. 285; Cattermole and Woodward, 'Public Access Restrictions', p.11; Woodward, 'Gunning for Rural England', pp. 18–19; Nugent Report (1973) cited in Woodward, 'Gunning for Rural England', p. 18.

21 Cattermole and Woodward, 'Public Access Restrictions', p. 3; Woodward, 'Gunning for Rural England', p. 21; Richard Austin, Guy Garrod and Nicola Thompson, 'The Impact and Legacy of the Otterburn Public Inquiry, Northumberland National Park, England', *Northern History*, 55, No. 1 (2018), pp. 92–110; MoD planning consultant (1998) cited by Woodward, 'Gunning for Rural England', p. 31.

22 Sharon Culinane, 'Traffic Management in Britain's National Parks', *Transport Reviews*, 17, No. 3 (1997), p. 268; Revitalizing Redesdale Landscape Partnership, 'Revitalizing Redesdale', pp. 22; 26.

23 http://www.redesdale-arms.co.uk

24 Michael Muncaster, 'Revealed: The two North East roads which are among the most dangerous in Britain', *Newcastle Chronicle* (30 January, 2018).

25 Revitalizing Redesdale Landscape Partnership, 'Revitalizing Redesdale', p. 22; Sheail, *An Environmental History*, pp. 79–81.

26 'Finding the Way in West Northumberland's Eternal Horizons. From the Wall to the Border'; John Darnton, 'After 460 Years, the Anglicans

Ordain Women', *New York Times* (13 March, 1994), p. 1; Hattie Williams, 'More women than men enter clergy training, latest figures show', *Church Times* (27 September, 2017).

27 Tom Stephenson, 'Wanted – A Long Green Trail', *Daily Herald* (22 June, 1935), p. 10.

28 Cited in Robin S. Henshaw, 'The Development and Impact of Formal Long-Distance Footpaths in Great Britain', University of Edinburgh PhD (1984), p. 238.

29 Northumberland International Dark Sky Park, '2015 Annual Report'.

30 https://astro.ventures/public-observatory/; John E. Bortle, 'Introducing the Bortle Dark-Sky Scale', *Sky and Telescope*, 60 (2001), pp. 126–9; http://unihedron.com/projects/darksky/; Dan Duriscoe, 'Protecting Dark Skies. Preserving Pristine Night Skies in National Parks and the Wilderness Ethic', *The George Wright Forum*, 18, 4 (2001), pp. 30–6; Bob Mizon, 'The BAA Campaign for Dark Skies: Twenty years on', *Journal of the British Astronomical Association*, 119, No. 3 (2009), pp. 159–61.

31 LUC, 'England's light pollution and dark skies. Final report prepared by LUC' (May 2016); F. M. Wartmann et al., 'Towards an interdisciplinary understanding of landscape qualities: wilderness, tranquillity and dark skies', in L. Müller and F. Eulenstein (eds.), *Current Trends in Landscape Research. Innovations in Landscape Series* (Cham: Springer International Publishing, 2019), pp. 209–20; Campaign for Rural England, 'Night Blight: Mapping England's light pollution and dark skies' (2016).

32 Northumberland National Park and Kielder Water and Forest Park Dark Sky Park application (2013).

33 'Northumberland National Park and Kielder Water and Forest Park Dark Sky Park Annual Report' (2018); Northumberland International Dark Sky Park, '2019 Annual Report'; DEFRA, '8-Point Plan for England's National Parks' (2016), pp. 11–12.

34 https://www.egger.com/shop/en_GB/about-us/group/history

35 David Byrne and Adrian Doyle cited in Tim Strangleman, ' "Smokestack Nostalgia", "Ruin Porn" or Working-Class Obituary: The Role and Meaning of Deindustrial Representation', *International Labor and Working Class History*, 84 (2013), p. 29.

36 Anna Woodford, 'I See Public Artwork. County Durham 1973–2009' (Commissions North, 2009).

37 Kenneth Warren, 'Recent Changes in the Geographical Location of the British Steel Industry', *Geographical Journal*, 135, No. 3 (1969), p. 359; M. I. A. Bulmer, 'Mining Redundancy: A Case Study of the Workings

of the Redundancy Payments Acts in the Durham Coalfield', *Industrial Relations Journal*, 2, No. 4 (1971), p. 5; Katy Bennett, 'Emotion and Place Promotion: Passionate about a Former Coalfield', *Emotion, Space and Society*, 8 (2013), pp. 1–10; Paul Greenhalgh, 'Coalfield Regeneration: May the Task Force be with you', *Northern Economic History* (1999), pp. 82–96.

38 Ray Hudson, 'Making Music Work? Alternative Regeneration Strategies in a Deindustrialized Locality: The Case of Derwentside', *Transactions of the Institute of British Geographers*, 20, No. 4 (1995), pp. 460–73; Peter Boulding, Ray Hudson and David Sadler, 'Consett and Corby: What Kind of New Era?', *Public Administration Quarterly*, 12, No. 2 (1988), pp. 235–55; A. E. Green, 'Considering Long-Term Unemployment as a Criterion for Regional Policy Aid', *Area* 16, No. 3 (1984), pp. 209–18; Bennett, 'Emotion and Place Promotion', p. 3.

39 CPRE, 'Mapping Tranquillity. Defining and assessing a valuable resource' (2005).

CHAPTER 11: LOWLANDS OF SCOTLAND

1 *About Britain No. 11*, pp. 77–8. Unless noted, other references to the guidebook in this chapter come from these pages.

2 https://www.google.com/streetview/

3 Francesco Lapenta, 'Geomedia: On location-based media, the changing status of collective image production and the emergence of social navigation systems', *Visual Studies*, 26, 1 (2011), pp. 14–24.

4 *About Britain No. 11*, p. 24.

5 'Traffic over the Forth', *The Times* (25 April, 1936), p. 17; Gillian Bowditch, 'Backing by Lang for new Forth bridge', *The Times* (11 January, 1995), p. 6; Kaya Burgess, 'A Tale of Two Bridges', *The Times* (3 December, 2011), pp. 46–7; 'Forth Bridge "Not Doing Badly"', *The Times* (8 September, 1965), p. 6; 'Window on Britain', *The Times* (6 January, 2009); Angus Macleod, '£1bn pledge for Forth bridge replacement', *The Times* (15 February, 2007), p. 31; 'Hovercraft cuts Forth crossing time', *The Times* (14 July, 2007), p. 24.

6 Transport Scotland, 'Queensferry Crossing and Forth Road Bridge Users' Guide' (January 2018), pp. 14, 3–5.

7 Julie Currie, 'A behind the scenes tour of Traffic Scotland's National Control Centre', *Falkirk Herald* (17 February, 2019).

8 Sue Weekes, 'Scotland demonstrates full-size autonomous bus', *Smart Cities World* (18 November, 2019); 'Forth Road Bridge driverless buses: Here's how the technology works', *Edinburgh Evening News* (22

November, 2018); Simon Calder, 'Driverless Buses and Taxis to be Launched in Britain by 2021', *Independent* (23 November, 2018).

9 *About Britain No. 11*, p. 29.

10 Jim Phillips, 'The Closure of Michael Colliery in 1967 and the Politics of Deindustrialization in the East Fife Coalfield, 1947–67', *Twentieth Century British History*, 26, 4 (2015), pp. 551–72; Tim Webb, 'Government ready to rescue UK Coal and save thousands of mining jobs', *The Times* (29 June, 2013), p. 53; David Henderson, 'Inside the once-mighty Longannet Power Station', BBC News (22 August, 2019).

11 https://www.mrsl.co.uk

12 *About Britain No. 11*, p. 54.

13 'New Mining Town in Fife', *The Times* (23 January, 1951), p. 2; 'Uncertainty for Scottish Town', *The Times* (24 August, 1954), p. 3; 'American Electronics Factory in Fife', *The Times* (18 November, 1959), p. 7; 'American Business Invasion Aids Scotland's Economy,' *The Times* (4 August, 1961), p. 14; 'More US Industry for Glenrothes', *The Times* (15 October, 1963), p. 8; 'The Scottish Plan. Big Population Expansion', *The Times* (15 November, 1963), p. 8; 'Airfield Puts Scots New Town Ahead', *The Times* (7 August, 1964), p. 6; Gerald Ely, 'Exhibition will make work progress', *The Times* (12 June, 1967), p. 15; Maurice Baggot, 'Year of doubts and delays', *The Times* (18 June, 1974), p. iv.

14 https://scotchwhisky.com/whiskypedia/2627/john-haig-company/; 'John Haig Whisky (Markinch)' House of Commons Debate (4 March 1983), *Hansard*, Volume 38, cc 537–44.

15 https://www.edenmill.com; 'Scotland's New Distillery Boom', *The Drinks Business* (19 December, 2017); https://www.thedrinksbusiness.com/2017/12/scotlands-new-distillery-boom/

16 https://www.st-andrews.ac.uk/about/sustainability/eden-campus/

17 'Bomb scare before Tay bridge opening', *The Times* (19 August, 1966), p. 9.

18 *About Britain No. 11*, p. 66.

19 'Dundee's Olympia pool full of history', *Dundee Evening Telegraph* (25 January, 2014).

20 *About Britain No. 11*, p. 58.

21 Brian McCleendon, 'Explore the world with Street View, now on all seven continents' (30 September, 2010); https://googleblog.blogspot.com/2010/09/explore-world-with-street-view-now-on.html

22 *About Britain No. 11*, p. 55.

23 Henry M. Leppard, 'Carse Agriculture: The Carse of Gowrie', *Economic Geography*, 10, 3 (1934), pp. 228–9; Forbes W. Robertson, 'A History of Apples in Scottish Orchards', *Garden History*, 35, 1 (2007), p.

43; Crispin W. Haye, 'Historic Orchards of the Carse of Gowrie. Phase 1 Survey 2007. Report to Perth and Kinross Countryside Trust' (2007); https://www.cairnomohr.com/about

24 *About Britain No. 11*, p. 90.

25 Viscount Templewood, *The Shadow of the Gallows* (London: Victor Gollancz Ltd, 1951), p. 13.

26 https://www.sps.gov.uk/Corporate/Prisons/Perth/HMP-Perth.aspx; 'Prison gallows removed', *The Times* (7 June, 1995), p. 2.

27 https://historic-hospitals.com/gazetteer/perth-and-kinross/

28 'Need to know', *The Times* (11 March, 2010), p. 42.

29 https://www.amazingresults.com/property/balado-bridge-by-kinross/; 'Iconic satellite for sale', BBC News (31 July, 2006); Pearce Wright, 'Ancient shape of new technology', *The Times* (3 May, 1990), p. 33.

30 Lisa Verrico, 'Oasis, and sunshine, cheer Scots', *The Times* (16 July, 2002), p. 17.

31 'Forth Road Bridge Opening', *The Times* (20 October, 1936), p. 13.

32 'Scottish fact of the day: M8 motorway sculptures', *The Scotsman* (1 December, 2014); Severin Carrell, 'Meet the Kelpies, Scotland's giant addition to the UK sculptural skyline', *Guardian* (24 November, 2008).

33 Chris Partridge, 'Making a dramatic statement', *The Times* (29 January, 2009), p. 62.

34 Peter Marsh, 'Falkirk keeps iron in fire of metals trade', *The Financial Times* (18 November, 2012).

35 https://www.spenergynetworks.co.uk/pages/bonnybridge.aspx

36 'Government to Close Canal', *The Times* (7 June, 1961), p. 7; Gillian Bowditch, 'New era for canals heralds 4,000 jobs', *The Times* (25 October, 1994), p. 12; Mary Fagan, 'Fibreway opens new trade on canals', *Independent* (9 March , 1994).

37 Ben Webster, 'Canals to be revived by a £500m flow of cash', *The Times* (19 March, 2002), p. 8; Chris Partridge, 'Britain's Waterways', *The Times* (28 January, 2009), p. 55; https://www.flickr.com/photos/23666168@N04/37596455865

CHAPTER 12: HIGHLANDS AND ISLANDS OF SCOTLAND

1 *About Britain No. 12*, pp. 80–1. Unless noted, other references to the guidebook in this chapter come from these pages.

2 *About Britain No. 12*, pp. 7–8; *About Britain No. 11*, p. 90.

3 https://www.audleytravel.com/united-kingdom/scotland/accommodation/methven-castle

4 'Being There', *The Times* (10 May, 2002), p. 31; Warren Pole, 'Think of it as a spiritual journey', *The Times* (18 November, 2010), p. 10; Ian Buxton, 'Scotland's top whisky tours', *The Times* (25 January, 2014), pp. 42–3; Felipe Schrieberg, 'Lalique Crystal Owner Buys Glenturret Whisky Distillery', *Forbes* (26 December, 2018); https://theglenturret.com/pages/our-story

5 *About Britain No. 11*, p. 79; *About Britain No. 12*, p. 58; Gemma Howard-Vyse, 'Visit Scotland Marks 50 Years of Scottish Tourism', *Scottish Field* (23 July, 2019).

6 House of Commons Debates (18 April, 1961), *Hansard*, Volume 638, 88; 'Seat of learning for young farmers', *Daily Record* (15 February, 2008).

7 http://comriedevelopmenttrust.org.uk/; 'Tech Firm Bogons buys Cultybraggan nuclear bunker', BBC News Online (21 May, 2014).

8 Report by the Scottish National Parks Committee and the Scottish Wild Life Conservation Committee, *National Parks and the Conservation of Nature in Scotland* (Edinburgh: HMSO, 1947), pp. 21–2, 39, 4.

9 Sheail, *An Environmental History*, pp. 141–2; *About Britain No. 12*, p. 19.

10 *National Parks and the Conservation of Nature in Scotland*, pp. 20–1; 26–7; Anniko Dahberg, Rick Rohde and Klas Sandell, 'National Parks and Environmental Justice: Comparing Access Rights and Ideological Legacies in Three Countries', *Conservation and Society*, 8, 3 (2010), pp. 209–24; Phil Back, ' "If you build it, they will come." The origins of Scotland's Country Parks' (University of Sheffield PhD thesis, 2018), pp. 75–6; Murray P. Ferguson, 'National parks for Scotland?', *Scottish Geographical Magazine*, 104, 1 (1988), pp. 36–40; Joanne Connell and Stephen J. Page, 'Exploring the spatial patterns of car-based tourist travel in Loch Lomond and Trossachs National Park, Scotland', *Tourism Management*, 29 (2008), pp. 561–80.

11 *About Britain No. 12*, p. 84.

12 https://www.gov.uk/government/statistical-data-sets/ras52-international-comparisons

13. https://www.gov.scot/binaries/content/documents/govscot/publications/foi-eir-release/2019/02/foi-19-00222/documents/foi-19-00222-annexes-a-to-i/foi-19-00222-annexes-a-to-i/govscot%3Adocument/foi-19-00222%2BAnnexes%2BA%2Bto%2BI.pdf; https://www.gov.scot/publications/foi-17-01451/; Angus Macleod, 'Plans for bilingual signs in Scotland', *The Times* (25 November, 2002), p. 7; N. Kinnear, S. Helman, S. Buttress, L. Smith, E.

Delmonte, L. Lloyd and B. Sexton, 'Analyses of the effects of bilingual signs on road safety in Scotland – final report' (Transport Research Laboratory, 2012).

14 George Blake, 'Lowland Scotland', in *The Beauty of Britain. A Pictorial Survey* (London: B. T. Batsford, 1937), pp. 229–30.

15 North of Scotland Hydro-Electric Board, *Loch Sloy Hydro-Electric Scheme 1950* (commemorative book, 1950).

16 *About Britain No. 12*, pp. 36, 40–1, 60–2.

17 *About Britain No. 12*, pp. 36, 29; Sheail, *An Environmental History*, pp. 94–8.

18 Craig Borland, 'Jobs lost in Arrochar and Tarbet as two hotels close after holiday firm's collapse', *Helensburgh Advertiser* (22 May 2020).

19 *About Britain No. 11*, p. 80; TNA, Works FULL REF C/2/507, Correspondence with Alistair Dunnett (August-October, 1950).

20 https://www.rias.org.uk/for-the-public/practices/norr-consultants-ltd-glasgow/ben-arthur-resort-arrochar; 'A chapter of history ends', *Helensburgh Advertiser* (16 January, 1987); https://www.rias.org.uk/for-the-public/practices/norr-consultants-ltd-glasgow/ben-arthur-resort-arrochar Andy Galloway, 'Argyll and Bute Councillors back Ben Arthur resort in Arrochar', *Helensburgh Advertiser* (24 December, 2018).

21 'Polaris Project is on Target', *The Times* (1 July, 1966), p. 14; 'Water Seeped into Polaris Base', *The Times* (4 April, 1967), p. 2; Ronald Faux, 'Sevenfold growth for Trident base announced', *The Times* (21 May, 1981), p. 6.

22 *About Britain No. 12*, p. 84; Gordon Cruickshank, 'Track Tests. Rest and Be Thankful', *Motor Sport* (December 2003), pp. 66–72.

23 Stefano B. Longo, Rebecca Clausen and Brett Clark, *The Tragedy of the Commodity: Oceans, Fisheries and Aquaculture* (New Brunswick: Rutgers University Press, 2015) pp. 106–43; *About Britain No. 12*, pp. 18, 9–10.

24 Richard J. Gowen and Harald Rosenthal, 'The Environmental Consequences of Intensive Coastal Aquaculture in Developed Countries: What Lessons Can Be Learnt', in R. S. V. Pullin, H. Rosenthal and J. L. Maclean (eds.), *Environment and Aquaculture in Developing Countries, ICLARM Conf. Proc. 31* (1991), pp. 102–15; Les Wood, Karen Anutha and Achim Peschken, 'Marine Farming of Atlantic Salmon', *Geography*, 75. 3 (1990), pp. 211–21; Mike Harvey, 'Farming the ocean as we farm the land', *The Times* (12 September, 2009), p. 63; Peter J. W. N. Bird, 'Econometric Estimation of World Salmon Demand', *Marine Resource*

Economics, 3, No. 2 (1986), pp. 169–82; https://www.gov.scot/publications/scottish-fish-farm-production-survey-2018/pages/5/; https://www.gov.scot/binaries/content/documents/govscot/publications/factsheet/2019/11/marine-scotland-topic-sheets-aquaculture/documents/the-value-of-scotlands-aquaculture-updated-june-2017/the-value-of-scotlands-aquaculture-updated-june-2017/govscot%3Adocument/value-aquaculture.pdf; https://assets.publishing.service.gov.uk/government/uploads/system/uploads/attachment_data/file/271295/pfn-scottish-wild-salmon-pgi.pdf; https://www2.gov.scot/Publications/2010/03/08154833/2; https://assets.publishing.service.gov.uk/government/uploads/system/uploads/attachment_data/file/891035/pfn-scottish-farmed-salmon-spec.pdf; *About Britain No. 12*, p. 55.

25 Angela Jameson, 'Watchdog to get its teeth into Scottish Salmon farm merger', *The Times* (7 July, 2006), p. 50; Andrew Morgan, 'Escaped Salmon "might breed hybrids"', *The Times* (17 May, 1989), p. 3; Magnus Linklater and Michael Wigan, 'Interlopers threaten Scottish Salmon's good name', *The Times* (4 January, 2011), p. 14; https://www.gov.scot/publications/fish-health-inspectorate-mortality-information/; Ronald A. Hites et al., 'Global Assessment of Organic Contaminants in Farmed Salmon', *Science*, 303, 5655 (9 January, 2004), pp. 226–9; Laura Peeke, 'Salmon shunned despite price cuts and reassurances', *The Times* (12 January, 2004), p. 7; https://scottishsalmonwatch.org

26 'Obituaries. John Noble', *The Times* (18 February, 2002), p. 39.

27 'Argyll Estate Sale to Meet Duties', *The Times* (17 November, 1951), p. 8; 'Summer Opening of Country Houses', *The Times* (19 April, 1954), p. 8; 'Restoring Historic Inveraray', *The Times* (29 May, 1957), p. 7; 'Duke of Argyll to Let Castle', *The Times* (14 April, 1961), p.9; Philip Howard, 'Magnificent Seven form stately co-op', *The Times* (2 May, 1975), p. 5; Ronald Faux, 'Heavy loss in castle fire but Scottish relics saved', *The Times* (7 November, 1975), p. 3; John Young, 'Visits to top historic houses are up 14%', *The Times* (21 January, 1986); 'Obituary. The Duke of Argyll', *The Times* (23 April, 2001), p. 19; Mandler, *The Fall and Rise*; Kerry Gill, 'Jail welcomes tourists to its cells', *The Times* (1 September, 1992), p. 3.

28 *About Britain No. 12*, pp. 46–7; 85.

29 A. A. Fulton, 'The Cruachan Pumped-Storage Development', *Electronics and Power* (July 1966), pp. 220–4; Emma Newlands, '"Iconic"

Cruachan Power Station to help safeguard Britain's energy supply', *Scotsman* (16 July, 2020).

30 *About Britain No. 12*, p. 21.

31 *About Britain No. 12*, p. 51.

BACK ABOUT BRITAIN

1 *About Britain No. 1*, p. 6.

2 See for example Patrick Wright, *On Living in an Old Country* (London: Verson, 1985).

Acknowledgements

One of the joys of writing this book, like any other, is that it has been a collective project. This has been especially true as I was joined on many of my journeys by others who helped me see the landscape through their eyes. Thanks to Julie, Alisha and Lauren who joined me on the first and last route, as well as a number in between. Thanks also to Barney and Lucy who accompanied me in a mid-summer hunt for mayflies along the River Test, and Matthew who joined me on the drive to, and through, the centre of England. Along the way, many others have assisted by sending books or newspaper articles my way or reading draft chapters. Special thanks to my colleague and friend Robert Bickers for accompanying me along the journey of writing this book, to Lucy Telling, Faye Salt and Matthew Sleeman who read and commented on chapters and to my mum – Christine Cole – for proofreading the draft manuscript. Thanks to my department for granting me a semester of leave to complete the final journeys and writing of this book.

Authors are not only dependent on the support and help of family and friends, but also their publishers. I have been very lucky to have in Robin Baird-Smith and Jamie Birkett at Bloomsbury two commissioning editors who believe in me and my ideas. They were key to the last book, were keen champions of this one, and I hope will encourage me to write the next. Jamie's editorial comments were especially astute and incisive. He sharpened my prose, and encouraged me to edit as a good editor does. I am hugely grateful to him for making this a better book than it would otherwise have been. Thanks also to Martin Bryant for his sharp copy-editing skills and Emily Faccini for her beautiful opening map. I am thankful to members of the whole team at Bloomsbury who have shepherded this book from initial idea to finished product with professionalism and humour.

Sadly, finishing this book coincided with my dad's death. The book is dedicated to him, as well as to his parents: my paternal grandparents. They first packed me into the back of the car and took me around Britain. We never went on foreign holidays as kids, but each Easter and summer break would see us journeying down the M6 and M5 to Somerset where my grandparents had retired to and then on to Devon or Cornwall, where my love of coast-path walking was developed. I have wonderful childhood memories of those days in Somerset at the beginning and end of our holiday in Devon or Cornwall. In the morning, we'd 'help' in the garden or around the house. In the afternoon, we'd cram into the back of my grandparents' car and head off to explore a wood or hillfort in Somerset or Dorset. My grandparents had met studying botany and zoology at university in Bangor, so they were the ideal guides to the flora and fauna we found along the way. I thought of them, and school holidays spent with them, as I travelled through the landscape of their childhood and young adulthood in North Wales. I also thought of my dad when I drove. Not simply because he was generally the person in the driving seat on those long motorway journeys, but also because he had spent his life working on roads like these. Rather than botany and zoology, he studied civil engineering, and spent his career designing bridges that spanned Lancashire's roads and growing network of motorways. I sent him early chapter drafts to read as I finished them, but sadly he died before the book was complete. *About Britain* is shaped by him and his parents, and dedicated to them.